From the staff of GUINNESS ("the world's leading record keepers")* comes this fully-packed photographically illustrated volume, with every record worth knowing in 81 sports and games. Here are all the gold medal winners of the 1984 summer and winter Olympics, along with the world record holders in every sport.

Besides there are year-by-year lists of tournament sports winners (golf, tennis, etc.) and even some minor sports (croquet, orienteering, darts, hang gliding, lacrosse, etc.) as well as the most celebrated race winners (Indy 500, LeMans, Kentucky Derby, etc.).

Not content with all that, the editors include the little odd events that the Guinness Books are famous for: the fly ball that never came down, the longest and shortest touchdown passes, the woman who took 166 strokes on one hole, the largest fish ever harpooned, the youngest swimmer to double-cross the English Channel, how a rule change revolutionized basketball, and hundreds of other sports facts worth knowing.

From aerobatics to yachting, you get the broad picture of sports and games, and you find in-depth coverage of the typically American sports—basketball, hockey, bowling and, of course, baseball and football, including World Series and Super-Bowl records.

Reliable information, facts you can depend on have come from experts in each field, heads of leagues and associations and newspaper editors that the Guinness editors consult in their quest for authentic verified records.

Photos abound, new from the 1984 Olympics, as well as outstanding action shots, and old-time classic pictures (boxing with bare knuckles, girls playing basketball in bloomers in 1900, polo on elephant back, etc.).

As you glance through the pages you will see why we say there is no other one-volume illustrated sports encyclopedia that holds so many surprising facts, records and pictures. This edition has been brought up to date to 1985 for your enjoyment and future reference. If it's a record, look it up here. If you can't find it here, you probably can't find it anywhere.

* Sports Illustrated

GUINNESS
SPORTS
RECORD
B·O·O·K
1985-86

Compilers
Norris McWhirter
(Ross McWhirter 1955-1975)
Stan Greenberg
Maris Cakars
Jim Benagh

Editor
David A. Boehm

To Bhai From Mitu OKLAHOMA

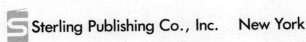 Sterling Publishing Co., Inc.   New York

Library of Congress Cataloging in Publication Data

Guinness sports record book / by Norris and Ross McWhirter.—
  [1972] — New York, N.Y. : Sterling Pub. Co., [c1972-

  v. : ill. ; 23 cm.
Annual.
"Taken in part from the Guinness book of world records."

  1. Sports—Records—Periodicals. I. McWhirter, Norris, 1925-   II.
McWhirter, Ross, 1925-1975. III. Guinness book of world records.
GV741.G843   796'.0212—dc19   82-642136
                                                    AACR 2   MARC-S

Library of Congress   [8301]

CONTENTS

The Sports World

Earliest

The origins of sport stem from the time when self-preservation ceased to be the all-consuming human preoccupation. Archery was a hunting skill in Mesolithic times (by *c.* 8000 BC), but did not become an organized sport until later, certainly by about 300 AD, among the Genoese and possibly as early as the 12th century BC, as an archery competition is described in Homer's *Iliad*. The earliest dated evidence for sport is *c.* 2750–2600 BC for wrestling. Ball games by girls, depicted on Middle Kingdom murals at Beni Hasan, Egypt, have been dated to *c.* 2050 BC.

Fastest

The highest speed reached in a non-mechanical sport is in sky-diving, in which a speed of 185 mph is attained in a head-down free-falling position, even in the lower atmosphere. In delayed drops, a speed of 625 mph has been recorded at high rarefied altitudes. The highest projectile speed in any moving ball game is *c.* 188 mph in pelota (jai-alai). This compares with 170 mph (electronically timed) for a golf ball driven off a tee.

Slowest

In amateur wrestling, before the rules were modified toward "brighter wrestling," contestants could be locked in holds for so long that a single bout once lasted for 11 hours 40 min. In the extreme case of the 2-hour-41-min pull in the regimental tug o'war in Jubbulpore, India, Aug 12, 1889, the winning team moved a net distance of 12 ft at an average speed of 0.00084 mph.

Longest

The most protracted sporting contest was an automobile duration test of 222,621 miles (equivalent to 8.93 times around the equator) by Appaurchaux and others in a Ford Taunus at Miranas, France. This was contested over 142 days (July–Nov) in 1963.

The most protracted non-mechanical sporting event is the *Tour de France* cycling race. In 1926 this was over 3,569 miles, lasting 29 days, but is now reduced to 23 days.

Largest Field

The largest field for any ball game is that for polo with 12.4 acres, or a maximum length of 300 yd and a width, without side-boards, of 200 yd (with boards the width is 160 yd).

MOST VERSATILE WOMEN ATHLETES: Lottie Dod (left) and Babe Didrikson Zaharias (right) were two of the best all-around athletes. Dod won the first of five Wimbledon titles before she was 16, and she also excelled at golf, archery, field hockey, skating and tobogganing. Didrikson was a basketball All-American, an Olympic gold medalist in track and field, a successful golfer and a talented baseball player. Her 296-foot baseball throw is the longest ever by a woman.

Biggest Sports Contract

In March 1982 the National Football League concluded a deal worth $2 billion for 5 years coverage of their games by the 3 major TV networks (ABC, CBS and NBC). This represents $14.2 million for each team in the league.

Largest Crowd

The greatest number of live spectators for any sporting spectacle is the estimated 2,500,000 who annually line the route of the New York Marathon. However, spread over 23 days, it is estimated that more than 10 million see the annual *Tour de France* along the route.

The largest crowd traveling to any single sporting event is "more than 400,000" for the annual *Grand Prix d'Endurance* motor race on the Sarthe circuit near Le Mans, France. The record stadium crowd was one of 199,854 for the Brazil vs Uruguay soccer match in the Maracaña Municipal Stadium, Rio de Janeiro, Brazil, July 16, 1950.

The largest television audience for a single sporting event (excluding Olympic events) was the estimated 1.5 billion who watched the final game of the 1982 World Cup soccer competition.

Most Participants

The *Round the Bays* 6.5-mile run in Auckland, NZ attracted an estimated 80,000 runners on March 27, 1982. The 1983 WIBC Championship Tournament attracted 75,480 women bowlers (all of whom paid entry fees) for the 83-day event held Apr 7–July 1 at Showboat Lanes, Las Vegas, Nev.

The most runners in a marathon were the 18,469 in the London Marathon May 13, 1984, of whom 16,580 finished.

In May 1971, the "Ramblin' Raft Race" on the Chattahoochee River at Atlanta, Ga, attracted 37,683 competitors on 8,304 rafts.

Most Sportsmen

According to a report in 1978, 55 million people are active in sports in the USSR. The country has 3,282 stadiums, 1,435 swimming pools and over 66,000 indoor gymnasia. It is estimated that some 29 percent of the population of E Germany participate in sport regularly.

Worst Disasters

The worst disaster in recent history was when an estimated 604 were killed after some stands at the Hong Kong Jockey Club race course collapsed and caught fire on Feb 26, 1918. During the reign of Antoninus Pius (138–161 AD) the upper wooden tiers in the Circus Maximus, Rome, collapsed during a gladiatorial combat, killing 1,112 spectators.

Greatest Earnings

The greatest fortune amassed by an individual in sport is an estimated $69 million by the boxer Muhammad Ali Haj to the end of 1981.

The highest-paid woman athlete is tennis player Martina Navratilova (b Prague, Czechoslovakia, Oct 18, 1956) whose career earnings passed $8 million in 1984.

Most Versatile Athletes

Charlotte "Lottie" Dod (1871–1960) won the Wimbledon singles title (1887 to 1893) 5 times, the British Ladies Golf Championship in 1904, an Olympic silver medal for archery in 1908, and represented England at hockey in 1899. She also excelled at skating and tobogganing.

Mildred (Babe) Didrikson Zaharias (US) (1914–56) was an All-American basketball player, took the silver medal in the high jump, and gold medals in the javelin throw and hurdles in the 1932 Olympics. Turning professional, she first trained as a boxer, and then, switching to golf, eventually won 19 championships, including the US Women's Open and All-American Open. She holds the women's world record also for longest throw of a baseball—296 ft.

Jim Thorpe (US) (1888–1953) excelled at football, baseball, the 10-event decathlon, and the 5-event pentathlon. He won two gold medals in the 1912 Olympics and was declared "the greatest athlete in the world" by King Gustav of Sweden.

Most Prolific Recordbreaker

Between Jan 24, 1970, and Nov 1, 1977, Vasili Alexeyev (USSR) (b Jan 7, 1942) broke 80 official world records in weight lifting.

Longest Reign

The longest reign as a world champion is 33 years (1829–62) by Jacques Edmond Barre (France, 1802–73) at the rarely played real (royal) tennis.

Shortest Reign

Olga Rukavishnikova (USSR) (b Mar 13, 1955) held the pentathlon world record for only 0.4 sec at Moscow on July 24, 1980. That is the difference between her second place time of 2 min 04.8 sec in the final 800m event of the Olympic five-event competition, and that of the third-placed Nadezda Tkachenko (USSR), whose overall points came to more than Rukavishnikova's total—5,083 points to 4,937 points.

Heaviest Sportsmen

The heaviest sportsman of all time was the wrestler William J. Cobb of Macon, Ga, who in 1962 was billed as the 802-lb "Happy Humphrey." The heaviest player of a ball game was Bob Pointer, the 487-lb tackle on the 1967 Santa Barbara High School football team.

Most Determined Competitors

The Italian rider Raimondo d'Inzeo competed in a record eight Olympic Games from 1948 to 1976, winning one gold, 2 silver and 3 bronze medals. The equivalent female record is six Games by fencer Janice Lee York-Romary (US) from 1948 to 1968, and by discus thrower Lia Manoliu (Rom) who competed from 1952 to 1972, winning a gold in 1968, and bronzes in 1960 and 1964. The Danish fencer Ivan Osier competed over a span of 40 years (winning a silver medal in 1912) from 1908 to 1948 (he missed out in 1936), and he was matched by 1912 and 1920 gold medalist yachtsman Magnus Konow (Nor) also from 1908 to 1948 (but he missed out in 1924, 1928 and 1932). The greatest span of years by a woman was 24 by fencer Ellen Muller-Preis (Austria) from 1932 to 1956, during which time she won one gold and 3 bronze medals.

Youngest and Oldest Recordbreakers

The youngest age at which any person has broken a non-mechanical world record is 12 years 298 days for Gertrude Caroline Ederle (b Oct 23, 1906) of the US, who broke the women's 880-yd freestyle swimming world record with 13 min 19.0 sec at Indianapolis, Ind, Aug 17, 1919.

The oldest person to break a world record is Gerhard Weidner (W Germany) (b Mar 15, 1933) who set a 20-mi walk record on May 25, 1974, aged 41 years 71 days.

Youngest and Oldest Champions

The youngest person to have successfully participated in a world title event was a French boy, whose name is not recorded, who coxed the

CZECH ROOM: Strahov Stadium in Prague, Czechoslovakia, is the largest in the world, with space for 240,000 spectators to view mass displays of up to 40,000 gymnasts.

winning Netherlands Olympic pair in rowing at Paris on Aug 26, 1900. He was not more than 10 and may have been as young as 7. The youngest individual Olympic winner was Marjorie Gestring (US) (b Nov 18, 1922), who took the springboard diving title at the age of 13 years 268 days at the Olympic Games in Berlin, Aug 12, 1936. Oscar G. Swahn (see below) was aged 64 years 258 days when he won the gold medal in the 1912 Olympic Running Deer team shooting competition.

Youngest and Oldest Internationals

The youngest age at which any person has won international honors is 8 years in the case of Joy Foster, the Jamaican singles and mixed doubles table tennis champion in 1958. It would appear that the greatest age at which anyone has actively competed for his country is 72 years 280 days in the case of Oscar Gomer Swahn (Sweden) (1847–1927), who won a silver medal for shooting in the Olympic Games at Antwerp on July 26, 1920. He qualified for the 1924 Games, but was unable to participate because of illness.

Largest Stadiums

The largest stadium is the Strahov Stadium in Praha (Prague), Czechoslovakia. It was completed in 1934 and can easily accommodate 240,000 spectators for mass displays of up to 40,000 Sokol gymnasts.

The largest football (soccer) stadium is the Maracaña Municipal Stadium in Rio de Janeiro, Brazil, which has a normal capacity of 205,000, of whom 155,000 may be seated. A crowd of 199,854 was accommodated for the World Cup final between Brazil and Uruguay on July 16, 1950. A dry moat, 7 ft wide and over 5 ft deep, protects players from spectators and *vice versa*.

Largest One-Piece Roof

The transparent acrylic glass "tent" roof over the Munich Olympic Stadium, W Germany, measures 914,940 sq ft in area. It rests on a steel net supported by masts. The roof of longest span is the 680-ft diameter of the Louisiana Superdome. The major axis of the elliptical Texas Stadium, Irving, Tex, completed in 1971 is, however, 784 ft 4 in.

Largest Indoor Arena

The largest indoor stadium is the 13-acre $173-million 273-ft-tall Superdome in New Orleans, La, completed in May 1975. Its maximum seating capacity for conventions is 97,365 or 76,791 for football. Box suites rent for $35,000, excluding the price of admission. A gondola with six 312-in TV screens produces instant replay.

AEROBATICS

Earliest

The first aerobatic maneuver is generally considered the sustained inverted flight in a Blériot of Célestin-Adolphe Pégoud (1889–1915) at Buc, France, Sept 21, 1913, but Lieut Peter Nikolayevich Nesterov (1887–1914), of the Imperial Russian Air Service, performed a loop in a Nieuport Type IV monoplane at Kiev, USSR, Aug 27, 1913.

World Championships

Held biennially since 1960 (excepting 1974), scoring is based on the system devised by Col José Aresti of Spain. The competitions consist of two compulsory and two free programs. Team competition has been won on 5 occasions by the USSR. No individual has won more than one title, the most successful competitor being Igor Egorov (USSR) who won in 1970, was second in 1976, fifth in 1972 and eleventh in 1968. The most successful in the women's competition has been Betty Stewart (US) who has won twice, 1980 and 1982. The US had a clean sweep of all the medals in 1980.

Inverted Flight

The duration record for inverted flight is 4 hours 9 min 5 sec by John "Hal" McClain in a Swick Taylorcraft on Aug 23, 1980 over Houston Raceways, Tex.

Loops

On June 21, 1980, R. Steven Powell performed 2,315⅝ inside loops in a Bellanca Decathlon over Almont, Mich. John McClain achieved 180 outside loops in a Bellanca Super Decathlon on Sept 2, 1978, over Houston, Tex. Ken Ballinger (GB) completed 155 consecutive loops in a Bellanca Citabria on Aug 6, 1983 over Staverton Airport, Cheltenham, Eng.

TOPFLIGHT: Using a handbow, April Moon (left) shot an arrow over 1,039 yd to set a women's record. Harry Drake (right) launched an arrow 1 mile 268 yd with a foot-bow. Drake also holds the crossbow record with a flight of nearly 1,360 yd.

ARCHERY

Earliest References

Though the earliest evidence of the existence of bows is seen in the Mesolithic cave paintings in Spain, archery as an organized sport appears to have developed in the 3rd century AD. Competitive archery may, however, date back to the 12th century BC. The world governing body is the *Fédération Internationale de Tir à l'Arc* (FITA), founded in 1931.

Highest Championship Scores

The highest scores achieved in either a world or Olympic championship for Double FITA rounds are: Men, 2,617 points (possible 2,880) by Richard McKinney (US) and Darrell Pace (US) and Women, 2,616 points by Kim Jin Ho (N Korea) at the World Championships in Long Beach, Calif on Oct 21–22, 1983.

Highest 24-Hour Scores

The record score at target archery over 24 hours by a pair of archers is 51,633 during 48 Portsmouth Rounds (60 arrows at 20 yd with a 2-in-diameter 10 ring) shot by Jimmy Watt and Gordon Danby at the Epsom Showgrounds, Auckland, NZ, Nov 18–19, 1977.

The highest recorded score at field archery is 123,724 by six members of the Holland Moss Field Archery Club at Holland Moss Field, Pimbo, Lancashire on Apr 28–29, 1983. Bill Chambers set an individual record score of 30.506.

Most Titles

The greatest number of world titles (instituted 1931) ever won by a man is 4 by Hans Deutgen (b Feb 28, 1917) (Sweden), 1947–50. The greatest number won by a woman is 7 by Mrs Janina Spychajowa-Kurkowska (b Feb 8, 1901) (Poland), 1931–34, 36, 39 and 47.

Oscar Kessels (Belgium) participated in 21 world championships.

ARCHERY WORLD RECORDS

MEN

Event	Name	Record/Maximum	Year
FITA	Darrell Pace (US)	1341/1440	1979
90 m.	Vladimir Esheyev (USSR)	322/360	1980
70 m.	Tomi Poikolainen (Finland)	339/360	1983
50 m.	Richard McKinney (US)	345/360	1982
30 m.	Darrell Pace (US)	356/360	1978
Team	US (Richard McKinney, Darrell Pace, Jerry Pylypchuk)	3908/4320	1983

WOMEN

Event	Name	Record/Maximum	Year
FITA	Ludmila Arzhannikova (USSR)	1325/1440	1984
70 m.	Natalia Butuzova (USSR)	328/360	1979
60 m.	Ludmila Arzhannikova (USSR)	338/360	1984
50 m.	Paivi Meriduoto (Fin)	331/360	1982
30 m.	Valentina Radonova (USSR)	353/360	1981
Team	USSR (Natalia Butuzova, Ludmila Arzhannikova, Sebinsio Rustamova)	3925/4320	1983

Olympic Medals

Hubert van Innis (Belgium) (1866–1961) won 6 gold and 3 silver medals in archery events at the 1900 and 1920 Olympic Games.

In 1984, the winners of gold medals were: Darrell Pace (US) with 2,616 points in the men's competition, and Seo Hyang-Soon (S Korea) with 2,568 points in the women's.

Flight Shooting

The longest flight shooting records are achieved in the footbow class. In the unlimited footbow division, Harry Drake (b May 7, 1915) of Lakeside, Calif, holds the record at 1 mile 268 yd, shot at Ivanpah Dry Lake, Calif, Oct 24, 1971. He also holds the regular footbow record with 1,542 yd 34 in set on Oct 6, 1979. The crossbow record is 1,359 yd 29 in, held by Drake set Oct 14–15, 1967. The female footbow record is 1,113 yd 30 in by Arlyne Rhode (b May 4, 1936) at Wendover, Utah, on Sept 10, 1978. Alan Webster (Eng) set the flight record for the handbow with 1,231 yd 1 ft 10 in on Oct 2, 1982, and April Moon (US) set a women's record of 1,039 yd 13 in on Sept 13, 1981, both at Ivanpah Dry Lake.

Greatest Pull

Gary Sentman of Roseburg, Ore, drew a longbow weighing a record 176 lb to the maximum draw on the arrow (28¼ in) at Forksville, Pa, Sept 20, 1975.

AUTO RACING*

Earliest Races

There are various conflicting claims, but the first automobile race was the 201-mile Green Bay-to-Madison, Wis, run in 1878, won by an Oshkosh steamer.

In 1887, Count Jules Felix Philippe Albert de Dion de Malfiance (1856–1946) won the *La Velocipede* 19.3-mile race in Paris in a De Dion steam quadricycle in which he is reputed to have exceeded 37 mph.

The first "real" race was from Paris to Bordeaux and back (732 miles) June 11–13, 1895. The winner was Emile Levassor (1844–97) (France) driving a Panhard-Levassor two-seater with a 1.2-liter Daimler engine developing 3½ hp. His time was 48 hours 47 min (average speed 15.01 mph). The first closed-circuit race was held over 5 laps of a mile dirt track at Narragansett Park, Cranston, RI on Sept 7, 1896. It was won by A. H. Whiting, who drove a Riker electric.

The oldest auto race in the world still being regularly run is the R.A.C. Tourist Trophy, first staged on the Isle of Man on Sept 14, 1905. The oldest continental race is the French Grand Prix first held June 26–27, 1906. The Coppa Florio, in Sicily, has been irregularly held since 1900.

Fastest Circuits

The highest average lap speed attained on any closed circuit is 250.958 mph in a trial by Dr Hans Liebold (b Oct 12, 1926) (Germany) who lapped the 7.85-mile high-speed track at Nardo, Italy, in 1 min 52.67 sec in a Mercedes-Benz C111-IV experimental coupé on May 5, 1979. It was powered by a V8 engine with two KKK turbochargers with an output of 500 hp at 6,200 rpm.

The highest average race lap speed for a closed circuit is 214.158 mph by Mario Gabriele Andretti (US) (b Trieste, Italy, Feb 28, 1940) driving a 2.6-liter turbocharged Viceroy Parnelli-Offenhauser on the 2-mile 22-degree banked oval at Texas World Speedway, College Station, Tex, Oct 6, 1973.

The fastest road circuit was the Francorchamps circuit near Spa, Belgium, then 14.10 km (8 miles 1,340 yd) in length. It was lapped in 3 min 13.4 sec (average speed of 163.086 mph) on May 6, 1973, by Henri Pescarolo (b Paris, France, Sept 25, 1942) driving a 2,933-cc V12 Matra-Simca MS 670 Group 5 sports car. The race lap average speed record at Berlin's AVUS track was 171.75 mph by Bernd Rosemeyer (Germany) (1909–38) in a 6-liter V16 Auto Union in 1937.

The Motor Industry Research Association (MIRA) High Speed Circuit (2.82-mile lap with 33-degree banking on the bends) at Lindley, Warwickshire, England, was lapped in 1 min 2.8 sec (average speed 161.655 mph) by David Wishart Hobbs (b Leamington, England, June 9, 1939) driving a 4,994-cc V12 Jaguar XJ13 Group 6 prototype sports car in Apr 1967.

---

* For more detailed information about auto racing, see *The Guinness Guide to Grand Prix Motor Racing* (Sterling).

LE MANS: Record-breaking crowd of 400,000 watches the start of the 24-hour race for touring cars called the Grand Prix d'Endurance.

MAN OF LE MANS (left): Jackie Ickx roared to 6 wins in this race, turned in the fastest practice lap at almost 147 mph and has been a contender since 1969.

Fastest Races

The fastest race in the world is the NASCAR Busch Clash, a 125-mile all-out sprint on the 2½-mile 31-degree banked tri-oval at Daytona International Speedway, Daytona Beach, Fla. In the 1979 event, Elzie Wylie "Buddy" Baker (b Jan 25, 1941) of Charlotte, NC, averaged 194.384 mph in an Oldsmobile. Baker also set the world record for a 500-mile race in 1980 when he won the Daytona 500 at an average speed of 177.602 mph.

The NASCAR qualifying record was set in May 1983 at 202.650 mph by Caleb "Cale" Yarborough (b Mar 27, 1939) at the Alabama International Motor Speedway.

The fastest average speed for a Grand Prix race is 139.218 mph in the British Grand Prix by Alain Prost (France) in a Renault Elf Turbo RE30 on July 16, 1983 over 67 laps (196.44 miles). The race lap record is 1 min 14.21 sec (av. speed 142.291 mph), also by Alain Prost in 1983. The practice lap record is 1 min 09.462 sec (151.956 mph) by Renée Arnoux (France) (b July 4, 1948) in a Ferrari 126C3 on July 15, 1983, all set at Silverstone.

Toughest Circuit

The most grueling and slowest Grand Prix circuit is that for the Monaco Grand Prix (first run Apr 14, 1929), run through the streets and around the harbor of Monte Carlo. It is 3.312 km (2.058 miles) in length and has 11 pronounced corners and several sharp changes of gradient. The race is run over 76 laps (156.4 miles) and involves on average about 1,600 gear changes.

The record for the race is 1 hour 54 min 11.259 sec (average speed 82.21 mph) by Riccardo Patrese (b Italy, Apr 17, 1954) in a Brabham-Ford, May 23, 1982. The race lap record is 1 min 26.35 sec (average speed 85.79 mph) by Patrese in 1980. The practice lap record is 1 min 22.66 sec (average speed 89.63 mph) by Alain Prost (France) in a McLaren TAG Porsche on June 2, 1984.

Le Mans

The greatest distance ever covered in the 24-hour *Grand Prix d'Endurance* (first held May 26–27, 1923) on the old Sarthe circuit (8 miles 650 yd) at Le Mans, France, is 3,314.222 miles by Dr Helmut Marko (b Graz, Austria, Apr 27, 1943) and Jonkheer Gijs van Lennep (b Bloemendaal, Netherlands, March 16, 1942) driving a 4,907-cc flat-12 Porsche 917K Group 5 sports car June 12–13, 1971. The record for the current circuit is 3,136 miles by Al Holbert, Hurley Haywood, and Vern Schuppan (average speed 130.69 mph) in a Porsche 956 June 18–19, 1983. The race lap record (8.475-mile lap) is 3 min 28.9 sec (average speed 145.16 mph) by Bob Wollek in a Lancia C2-84 in 1984. The practice lap record is 3 min 27.6 sec (average speed 146.97 mph) by Jacques-Bernard "Jackie" Ickx (b Belgium, Jan 1, 1945) in a turbocharged 2.1-liter Porsche 936/78 on June 7, 1978.

The race has been won by Ferrari cars nine times, in 1949, 54, 58 and 60–65. The most wins by one man is 6 by Jackie Ickx (Belgium), who won in 1969, 75–77 and 81–82.

Indianapolis 500

The Indianapolis 500-mile race (200 laps) was inaugurated on May 30, 1911. The most successful driver has been Anthony Joseph "A. J." Foyt, Jr (b Houston, Tex, Jan 16, 1935), who won in 1961, 64, 67 and 77.

The record time is 3 hours 3 min 21 sec (average speed 163.612 mph) by Rick Mears (b 1952, Calif) on May 26, 1984, driving a Pennzoil Z-7 special, powered by a Cosworth engine. This was a new record for highest average speed. Also, Mears won by the widest margin in 17 years.

The race lap record is 46.41 sec (average speed 193.924 mph) by Mario Andretti (b Trieste, Feb 28, 1940) (US) driving a Penske-Cosworth PC6 in 1978. The qualifying lap record speed is 210.689 mph by Tom Sneva (US) (b June 1, 1948) driving a March-Cosworth on May 18, 1984.

The first and only woman to qualify for and compete in the Indianapolis 500 is Janet Guthrie (b Mar 7, 1938). She passed her rookie test in May

1976, and earned the right to compete in the qualifying rounds, but was unable to win a place on the starting line when the Vollstedt-Offenhauser she drove was withdrawn from the race after repeated mechanical failures. In the 61st running of the Indianapolis 500, in 1977, Guthrie became the first woman to compete, although her car developed mechanical problems which forced her to retire after 27 laps. In 1978, she completed the race, finishing in ninth place after 190 laps.

The record prize fund was $2,800,000 for the 1984 race, the 68th. The individual prize record is the $434,000 won by Rick Mears in 1984.

Fastest Pit Stop

Bobby Unser (US) took 4 sec to take on fuel on lap 10 of the Indianapolis 500 on May 30, 1976.

Most Successful Drivers

Based on the World Drivers' Championships, inaugurated in 1950, the most successful driver is Juan-Manuel Fangio (b Balcarce, Argentina, June 24, 1911), who won five times in 1951, 54–57. He retired in 1958, after having won 24 Grand Prix races (2 shared).

The most successful driver in terms of race wins is Richard Lee Petty (b Randleman, NC, July 2, 1937) with 200 NASCAR Grand National wins, 1958–84. (See also *Stock Car Racing.*) His best season was 1967 with 27 wins. His total earnings reached $5,504,977 by July 25, 1984. Geoff Bodine won 55 races in 1978.

The most Grand Prix victories is 27 by Jackie Stewart (b June 11, 1939) of Scotland between Sept 12, 1965 and Aug 5, 1973. Jim Clark (1936–1968) of Scotland holds the record of Grand Prix victories in one year with 7 in 1963. He won 61 Formula One and Formula Libre races between 1959 and 1968. The most Grand Prix starts is 176 (out of a possible 184) between May 18, 1958, and Jan 26, 1975, by (Norman) Graham Hill (1929–1975). He took part in 90 *consecutive* Grands Prix between Nov 20, 1960 and Oct 5, 1969.

Oldest and Youngest World Champions

The oldest was Juan-Manuel Fangio, who won his last World Championship Aug 18, 1957, aged 46 years 55 days. The youngest was Emerson Fittipaldi (b São Paulo, Brazil, Dec 12, 1946) who won his first World Championship Sept 10, 1972, aged 25 years 273 days.

Youngest and Oldest Grand Prix Winners and Drivers

The youngest Grand Prix winner was Bruce Leslie McLaren (1937–70) of New Zealand, who won the US Grand Prix at Sebring, Fla, on Dec 12, 1959, aged 22 years 104 days. The oldest Grand Prix winner was Tazio Giorgio Nuvolari (1892–1953) of Italy, who won the Albi Grand Prix at Albi, France, on July 14, 1946, aged 53 years 240 days.

The oldest Grand Prix driver was Louis Alexandre Chiron (Monaco, 1899–1979), who finished 6th in the Monaco Grand Prix on May 22, 1955, aged 55 years 292 days. The youngest Grand Prix driver was Michael Christopher Thackwell (b New Zealand, March 30, 1961) who took part in the Canadian Grand Prix in Sept 28, 1980, aged 19 years 182 days.

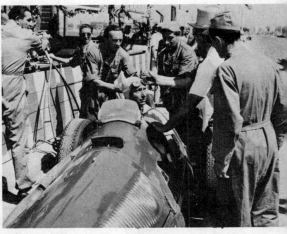

MOST SUCCESSFUL DRIVERS: (Left) Richard Petty has won 200 NASCAR races and earned $5.5 million. Juan-Manuel Fangio (above) won 24 Grand Prix races before retiring in 1958. He won his last race when more than 46 years old.

Stock Car Racing

Richard Petty was the first stock car driver to attain $1 million lifetime earnings on Aug 1, 1971. Also see *Most Successful Drivers*.

Closest Finishes

The closest finish to a World Championship race was in the Italian Grand Prix at Monza on Sept 5, 1971. Just 0.61 sec separated winner Peter Gethin (GB) from the fifth placer.

The closest finish in the Indianapolis 500 was in the 1982 race when the winner, Gordon Johncock, crossed the finish line just 0.16 sec before runner-up Rick Mears.

Manufacturers

Ferraris have won a record eight manufacturers' world championships, 1961, 1964, 1975–7, 1979, 1982–3. Ferraris have 88 race wins in 359 Grands Prix, 1950–1983.

Duration Record

The greatest distance ever covered in one year is 400,000 km (248,548.5 miles) by François Lecot (1879–1949), an innkeeper from Rochetaillée, France, in a 1,900-cc 66-bhp Citroën 11 sedan mainly between Paris and Monte Carlo, from July 22, 1935 to July 26, 1936. He drove on 363 of the 370 days allowed.

Indianapolis 500

Winners since 1946 (all US except where stated):

	Driver	Car	Speed (mph)
1946	George Robson	Thorne Engineering	114.820
1947	Mauri Rose	Blue Crown Special	116.338
1948	Mauri Rose	Blue Crown Special	119.814
1949	Bill Holland	Blue Crown Special	121.327
1950	Johnny Parsons	Wynn Kurtis Kraft	124.002
1951	Lee Wallard	Belanger	126.224
1952	Troy Ruttman	Agajanian	128.922
1953	Bill Vukovich	Fuel Injection	128.740
1954	Bill Vukovich	Fuel Injection	130.840
1955	Bob Sweikert	John Zink Special	128.209
1956	Pat Flaherty	John Zink Special	128.490
1957	Sam Hanks	Belond Exhaust	135.601
1958	Jimmy Bryan	Belond A. P.	133.791
1959	Rodger Ward	Leader Card Special	135.857
1960	Jim Rathmann	Ken-Paul Special	138.767
1961	A. J. Foyt	Bowes Seal Fast	139.130
1962	Rodger Ward	Leader Card Special	140.293
1963	Parnelli Jones	Agajanian Special	143.137
1964	A. J. Foyt	Sheraton-Thompson Special	147.350
1965	Jim Clark (GB)	Lotus-Ford	150.686
1966	Graham Hill (GB)	American Red Ball	144.317
1967	A. J. Foyt	Sheraton-Thompson Special	151.207
1968	Bobby Unser	Rislone Special	152.882
1969	Mario Andretti	STP Oil Treatment Special	156.867
1970	Al Unser	Johnny Lightning Special	155.749
1971	Al Unser	Johnny Lightning Special	157.735
1972	Mark Donohue	Sunoco McLaren	162.962
1973	Gordon Johncock	STP Double Oil Filter	159.036
1974	Johnny Rutherford	McLaren	158.589
1975	Bobby Unser	Jorgensen Eagle	149.213
1976	Johnny Rutherford	Hygain McLaren	148.725
1977	A. J. Foyt	Gilmore Coyote-Foyt	161.331
1978	Al Unser	Lola-Chapparal Cosworth	161.363
1979	Rick Mears	Penske-Cosworth	158.899
1980	Johnny Rutherford	Chapparal Cosworth	142.862
1981	Bobby Unser	Penske-Cosworth	139.084
1982	Gordon Johncock	Wildcat-Cosworth	162.025
1983	Tom Sneva	March-Cosworth	162.117
1984	Rick Mears	March-Cosworth	163.612

Le Mans 24-Hour Race

The world's most important race for sports cars was first held in 1923. Winners since 1949 when the race was revived after the Second World War:

	Driver	Car	Speed (mph)
1949	Luigi Chinetti/Lord Peter Selsdon	Ferrari	82.27
1950	Louis Rosier/Jean-Louis Rosier	Talbot	89.73
1951	Peter Walker/Peter Whitehead	Jaguar	93.50
1952	Hermann Lang/Fritz Riess	Mercedes	96.67
1953	Anthony Rolt/Duncan Hamilton	Jaguar	105.85
1954	José Froilan Gonzalez/Maurice Trintignant	Ferrari	105.15
1955	Mike Hawthorn/Ivor Bueb	Jaguar	107.07
1956	Ron Flockhart/Ninian Sanderson	Jaguar	104.46
1957	Ron Flockhart/Ivor Bueb	Jaguar	113.85
1958	Phil Hill/Olivier Gendebien	Ferrari	106.20
1959	Roy Salvadori/Carroll Shelby	Aston Martin	112.57
1960	Paul Frère/Olivier Gendebien	Ferrari	109.19
1961	Phil Hill/Olivier Gendebien	Ferrari	115.90
1962	Phil Hill/Olivier Gendebien	Ferrari	115.24
1963	Ludovico Scarfiotti/Lorenzo Bandini	Ferrari	118.10
1964	Jean Guichet/Nino Vaccarella	Ferrari	121.55
1965	Masten Gregory/Jochen Rindt	Ferrari	121.09
1966	Bruce McLaren/Chris Amon	Ford	126.01

Le Mans (continued)

Year	Driver	Car	
1967	Anthony Joseph Foyt/Dan Gurney	Ford	132.49
1968	Pedro Rodriguez/Lucien Bianchi	Ford	115.29
1969	Jackie Ickx/Jackie Oliver	Ford	125.44
1970	Hans Herrmann/Richard Attwood	Porsche	119.29
1971	Helmut Marko/Gijs van Lennep	Porsche	138.142
1972	Graham Hill/Henri Pescarolo	Matra-Simca	121.47
1973	Henri Pescarolo/Gerard Larrousse	Matra-Simca	125.68
1974	Henri Pescarolo/Gerard Larrousse	Matra-Simca	119.27
1975	Jackie Ickx/Derek Bell	Gulf Ford	118.99
1976	Jackie Ickx/Gijs van Lennep	Porsche	123.50
1977	Jackie Ickx/Jurgen Barth/Hurley Haywood	Porsche	120.95
1978	Didier Peroni/Jean-Pierre Jaussaud	Renault Alpine	130.60
1979	Klaus Ludwig/Bill and Don Whittington	Porsche	108.06
1980	Jean-Pierre Jaussaud/Jean Rondeau	Rondeau	119.17
1981	Jackie Ickx/Derek Bell	Porsche	124.87
1982	Jackie Ickx/Derek Bell	Porsche	126.84
1983	Vern Schuppan/Hurley Haywood/Al Holbert	Porsche	130.70
1984	Klaus Ludwig/Henri Pescarolo	Porsche	126.88

Daytona 500

Year	Driver	Car	Average Speed
1959	Lee Petty	59 Oldsmobile	135.521
1960	Junior Johnson	59 Chevrolet	124.740
1961	Marvin Panch	60 Pontiac	149.601
1962	Fireball Roberts	62 Pontiac	152.529
1963	Tiny Lund	63 Ford	151.566
1964	Richard Petty	64 Plymouth	154.334
1965*	Fred Lorenzen	65 Ford	141.539
1966**	Richard Petty	66 Plymouth	160.627
1967	Mario Andretti	67 Ford	146.926
1968	Cale Yarborough	68 Mercury	143.251
1969	LeeRoy Yarborough	69 Ford	157.950
1970	Pete Hamilton	70 Plymouth	149.601
1971	Richard Petty	71 Plymouth	144.462
1972	A. J. Foyt	71 Mercury	161.550
1973	Richard Petty	73 Dodge	157.205
1974	Richard Petty	74 Dodge	140.894
1975	Benny Parsons	Chevrolet	153.649
1976	David Pearson	Mercury	152.181
1977	Cale Yarborough	Chevrolet	153.218
1978	Bobby Allison	Ford	159.730
1979	Richard Petty	Oldsmobile	143.977
1980	Buddy Baker	Oldsmobile	177.602
1981	Richard Petty	Buick	169.651
1982	Bobby Allison	Buick	153.991
1983	Cale Yarborough	Pontiac	155.979
1984	Cale Yarborough	Chevrolet	150.994

* 332½ miles because of rain
** 495 miles because of rain

Rocket or Jet-Engined Dragsters

Terminal velocity is the speed attained at the end of a 440-yd run made from a standing start, and elapsed time is the time taken for the run.

The highest terminal velocity recorded by any dragster is 392.54 mph by Kitty O'Neil (US) at El Mirage Dry Lake, Calif, on July 7, 1977. The lowest elapsed time was 3.72 sec also by Kitty O'Neil on the same occasion.

Piston-Engined Dragsters

The highest terminal velocity recorded is 257.14 mph by Rocky Epperly (US) at Irvine, Calif on Oct 15, 1983.

Donald Glenn "Big Daddy" Garlits (US) (b 1932) set an American Hot Rod Association record (not accepted by the National Hot Rod Assoc) of 260.49 mph on July 11, 1982 at Gary, Ind in an AHRA-approved top fuel dragster powered by a 480-cu in, supercharged, fuel-injected Dodge V8 engine.

The world record for two runs in opposite directions over 440 yd from a standing start is 6.70 sec by Dennis Victor Priddle (b 1945) of Yeovil, Somerset, England, driving his 6,424-cc supercharged Chrysler dragster, developing 1,700 bhp using nitromethane and methanol, at Elvington Airfield, England, Oct 7, 1972. The faster run took 6.65 sec.

The lowest elapsed time recorded by a piston-engined dragster is 5.484 sec by Gary Beck (US) at the 28th annual US Nationals at Indianapolis in 1982.

Land Speed Records

The highest speed attained by any wheeled land vehicle is 739.666 mph or Mach 1.0106 (making it the only land vehicle to break the sound barrier) *in a one-way stretch* by the rocket-engined *Budweiser Rocket,* designed by William Frederick, and driven by Stan Barrett at Edwards Air Force Base, California, on Dec 17, 1979. The vehicle, owned by Hal Needham, has a 48,000-hp rocket engine with 6,000 lb of extra thrust from a sidewinder missile. The rear wheels (100-lb solid discs) lifted 10 in off the ground above Mach 0.95, acting as 7,500-rpm gyroscopes.

The official land speed record, which is for the average of a two-way run, was set on Oct 4, 1983 when Richard Noble (GB) drove a jet-powered car, *Thrust 2,* at 633.468 mph at Black Rock Desert, Gerlach, Nev. The previous record, 622.287, was set by Gary Gabelich and had stood for 13 years.

The most successful land speed record breaker was Major Malcolm Campbell (1885–1948) (UK). He broke the official record nine times between Sept 25, 1924, with 146.157 mph in a Sunbeam, and Sept 3, 1935, when he achieved 301.129 mph in the Rolls-Royce-engined *Bluebird.*

The world speed record for compression-ignition-engined cars is 190.344 mph (average of two runs over measured mile) by Robert Havemann of Eureka, Calif, driving his *Corsair* streamliner, powered by a turbocharged 6.981-cc 6-cylinder GMC 6-71 diesel engine developing 746 bhp, at Bonneville Salt Flats, Utah, in Aug, 1971. The faster run was made at 210 mph.

Pikes Peak Race

The Pikes Peak Auto Hill Climb, Colorado (instituted 1916) has been won by Bobby Unser 13 times between 1956 and 1974 (10 championship, 2 stock and 1 sports car title). In the 1979 race Dick Dodge set a record time of 11 min 54.18 sec in a Chevrolet-powered Wells Coyote over the 12.42-mile course, rising from 9,402 to 14,110 ft through 157 curves.

633.468 MPH is the "official" land speed record for a jet-powered car, set in a two-way run at Black Rock Desert, Nev, on Oct 4, 1983 by Richard Noble of England in his "Thrust 2." His average speed works out to a mile in 5.683 sec. (Photos by Franklin Berger.)

Earliest Rally

The earliest long rally was promoted by the Parisian daily *Le Matin* in 1907 from Peking to Paris, over about 7,500 miles on June 10. The winner, Prince Scipione Borghese (1871–1927), arrived in Paris on Aug 10, 1907 in his 40-hp Itala accompanied by his chauffeur, Ettore, and Luigi Barzini.

Longest Rallies

The longest rally ever was the *Singapore Airlines* London-Sydney Rally over 19,329 miles, from Covent Garden, London, on Aug 14, 1977, to the Sydney Opera House, won Sept 28, 1977, by Andrew Cowan, Colin Malkin and Michael Broad in a Mercedes 280E.

The longest rally held annually is the Safari Rally (first run 1953 through Kenya, Tanzania and Uganda), which is up to 3,874 miles long, as in the 17th Safari held Apr 8–12, 1971. It has been won a record 5 times by Shekhar Mehta (Uganda) in 1973, 79–82.

FASTEST EXPERIMENTAL CAR: This Mercedes-Benz C III–IV coupe reached 250.958 mph on May 5, 1979 to set a record for highest average lap speed on a closed circuit.

Monte Carlo

The Monte Carlo Rally (first run 1911) has been won a record 4 times by Sandro Munari (Italy) in 1972, 75–77; and by Walter Röhrl (b Mar 7, 1947) (with co-driver Christian Geistdorfer) in 1980, 1982–84, each time in a different car. Walter Röhrl is also the only man to win two drivers' world championships (inst 1979), 1980 and 1982.

The smallest car to win was an 851-cc Saab driven by Erik Carlsson (b Sweden, March 5, 1929) and Gunnar Häggbom of Sweden, in 1962, and by Carlsson and Gunnar Palm in 1963.

Worst Disaster

Drivers have hit spectators with appalling regularity throughout the history of racing, first place doubtless going to Pierre Levegh, who killed 81 spectators as well as himself at Le Mans in 1955.

BADMINTON

Origins

A game similar to badminton was played in China in the 2nd millennium BC. The modern game may have evolved *c.* 1870 at Badminton Hall in Avon, England, the seat of the Dukes of Beaufort, or from a game played in India. The first modern rules were codified in Poona, India in 1876.

International Championships

The International Championship or Thomas Cup (instituted 1948) has been won 8 times by Indonesia, in 1958, 61, 64, 70, 73, 76, 79, and 1984. Indonesians have also won all-England titles 12 times in the last 16 years.

The Ladies International Championship or Uber Cup (instituted 1956) had been won 5 times by Japan (1966, 69, 72, 78 and 81).

Most Titles

The record for men's singles in the All-England Championship is 8 by Rudy Hartono Kurniawan (b Aug 18, 1948) of Indonesia (1968–74, 76). The most, including doubles, by women is 17, a record shared by Muriel Lucas (later Mrs King Adams) (1899–1910) and Mrs G. C. K. Hashman (*née* Judy Devlin) (US) (b Oct 22, 1935), whose wins came from 1954 to 1967, including a record 10 singles titles. Judy Hashman also won 29 US titles.

Marathons

The longest singles match is 74 hours 41 min by Mike Watts and Bryan Garnham at Llansamlet Parish Hall, Swansea, Wales, Oct 15–18, 1981.

The longest doubles is 77 hours 1 min by Paul Farmer, Andrew Hood, Ben Smith and Loraine Stoney in Nottingham, Eng, May 29–June 1, 1984.

Longest Hit

Frank Rugani drove a shuttlecock 79 ft 8½ in in indoor tests at San Jose, Calif, Feb 29, 1964.

BADMINTON CHAMPION: Indonesian Rudy Hartono won the men's singles world title in 1980, captured 8 singles titles in the All-England championships and has been the mainstay of Indonesia's successful Thomas Cup teams.

BASEBALL

Earliest Games

The Reverend Thomas Wilson, of Maidstone, Kent, England, wrote disapprovingly, in 1700, of baseball being played on Sundays. The earliest game on record under the Cartwright (Alexander Joy Cartwright, Jr, 1820–92) rules was on June 19, 1846, in Hoboken, NJ, where the "New York Nine" defeated the Knickerbockers 23 to 1 in 4 innings. The earliest all-professional team was the Cincinnati Red Stockings in 1869, who had 56 wins and 1 tie that season.

In 1893, there was an important rules change that must be considered when looking at batting records. In the early days of the game, pitching was viewed merely as a matter of trying to get the ball over the plate. Any outfielder might be called upon to pitch. But as managers discovered that there was a decisive advantage to having a pitcher who knew how to throw a knuckleball or a spitball, batting averages declined drastically. Thus in 1893 the distance between home plate and the pitcher's rubber was changed from 50 ft to the current 60 ft 6 in. Batting averages soared.

Home Runs

Henry L. (Hank) Aaron (b Feb 5, 1934, Mobile, Ala) broke the major league record set by George H. (Babe) Ruth of 714 home runs in a lifetime when he hit No. 715 on Apr 8, 1974. Between 1954 and 1974 he hit 733 home runs for the Milwaukee and Atlanta Braves in the National League. In 1975, he switched to the Milwaukee Brewers in the American League and in that year and 1976, when he finally retired, he hit 22 more, bringing his lifetime total to 755, the major league record.

A North American record of almost 800 in a lifetime has been claimed for Josh Gibson (1911–47), mostly for the Homestead Grays of the Negro National League, who was elected in 1972 to the Baseball Hall of Fame in Cooperstown, NY. Gibson is said to have hit 75 round-trippers in one season, in 1931, but no official records were kept.

The most officially recorded home runs hit by a professional player in the US in one season is 72, by Joe Bauman, of the Roswell, NM team, a minor league club, in 1954. The major league record is 61 in 162 games by Roger Maris (b Sept 10, 1934), of the NY Yankees, in 1961. George Herman "Babe" Ruth (1895–1948) hit 60 in a 154-game season in 1927.

The longest home run ever measured was one of 618 ft by Roy Edward "Dizzy" Carlyle (1900–56) in a minor league game at Emeryville Ball Park, Calif, July 4, 1929. Babe Ruth hit a 587-ft homer for the Boston Red Sox vs NY Giants in an exhibition game at Tampa, Fla, in 1919. The longest measured home run in a regular-season major league game is 565 ft by Mickey Mantle (b Oct 20, 1931) for the NY Yankees vs Washington Senators on Apr 17, 1953, at Griffith Stadium, Wash DC.

LONGBALL: Josh Gibson (left, above) died only 3 months before Jackie Robinson became the first black man to play in the major leagues (1947). If Josh had been welcome in the majors, he might have rewritten the record books. He was credited with 800 home runs in the Negro leagues. Hank Aaron (right) did rewrite the record book. The great outfielder hit 755 homers in the major leagues and collected a lifetime record of 2,297 rbi's.

SWAT TEAM: Roger Maris (left, below) watches his 60th home run fly into the seats at Yankee Stadium. Maris then hit his record-breaking 61st in the last game of the 1961 season. Hounded by the press, Maris gained an undeserved reputation for surliness. Although his home run records have been surpassed, Babe Ruth (right) is unlikely to be forgotten. His .625 batting average in the 1928 World Series is the best ever, as is his career slugging percentage of .690.

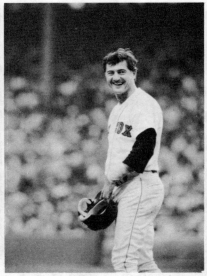

868 HOMERS was the record set in Japanese baseball by Sadaharu Oh (left). A new MOST GAMES PLAYED record was set in 1983 by Carl Yastrzemski, Boston AL (right), only to have that record beaten by Pete Rose (see next page) in 1984. (Photo by Steve Babineau.)

Shortest and Tallest Players

The shortest major league player was surely Eddie Gaedel, a 3-ft-7-in, 65-lb midget, who pinch hit for the St Louis Browns vs the Detroit Tigers on Aug 19, 1951. Wearing number ⅛, the batter with the smallest ever major league strike zone walked on four pitches. Following the game, major league rules were hastily rewritten to prevent the recurrence of such an affair.

The tallest major leaguer was John Alexander Gee (b Dec 7, 1915), a 6-ft-9-in pitcher who spent 6 seasons in the National League: 1939, 41, 43–46.

Fastest Base Runner

Ernest Evar Swanson (1902–73) took only 13.3 sec to circle the bases at Columbus, Ohio, in 1932, averaging 18.45 mph.

Sadaharu Oh played for 22 years in the Japanese majors after gaining fame as a schoolboy star, starting out as a lefty pitcher (like Babe Ruth), and winding up as a first baseman to keep his bat in the lineup daily. With a strange one-legged stance, he would step into the ball and gain impetus by swinging his bat like a Samurai sword, a discipline he learned from a master of the martial arts. He reveals in his autobiography (Times Books, 1984) that he also practiced Zen for mental strength. He played with and against many US ball players in Japanese leagues, and would have been a star in the US, in the opinion of 30 American players who are quoted in the book's appendix.

MOST AT-BATS, MOST GAMES: Pete Rose, spark plug of the Cincinnati Reds for 15 years and with the Phillies for 5 years after that, now manager of the Reds, is still aiming to beat Ty Cobb's record of 4,191 hits in his career. (UPI-Bettman Archive)

Youngest and Oldest Players

The youngest major league player of all time was the Cincinnati pitcher Joe Nuxhall, who started his career in June 1944, aged 15 years 10 months 11 days.

Leroy Satchel Paige (1906?–82) pitched three scoreless innings for the Kansas City Athletics at age 59 in 1965. Baseball's color barrier had kept him out of the major leagues until 1948, when he was a 42-year-old "rookie," and his record of 6 wins and 1 loss helped the Cleveland Indians win the pennant. His birthday is listed as July 7, 1906, but many believe he was born earlier. The Atlanta Braves carried Paige on their roster in 1968 to allow him to qualify for a pension.

Hit by Pitch

Ron Hunt, an infielder who played with various National League teams from 1963 to 1974, led the league in getting hit by pitched balls for a record 7 consecutive years. His career total is 243, also a major league record.

World Series Attendance

The World Series record attendance is 420,784 (6 games with total gate receipts of $2,626,973.44) when the Los Angeles Dodgers beat the Chicago White Sox 4 games to 2, Oct 1–8, 1959.

The single game record is 92,706 for the fifth game (gate receipts $552,774.77) at the Memorial Coliseum (no longer used for baseball), LA, Oct 6, 1959.

BASE STEALER SUPREME: Rickey Henderson (left) while with the Oakland A's in 1982, stole 130 bases in 149 games. (Steve Babineau photo.) HIT IN EVERY GAME for 56 games is the record Joe DiMaggio of the Yankees set in 1941, collecting 91 hits in those 2 months.

Do-Nothing Record

Toby Harrah of the Texas Rangers (AL) played an entire double-header at shortstop on June 26, 1976, without having a chance to make any fielding plays, assists or putouts.

Do-Everything Record

Two major league ballplayers, Bert Campaneris (b Mar 12, 1942) and Cesar Tovar (b July 3, 1940), have the distinction of playing each of the nine field positions in a single major league game. Campaneris did it first, on Sept 8, 1965, when his team, the Kansas City Athletics, announced he would. He played one inning at each position, including the full eighth inning as a pitcher and gave up just one run. Tovar duplicated the feat on Sept 22, 1968, when he played for the Minnesota Twins. He pitched a scoreless first inning and retired the first batter, none other than Campaneris. On June 4, 1983, Mike Ashman, a minor league player for the Albany-Colonie A's of the Eastern League, improved upon the Campaneris-Tovar feat by playing 10 positions, including designated hitter, in a game against Nashua.

Tale of Two Cities Record

Joel Youngblood (b Aug 28, 1951) started a day game at Wrigley Field in Chicago on Aug 4, 1982, as a NY Met, hit a single in the 3rd inning, left the game when he received word that he had been traded to the Montreal Expos, and immediately made plane reservations to Philadelphia where the Expos were playing a night game. He had dinner on the plane, took a taxi from the airport, arrived at the field in the 3rd inning, was substituted for the Expos' right fielder in the 6th inning, and got a single in his one time at bat. His record: playing (and getting a hit) for two different teams in two different cities in the same day. Other major leaguers have played for two teams in one day, but in only one city as they were swapped between games of a doubleheader.

Managers

Connie Mack (1892–1956) managed in the major leagues for 53 seasons—3 with Pittsburgh (NL), 1894–96, and 50 with the Philadelphia Athletics (AL), the team he owned, 1901–50. He amassed a record 3,776 regular-season victories (952 victories ahead of John McGraw). Eddie Stanky managed the Texas Rangers (AL) for one day (June 23, 1977) before deciding he did not want the job—even though his team beat Minnesota, 10–8. It is believed to be the shortest term for anyone who signed a managerial contract (that is, excluding interim managers).

Charles D. "Casey" Stengel (1890–1975) set records by managing the NY Yankees (AL) in 10 World Series and winning 7 of them, including 5 in a row (1949–53).

Longest Throw

The longest throw of a 5–5¼-oz (regulation) baseball is 445 ft 10 in by Glen Gorbous (b Canada) Aug 1, 1957. Mildred "Babe" Didrikson (later Mrs George Zaharias) (1914–56) threw a ball 296 ft at Jersey City, NJ, July 25, 1931.

LITTLEST MAJOR LEAGUER: In their quest for a leadoff base runner, the St. Louis Browns sent 3-ft-7-in Eddie Gaedel to the plate as a pinch hitter in the first inning of the second game of a doubleheader against the Detroit Tigers on Aug 19, 1951. The 26-year-old midget walked on four pitches. Nonetheless, the hapless Browns were unable to score that inning.

STRIKEOUT SPECIALISTS: Walter Johnson (left, above) of the Wash Senators pitched 113 shutouts and struck-out 3,508 batters, 1907–27. (UPI.) Nolan Ryan (right, above) had 3,874 strikeouts to the end of the 1984 season, followed closely at 3,872 by Steve Carlton (right, below). (Calif Angels, Phila Phillies) KNUCKLEBALL PITCHER Hoyt Wilhelm (left, below) pitched in 1,070 games, 1952–72, and finished 651 games.

Fastest Pitcher

The fastest recorded pitcher is Lynn Nolan Ryan (b Jan 31, 1947) who, on Aug 20, 1974 (then of the California Angels, now of the Houston Astros) at Anaheim Stadium, Calif, was measured to pitch at 100.9 mph.

Most Strikeouts, Career

Steve Carlton and Nolan Ryan, both still active, are in a race to see who will finish his career with the record number of strikeouts. Carlton completed the 1984 season with 3,872 with Ryan slightly ahead with 3,874. On April 27, 1983, in Montreal, Ryan was the first to eclipse Walter Johnson's record of 3,508 which he had set between 1907 and 1927 and which stood for 55 years. Carlton passed Ryan on June 7, 1983, when he notched his 3,526th strikeout. Carlton played with St L (NL) 1965–71 and Phil (NL) 1972–84; Ryan was with NY (NL) 1966, 1968–71; Calif (AL) 1972–79, and Houston (NL) 1980–84; Johnson spent his entire career with the Washington Senators (AL).

MAJOR LEAGUE ALL-TIME RECORDS
(including 1984 season)

Individual Batting

Highest percentage, lifetime (5,000 at-bats)
.367   Tyrus R. Cobb, Det AL, 1905–26; Phil AL, 1927–28

Highest percentage, season (500 at-bats) (Leader in each league)
.438   Hugh Duffy, Bos NL, 1894
.422   Napoleon Lajoie, Phil AL, 1901

Most games played
3,371   Peter Rose, Cin NL, 1963–78; Phil NL, 1979–83; Cin 1984

Most consecutive games played
2,130   Henry Louis Gehrig, NY AL, June 1, 1925 through Apr 30, 1939

Most runs batted in, season
190   Lewis R. (Hack) Wilson, Chi NL, 155 games, 1930

Most runs batted in, game
12   James L. Bottomley, St L NL, Sept 16, 1924

Most runs batted in, inning
7   Edward Cartwright, St L AA, Sept 23, 1890

Most runs batted in, lifetime
2,297   Henry L. Aaron, Mil NL, 1954–65, Atl NL, 1966–74; Mil AL, 1975–76

Most runs, lifetime
2,245   Tyrus R. Cobb, Det AL, 1905–26; Phil AL, 1927–28

Most base hits, lifetime
4,191   Tyrus R. Cobb, Det AL, 1905–26; Phil AL, 1927–28; 24 years

Most base hits, season
257   George H. Sisler, St L AL, 154 games, 1920

Most hits in succession
12   M. Frank (Pinky) Higgins, Bos AL, June 19–21 (4 games), 1938
Walter Dropo, Det AL, July 14, July 15, 2 games, 1952

Most base hits, consecutive, game
7   Wilbert Robinson, Balt NL, June 10, 1892, 1st game (7-ab), 6-1b, 1-2b
Renaldo Stennett, Pitt NL, Sept 16, 1975 (7-ab), 4-1b, 2-2b, 1-3b
Cesar Gutierrez, Det AL, June 21, 1970, 2nd game (7-ab) 6-1b, 1-2b (extra-inning game)

Most times at bat, lifetime
13,411   Peter Rose, Cin NL, 1963–78; Phil NL, 1979–83; Cin 1984

Most consecutive games batted safely, season
56   Joseph P. DiMaggio, NY AL (91 hits—16-2b, 4-3b, 15 hr), May 15 to July 16, 1941

Most total bases, lifetime
6,856   Henry L. Aaron, Mil NL, 1954–65; Atl NL, 1966–74; Mil AL, 1975–76

Most total bases, season
457   George H. (Babe) Ruth, NY AL, 152 gs (85 on 1b, 88 on 2b, 48 on 3b, 236 on hr), 1921

Most total bases, game
18   Joseph W. Adcock, Mil NL (1-2b, 4-hr), July 31, 1954

Individual Batting (*continued*)

Most one-base hits (singles), season
202　William H. Keeler, Balt NL, 128 games, 1898

Most two-base hits, season
67　Earl W. Webb, Bos AL, 151 games, 1931

Most three-base hits, season
36　J. Owen Wilson, Pitts NL, 152 games, 1912

Most home runs, season
61　Roger E. Maris, NY AL (162-game schedule) (30 home, 31 away), 161 gs, 1961
60　George H. (Babe) Ruth, NY AL (154-game schedule) (28 home, 32 away), 151 gs, 1927

Most home runs, lifetime
755　Henry L. Aaron, Mil NL, 1954 (13), 1955 (27), 1956 (26), 1957 (44), 1958 (30), 1959 (39), 1960 (40), 1961 (34), 1962 (45), 1963 (44), 1964 (24), 1965 (32); Atl NL, 1966 (44), 1967 (39), 1968 (29), 1969 (44), 1970 (38), 1971 (47), 1972 (34), 1973 (40), 1974 (20); Mil AL, 1975 (12), 1976 (10)

Most home runs, bases filled, lifetime
23　Henry Louis Gehrig, NY AL, 1927–1938

Most home runs, with bases filled, game
2　Anthony M. Lazzeri, NY AL, May 24, 1936
　　James R. Tabor, Bos AL (2nd game), July 4, 1939
　　Rudolph York, Bos AL, July 27, 1946

James E. Gentile, Balt AL, May 9, 1961 (consecutive at-bats)
Tony L. Cloninger, Atl NL, July 3, 1966
James T. Northrup Det AL, June 24, 1968 (consecutive at-bats)
Frank Robinson, Balt AL, June 26, 1970 (consecutive at-bats)

Most home runs with bases filled, season
5　Ernest Banks, Chi NL, May 11, 19, July 17 (1st game), Aug 2, Sept 19, 1955
　　James E. Gentile, Balt AL, May 9 (2), July 2, 7, Sept 22, 1961

Most consecutive games hitting home runs
8　R. Dale Long, Pitt NL, May 19–28, 1956

Most home runs, one doubleheader
5　Stanley F. Musial, St L NL, 1st game (3), 2nd game (2), May 2, 1954
　　Nathan Colbert, SD NL, 1st game (2), 2nd game (3), Aug 1, 1972

Most bases on balls, game
6　James E. Foxx, Bos AL, June 16, 1938

Most bases on balls, season
170　George H. (Babe) Ruth, NY AL, 152 games, 1923

Most hits, pinch-hitter, lifetime
150　Manuel R. Mota, SF NL, 1962; Pitt NL, 1963–1968; Mont NL, 1969; LA NL, 1969–1980

Most consecutive home runs, pinch-hitter
3　Del Unser, Phil NL, June 30, July 5, 10, 1979
　　Lee Lacy, LA NL, May 2, 6, 17, 1978 (one walk in between)

Fly Ball Stays Up

When the architects planned the Metrodome in Minneapolis they didn't know they had to contend with Dave Kingman, the slugger who has played in the American and National Leagues, who has been known previously for his many home runs and many strike-outs. Now Kingman has entered the *Guinness Book* with a record for a fly ball he hit that went straight up and didn't come down. It happened when he came up to bat for the Oakland Athletics against the Minneapolis Twins on the night of May 4, 1984.

The ball penetrated the netting of the fabric ceiling of the dome 180 feet up and rolled around. When it didn't drop down for an in-fielder to catch it, the umpires didn't know what to call it. It wasn't in the rule book, of course. Was Kingman out, on the supposition that the fly ball would have been caught? They decided that the ball park was at fault and ruled it a "ground rule double." Fair? The A's lost the game anyway, 3–1.

P.S. When the groundskeeper got the ball down, it was sent to the Baseball Hall of Fame in Cooperstown, NY.

CAPTURING THE FLAG: Stan "The Man" Musial (left) helped the St. Louis Cardinals to 4 pennants in 5 years, hit 5 home runs in one day, and was selected as the National League MVP 3 times. Lou Gehrig (right) played in 2,130 consecutive games, helping the Yankees to 6 of their record 22 championships. The Iron Man's 23 grand-slam home runs is a career record.

Most consecutive pinch hits, lifetime
9   David E. Philley, Phil NL, Sept 9, 11, 12, 13, 19, 20, 27, 28, 1958; Apr 16, 1959

Base Running

Most stolen bases, lifetime
938   Louis C. Brock, Chi-St L NL, 1961–79

Most stolen bases, season since 1900
130   Rickey Henderson, Oak AL, 149 games, 1982

Most stolen bases, game
7   George F. (Piano Legs) Gore, Chi NL, June 25, 1881
William R. (Sliding Billy) Hamilton, Phil NL, 2nd game, 8 inn, Aug 31, 1894

Modern record
6   Edward T. Collins, Phil AL, Sept 11 and again 22, 1912

Most times stealing home, lifetime
35   Tyrus R. Cobb, Det-Phil AL, 1905–28

Fewest times caught stealing, season (50+ attempts)
2   Max Carey, Pitt NL, 1922 (53 atts)

Pitching

In 1893 the distance from home plate to where the pitcher must stand was changed from 50 feet to the current 60 feet, 6 in.

Most years
25   James Kaat, Minn AL 1959–73; Chi AL 1973–75; Phil NL 1976–79; NY AL 1979–80; St L NL 1980–83

WORLD SERIES SLUGGING gave Reggie Jackson the nickname "Mr. October." He hit 5 homers in the 1977 Series (including first-pitch 4-baggers in one game) and has a record slugging average of .755.

Pitching (continued)
Most games, lifetime
1,070 J. Hoyt Wilhelm, NY-St L-Atl-
Chi-LA (448) NL, 1952–57,
69–72; Clev-Balt-Chi-Cal (622)
AL, 1957–69

Most complete games, lifetime
751 Denton T. (Cy) Young, Clev-St L-
Bos NL (428); Bos-Clev AL
(323), 1890–1911

Most games, season
106 Mike Marshall, LA NL, 1974

Most complete games, season
74 William H. White, Cin NL, 1879

Most innings pitched, game
26 Leon J. Cadore, Bklyn NL, May 1,
1920
Joseph Oeschger, Bos NL, May 1,
1920

Lowest earned run average, season
0.90 Ferdinand M. Schupp, NY NL,
1916 (140 inn)
1.01 Hubert B. (Dutch) Leonard, Bos
AL, 1914 (222 inn)
1.12 Robert Gibson, St L NL, 1968 (305
inn)

Most games won, lifetime
511 Denton T. (Cy) Young, Clev NL
(239) 1890–98; St L NL (46)
1899–1900; Bos AL (193)
1901–08; Clev AL (29) 1909–11;
Bos NL (4) 1911

Most games won, season
60 Charles Radbourn, Providence NL,
1884

Most consecutive games won, lifetime
24 Carl O. Hubbell, NY NL, 1936 (16);
1937 (8)

Most consecutive games won, season
19 Timothy J. Keefe, NY NL, 1888
Richard W. Marquard, NY NL,
1912

Most shutout games, season
16 George W. Bradley, St L NL, 1876
Grover C. Alexander, Phil NL,
1916

Most shutout games, lifetime
113 Walter P. Johnson, Wash AL, 21
years, 1907–27

Most consecutive shutout games, season
6 Donald S. Drysdale, LA NL, May
14, 18, 22, 26, 31, June 4, 1968

Most consecutive shutout innings
58 Donald S. Drysdale, LA NL, May
14–June 8, 1968

Most saves, season
45 Daniel Quisenberry, KC AL 1983
Bruce Sutter, St L NL, 1984

Most saves, lifetime
324 Roland Fingers, Oak AL, 1968–76;
SD NL 1977–80; Mil AL 1981–84

Perfect game—9 innings
1880 John Lee Richmond, Worcester vs
Clev NL, June 12   1–0
John M. Ward, Prov vs Buff NL,
June 17 AM   5–0
1904 Denton T. (Cy) Young, Bos vs Phil
AL, May 5   3–0
1908 Adrian C. Joss, Clev vs Chi AL,
Oct 2   1–0
†1917 Ernest G. Shore, Bos vs Wash AL,
June 23 (1st g)   4–0
1922 C. C. Robertson, Chi vs Det AL,
Apr 30   2–0
*1956 Donald J. Larsen, NY AL vs Bklyn
NL, Oct 8   2–0
1964 James P. Bunning, Phil NL vs NY,
June 21 (1st g)   6–0
1965 Sanford Koufax, LA NL vs Chi,
Sept 9   1–0
1968 James A. Hunter, Oak AL vs
Minn, May 8   4–0
1981 Leonard H. Barker II, Cleve AL vs
Tor, May 15   3–0

Special mention
1959 Harvey Haddix, Jr, Pitt vs Mil NL,
May 26, pitched 12 perfect innings, allowed hit in 13th and
lost.

Most strikeouts, season
505 Matthew Kilroy, Balt AA, 1886
(Distance 50 ft)

383 L. Nolan Ryan, Cal AL, 1973 (Distance 60 ft 6 in)

Most strikeouts, game (9 inn) since 1900
19 Steven N. Carlton, St L NL vs NY,
Sept 15, 1969 (lost)
G. Thomas Seaver, NY NL vs SD,
Apr 22, 1970
L. Nolan Ryan, Cal AL, vs Bos,
Aug 12, 1974

Most strikeouts, extra-inning game
21 Thomas E. Cheney, Wash AL vs
Balt (16 inns), Sept 12, 1962
(night)

Most no-hit games, lifetime
5 L. Nolan Ryan, Cal AL, 1973
(2)–74–75; Hou NL, 1981

Most consecutive no-hit games
2 John S. Vander Meer, Cin NL,
June 11–15, 1938

---

†Starting pitcher, "Babe" Ruth, was banished
from game by Umpire Brick Owens after an ar-
gument. He gave the first batter, Ray Morgan, a
base on balls. Shore relieved and while he pitched
to second batter, Morgan was caught stealing.
Shore then retired next 26 batters to complete the
"perfect" game.
*World Series game.

OLDTIMER: Denton T. (Cy for "Cyclone") Young pitched an astounding 751 complete games in his 22-year career, and notched an equally astounding 511 wins (including one perfect game). Young averaged nearly 24 wins a season. Each year the outstanding pitcher in each league is given a Cy Young award.

IDOL OF THE GIANTS: Christy Mathewson pitched 3 shutouts in the 1905 World Series. His best pitch was a fadeaway, a screwball-like pitch that broke away from left-handed batters.

World Series Records

Most series played
14 Lawrence P. (Yogi) Berra, NY, AL, 1947, 49–53, 55–58, 60–63

Highest batting percentage (20 g min.), total series
.391 Louis C. Brock, St L NL, 1964, 67–68 (g-21, ab-87, h-34)

Highest batting percentage, 4 or more games, one series
.625 4-game series, George H. (Babe) Ruth, NY AL, 1928

Most runs, total series
42 Mickey C. Mantle, NY AL, 1951–53, 55–58, 60–64

Most runs, one series
10 Reginald M. Jackson, NY AL, 1977

Most runs batted in, total series
40 Mickey C. Mantle, NY, AL, 1951–53, 55–58, 60–64

Most runs batted in, consecutive times at bat
7 James L. (Dusty) Rhodes, NY NL, first 4 times at bat, 1954

Most base hits, total series
71 Lawrence P. (Yogi) Berra, NY AL, 1947, 49–53, 55–58, 60–61

Most home runs, total series
18 Mickey C. Mantle, NY AL, 1952 (2), 53 (2), 55, 56 (3), 57, 58 (2), 60 (3), 63, 64 (3)

Most home runs, one series
5 Reginald M. Jackson, NY AL, 1977

Most home runs, game
3 George H. (Babe) Ruth, NY AL, Oct 6, 1926; Oct 9, 1928
Reginald M. Jackson, NY AL, Oct 18, 1977

Pitching in most series
11 Edward C. (Whitey) Ford, NY AL, 1950, 53, 55–58, 60–64

Most victories, total series
  10 Edward C. (Whitey) Ford, NY AL,
      1950 (1), 55 (2), 56 (1), 57 (1), 60
      (2), 61 (2), 62 (1)

Most victories, no defeats
   6 Vernon L. (Lefty) Gomez, NY AL,
      1932 (1), 36 (2), 37 (2), 38 (1)

Most games won, one series
   3 games in 5-game series
      Christy Mathewson, NY NL, 1905
      J. W. Coombs, Phil AL, 1910
   Many others won 3 games in series of
   more games.

Most shutout games, total series
   4 Christy Mathewson, NY NL 1905
      (3), 1913

Most shutout games, one series
   3 Christy Mathewson, NY NL 1905

Most strikeouts, one pitcher, total series
  94 Edward C. (Whitey) Ford, NY AL,
      1950, 53, 55–58, 60–64

Most strikeouts, one series
  23 in 4 games
      Sanford Koufax, LA NL, 1963
  18 in 5 games
      Christy Mathewson, NY NL, 1905
  20 in 6 games
      C. A. (Chief) Bender, Phil AL, 1911
  35 in 7 games
      Robert Gibson, St L NL, 1968
  28 in 8 games
      W. H. Dinneen, Bos AL, 1903

Most strikeouts, one pitcher, game
  17 Robert Gibson, St L NL, Oct 2, 1968

Most runs batted in, game
   6 Robert C. Richardson, NY AL, (4)
      1st inn, (2) 4th inn, Oct 8, 1960

Most Series Won
  22 New York AL, 1923, 1927, 1928,
      1932, 1936–39, 1941, 1943, 1947,
      1949–53, 1956, 1958, 1961, 1962,
      1977, 1978

58 CONSECUTIVE SHUTOUT IN-NINGS: Don Drysdale of the Dodgers, now a broadcast announcer, in 1968 entered the record book. (LA Dodgers photo)

Longest and Shortest Games

The Brooklyn Dodgers and Boston Braves played to a 1–1 tie after 26 innings on May 1, 1920.

The NY Giants needed only 51 min to beat the Philadelphia Phillies, 6–1, in 9 innings on Sept 28, 1919.

The Chicago White Sox played the longest ball game in elapsed time—8 hours 6 min—before beating the Milwaukee Brewers, 7–6, in the 25th inning on May 9, 1984 in Chicago. The game was ended with a homer by Harold Baines, making Tom Seaver the winning pitcher for pitching the last inning. The game took 2 days, actually. It started on Tuesday night and was still tied at 3–3 when the 1 a.m. curfew caused suspension until Wednesday night.

BASKETBALL

Origins

Ollamalitzli was a 16th century Aztec precursor of basketball played in Mexico. If the solid rubber ball was put through a fixed stone ring placed high on one side of the stadium, the player was entitled to the clothing of all the spectators. The captain of the losing team often lost his head (by execution). Another game played much earlier, in the 10th century BC by the Olmecs in Mexico, called *Pok-ta-Pok,* also resembled basketball in its concept of a ring through which a round object was passed.

Modern basketball was devised by the Canadian-born Dr James Naismith (1861–1939) at the Training School of the International YMCA College at Springfield, Mass, in Dec 1891. The first game played under modified rules was on Jan 20, 1892. The first public contest was on March 11, 1892.

The International Amateur Basketball Federation (FIBA) was founded in 1932.

Rule Change

In the 1940's coaches devised a new tactic, "freezing the ball," in order to maintain a leading score. It consisted of dribbling the ball and avoiding shooting it at the basket in order to maintain possession. In a short time this strategy became part of the entire game resulting in slow play and low scores. The lowest ever was when the Fort Wayne Pistons beat the Minneapolis Lakers 19–18, Nov 22, 1950. As attendance dropped as a result of boring play, Danny Biasone, a team owner, conceived of the "24-second rule" which requires a team to make a try at a basket within 24 seconds of gaining possession of the ball or turn possession over to the opposing team. In 1954, the NBA adopted the rule and scores increased dramatically—as did attendance. In international amateur play the 30-second rule is enforced. There is no such rule in US college play.

Most Accurate Shooting

The greatest goal-shooting demonstration was made by a professional, Ted St. Martin, now of Jacksonville, Fla, who, on June 25, 1977, scored 2,036 consecutive free throws.

In a 24-hour period, May 31–June 1, 1975, Fred L. Newman of San Jose, Calif, scored 12,874 baskets out of 13,116 attempts (98.15%). Newman has also made 88 consecutive free throws while blindfolded at the Central YMCA, San Jose, Calif, Feb 5, 1978.

Using 2 basketballs and 2 rebounders, Ted St. Martin made 258 free throws (of 297 attempts) in 10 min in Orange Park, Fla, on Nov 13, 1982 (average 86.8%). This record was surpassed by Fred Newman on May 19, 1984 at the Calif Institute of Technology gymnasium, Pasadena, Calif, when he made 314 free throws out of 353 attempts in 10 min (88.9% accuracy).

The longest reported string of consecutive free throws made at any level of organized game competition is 126 by Daryl Moreau over 2 seasons (Jan 17, 1978–Jan 9, 1979) of high school play for De La Salle in

BUCKET BRIGADE: Bevo Francis (left) scored 113 points in one game for tiny Rio Grande College in 1954. That season, he averaged 46.5 points per game. Starring for Francis Marion College, Pearl Moore (above) topped all collegiate players with 4,061 career points.

New Orleans, La. The best reported one-game free throw performance was by Chris McMullin who made all 29 of his foul shots for Dixie College (St. George, Utah) in the NJCAA National Finals on March 16, 1982.

Longest Field Goal

The longest *measured* field goal in a college game was made from a distance of 89 ft 10 in by Bruce Morris for Marshall Univ vs Appalachian St, Feb 7, 1985. In an AAU game at Pacific Lutheran University on Jan 16, 1970, Steve Myers sank a shot while standing out of bounds at the other end of the court. Though the basket was illegal, the officials gave in to crowd sentiment and allowed the points to count. The distance is claimed to be 92 ft 3½ in from measurements made 10 years later.

Individual Scoring

Marie Boyd (now Eichler) scored 156 points in a girls' high school basketball game for Central HS, Lonaconing, Md, in a 163–3 victory over Ursuline Academy, on Feb 25, 1924. The boys' high school record is 135 points by Danny Heater of Burnsville, W Va, on Jan 26, 1960.

In college play, Clarence (Bevo) Francis of Rio Grande College, Ohio, scored 113 points against Hillsdale on Feb 2, 1954. One year earlier, Francis scored 116 points in a game, but the record was disallowed because the competition was with a two-year school.

Wilton Norman (Wilt) Chamberlain (b Aug 21, 1936) holds the professional record with 100 points for the Philadelphia Warriors vs NY Knicks, scored on March 2, 1962. During the same season, Wilt set the record for points in a season (4,029) and he also held the career record (31,419) until 1984.

Pearl Moore of Francis Marion College, Florence, SC, scored a record 4,061 points during her college career, 1975–79. The men's college career scoring record is 4,045 points by Travis Grant for Kentucky State, 1969–72.

Mats Wermelin (Sweden), 13, scored all 272 points in a 272–0 win in a regional boys' tournament in Stockholm, Sweden, on Feb 5, 1974.

Team Scoring

The highest game total in the NBA is 370 points in the Detroit Pistons' victory over the Denver Nuggets 186–184 in 1983.

Youngest and Oldest

Bill Willoughby (b May 20, 1957) made his NBA debut for the Atlanta Hawks on Oct 23, 1975, when he was 18 years 5 months 3 days old. The oldest NBA player was Bob Cousy (b Aug 9, 1928), who was 41 years 6 months 2 days old when he appeared in the last of seven games he played for the team he was coaching (Cincinnati Royals) during 1969–70.

Tallest Players

The tallest player of all time is reputed to be Suleiman Ali Nashnush (b 1943) who played for the Libyan team in 1962 when he measured 8 ft tall. Aleksandr Sizonenko of the USSR national team is 7 ft 9¼ in tall. The tallest woman player is Iuliana Semenova (USSR) who played in the 1976 Olympics and is reputed to stand 7 ft 2 in tall and weigh 281 lb.

Olympic Champions

The US won all 7 Olympic titles from the time the sport was introduced to the Games in 1936 until 1968, without losing a single contest. In 1972, in Munich, the US run of 63 consecutive victories was broken when its team lost, 51–50, to the USSR in a much-disputed final game. The US regained the Olympic title in Montreal in 1976, again without losing a game. In 1980 Yugoslavia took the Olympic gold, but the US came back once more in 1984 for a record 9th title.

In women's Olympics, the USSR won in 1976 and 1980, but the US took the gold in 1984.

World Champions

The USSR has won most titles at both the Men's World Championships (inst. 1950) with three (1967, 1974 and 1982) and Women's (inst. 1953) with six (1959, 1964, 1967, 1971, 1975 and 1983).

TOP SCORERS: Kareem Abdul-Jabbar, Mil-LA, (left) compiled 31,527 points with 13,006 field goals through 1983–84, beating the 31,419 point record of Wilt Chamberlain (below, # 13 in Phila uniform) who scored 100 points in one game and never fouled out of his 1,045 games played. Here he is seen jumping over Bill Russell of the Celtics.

NBA REGULAR SEASON RECORDS (INCLUDING 1983–84)

The National Basketball Association's Championship series was established in 1947. Prior to 1949, when it joined with the National Basketball League, the professional circuit was known as the Basketball Association of America.

SERVICE

Most Games, Lifetime
1,303   Elvin Hayes SD-Hou-Balt/Wash-Hou 1969–84

Most Games, Consecutive, Lifetime
906   Randy Smith, Buf-SD-Cleve-NY 1972–1983

Most Complete Games, Season
79   Wilt Chamberlain, Phil 1962

Most Minutes, Lifetime
50,000   Elvin Hayes, SD-Hou-Balt/Wash-Hou 1969–84

Most Minutes, Season
3,882   Wilt Chamberlain, Phil 1962

SCORING

Most Seasons Leading League
7   Wilt Chamberlain, Phil 1960–62; SF 1963–64; SF-Phil 1965; Phil 1966

Most Points, Lifetime
31,527   Kareem Abdul-Jabbar, Mil 1970–75, LA 1976–84

Most Points, Season
4,029   Wilt Chamberlain, Phil 1962

Scoring (continued)

Most Points, Game
100 Wilt Chamberlain, Phil vs NY, Mar 2, 1962

Most Points, Half
59 Wilt Chamberlain, Phil vs NY, Mar 2, 1962

Most Points, Quarter
33 George Gervin, SA vs NO, Apr 9, 1978

Most Points, Overtime Period
13 Earl Monroe, Balt vs Det, Feb 6, 1970
Joe Caldwell, Atl vs Cin, Feb 18, 1970

Highest Scoring Average, Lifetime (400+ games)
30.1 Wilt Chamberlain, Phil-SF-LA 1960–73

Highest Scoring Average, Season
50.4 Wilt Chamberlain, Phil 1962

Field Goals Made

Most Field Goals, Lifetime
13,006 Kareem Abdul-Jabbar, Mil 1970–75; LA 1976–84

Most Field Goals, Season
1,597 Wilt Chamberlain, Phil 1962

Most Field Goals, Game
36 Wilt Chamberlain, Phil vs NY, Mar 2, 1962

Most Field Goals, Half
22 Wilt Chamberlain, Phil vs NY, Mar 2, 1962

Most Field Goals, Quarter
13 David Thompson, Den vs Det, Apr 9, 1978

Most 3-Point Field Goals, Game
8 Rick Barry, Hou vs Utah, Feb 9, 1980
John Roche, Den vs Sea, Jan 9, 1982

Most 3-Point Field Goals, Season
91 Darrell Griffith, Utah 1984

Field Goal Percentage

Most Seasons Leading League
9 Wilt Chamberlain, Phil 1961; SF 1963; SF-Phil 1965; Phil 1966–68; LA 1969, 72–73

Highest Percentage, Lifetime
.596 Artis Gilmore, Chi 1977–82; SA 1983–84

Highest Percentage, Season
.727 Wilt Chamberlain, LA 1973

NBA Championships

The most National Basketball Association titles have been won by the Boston Celtics with 15 championships between 1957 and 1984. The Celtics also hold the record for consecutive championships with 8 (1959–66).

Free Throws Made

Most Free Throws Made, Lifetime
7,694 Oscar Robertson, Cin-Mil 1961–74

Most Free Throws Made, Season
840 Jerry West, LA 1966

Most Free Throws Made, Consecutive, Season
78 Calvin Murphy, Hou Dec 27, 1980–Feb 28, 1981

Most Free Throws Made, Game
28 Wilt Chamberlain, Phil vs NY, Mar 2, 1962
Adrian Dentley, Utah vs Hou, Jan 5, 1984

BULLS' EYE: Artis Gilmore, the 7-ft-2-in center for the Chicago Bulls, leads the NBA with a .596 lifetime field goal percentage.

REBOUNDS

Most Seasons Leading League
11   Wilt Chamberlain, Phil 1960–62; SF 1963; Phil 1966–68; LA 1969, 71–73

Most Rebounds, Lifetime
23,924   Wilt Chamberlain, Phil-SF-LA 1960–73

Most Rebounds, Season
2,149   Wilt Chamberlain, Phil 1961

Most Rebounds, Game
55   Wilt Chamberlain, Phil vs Bos, Nov 24, 1960

Most Rebounds, Half
32   Bill Russell, Bos vs Phil, Nov 16, 1957

Most Rebounds, Quarter
18   Nate Thurmond, SF vs Balt, Feb 28, 1965

Highest Average (per game), Lifetime
22.9   Wilt Chamberlain, Phil-SF-LA 1960–73

Highest Average (per game), Season
27.2   Wilt Chamberlain, Phil 1961

TALL STORIES: The Harlem Globetrotters, as typified by court jester Meadowlark Lemon, have attracted over 80 million fans with their witty basketball antics.

Most Free Throws Made (No Misses), Game
19   Bob Pettit, St L vs Bos, Nov 22, 1961
Bill Cartwright, NY vs KC, Nov 17, 1981

Most Free Throws Made, Half
19   Oscar Robertson, Cin vs Balt, Dec 27, 1964

Most Free Throws Made, Quarter
14   Rick Barry, SF vs NY, Dec 6, 1966
Pete Maravich, At vs Buff, Nov 28, 1973

Free Throw Percentage

Most Seasons Leading League
7   Bill Sharman, Bos 1953–57, 59, 61

Highest Percentage, Lifetime
.900   Rick Barry, SF-GS-Hou 1966–67, 73–80

Highest Percentage, Season
.958   Calvin Murphy, Hou 1981

MURPHY'S LAW: It didn't pay to foul Calvin Murphy during the 1980–81 season. That season, the 5-foot-10-inch guard made 95.8% of his free throws, including 78 straight without a miss.

ASSISTS

Most Seasons Leading League
8   Bob Cousy, Bos 1953–60

Most Assists, Lifetime
9,887   Oscar Robertson, Cin-Mil 1961–74

Most Assists, Season
1,099   Kevin Porter, Det 1979

Most Assists, Game
29   Kevin Porter, NJ vs Hou, Feb 24, 1978

Most Assists, Half
19   Bob Cousy, Bos vs Minn, Feb 27, 1959

Most Assists, Quarter
12   Bob Cousy, Bos vs Minn, Feb 27, 1959
   John Lucas, Hou vs Mil, Oct 27, 1977
   John Lucas, GS vs Chi, Nov 17, 1978
   Earvin (Magic) Johnson, LA vs Seattle, Feb 21, 1984

Highest Average (per game), Lifetime
9.5   Oscar Robertson, Cin-Mil 1961–74

Highest Average (per game), Season
13.4   Kevin Porter, Det 1979

PERSONAL FOULS

Most Personal Fouls, Lifetime
4,193   Elvin Hayes, SD-Hou-Balt/Wash-Hou 1969–84

Most Personal Fouls, Season
386   Darryl Dawkins, NJ 1984

Most Personal Fouls, Game
8   Don Otten, TC vs Sheb, Nov 24, 1949

DISQUALIFICATIONS
(Fouling Out of Game)

Most Disqualifications, Lifetime
127   Vern Mikkelsen, Minn, 1950–59

Most Disqualifications, Season
26   Don Meineke, Ft W 1953

Most Games, No Disqualifications, Lifetime
1,045   Wilt Chamberlain, Phil-SF-LA 1960–73 (Entire Career)

Marathon

The longest game is 102 hours by two teams of five from the Sigma Nu fraternity at Indiana Univ of Pennsylvania, Indiana, Penn, April 13–17, 1983.

Greatest Attendances

The Harlem Globetrotters played an exhibition to 75,000 in the Olympic Stadium, West Berlin, Germany, in 1951. The largest indoor basketball crowd was at the Superdome, New Orleans, La, where admissions of 61,612 were recorded for both the semi-final doubleheader (Mar 27, 1982) and final game (UNC vs Georgetown, Mar 29, 1982) of the 1982 NCAA Division I Tournament.

BASKETBALL at Barnard College in 1900, only 8 years after the game was invented.

BIATHLON

(See Skiing)

BOBSLEDDING, LUGING AND TOBOGGANING

Origins

The oldest known sled is dated *c.* 6500 BC and came from Heinola, Finland. The first known bobsled race took place at Davos, Switzerland, in 1889.

Bobs have two pairs of runners and streamlined cowls. Steering is by means of cables attached to the front runners, which are flexible. The International Federation of Bobsleigh and Tobogganing was formed in 1923, followed by the International Bobsleigh Federation in 1957.

Official international luging competition began at Klosters, Switzerland, in 1881. The first European championships were at Reichenberg (now East) Germany, in 1914 and the first world championships at Oslo, Norway, in 1953. The International Luge Federation was formed in 1957. Luging became an Olympic sport in 1964.

Olympic and World Titles

The Olympic 4-man bob title (instituted 1924) has been won 4 times by Switzerland (1924, 36, 56, 72). The US (1932, 36), Switzerland (1948, 80), Italy (1956, 68) W Germany (1952, 72) and E Germany (1976, 84) have won the Olympic boblet event (instituted 1932) twice. The most gold medals won by an individual is 3 by Meinhard Nehmer (b June 13, 1941) (E Germany) and Bernhard Germeshausen (b Aug 21, 1951) (E Germany) in the 1976 two-man, 1976 and 1980 four-man events. The most medals won is 6 (2 gold, 2 silver, 2 bronze) by Eugenio Monti (Italy) (b Jan 23, 1928) from 1956 to 1968.

In Olympic years, the Olympic champion is also world champion.

The world 4-man bob has been won 15 times by Switzerland (1924, 36, 39, 47, 54–57, 71–73, 75, 82, 83, 84). Italy won the 2-man title 14 times (1954, 56–63, 66, 68–69, 71, 75). Eugenio Monti has been a member of 11 world championship crews, 8 two-man and 3 four-man.

Tobogganing

The word "toboggan" comes from the Micmac American Indian word *tobaakan*. The St Moritz Tobogganing Club, Switzerland, founded in 1887 is the oldest toboggan club in the world. It is unique in being the home of the Cresta Run, which dates from 1884, and for the introduction of the one-man racing toboggan skeleton. The course is 3,977 ft long with a drop of 514 ft and the record is 51.75 sec (av. 52.40 mph) by Franco Gansser of Switzerland on Feb 19, 1984. On the same day Gansser set a record from Junction (2,920 ft) of 41.99 sec.

Speeds of 90 mph are sometimes reached.

The greatest number of wins in the Grand National (instituted 1885) is

BOB TALE: Meinhard Nehmer and Bernhard Germeshausen, the pilots of this East German 2-man bobsled, have each won 3 Olympic gold medals. Between them, they have also accumulated 4 world titles.

eight by the 1948 Olympic champion Nino Bibbia (Italy) (b Sept 9, 1924) in 1960–64, 66, 68, 73. The greatest number of wins in the Curzon Cup (instituted in 1910) is eight by Bibbia in 1950, 57–58, 60, 62–64, 69, who hence won the double in 1960, 62–64.

Luge

In luging the rider adopts a reclining, as opposed to a prone, position. Luging was first competed in 1883 in Switzerland, first in world competition in 1955, and first in the Olympics in 1964.

The most successful rider in the world championships is Thomas Köhler (E Germany) (b June 25, 1940), who won the single-seater title in 1962, 64 (Olympic), 66, and 67, and shared the two-seater title in 1967 and 68 (Olympic). Margit Schumann (E Germany) (b Sept 14, 1952) has won the women's championship 5 times—in 1973, 74, 75, 76 (Olympic) and 77.

Highest Luge Speed

The highest recorded photo-timed speed is 85.38 mph by Asle Strand (Norway) at Tandådalens Linbane, Sälen, Sweden, on May 1, 1982.

1984 Olympic Gold Medalists

Bobsledding
2-Man

1. E Ger II (Wolfgang Hoppe & Dietmar Schauerhammer) 3 min 25:56 sec
2. E Ger I (Bernhard Lehmann & Bogdan Musiol) 3 min 26:04 sec
3. USSR II (Zintis Ekmanis & Vladimir Aleksandrov) 3 min 26:16 sec

4-Man

1. E Ger I 3 min 2:22 sec
2. E Ger II 3 min 20:78 sec
3. Switzerland I 3 min 21:39 sec

Luge
Men's Singles

Paul Hildgartner (Ita) 3 min 04:258 sec

2-Man

W Germany (Hans Stanggassinger & Franz Wembecher) 1 min 23:620 sec

Women's Singles

Steffi Martin (E Germany) 2 min 46:570 sec

BOWLING

Origins

Bowling can be traced to articles found in the tomb of an Egyptian child of 5200 BC where there were nine pieces of stone to be set up as pins at which a stone "ball" was rolled. The ball first had to roll through an archway made of three pieces of marble. In the Italian Alps about 2,000 years ago, the underhand tossing of stones at an object is believed the beginnings of *bocci,* a game still widely played in Italy and similar to bowling. Martin Luther is credited with the statement that nine was the ideal number of pins. In the British Isles, lawn bowls was preferred to bowling at pins. In the 16th century, bowling at pins was the national sport in Scotland. Early British settlers probably brought lawn bowls to the US and set up what is known as Bowling Green at the tip of Manhattan Island in NY but perhaps the Dutch under Henry Hudson were the ones to be credited.

Organizations

The American Bowling Congress (ABC), established in NY on Sept 9, 1895, was the first body to standardize rules, and the organization now comprises 3,700,000 men who bowl in leagues and tournaments. The Women's International Bowling Congress (WIBC) has a membership of 3,800,000. The Professional Bowlers Association (PBA), formed in 1958, comprises nearly 2,700 of the world's best bowlers.

Lanes

In the US there were 8,404 bowling establishments with 153,630 lanes in 1983 and about 68 million bowlers, down from the previous year by about 4%.

The world's largest bowling center (now closed) was the Tokyo World Lanes Center, Japan, with 252 lanes. Currently the largest center is Fukuyana Bowl, Osaka, Japan, which has 144 lanes.

World Championships

The Fédération Internationale des Quilleurs world championships were instituted in 1954. The highest pinfall in the individual men's event is 5,963 for 28 games by Ed Luther (US) at Milwaukee, Wis on Aug 28, 1971. In the current schedule of 24 games, the men's record is 5,242 by Mats Karlsson (Sweden) and 4,806 by Bong Coo (Philippines) is the women's record, both set in Nov 1983 at Caracas, Venezuela.

Marathons

Bob Atheney Jr of St Petersburg, Fla bowled 1,976 games in 265 hours non-stop Nov 9–21, 1975, an average of 7½ games per hour, according to the ABC, which is not sanctioning this category any longer. AMF-Australia reports that a "record" of 195 hours 1 min was set there by Jim Webb in Feb 1984, and the US newspapers reported a "record" of 168 hours 25 min set by a Navy man, Richard C. King, Jr in May 1984.

BEST FINISHES: Les Schissler of Denver (bowling here) bowled a 300 game, won 3 ABC crowns in one year in 1966 after winning the singles, All-Events, and being on the winning team in one tournament.

ABC LEAGUE RECORDS

Highest Scores

The highest individual score for three games is 886 by Allie Brandt of Lockport, NY, on Oct 25, 1939. Glenn Allison (b 1930) rolled a perfect 900 in a 3-game series in league play on July 1, 1982, at La Habra Bowl, LA, Calif, but the ABC refused to recognize the record when an ABC inspector examined the lanes and determined they had been illegally oiled (for other 900 series see *Most Perfect Scores,* below). Highest team score is 3,858 by Budweisers of St Louis on March 12, 1958.

The highest season average attained in sanctioned competition is 242 by John Rogard of Susquehanna, Pa, for 66 games in 1981–82.

Consecutive Strikes

The record for consecutive strikes in sanctioned match play is 33 by John Pezzin (b 1930) at Toledo, Ohio, on March 4, 1976.

Most Perfect Scores

The highest number of sanctioned 300 games is 27 (through 1982) by Elvin Mesger of Sullivan, Mo. The maximum 900 for a three-game series has been recorded five times in unsanctioned games—by Leon Bentley at Lorain, Ohio, on March 26, 1931; by Joe Sargent at Rochester, NY, in

1934; by Jim Margie in Philadelphia, on Feb 4, 1937; by Bob Brown at Roseville Bowl, Calif, on Apr 12, 1980; and by Glenn Allison at Whittier, Calif, on July 1, 1982.

ABC TOURNAMENT RECORDS

Highest Individual

Highest three-game series in singles is 801 by Mickey Higham of Kansas City, Mo, in 1977. Best three-game total in any ABC event is 833 by Fran Bax of Niagara Falls, NY, in team in 1983. Jim Godman of Lorain, Ohio, holds the record for a nine-game All-Events total with 2,184 (731–749–704) set in Indianapolis, Ind, in 1974. ABC Hall of Famers Fred Bujack of Detroit, Bill Lillard of Houston, and Nelson Burton Jr of St Louis, have won the most championships with 8 each. Bujack shared in 3 team and 4 team All-Events titles between 1949 and 1955, and also won the individual All-Events title in 1955. Lillard bowled on Regular and team All-Events champions in 1955 and 1956, the Classic team champions in 1962 and 1971, and won regular doubles and All-Events titles in 1956. Burton shared in 3 Classic team titles, 2 Classic doubles titles and has won Classic singles twice and Classic All-Events.

Highest Doubles

The ABC record of 558 was set in 1976 by Les Zikes of Chicago and Tommy Hudson of Akron, Ohio. The record score in a doubles series is 1,453, set in 1952 by John Klares (755) and Steve Nagy (698) of Cleveland.

Perfect Scores

Les Schissler of Denver scored 300 in the Classic team event in 1967, and Ray Williams of Detroit scored 300 in Regular team play in 1974. In all, there have been only thirty-nine 300 games in the ABC tournament through 1980. There have been 20 perfect games in singles, 15 in doubles, and four in team play.

Best Finishes in One Tournament

Les Schissler of Denver won the singles, All-Events, and was on the winning team in 1966 to tie Ed Lubanski of Detroit and Bill Lillard of Houston as the only men to win three ABC crowns in one year. The best four finishes in one ABC tournament were third in singles, second in doubles, third in team and first in All-Events by Bob Strampe, Detroit, in 1967, and first in singles, third in team and doubles and second in All-Events by Paul Kulbaga, Cleveland, in 1960.

Strikes and Spares in a Row

In the greatest finish to win an ABC title, Ed Shay set a record of 12 strikes in a row in 1958, when he scored a perfect game for a total of 733 in singles. Most strikes in a row is 20 by Lou Vilt of Milwaukee in 1977.

HALL OF FAMER: Marion Ladewig of Grand Rapids, Mich, won 14 major championships: 8 All-Star titles, 4 World's Invitational titles, and 2 WIBC titles. She was also named "Woman Bowler of the Year" 9 times. (Photo Stephen Walker Press)

The most spares in a row is 23, a record set by Lt Hazen Sweet of Battle Creek, Mich, in 1950.

Most Tournament Appearances

Bill Doehrman of Fort Wayne, Ind, competed in 71 consecutive ABC tournaments, beginning in 1908. (No tournaments were held 1943–45.)

Attendance

Largest spectator attendance on one day for an ABC Tournament was 5,257 in Milwaukee in 1952. The total attendance record was set at Reno, Nev, in 1977 with 174,953 in 89 days.

Youngest and Oldest Winners

The youngest champion was Ronnie Knapp of New London, Ohio, who was a member of the 1963 Booster team champions when he was 16 years old. The oldest champion was Joe Detloff of Chicago, Ill, who, at the age of 72, was a winner in the 1965 Booster team event. The oldest doubles team in ABC competition totaled 165 years in 1955: Jerry Ameling (83) and Joseph Lehnbeutter (82), both from St Louis.

EARL ANTHONY

FRAME AND FORTUNE: Earl Anthony of Dublin, Calif (left) is the PBA career champion with a lifetime total of 42 titles and earnings of more than $1¼ million. Mark Roth of N Arlington, NJ, (right) set a PBA season mark in 1978 when he won 8 titles.

WIBC RECORDS

Highest Scores

The highest individual score for three games is 853 by Sherrie Langford, 25, in the Clearwater Classic Tournament, Clearwater, Fla, on Feb 19, 1982. Patty Ann of Springfield, Ill, had a record 232 average in league play in the 1983–84 season.

The highest 5-woman team score for a 3-game series is 3,379 by Freeway Washer of Cleveland in 1960. The highest game score by a 5-woman team is 1,210 by Sheraton Inn, Scranton, Pa in 1981–82.

The highest lifetime average is 199.14 by Dorothy Fothergill of Lincoln, RI, who has bowled for 10 years but is now inactive.

Perfect Games

The most 300 games rolled in a career is 9 by Jeanne Maiden of Solon, Ohio. The oldest woman to bowl a perfect game was Helen Duval of Berkeley, Calif, at age 66 in 1982. Of all the women who rolled a perfect game, the one with the lowest average was Diane Ponza of Santa Cruz, Calif, who had a 112 average in the 1977–78 season.

Consecutive Strikes, Spares and Splits

The record for most consecutive strikes is 26 by Robin Romeo of Beverly Hills, Calif. Joan Taylor of Syracuse, NY, made 27 consecutive spares. Shirley Tophigh of Las Vegas, Nev, holds the unenviable record of rolling 14 consecutive splits.

Championship Tournament

The highest score for a 3-game series in the annual WIBC Championship Tournament is 737 by D. D. Jacobson in the 1972 singles competition. The record for one game is 300 (the only perfect game) by Lori Gensch in the 1979 doubles event.

Myrtle Schulte of St Louis has participated in 54 tournaments through 1982. The oldest participant was Ethel Brunnick (b Aug 30, 1887) of Santa Monica, Calif, at age 96 in 1984. Mary Ann Keiper of St Louis was only 5 years old when she participated in the 1952 tournament. The youngest champion was Leila Wagner (b July 12, 1960) of Seattle, Wash, who was 18 when she was a member of the championship 5-woman team in 1979.

PBA RECORDS

Perfect Games

A total of 119 perfect (300-pin) games were bowled in PBA tournaments in 1979. Dick Weber rolled 3 perfect games in one tournament (Houston) in 1965, as did Billy Hardwick of Louisville, Ky (in the Japan Gold Cup competition) in 1968, Roy Buckley of Columbus, Ohio (at Chagrin Falls, Ohio) in 1971, John Wilcox (at Detroit), Norm Meyers of St Louis (at Peoria, Ill) in 1979, and Shawn Christensen of Denver (at Denver) in 1984.

Don Johnson of Las Vegas, Nev, bowled at least one perfect game in 11 consecutive seasons (1965–1975). Guppy Troup, of Savannah, Ga, rolled 6 perfect games on the 1979 tour.

Most Titles

Earl Anthony of Dublin, Calif, has won a lifetime total of 42 PBA titles through Oct 1984. The record number of titles won in one PBA season is 8, by Mark Roth of North Arlington, NJ, in 1978.

Consecutive Titles

Only three bowlers have ever won three consecutive professional tournaments—Dick Weber in 1961, Johnny Petraglia in 1971, and Mark Roth in 1977.

Highest Earnings

The greatest lifetime earnings on the Professional Bowlers Association circuit have been won by Earl Anthony who has taken home $1,257,021 to Oct 15, 1984. Anthony also holds the season earnings record with $164,735 in 1981.

Television Bowling

Nelson Burton Jr, St Louis, rolled the best series, 1,050, for four games (278-279-257-236) at Dick Weber Lanes in Florrisant, Mo, Feb 11, 1984.

BOXING THE WAY IT USED TO BE: No overstuffed gloves, just a taped-off dirt ring. Just $22,500 was the record prize in 1889 for a fight-till-you-drop that went 27 rounds in Port Elizabeth, S Africa, between Jack Cooper and Wolf Bendoff.

BOXING

Boxing with gloves was depicted on a fresco from the Isle of Thera, Greece, which has been dated to 1520 BC. The earliest prize-ring code of rules was formulated in England, Aug 16, 1743, by the champion pugilist Jack Broughton (1704–89), who reigned from 1729 to 1750. Boxing, which had in 1867 come under the Queensberry Rules, formulated for John Sholto Douglas, 9th Marquess of Queensberry, was not established as a legal sport in Britain until after a ruling of Mr Justice Grantham following the death of Billy Smith (Murray Livingstone) due to a fight on Apr 24, 1901, at Covent Garden, London.

There are two governing bodies, the World Boxing Association (formed as the National Boxing Association in the US in 1920) and the World Boxing Council (formed in 1963). At most weights separate champions are recognized by these two organizations.

Longest Fight

The longest recorded fight with gloves was between Andy Bowen of New Orleans and Jack Burke in New Orleans, Apr 6–7, 1893. The fight lasted 110 rounds (7 hours 19 min from 9:15 p.m. to 4:34 a.m.) but was declared no contest (later changed to a draw) when both men were unable to continue. The longest recorded bare knuckle fight was one of 6 hours 15 min between James Kelly and Jack Smith at Fiery Creek, Dalesford, Australia, Dec 3, 1855. The greatest recorded number of rounds is 276 in 4 hours 30 min, when Jack Jones beat Patsy Tunney in Cheshire, England, in 1825. The longest world title fight was in 1906 when Joe Gans (US) beat Battling Nelson (Den) when Nelson was disqualified in the 42nd round of a scheduled 45-round contest.

Shortest Fight

There is a distinction between the quickest knockout and the shortest fight. A knockout in 10½ sec (including a 10-sec count) occurred on Sept 26, 1946, when Al Couture struck Ralph Walton while the latter was adjusting his mouthpiece in his corner at Lewiston, Me. If the time was accurately taken it is clear that Couture must have been more than half-way across the ring from his own corner at the opening bell.

The shortest fight on record appears to be one in a Golden Gloves tournament in Minneapolis, Minn, Nov 4, 1947, when Mike Collins floored Pat Brownson with his first punch and the contest was stopped, without a count, 4 sec after the bell.

The shortest world heavyweight title fight was when the referee stopped the fight after 63 sec when Michael Dokes (US) (b Aug 10, 1958) beat Mike Weaver (US) for the WBA title on Dec 10, 1982. The shortest world title fight was when Al McCoy knocked out George Chip in 45 sec for the middleweight crown in NYC on Apr 7, 1914.

Tallest Boxer

The tallest boxer to fight professionally was Gogea Mitu (b 1914) of Rumania in 1935. He was 7 ft 4 in and weighed 327 lb. John Rankin, who won a fight in New Orleans, in Nov 1967, also claimed 7 ft 4 in.

WORLD HEAVYWEIGHT CHAMPIONS

Earliest Title Fight

The first world heavyweight title fight, with gloves and 3-minute rounds, was between John L. Sullivan (1858–1918) and "Gentleman" James J. Corbett (1866–1933) in New Orleans, Sept 7, 1892. Corbett won in 21 rounds.

Heavyweight Champions through the Years

1882 John L. Sullivan (US)
1892 James J. Corbett (US)
1897 Bob Fitzsimmons (GB)
1899 James J. Jeffries (US)
1905 Marvin Hart (US)
1906 Tommy Burns (Can)
1908 Jack Johnson (US)
1915 Jess Willard (US)
1919 Jack Dempsey (US)
1926 Gene Tunney (US)
1930 Max Schmeling (Ger)
1932 Jack Sharkey (US)
1933 Primo Carnera (Ita)
1934 Max Baer (US)
1935 James J. Braddock (US)
1937 Joe Louis (US)
1949 Ezzard Charles (US)
1951 Jersey Joe Walcott (US)
1952 Rocky Marciano (US)
1956 Floyd Patterson (US)
1959 Ingemar Johansson (Swe)

1960 Floyd Patterson (US)
1962 Sonny Liston (US)
1964 Cassius Clay/Muhammad Ali (US)
1965 Ernie Terrell (US)—WBA only till 1967
1968 Joe Frazier (US)—NY State
1968 Jimmy Ellis (US)—WBA
1970 Joe Frazier (US)—undisputed
1973 George Foreman (US)
1974 Muhammad Ali (US)
1978 Leon Spinks (US)
1978 Ken Norton (US)—WBC
1978 Muhammad Ali (US)—WBA
1978 Larry Holmes (US)—WBC, IBF from 1983
1979 John Tate (US)—WBA
1980 Mike Weaver (US)—WBA
1982 Mike Dokes (US)—WBA
1983 Gerry Coetzee (So Afr)—WBA
1984 Tim Witherspoon (US)—WBC

TITLE DEEDS: Joe Louis (far left) kept the heavyweight title for over 11 years, the longest reign at any weight class. Known as the Brown Bomber, Louis successfully defended his title a record 25 times. Floyd Patterson (standing, right) was 1 month shy of his 22nd birthday when he beat Archie Moore to become the youngest heavyweight champion ever. Patterson later became the first heavyweight ever to recapture that title.

Heaviest and Lightest

The heaviest world champion was Primo Carnera (Italy) (1906–67), the "Ambling Alp," who won the title from Jack Sharkey in 6 rounds in NYC, on June 29, 1933. He scaled 267 lb for this fight. He had the longest reach at 85½ in and an expanded chest measurement of 53 in.

The lightest was Robert James Fitzsimmons (1863–1917), (b Helston, Cornwall, England) who, at a weight of 167 lb, won the title by knocking out James J. Corbett in 14 rounds at Carson City, Nev, March 17, 1897.

The greatest differential in a world title fight was 86 lb between Carnera (270 lb) and Tommy Loughran (184 lb) of the US, when the former won on points at Miami, Fla, March 1, 1934.

Tallest and Shortest

The tallest world champion was Primo Carnera, who was measured at 6 ft 5.4 in by the Physical Education Director at the Hemingway Gymnasium of Harvard, although he was widely reported and believed in 1933 to be 6 ft 8½ in tall. Jess Willard (1881–1968), who won the title in 1915, was often described as being 6 ft 6¼ in tall, but was in fact 6 ft 5¼ in. The shortest was Tommy Burns (1881–1955) of Canada, world champion from Feb 23, 1906, to Dec 26, 1908, who stood 5 ft 7 in and weighed 179 lb.

Longest and Shortest Reigns

The longest reign of any world heavyweight champion is 11 years 8 months and 7 days by Joe Louis (b Joseph Louis Barrow, 1914–81), from June 22, 1937, when he knocked out James J. Braddock in the 8th round at Chicago until announcing his retirement on March 1, 1949. During his reign Louis made a record 25 defenses of his title. The shortest reign was by Leon Spinks (US) (b July 11, 1953) for 212 days, Feb 15–Sept 15, 1978. Ken Norton (US) (b Aug 6, 1945) was recognized by the WBC as champion for 83 days, March 18–June 9, 1978.

Oldest and Youngest

The oldest man to win the heavyweight crown was Jersey Joe Walcott (b Arnold Raymond Cream, Jan 31, 1914, at Merchantville, NJ), who knocked out Ezzard Charles on July 18, 1951, in Pittsburgh, when aged 37 years 5 months 18 days. Walcott was the oldest title holder at 38 years 7 months 23 days when he lost to Rocky Marciano on Sept 23, 1952. The youngest age at which the world heavyweight title has been won is 21 years 331 days by Floyd Patterson (b Waco, NC, Jan 4, 1935), who won the vacant title by beating Archie Moore in 5 rounds in Chicago on Nov 30, 1956.

Undefeated

Rocky Marciano (b Rocco Francis Marchegiano) (1923–69) is the only heavyweight champion to have been undefeated in his entire professional career (1947–1956). His record was 49 wins (43 by KO) and no losses or draws. (It should be noted that Larry Holmes has won all 45 of his professional fights through July 1984.)

LORDS OF THE RING: Rocky Marciano (far left) is the only heavyweight champion to go through his entire professional career without a loss. Marciano won all 49 of his bouts, including 43 knockouts. The youngest man to win a world title was Wilfredo Benitez (far right), who captured the light-welterweight title when he was only 17½ years old. Benitez is one of only a handful of fighters who have won world titles in 3 different weight classes.

THE HARDER THEY FALL: Muhammad Ali is seated on the canvas (left) during his unsuccessful attempt to regain the heavyweight crown from Joe Frazier in New York's Madison Square Garden in 1971. Three years later, Ali knocked out George Foreman in the 8th round (above) in Zaire for the first of his record two recaptures.

MUHAMMAD ALI (right, below) seems to be knocking the stuffing out of Joe Frazier in the "thriller in Manila" when he won $6½ million. Ali's earnings in his 61 fights totaled about $69 million, making him the highest paid in any sport. (AP)

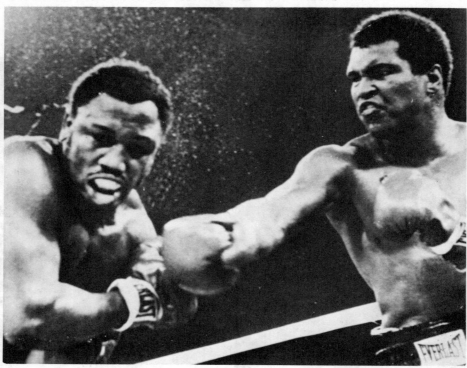

Most Recaptures

Muhammad Ali Haj (b Cassius Marcellus Clay, in Louisville, Ky, Jan 17, 1942) is the only man to regain the heavyweight title twice. Ali first won the title on Feb 25, 1964, defeating Sonny Liston. He defeated George Foreman on Oct 30, 1974, having been stripped of his title by the world boxing authorities on Apr 28, 1967. He lost his title to Leon Spinks on Feb 15, 1978, but regained it on Sept 15, 1978 by defeating Spinks in New Orleans.

Knockout Percentage

George Foreman (b Jan 10, 1949) had the highest career knockout percentage of any heavyweight champion. In his 47 professional fights, Foreman KO'd 42 opponents, thus winning 89.36% of his bouts by knockout.

George Foreman is the only US champion in any weight class to have won, defended, and lost his crown all outside the US. To win his title he defeated Joe Frazier in Kingston, Jamaica, Jan 22, 1973. He defended it against Joe Roman in Tokyo, Japan, Sept 1, 1973 and against Ken Norton in Caracas, Venezuela, Mar 26, 1974. He lost it to Muhammad Ali in Kinshasa, Zaire, Oct 30, 1974. As world champion, this native of Marshall, Tex never fought in his own country.

WORLD CHAMPIONS (ANY WEIGHT)

Longest and Shortest Reign

Joe Louis's heavyweight duration record stands for all divisions. The shortest reign has been 33 days by Tony Canzoneri (US) (1908–59) who was junior welterweight champion from May 21 to June 23, 1933.

Youngest and Oldest

The youngest at which any world championship has been won is 17 years 176 days by Wilfredo Benitez (b Sept 12, 1958) of Puerto Rico, who won the WBA light-welterweight title in San Juan, March 6, 1976.

The oldest world champion was Archie Moore (b Archibald Lee Wright, Collinsville, Ill, Dec 13, 1913 or 1916), who was recognized as a light-heavyweight champion up to Feb 10, 1962, when his title was removed. He was then between 45 and 48. Bob Fitzsimmons (1863–1917) had the longest career of any official world titleholder with over 32 years from 1882 to 1914. He won his last world title aged 40 years 183 days in San Francisco on Nov 25, 1903.

Greatest "Tonnage"

The greatest "tonnage" in a world title fight was 488¾ lb when Primo Carnera (259¼ lb) fought Paolino Uzcudun (229½ lb) of Spain, in Rome, Italy, Oct 22, 1933.

The greatest "tonnage" recorded in any fight is 700 lb, when Claude "Humphrey" McBride of Okla at 340 lb knocked out Jimmy Black of Houston at 360 lb in the 3rd round at Oklahoma City, June 1, 1971.

Smallest Champions

The smallest man to win any world title has been Netranoi Vorsingh (b Apr 22, 1959) (Thailand), WBC light-flyweight champion from May to Sept 1978, at 4 ft 11 in tall. Jimmy Wilde (b Merthyr Tydfil, 1892, d 1969, UK), who held the flyweight title from 1916 to 1923, was reputed never to have fought above 108 lb.

Longest Fight

The longest world title fight (under Queensberry Rules) was between the lightweights Joe Gans (1874–1910), of the US, and Oscar "Battling" Nelson (1882–1954), the "Durable Dane," at Goldfield, Nev, Sept 3, 1906. It was terminated in the 42nd round when Gans was declared the winner on a foul.

Most Recaptures

The only boxer to win a world title five times at one weight is Sugar Ray Robinson (b Walker Smith, Jr, in Detroit, May 3, 1920) who beat Carmen Basilio (US) in the Chicago Stadium on March 25, 1958, to regain the world middleweight title for the fourth time. The other title wins were over Jake LaMotta (US) in Chicago on Feb 14, 1951; Randy Turpin (UK) in NYC on Sept 12, 1951; Carl "Bobo" Olson (US) in Chicago on Dec 9, 1955; and Gene Fullmer (US) in Chicago on May 1, 1957. The record number of title bouts in a career is 33 or 34 (at bantam and featherweight) by George Dixon (1870–1909), *alias* "Little Chocolate," of Canada, between 1890 and 1901.

Most Titles Simultaneously

The only man to hold world titles at three weights simultaneously was "Hammerin' " Henry Armstrong (b Dec 12, 1912) of the US, at featherweight, lightweight and welterweight from Aug to Dec 1938.

Most Knockdowns in Title Fights

Vic Toweel (South Africa) knocked down Danny O'Sullivan of London 14 times in 10 rounds in their world bantamweight fight at Johannesburg, Dec 2, 1950, before the latter retired.

Amateur World Championships

Two boxers have won two world championships (instituted 1974): Teofilo Stevenson (Cuba), heavyweight 1974 and 1978, and Angel Herrera (b Aug 2, 1952), featherweight 1978 and lightweight 1982.

FISTFUL OF DOLLARS: Sugar Ray Leonard (left) and Thomas Hearns fought to unite the WBA and WBC welterweight titles in a fight that set the world's record for the largest total purse for both fighters of $17.1 million, of which Leonard earned a record share with an estimated $11 million (almost three times greater than Joe Louis' lifetime earnings of $3.8 million for 71 fights). The discovery of a detached retina in his left eye in May 1982 caused Leonard to announce his retirement from boxing. (All-Sport).

ALL FIGHTS

Largest Purse

The greatest purse received is an estimated $11 million by Sugar Ray Leonard (US) (b May 17, 1956) when he beat Thomas Hearns (US) for the undisputed world welterweight title at Las Vegas, Nev, on Sept 16, 1981. The total purse for both fighters was a record $17.1 million.

The largest stake ever fought for in the bare-knuckle era was $22,500 in a 27-round fight when Jack Cooper beat Wolf Bendoff at Port Elizabeth, South Africa, July 26, 1889.

Highest Earnings in Career

The largest known fortune ever made in a fighting career (or any sports career) is an estimated $69 million (including exhibitions) amassed by Muhammad Ali from Oct 1960 to Dec 1981, in 61 fights comprising 549 rounds.

Highest and Lowest Attendances

The greatest paid attendance at any boxing fight has been 120,757 (with a ringside price of $27.50) for the Tunney vs Dempsey world heavyweight title fight at the Sesquicentennial Stadium, Philadelphia, Sept 23, 1926. The indoor record is 63,360 for the Spinks vs Ali world heavyweight title fight at the Louisiana Superdome in New Orleans, Sept 15, 1978. The record for live gate receipts is $7,293,600 for the Larry

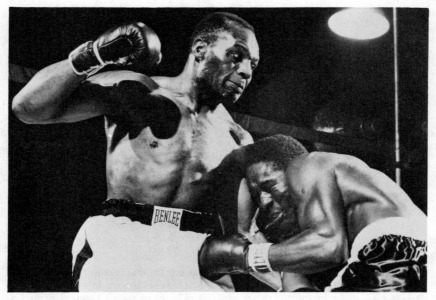

OLDEST WORLD HEAVYWEIGHT CHAMPION: Jersey Joe Walcott (left) in the process of knocking out Ezzard Charles to gain the heavyweight championship in 1951. Walcott was 37½ at the time. (AP)

Holmes vs Gerry Cooney WBC heavyweight title bout in Las Vegas, Nev, on June 11, 1982. The highest non-paying attendance is 135,132 at the Tony Zale vs Billy Pryor fight at Juneau Park, Milwaukee, Wis, Aug 18, 1941.

The smallest attendance at a world heavyweight title fight was 2,434 at the Ali vs Liston fight at Lewiston, Me, May 25, 1965.

Most Knockouts

The greatest number of knockouts in a career is 145 by Archie Moore (1936 to 1963). The record for consecutive KO's is 44, set by Lamar Clark of Utah at Las Vegas, Nev, Jan 11, 1960. He knocked out 6 in one night (5 in the first round) in Bingham, Utah, on Dec 1, 1958.

Most Fights

The greatest recorded number of fights in a career is 1,024 by Bobby Dobbs (US) (1858–1930), who is reported to have fought from 1875 to 1914, a period of 39 years. Abraham Hollandersky, *alias* Abe the Newsboy (US), is reputed to have had 1,309 fights in the 14 years from 1905 to 1918, but many of them were exhibition bouts.

Most Fights Without Loss

Edward Henry (Harry) Greb (US) (b June 6, 1894) was unbeaten in 178 bouts, including 117 "no decisions," 1916–23. Of boxers with complete records Packey McFarland (US) (1888–1936) had 97 fights (five draws) in 1905–15 without a defeat. Pedro Carrasco (b Spain, Nov 7, 1943) won 83 consecutive fights from Apr 22, 1964 to Sept 3, 1970, and then drew once and had a further nine wins before his loss to Armando Ramos in a WBC lightweight contest on Feb 18, 1972.

Olympic Gold Medals

In the 1984 Olympics, US boxers won a record total of 9 of the 12 gold medals.

Only two boxers have won three Olympic gold medals: southpaw László Papp (b 1926, Hungary), who took the middleweight (1948) and the light-middleweight titles (1952 and 56), and Cuban heavyweight Teofilo Stevenson (b Mar 23, 1952), who won the gold medal in his division for three successive Games (1972, 76 and 80). The only man to win two titles in one meeting was Oliver L. Kirk (US), who took both the bantam and featherweight titles at St Louis, Mo, in 1904, when the US won all the titles.

The oldest man to win an Olympic gold medal in boxing was Richard K. Gunn (b 1870) (GB), who won the featherweight title on Oct 27, 1908, in London, aged 38.

Olympic Gold Medalists 1984

Light Flyweight	*Welterweight*
Paul Gonzales (US)	Mark Breland (US)
Flyweight	*Light Middleweight*
Steve McCrory (US)	Frank Tate (US)
Bantamweight	*Middleweight*
Maurizio Stecca (Ita)	Shin Joon-Sup (S Kor)
Featherweight	*Light Heavyweight*
Meldrick Taylor (US)	Anton Josipovic (Yug)
Lightweight	*Heavyweight*
Pernell Whitaker (US)	Henry Tillman (US)
Light Welterweight	*Super Heavyweight*
Jerry Page (US)	Tyrell Biggs (US)

Time-Keeping

There is a little known variable in the sport of boxing. While all rule books agree that, under the Queensberry rules, a round lasts 3 min, in fact they often do not. At the Gerrie Coetzee-Michael Dokes heavyweight championship fight (Sept 23, 1984) the rounds were about 3 min, 2 sec. If the correct time had been kept the fighters would have been in their corners when Coetzee knocked out Dokes at 2:58 of round 10. It is not unusual for a timekeeper to be off by as much as a minute. The chairman of the NY State Athletic Commission explained it this way: "With all the excitement, it's sometimes hard to keep exact time."

CANOEING AND KAYAKING

Origins

Modern canoes and kayaks originated with the Indians and Eskimos of North America. French trappers were the first to compete in canoe races (1790).

The acknowledged pioneer of canoeing as a modern sport was John Macgregor (1825–92), a British barrister, in 1865. The Canoe Club was formed on July 26, 1866.

Olympic and World Titles

Gert Fredriksson (b Nov 21, 1919) of Sweden has won the most Olympic gold medals with 6 (1948, 52, 56, 60). The most by a woman is 3 by Ludmila Pinayeva (*née* Khvedosyuk, b Jan 14, 1936) (USSR) in the 500-m K.1 in 1964 and 1968, and the 500-m K.2 in 1972. The most gold medals at one Games is 3 by Vladimir Parfenovich (b Dec 2, 1958) (USSR) in 1980 and by Ian Ferguson (NZ) (b July 20, 1952) in the 1984 Olympics (one individually at 500 m and 2 on New Zealand boat at 500 m and 1,000 m).

Twelve world titles have been won by Vladimir Parfenovich, 1979–83. The women's record is ten by Birgit Fischer (E Germany) (b Feb 25, 1962), 1980–3.

Highest Speed

The Olympic 1,000-m best performance of 3 min 02.70 sec by the 1980 USSR K4 on July 31, 1980, represents a speed of 12.24 mph. They achieved 13.14 mph over the first quarter of the course.

The record for canoeing down the Mississippi from Lake Itasca, Minn to the Gulf of Mexico is 23 days 10 hours 20 min by Valerie Fons and Verlen Kruger, Apr 27–May 20, 1984.

ALONE TOGETHER: Ken Beard and Steve Benson paddle in the Gulf Stream, looking very vulnerable. Along with Beatrice and John Dowd, they completed the longest open sea voyage ever made by canoe.

Olympic Gold Medalists 1984

Men

500 meters K-1	
Ian Ferguson (NZ) 1 min 47:84 sec	
1,000 meters K-1	
Alan Thompson (NZ) 3 min 45:73 sec	
500 meters K-2	
New Zealand 1 min 34:21 sec	
1,000 meters K-2	
Canada 3 min 24:22 sec	
1,000 meters K-4	
New Zealand 3 min 02:28 sec	
500 meters C-1	
Larry Cain (Can) 1 min 57:01 sec	
1,000 meters C-1	
Ulrich Eicke (W Ger) 4 min 06:32 sec	
500 meters C-2	
Yugoslavia 1 min 43:67 sec	
1,000 meters C-2	
Romania 3 min 40:60 sec	

Women

4500 meters K-1	
Agneta Andersson (Swe) 1 min 58:72 sec	
500 meters K-2	
Sweden 1 min 45:25 sec	
500 meters K-4	
Romania 1 min 38:34 sec	

LONGEST JOURNEY: Jerry Pushcar of Prior Lake, Minn paddled and carried his 17-ft, 78-lb canoe 8,880 miles from New Orleans to Nome, Alaska from 1975 to 1977. His Samoyed dog, Blizzard, was his only companion.

Longest Open Sea Voyage

Beatrice and John Dowd, Ken Beard and Steve Benson (Richard Gillett replaced him mid-journey) paddled 2,170 miles out of a total journey of 2,192 miles from Venezuela to Miami, Fla, via the West Indies from Aug 11, 1977, to Apr 29, 1978, in two Klepper Aerius 20 kayaks.

Longest Race

The longest regularly held canoe race in the US is the Texas Water Safari (instituted 1963) which covers 265 twisting mi from San Marcos to Seadrift, Tex, on the San Marcos and Guadalupe Rivers. Robert Chatham and Butch Hodges set the record of 37 hours 18 min, June 5–6, 1976.

Longest Journey

The longest canoe journey in history was one of 8,880 miles from New Orleans by paddle and portage *via* the Mississippi River, Prescott, Minnesota, Grand Portage, Lake Superior and across Canada to the Bering Sea and Nome, Alaska, by Jerry Robert Pushcar (b Nov 26, 1949), accompanied only by a Samoyed dog, from Jan 10, 1975, to Nov 12, 1977.

Downstream Canoeing

The longest journey without portage or aid of any kind is one of 6,102 miles by Richard H. Grant and Ernest "Moose" Lassey circumnavigating the eastern US from Chicago to New Orleans to Miami to NYC, returning back to Chicago *via* the Great Lakes, from Sept 22, 1930, to Aug 15, 1931.

River	Miles	Canoers	Location	Duration
Mississippi	2,552	Valerie Fons and Verlen Kruger (US)	Lake Itasca, Minnesota, to Gulf of Mexico, Apr 27–May 20, 1984	23 days 10 hours 20 min
Mississippi-Missouri	3,810	Nicholas Francis (GB)	Three Forks, Montana, to New Orleans, July 13–Nov. 25, 1977	135 days
	3,500	Beverly Gordon and Mary Schmidt (US) in 2 solo canoes	Dillon, Mont to New Orleans July 6–Oct 12, 1984	98 days
Congo	2,600	John and Julie Batchelor (GB)	Moasampanga to Banana, May 8–Sept. 12, 1974	128 days
Amazon	3,800	Alan Trevor Halman (GB/Aust)	Quitani, Peru to Cabo Maguari, Brazil Aug 9–Dec 3, 1982	116 days
Nile	4,000	John Goddard (US), Jean Laporte and André Davy (France)	Kagera to the Delta, Nov., 1953–July, 1954	9 months

Eskimo Rolls

Bruce Jeffery Parry (Australia) (b Sept 25, 1960) achieved 1,000 Eskimo rolls in a kayak in 52 min 37.7 sec at Carrara, Queensland, Australia on Oct 2, 1983. Julian Dean achieved 1,555 continuous rolls at Casterton Swimming Pool, Cumbria, England, taking 1 hour 49 min 45 sec on Dec 6, 1983. A "hand-rolling" record of 100 rolls in 3 min 23 sec was set by John Bouteloup at Crystal Palace, London, on Feb 25, 1980.

CROQUET

Origins

Some say croquet began in the 12th to 14th century in France when peasants used crude mallets to knock balls through hoops made of bent willow branches. Americans contend that, since one needed a large lawn, or at least a large backyard, peasants could not have invented the game.

It was probably first popular in England as a country-house game in the mid-1600's, when it was called "crokey." Professional groundskeepers were hired and lawns became "greenswards." Oddly enough (according to a recent book by Jack Osborn and Jesse Kornbluth), "one court was made of powdered cockleshell and its wickets were festooned with flowers."

The game has gone through several lapses into obscurity over the years, and in the last century was introduced from England into Australia and the US. The literary group that gathered around Herbert Bayard Swope and Alexander Woollcott in the 1920's (the Algonquin Round Table set which included George S. Kaufman and Dorothy Parker) brought croquet into the limelight. Croquet spread to Hollywood soon after, under the guidance of Darryl Zanuck and Samuel Goldwyn.

CROQUET is "the game" in Palm Beach, Fla, and The Breakers hotel where this photo was taken. John Young (right), #3 seed in the US Croquet Association, was a 3-time Olympic swimming star. (Courtesy US Croquet Gazette)

Today the U.S. Croquet Association has 175 clubs as members with 26 of them new in 1984. Australia, however, is the largest croquet-playing nation.

USCA National Ratings

These ratings are based on the final standings of all individual competitors entered in these major Class "A" 1982 USCA Championship tournaments:

USCA National Singles Championships—NYC
USCA National Doubles Championships—NYC
USCA National Club Team Championships—Palm Beach, Fla.

Annually hereafter, all USCA–sanctioned regional, sectional, district and club championship tournaments will be computed into the comprehensive overall rankings for all individuals entering these events.

1. J. Archie Peck, Fla
2. Richard Pearman, Bermuda
3. John Young, Bermuda
4. Ted Prentis, NY
5. Paul Kemmerly, Ariz
   Nelga Young, Bermuda
7. Archie Burchfield, Ky
   James Dushek, Ill
9. Arthur Bohner, NY
   William Hiltz, NY
   Jack Osborn, NY
   Mack Penwell, NC

(Based on the final standings in the National Singles Championships. Ties are listed in alphabetical order.)

US Croquet Hall of Fame

Each year the trustees of the Croquet Foundation of America consider individual nominees whose contributions to the growth and enjoyment of the game of croquet in the US would merit their induction in the US Croquet Hall of Fame. Since 1979, its inaugural year, the following distinguished American croquet players have been elected:

George Abbott
Paul Butler
Margaret Emerson
Raoul Fleischmann
Andrew Fuller
Samuel Goldwyn
John David Griffin
William Harbach
W. Averell Harriman
Moss Hart
Howard Hawks
William Hawks
Milton "Doc" Holden
Louis Jourdan
George S. Kaufman
John Lavalle
Mrs. Carvel (Susie) Linden
Duncan McMartin
Harpo Marx
Jean Negulesco
Jack Osborn
Mrs. Ogden (Lilian) Phipps
Edmund A. Prentis III
Richard Rodgers
Mrs. Richard (Dorothy) Rodgers
Michael Romanoff
George Sanders
Frederick Schock, Jr.
Herbert Bayard Swope, Jr.
Herbert Bayard Swope, Sr.
S. Joseph Tankoos
Francis O. Tayloe
Alexander Woollcott
Gig Young
John and Melga Young
Darryl F. Zanuck

USCA National Champions

SINGLES

Year	*Winners*	*Runners-Up*
1977	J. Archie Peck, Palm Beach	Jack Osborn, NY
1978	Richard Pearman, Bermuda	Jack Osborn, NY
1979	J. Archie Peck, Palm Beach	Richard Pearman, Bermuda
1980	J. Archie Peck, Palm Beach	Arthur Bohner, Westhampton, N.Y.
1981	Richard Pearman, Bermuda	Jack Osborn, NY
1982	J. Archie Peck, Palm Beach	Richard Pearman, Bermuda
1983	E. A. (Ted) Prentis IV, Florida & NY	Richard Pearman, Bermuda
1984	James Bast, Phoenix	Kiley Jones, NY

DOUBLES

Year	*Winners*	*Runners-Up*
1977	Jack Osborn & J. Archie Peck	Nelga & John Young, Bermuda
1978	E. A. (Ted) Prentis & Arthur Bohner	Jack Osborn & J. Archie Peck
1979	Jack Osborn & J. Archie Peck	E. A. Ted Prentis & Arthur Bohner
1980	Ted & Ned Prentis	Richard Pearman & John Young
1981	Ted & Ned Prentis	Richad Pearman & John Young
1982	Archie & Mark Burchfield (Kentucky)	Jack Osborn & J. Archie Peck
1983	Kiley Jones & Richard Illingsworth	Archie Peck & Dana Dribben
1984	James Bast & Ray Bell	Richard Pearman & John Young

International Challenge Cup

John C. (Jack) Osborn (US) and Kiley Jones (US) won their singles matches and, paired, won the doubles against Australia in 1984, but the US failed to win the Cup, 16–8.

CROSS-COUNTRY RUNNING

International Championships

The earliest international cross-country race was run between England and France on a course 9 miles 18 yd long from Ville d'Avray, outside Paris, on March 20, 1898 (England won by 21 points to 69). The inaugural International Cross-Country Championships took place at the Hamilton Park Racecourse, Scotland, on March 28, 1903. Since 1973 the race has been run under the auspices of the International Amateur Athletic Federation.

The greatest margin of victory in the International Cross-Country Championships has been 56 sec, or 390 yd, by Jack T. Holden (England) (b Mar 13, 1907) at Ayr Racecourse, Scotland, March 24, 1934. The narrowest win was that of Jean-Claude Fayolle (France) at Ostend, Belgium, on March 20, 1965, when the timekeepers were unable to separate his time from that of Melvyn Richard Batty (England).

The greatest men's team wins have been those of England, with a minimum of 21 points (the first six runners to finish) on two occasions, 1924 and 1932.

Most Appearances

The runner with the largest number of international championship appearances is Marcel Van de Wattyne of Belgium, who participated in 20 competitions in the years 1946–65.

Most Wins

The most victories is 5 in the women's race by Doris Brown-Heritage (US) (b Sept 17, 1942), 1967–71; and by Grete Waitz (Norway) (b Oct 1, 1953), 1978–81, 83.

The greatest number of men's individual victories is 4 by Jack Holden (England) in 1933–35, and 39; by Alain Mimoun-o-Kacha (b Jan 1, 1921) (France) in 1949, 52, 54 and 56; and Gaston Roelants (b Feb 5, 1937) (Belgium) in 1962, 67, 69 and 72.

Largest Field

The largest recorded field in any cross-country race was 11,763 starters (10,810 finishers) in the 18.6-mi Lidingoloppet near Stockholm, Sweden, Oct 3, 1982.

COUNTRY MILES: French runner Alain Mimoun (#1) streaks to one of his four world titles, a record he shares with Jack Holden and Gaston Roelants.

CYCLING

Earliest Race

The earliest recorded bicycle race was a velocipede race over 2 km (1.24 miles) at the Parc de St Cloud, Paris, on May 31, 1868, won by Dr James Moore (GB) (1847–1935).

The time-trial was devised in 1889–90 by F. T. Bidlake to avoid the congestion caused by ordinary mass road racing.

Highest Speed

Fred Markham recorded 8.80 sec for 200 m (50.84 mph) on a stream-lined bicycle at Ontario, Calif, May 6, 1979.

The greatest distance ever covered in one hour is 76 miles 604 yd by Leon Vanderstuyft (Belgium) on the Montlhéry Motor Circuit, France, Sept 30, 1928. This was achieved from a standing start paced by a motorcycle ahead. (Cycling rules permit a motorcycle to precede a bicycle in an event of over 10 km.) The 24-hour record behind pace is 860 miles 367 yd by Hubert Opperman in Melbourne, Australia on May 23, 1932.

The greatest distance covered in 60 min unpaced is 31 mi 1381 yd by Francesco Moser (Italy) at Mexico City on Jan 23, 1984. The 24-hour record on the road is 515.8 miles by Teuvo Louhivouri of Finland on Sept 10, 1974.

A record of 140.5 mph was achieved in 1973 behind a windshield in the wake of a speeding car, and a record of 62.28 mph behind a speeding train with the bike on a wooden surface in an 1899 stunting exhibition.

Tour de France

This race is the longest lasting non-mechanical sporting event in the world, taking 23 days to stage annually. The longest ever was in 1926 when it lasted for 29 days. It is estimated that as many as 10 million people watch some part of it, and the cost to the French economy has been estimated to be in excess of $1 billion.

The greatest number of wins in the Tour de France (inaugurated 1903)

ONE HOUR 76 MILES: Leon Vanderstuyft (wreathed, and looking somewhat the worse for wear) pedaled 76 miles 604 yards in one hour behind a pacing motorcycle.

SIX DAYS ON THE TRACK: Patrick Sercu (Belgium) (leading) won 88 six-day races out of 223 events for a 39% record. The durable cyclist also holds 3 professional speed records for 1 kilometer.

is 5 by Jacques Anquetil (b Jan 8, 1934) (France), who won in 1957, 1961–64; and Eddy Merckx (b June 17, 1945) (Belgium) who won five titles (1969–72, 1974).

The closest race ever was in 1968 when after 2,898.7 miles over 25 days (June 27–July 21) Jan Jannssen (Netherlands) (b May 19, 1940) beat Herman van Springel (Belgium) in Paris by 38 sec. The longest course was 3,569 miles on June 20 to July 18, 1926. The length of the course is usually about 3,000 miles, but varies from year to year.

The fastest average speed was 23.51 mph by Bernard Hinault (b Nov 14, 1954) (France) in 1981. The greatest number of participants was in 1982, when 170 started and 71 finished.

Six-Day Races

The greatest number of wins in six-day races is 88 out of 223 events by Patrick Sercu (b June 27, 1944), of Belgium, 1964–83.

Most Olympic Titles

The greatest number of gold medals ever won is 3 by Paul Masson (France) in 1896, Francisco Verri (Italy) in 1906 and Robert Charpentier (France) in 1936. Daniel Morelon (France) won two in 1968 and a third in 1972. He also won a bronze medal in 1964. Marcus Hurley (US) (1884–1950) won 4 events in the "unofficial" cycling competition in the 1904 Games.

1984 Olympic Winners

1,000 m Time Trials	
Fredy Schmidthe (W Ger)	1:06.10
1,000 m Sprint	
Mark Gorski (US)	
Individual Points Race	
Roger Ilegems (Belgium)	
4,000 m Individual Pursuit	
Steve Hegg (US)	4:39.35
4,000 m Team Pursuit	
Australia	4:25.99
Individual Road Race	
Alexi Grewal (US)	4 hr 59 min 57 sec
100 km Team Time Trial	
Italy	1 hr 58 min 28 sec
Women's Individual Road Race	
Connie Carpenter-Phinney (US)	2 hr 11 min 14 sec

GOLD MEDALIST: Alexi Grewal (US) (left) is jubilant as he wins the individual road race in 1984 Olympics. CYCLO-CROSS (right): The new activity requires the racers to carry their bikes over a ridge.

Longest One-Day Race

The longest single-day "massed start" road race is the Bordeaux-to-Paris, France, event of 342 to 385 miles. Paced over all or part of the route, the highest average speed in 1981 was 29.32 mph by Herman van Springel (Belgium) (b Aug 14, 1943) for 362.2 mi in 13 hours 35 min 18 sec. The longest unpaced single-day race is the Bristol-to-Bradford, England, 245-mile event.

Touring

The greatest number of participants in a bicycle tour is 17,344 in the 36-mile Citibank–AYH Five Borough Tour of NYC on Apr 25, 1982.

The longest cycle tour on record is the more than 402,000 miles amassed by Walter Stolle (b Sudetenland, 1926), an itinerant lecturer. From Jan 24, 1959 to Dec 12, 1976, he covered 159 countries, had 5 bicycles stolen and suffered 231 other robberies, along with over 1,000 flat tires. From 1922 to Dec 25, 1973, Tommy Chambers (1903–84) of Glasgow, Scotland, had ridden a verified total of 799,405 miles.

John Hathaway of Vancouver, Canada, covered 50,600 miles, visiting every continent from Nov 10, 1974 to Oct 6, 1976.

Veronica and Colin Scargill, of Bedford, England, traveled 18,020 miles around the world, on a tandem, Feb 25, 1974–Aug 27, 1975.

Endurance

Tommy Godwin (1912–75) (GB) in the 365 days of 1939 covered 75,065 miles or an average of 205.65 miles per day. He then completed 100,000 miles in 500 days to May 14, 1940.

Nicholas Mark Sanders (b Nov 26, 1957) of Glossop, England, circumnavigated the world (13,609 road miles) in 138 days, Feb 7–July 5, 1981.

Lon Haldeman was reported to have ridden from Santa Monica, Calif, to NYC (2,976 miles) in a record 9 days 20 hours 2 min in 1982. Susan Notorangelo set the women's trans-America cycling record when she completed the 2,932-mile journey from Santa Monica to NYC in 11 days 16 hours 15 minutes, July 1–13, 1982. Wayne Phillips of Richmond, BC, rode across Canada from Vancouver, BC, to Halifax, Nova Scotia, covering the 3,800 miles in 14 days 22 hours 47 min June 13–28, 1982.

Carlos Vieira cycled for 191 hours "non-stop" at Leiria, Portugal June 8–16, 1983. The distance covered was 1496.04 mi, and he was moving 98.7% of the time.

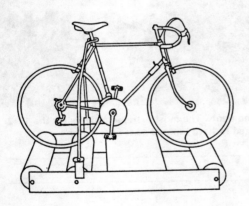

ROLLER CYCLING is performed on a device like this. (From the "Cyclist's Manual" by Doug Colligan and Dick Teresi—Sterling)

Roller Cycling

The four-man 12-hour record is 717.9 miles by a Northampton team at the Guildhall, Northampton, England, on Jan 28, 1978. The 24-hour solo record is 792.7 miles by Bruce W. Hall at San Diego University, Calif, Jan 22–23, 1977. Paul Swinnerton (GB) achieved a record 102 mph for 200 meters on rollers on Feb 12, 1982, at Stoke-on-Trent, England.

Stationary Cycling

Rudi Jan Jozef De Greef (b Dec 28, 1955) stayed stationary without support for 10 hours at Meensel-Kiezegem, Belgium, Nov 19, 1982.

STEEPLECHASE provides thrilling moments. The most extreme claim is for the 1912 Grand National winner who is alleged to have jumped 40 ft over water.

EQUESTRIAN SPORTS*

Origin

Men have ridden horses for 5,000 years. The Athenian general and historian Xenophon wrote a treatise on horsemanship 2,300 years ago, but it was not until the 16th century that schools of horsemanship, or equitation, became established, primarily in Italy and then in France. In Britain the first official competitions were held in 1865 under the auspices of the Royal Dublin Society, while the first jumping contest was at the Agricultural Hall, London in 1869. The dressage event was a direct outcome of the exercises taught in the early Italian and French academies. The Three-Day Event developed from cavalry endurance rides, one of the earliest being from Vienna to Berlin in 1892. There was a jumping

* For more detailed information about equestrian sports, see *The Guinness Guide to Equestrianism,* available from Sterling.

event in the Olympic Games of 1900, but a full equestrian program was not instituted until 1912.

Most Olympic Medals

The greatest number of Olympic gold medals is 5 by Hans-Günter Winkler (b July 24, 1926) (W Germany), who won 4 team gold medals as captain in 1956, 60, 64 and 72, and won the individual Grand Prix in 1956. The most team wins in the Prix des Nations is 5 by Germany in 1936, 56, 60, 64, and 1972.

The lowest score obtained by a winner for jumping was no faults, by Frantisek Ventura (Czechoslovakia) on "Eliot" in 1928, and by Alwin Schockemöhle (W Germany) on "Warwick Rex" in 1976. Pierre Jonqueres d'Oriola (France) is the only two-time winner of the individual gold medal, in 1952 and 1964.

In dressage, Henri St Cyr (Swe) has won four golds, including a unique two in the individual competition 1952–56. St Cyr was also a member of the winning Swedish team in 1948, but subsequently they were disqualified because one of them was not a military officer as the rules at that time decreed. Emphasizing the increasingly successful role of women in this sport, the most medals ever won is five by Liselott Linsenhoff (W Ger) between 1956 and 1972.

In the Three-Day Event, Charles Pahud de Mortanges (Hol) won a record four gold medals, including two individual titles, from 1924 to 1932, as well as a team silver.

The 1984 Olympic gold medal winners were: Joe Fargis (US) with 4 faults in the individual Grand Prix jumping; Reiner Klimke (W Ger) with 1,504 points in the Grand Prix dressage; Mark Todd (NZ) with 51.60 points in the individual Three-Day Event; and the US team won the Team Grand Prix Jumping by 12.00 faults to GB's 36.75, and the Team Three-Day Event by 186.00 points to GB's 189.20 points.

TWO FOR THE SHOW: Hans-Günter Winkler (West Germany) rode to 5 Olympic gold medals: 4 for team competition and the individual gold in 1956. The show-jumping champion also won 2 world titles.

"HEATHERBLOOM": Flying like a bird, this horse is said to have covered 37 feet in clearing an 8-foot-3-inch jump in 1903. She is here making a demonstration jump of 8 feet 2 inches in 1905.

World Titles

The men's world championship (instituted 1953) has been won twice by Hans-Günter Winkler of W Germany in 1954 and 1955, and Raimondo d'Inzeo of Italy in 1956 and 1960. The women's title (1965–74) was won twice by Jane "Janou" Tissot (*née* Lefebvre) of France on "Rocket" in 1970 and 1974.

Jumping Records

The official *Fédération Equestre Internationale* high jump record is 8 ft 1¼ in by "Huaso," ridden by Capt A. Larraguibel Morales (Chile) at Santiago, Chile, on Feb 5, 1949, but there are several reports of much higher jumps. The most extreme is a 9 ft 6 in clearance by "Ben Bolt" at the 1938 Royal Horse Show in Sydney, Australia.

The greatest height by a woman is 7 ft 8 in by Katrina Towns-Musgrove (Aust) on "Big John" in Cairns in 1978.

The greatest recorded height reached bareback is 7 ft by Michael Whitaker (b Mar 17, 1960) on "Red Flight" in Dublin, Eire, Nov 14, 1982.

The official long jump record is 27 ft 6¾ in by "Something" ridden by André Ferreira at Johannesburg, S Africa on April 26, 1975, but there have been many longer jumps recorded. The Australian record is 32 ft 10 in by "Monarch" at Brisbane in 1951, but "Solid Gold" jumped 36 ft 3 in at the Wagga Show, NSW, Australia, in 1936. In the US "Heatherbloom," ridden by Dick Donnelly, is reputed to have cleared 37 ft when high jumping 8 ft 3 in at Richmond, Va. in 1903. The most extreme claim made is for "Jerry M," the 1912 Grand National Steeplechase winner at Aintree, Eng, who is alleged to have jumped 40 ft over water there.

HIGHEST JUMP—7 FEET: Michael Whitaker of Yorkshire, England, on "Red Flight" is setting the bareback jump record in Dublin, Ireland, Nov 14, 1982. (Tony Parkes)

Longest Ride

Thomas L. Gaddie (US) rode 11,217.2 miles from Dallas, Tex, to Fairbanks, Alaska, and back in 295 days, Feb 12–Dec 2, 1980, with seven horses.

The Bicentennial "Great American Horse Race," begun on May 31, 1976, from Saratoga Springs, NY, to Sacramento, Calif (3,500 miles) was won by Virl Norton on "Lord Fauntleroy"—a mule—in 98 days. His actual riding time was 315.47 hours.

First Solo Transcontinental Journey

Nan Jane Aspinwall left San Francisco on horseback on Sept 1, 1910. She arrived in NYC on July 8, 1911, having covered 4,500 miles in 301 days, 108 of which she spent traveling.

Marathon

Paulette Standt rode at all paces (including jumping) for 100 hours at Shartlesville, Pa, June 13–17, 1984.

FOILED: Christian d'Oriola (left) merited his opponent's complete attention. The French foilist won 4 world titles and 2 Olympic golds. He was also a member of 2 gold-medal-winning French foil teams.

FENCING

Origins

Swords have been in use as combat weapons since ancient times. The first indication of fencing as a sport or pastime is on a relief in the temple of Medinet Habu, Luxor, Egypt built by Rameses III about 1190 BC, although it seems likely that it was used in religious ceremonies some two centuries before. The modern sport developed directly from the dueling, often to the death, of the Middle Ages. In the early 14th century the Marxbrüder Fencing Guild was flourishing in Frankfurt, Germany. In Britain, Edward I had specifically banned fencing tournaments in the City of London in 1285. Henry VIII, some 250 years later, founded the Corporation of Masters of Defence which was probably the first governing body of any sport in Britain. The mask was introduced by a Frenchman, La Boessière in about 1780.

There are three swords used today. With the foil, introduced in the 17th century, only the trunk of the body is acceptable as a target. The épée, established in the mid-19th century, is rather heavier and more rigid than the foil and has the whole body as a valid target. The saber, introduced in the late-19th century, has cutting edges on the front and back of the blade, and can only score on the whole body from the waist upwards. In foil and épée, hits are scored with the point of the weapon, but with the saber, scoring is allowed using all of the front edge and part of the back edge of the blade.

Most Olympic Titles

Fencing was included in the first modern Olympics in 1896.

The greatest number of individual Olympic gold medals won is 3 by Ramón Fonst (Cuba) (1883–1959) in 1900 and 1904 (2) and Nedo Nadi (Italy) (1894–1952) in 1912 and 1920 (2). Nadi also won 3 team gold medals in 1920 making a then unprecedented total of 5 gold medals at one Olympic meet.

Edoardo Mangiarotti (Italy) (b Apr 7, 1919) holds the record of 13 Olympic medals (6 gold, 5 silver, 2 bronze), won in the foil and épée competitions from 1936 to 1960.

The most gold medals won by a woman is four (one individual, three team) by Elena Novikova- Belova (USSR) (b July 28, 1947) from 1968 to 1976, and the record for all medals is 7 (2 gold, 3 silver, 2 bronze), by Ildikó Sagi-Retjö (formerly Ujlaki-Retjö) (Hungary) (b May 11, 1937) from 1960 to 1976.

The 1984 Olympics gold medalists were: Mauro Numa (Italy) in the foil, Philippo Boisse (France) in the épée, Jean-Francois Lamour (France) in the saber, Jujie Luan (China) in the women's foil. In the team events, Italy won the foil and saber, and W Germany took the épée and women's foil.

World Championships

Other than at the Olympic Games, genuine world championships were not introduced until 1937, although the European titles, inaugurated in 1921 for men, were styled "world championships."

The greatest number of individual world titles won is 5 by Aleksandr Romankov but note that Christian d'Oriola (France) won 4 world titles (1947, 49, 53–54) and also won 2 individual Olympic titles. Likewise, of the 3 women foilists with 3 world titles (Helene Mayer, Ellen Müller-Preiss and Ilona Schacherer-Elek) only Elek also won 2 individual Olympic titles.

FISHING

Origins

From time immemorial men have fished the seas and rivers of the world for food, but fishing for pleasure and leisure seems to have been practiced in Egypt, according to wall paintings, from the 5th Dynasty, 2470–2320 BC. On tomb inscriptions, Amenemhat, a prince of Beni Hasan, is described as "overseer of the swamps of enjoyment," a reference interpreted as fishing grounds.

Largest Catches

The largest fish ever caught on a rod is an officially ratified man-eating great white shark (*Carcharodon carcharias*) weighing 2,664 lb, and measuring 16 ft 10 in long, caught by Alf Dean at Denial Bay, near Ceduna, South Australia, on Apr 21, 1959. In June 1978 a great white shark measuring 29 ft 6 in in length and weighing over 10,000 lb was harpooned and landed by fishermen in the harbor of San Miguel, Azores.

A white pointer shark weighing 3,388 lb was caught on a rod by Clive Green off Albany, W Australia, on Apr 26, 1976, but this will remain unratified as whale meat was used as bait.

The largest marine animal ever killed by *hand* harpoon was a blue whale 97 ft in length by Archer Davidson in Twofold Bay, NSW, Australia, in 1910. Its tail flukes measured 20 ft across and its jaw bone 23 ft 4 in.

3,001 BASS caught in one season of 77 days is the record set by David Romeo of East Meadow, NY.

The biggest single freshwater catch ever ratified was on the Snake River, Idaho, in 1956 when Willard Cravens caught a white sturgeon weighing 360 lb. However, that may not be the last word as two years previously, in the same river, Glenn Howard claims to have caught one which weighed 394 lb.

Smallest Catch

The smallest fish ever to win a competition was a smelt weighing 1/16 of an oz, caught by Peter Christian at Buckenham Ferry, Norfolk, England, on Jan 9, 1977. This beat 107 other competitors who failed to catch anything.

Most Fish Caught in a Season

In 77 days of fishing from Apr 1 to Oct 31, 1984, David Romeo of East Meadow, NY, caught on rod and reel 3,001 largemouth bass in the fresh waters of NY State and Florida, the most ever caught in a season. Mr. Romeo, who doesn't like eating fish but enjoys catching them, threw back all but 24 of them for this and legal reasons. His log books helped the environment conservation people to make "informed bass management decisions."

World Championships

The *Confédération Internationale de la Pêche Sportive* championships were inaugurated as European championships in 1953. They were recognized as World Championships in 1957. France won 12 times between 1956 and 1981 and Robert Tesse (France) took the individual title uniquely three times, 1959–60, 65. The record weight (team) is 76 lb 8 oz in 3 hours by W Germany in the Neckar at Mannheim, W Germany on Sept 21, 1980. The individual record is 37 lb 7 oz by Wolf-Rüdiger Kremkus (W Germany) at Mannheim on Sept 20, 1980. The most fish caught is 652 by Jacques Isenbaert (Belgium) at Dunajvaros, Yugoslavia on Aug 27, 1967.

Freshwater Casting

The longest freshwater cast ratified under ICF (International Casting Federation) rules is 574 ft 2 in by Walter Kummerow (W Germany), for the Bait Distance Double-Handed 30-g event held at Lenzerheide, Switzerland, in the 1968 Championships.

The longest Fly Distance Double-Handed cast is 257 ft 2 in by Sverne Scheen (Norway) also set at Lenzerheide in Sept 1968.

Longest Fight

The longest recorded fight between a fisherman and a fish is 32 hours 5 min by Donal Heatley (NZ) (b 1938) with a black marlin (estimated length 20 ft and weight 1,500 lb) off Mayor Island off Tauranga, New Zealand, Jan 21–22, 1968. It towed the 12-ton launch 50 miles before breaking the line.

FISHING WORLD RECORDS

Selected Sea and Freshwater fish records taken by tackle as ratified by the International Game Fish Association to Nov 1984. For a more complete listing of IGFA all-tackle records, see the *Guinness Book of Sports Records, Winners & Champions* (Sterling), published in 1982.

Species	Weight in lb oz		Name of Angler	Location	Date
Amberjack	155	10	Joseph Dawson	Challenger Bank, Bermuda	June 24, 1981
Barracuda††	83	0	K. J. W. Hackett §§	Lagos, Nigeria	Jan 13, 1952
Bass (Giant Sea)	563	8	James D. McAdam, Jr	Anacapa Island, Calif	Aug 20, 1968
Bass (Striped)	78	8	Albert J. McReynolds	Atlantic City, NJ	Sept 21, 1982
Bluefish	31	12	James M. Hussey	Hatteras, NC	Jan 30, 1972
Carp†	57	13	David Nikolow	Potomac, Wash, DC	June 19, 1983
Cod	98	12	Alphonse J. Bielevich	Isle of Shoals, NH	June 8, 1969
Mackerel, Spanish	10	15	Heather J. Wadsworth	Oak Bluffs, Mass	Sept 18, 1983
Marlin (Black)	1,560	0	Alfred C. Glassell, Jr	Cabo Blanco, Peru	Aug 4, 1953
Marlin (Atlantic Blue)	1,282	0	Larry Martin	St Thomas, US VI	Aug 6, 1977
Marlin (Pacific Blue)	1,376	0	Jay Wm. deBeaubien	Kaaiwi Point, Kona, Hawaii	May 31, 1982
Marlin (Striped)	455	4	Bruce Jenkinson	Mayor Island, NZ	Mar 8, 1982
Marlin (White)	181	14	Evando Luiz Coser	Vitoria, Brazil	1980
Pike (Northern)	46	2	Peter Dubuc	Sacandaga Reservoir, NY	Sept 15, 1940
Sailfish (Atlantic)	128	1	Harm Steyn	Luanda, Angola	Mar 27, 1974
Sailfish (Pacific)	221	0	C. W. Stewart	Santa Cruz I, Galapagos Is	Feb 12, 1947
Salmon (Chinook)§	93	0	Howard C. Rider	Kelp Bay, Alaska	June 24, 1977
Salmon, Sockeye	12	8	Mike Boswell	Yakutat, Alaska	June 23, 1983
Shark (Blue)	437	0	Peter Hyde	Catherine Bay, NSW, Aust	Oct 2, 1976
Shark (Hammerhead)	991	0	Allen Ogle	Sarasota, Fla	May 30, 1982
Shark (Mako)**	1,080	0	James L. Melanson	Montauk, NY	Aug 26, 1979
Shark (White or Man-eating)	2,664	0	Alfred Dean	Ceduna, S Aust	Apr 21, 1959
Shark (Porbeagle)	465	0	Jorge Potier	Cornwall, England	July 23, 1976
Shark (Thresher)‡	802	0	Dianne North	Tutukaka, NZ	Feb 8, 1981
Shark (Tiger)	1,780	0	Walter Maxwell	Cherry Grove, SC	June 14, 1964
Sturgeon‡‡	468	0	Joey Pallatta, III	Benicia, Calif	July 9, 1983
Swordfish	1,182	0	L. E. Marron	Iquique, Chile	May 7, 1953
Tarpon	283	0	M. Salazar	Lago de Maracaibo, Venez	Mar 19, 1965
Trout (Brook)	14	8	Dr. W. J. Cook	Nipigon R, Ont, Can	July 1916
Trout (Lake)¶	65	0	Larry Daunis	Great Bear Lake, Can	Aug 8, 1970
Tuna (Allison or Yellowfin)	388	12	Curt Wiesenhutter	San Benedicto Is, Mex	Apr 1, 1977
Tuna (Atlantic Big-eyed)	375	8	Cecil Browne	Ocean City, Md	Aug 26, 1977
Tuna (Pacific Big-eyed)	435	0	Dr Russel V. A. Lee	Cabo Blanco, Peru	Apr 17, 1957
Tuna (Bluefin)	1,496	0	Ken Fraser	Aulds Cove, Nova Scotia	Oct 26, 1979
Wahoo	149	0	John Pirovano	Cat Cay, Bahamas	June 15, 1962
Weakfish	19	0	Philip W. Halstead	Chesapeake Bay, Va	May 19, 1983

†† A barracuda weighing 103 lb 4 oz was caught on an untested line by Chester Benet at West End, Bahamas, on Aug 11, 1932. Another weighing 48 lb 6 oz was caught barehanded by Thomas B. Pace at Panama City Beach, Fla, on Apr 19, 1974. §§ Hackett was only 11 years 137 days old at the time. † A carp weighing 83 lb 8 oz was taken (not by rod) near Pretoria, South Africa. A 60-lb specimen was taken by bow and arrow by Ben A. Topham in Wythe Co, Va, on July 5, 1970. § A salmon weighing 126 lb 8 oz was taken (not by rod) near Petersburg, Alaska. ** A 1,295-lb specimen was taken by two anglers off Natal, South Africa, on March 17, 1939, and a 1,500-lb specimen harpooned inside Durban Harbour, South Africa, in 1933. ‡ W. W. Dowding caught a 922-lb thresher shark in 1937 on an untested line. ‡‡ An 834-lb sturgeon was landed (not by a rod) by Garry Oling at Albion, BC, Canada, from the Fraser River on Aug 11, 1981. ¶ A 102-lb trout was taken from Lake Athabasca, northern Saskatchewan, Canada, on Aug 8, 1961.

Spear-fishing

The largest fish ever taken underwater was an 804-lb giant black grouper by Don Pinder of the Miami Triton Club, Fla, in 1955.

Bass, anyone?

If you're a bass-fisher, you should check into Indiana State University at Terre Haute, where 10,000 enrollees from ten states take courses sponsored by the school's Bass Fishing Institute.

REEL WINNERS: 1,282-lb Atlantic blue marlin (left) caught by Larry Martin in the Virgin Isles in 1977. (Center) MOST VALUABLE FISH—see box below. (Right) Ken Fraser with his 1,496-lb bluefin tuna landed after a 45-min fight off Nova Scotia, Canada, for an all-tackle record.

Most Valuable Fish

It was a modern version of an old fairy tale. When Al McReynolds went fishing one stormy night, the fish he caught brought fame and fortune. In this case, the magic was supplied by ABU-Garcia, a leading manufacturer of fishing tackle, through a contest that offered a $250,000 reward for landing an all-tackle world record fish in one of four categories.

McReynolds, 36, and his friend Pat Erdman were fishing from a jetty in their hometown, Atlantic City, NJ, on the night of Sept 21, 1982, when McReynolds hooked and, after a 2-hour fight, landed a 78-lb-8-oz striped bass—a world record for rod and reel. As one ordeal had ended, another began. McReynolds had to wait for the IGFA and ABU-Garcia to determine that the record was legitimate—a process that took nearly 5 months. Testing even included having the fish x-rayed to determine no stones or weights had been added to make the fish heavier.

It all ended happily on Feb 11, 1983, at the Explorers Club in NYC when McReynolds received a check for $250,000—the most money ever paid for a fish.

FOOTBALL

Origins

The origin of modern football stems from the "Boston Game" as played at Harvard. Harvard declined to participate in the inaugural meeting of the Intercollegiate Football Association in NYC in Oct 1873, on the grounds that the proposed rules were based on the non-handling "Association" code of English football. Instead, Harvard accepted a proposal from McGill University of Montreal, which played the more closely akin English Rugby Football. The first football match under the Harvard Rules was thus played against McGill at Cambridge, Mass, in May 1874. Most sports historians point to a contest between Rutgers and Princeton at New Brunswick, NJ, on Nov 6, 1869, as the first football game, but many American soccer historians regard this contest as the first intercollegiate *soccer* game. (Rutgers won the game, 6 goals to 4, and there were 25 players to a side.) In Nov 1876, a new Intercollegiate Football Association, with a pioneer membership of 5 colleges, was inaugurated at Springfield, Mass, to reconcile the conflicting versions of the sport. It was not until 1880 that the game, because of the organizational genius of Walter Camp of Yale, began to take its modern form. Among other things, he reduced the number of players on a side to 11, which it is today (and defined their positions), and also replaced the scrum with the line of scrimmage.

Professional football dates from the Latrobe, Pa vs Jeannette, Pa match at Latrobe, in Aug 1895. The National Football League was founded in Canton, Ohio, in 1920, although it did not adopt its present name until 1922. The year 1969 was the final year in which professional football was divided into separate National and American Leagues, for record purposes.

College Series Records

The oldest collegiate series still contested is that between Yale and Princeton dating from 1873, or 3 years before the passing of the Springfield rules, with 107 games played through 1983. The most regularly contested series is between Lafayette and Lehigh, who have met 119 times between 1884 and the end of 1984.

Yale University became the only college to win more than 700 games when it finished the 1979 season with a total of 701 victories in 107 seasons. Yale has 723 wins in 111 seasons to the end of 1983.

College Record Passer

Doug Flutie of Boston College became the first collegian to pass for more than 10,000 yards in a career. His next-to-last game of the 1984 season on Nov 23 saw him complete 34 of 46 passes for 472 yards and 3 touchdowns with no interceptions in a victory over the University of Miami, 47–45. The winning touchdown pass of 64 yards came in the last seconds of play in the Orange Bowl before 30,235 spectators and countless thousands on a national TV hookup. The receiver of the final pass and many other of Flutie's passes was Gerald Phelan, his roommate.

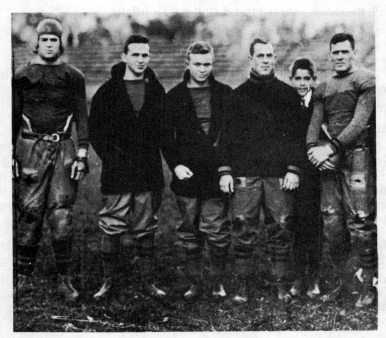

FAMOUS WEST POINTERS: Future President Dwight D. Eisenhower (third from left, above) when he played football for Army. Running backs for Army (below, left) in the 1940's were Glenn Davis (#41) and "Doc" Blanchard (#35), who won back-to-back Heisman Trophies. Davis' record of 59 touchdowns in a career still stands. FAMOUS COACH Amos Alonzo Stagg (below, right) coached or played football for 72 of his 102 years, mostly at the University of Chicago.

U.S. Presidents Who Played College Football

Eisenhower at West Point.
Kennedy tried out for the team at Harvard.
Nixon at Whittier College, in California.
Ford at Michigan, where he played on a national championship team and later captained the varsity.
Reagan at Eureka College, in Illinois.

All-America Brothers

Twice have three brothers made All-America at the same school. The first trio were the Wistert brothers at Mich, all of whom were tackles. Francis was honored in 1933, Albert in 1942, Alvin in 1948–49. At Oklahoma, defensive lineman Lucious Selmon was an All-America in 1973 and he was followed by his brothers Leroy, a defensive tackle, and Dewey, an offensive guard, in 1975.

Most Prolific Recordbreaker

After he finished his 4-year career at Portland State U in 1980, Neil Lomax held 90 NCAA football records and was tied for two other records, mostly on the basis of his passing feats. No other football player, past or present, has been remotely close to holding that many records—in any college sport.

Shortest Touchdown Pass

When the Dallas Cowboys had only 2 inches to go for a touchdown against the Washington Redskins on Oct 9, 1960, quarterback Eddie LeBaron did the unexpected. Knowing that everyone was looking to a powerful thrust at the line by the heaviest plunging back on his team, LeBaron took the ball from center and instead of handing it off to his fullback, slipped into the pocket and unleashed a short pass over the left side to his left end Bielski to set a world record for the shortest distance gained by a pass for a touchdown—2 inches. LeBaron today is a lawyer in Las Vegas.

Worst Attendance

The worst attendance for a college football game was recorded on Nov 12, 1955 at Pullman, Washington. The game was between Wash State and San Jose State. It was played in spite of high winds and a temperature of 0 °F. Total paid attendance: 1.

Coaching Records

The longest serving head coach was Amos Alonzo Stagg (1862–1965), who served Springfield in 1890–91, Chicago from 1892 to 1932 and College of the Pacific from 1933 to 1946, making a total of 57 years. He later served as an assistant coach to his son.

Paul "Bear" Bryant (1913–1983) was the winningest college coach with 323 victories from 1945 through 1982. Bryant was head coach at Maryland (1945), Kentucky (1946–1953), Texas A&M (1954–1957), and Alabama (1958–1982).

The record for most victories by a professional coach is 325, by George

MANY HAPPY RETURNS: George Halas (standing center, in raincoat and baseball hat) coached the Chicago Bears for 40 seasons, piling up a record 325 victories. Here he watches Gale Sayers take off around end. Sayers, who averaged 30.6 yards per kickoff return in his career, had a great rookie season in 1965 with 22 td's, including 6 in one game.

Halas (1895–1983), who coached the Chicago Bears, 1920–29, 33–42, 46–55, 58–67.

In 1948, Bennie Oosterbaan, an assistant coach at Mich, his alma mater, was elevated to head coach. He won all 9 games and the national championship, becoming the first and only man to do that as a first-year head coach.

Highest Score

The most points ever scored (by one team and both teams) in a college football game was 222 by Georgia Tech, Atlanta, Ga, against Cumberland University of Lebanon, Tenn on Oct 7, 1916. Tech also set records for the most points scored in one quarter (63), most touchdowns (32) and points after touchdown (30) in a game, and the largest victory margin (Cumberland did not score).

First Televised Football Game

Fordham U, NYC, was the host to Waynesburg, a Pa school, in the first football game ever televised—in 1939. Fordham won, 34–7.

Longest Streaks

The longest collegiate winning streak is 47 straight by Oklahoma. The longest unbeaten streak is 63 games (59 won, 4 tied) by Washington from 1907 to 1917. Macalaster University of St Paul, Minn, ended a record 50-game losing streak when, with 11 sec remaining in the game, a 23-yd field goal beat Mount Senario, 17–14, on Sept 6, 1980. It was Macalaster's first victory since Oct 11, 1974.

Ban Football!

Although remembered as one of the most athletic of presidents, Theodore Roosevelt threatened to ban college football in 1905. Eighteen players had died of injuries that year and 73 were seriously hurt. One of Roosevelt's sons, a freshman at Harvard, came home from the first day of practice with a black eye. At the President's urging, the flying wedge was outlawed as a move, and a neutral zone between opposing lines was instituted. Roosevelt's demands to outlaw rough play led to the Rules Committee legalizing the forward pass in 1906.

All-America Selections

The earliest All-America selections were made in 1889 by Caspar Whitney of *The Week's Sport* and later of *Harper's Weekly*.

Jim Thorpe vs Dwight D. Eisenhower

The two met in 1912 when Thorpe was playing for small, not well-endowed Carlisle School for Indians (Pa) and Eisenhower was playing for Army (West Point, NY). Eisenhower and another back were instructed to follow Thorpe wherever he went. In the third quarter of the game they both hit Thorpe so hard that the pair of them were dazed and were taken out of the game by their coach. Thorpe played to the end. Carlisle, then under the coaching of the legendary Glenn "Pop" Warner, won 27–6.

MODERN MAJOR-COLLEGE INDIVIDUAL RECORDS
(Through 1984 Season)

Points

Most in a Game	43	Jim Brown (Syracuse)	1956
Most in a Season	174	Lydell Mitchell (Penn State)	1971
	174	Mike Rozier (Nebraska)	1983
Most in a Career	368	Luis Zendejas (Ariz State)	1981–84

Touchdowns

Most in a Game	7	Arnold Boykin (Mississippi)	1951
Most in a Season	29	Lydell Mitchell (Penn State)	1971
	29	Mike Rozier (Nebraska)	1983
Most in a Career	59	Glenn Davis (Army)	1943–46
	59	Tony Dorsett (Pittsburgh)	1973–76

Field Goals

Most in a Game	7	Mike Prindle (W Mich)	1984
Most in a Season	28	Paul Woodside (West Virginia)	1982
Most in a Career	60	Obed Ariri (Clemson)	1977–80
Most Consecutively (Career)	30	Chuck Nelson (Washington)	1981–82

Other Season Records

Yards Gained Rushing	2,342 yd	Marcus Allen (So Cal)	1981
Highest Average Gain per Rush (min. 150 attempts)	9.35 yd	Greg Pruitt (Oklahoma)	1971
Most Passes Attempted	509	Bill Anderson (Tulsa)	1965
Most Passes Completed	296	Bill Anderson (Tulsa)	1965
Most Touchdown Passes	47	Jim McMahon (Brigham Young)	1980
Most Yards Gained Passing	4,571 yd	Jim McMahon (Brigham Young)	1980
Most Passes Caught	134	Howard Twilley (Tulsa)	1965
Most Yards Gained on Catches	1,779 yd	Howard Twilley (Tulsa)	1965
Most Touchdown Passes Caught	18	Tom Reynolds (San Diego St)	1969
Most Passes Intercepted by	14	Al Worley (Washington)	1968
Highest Punting Average (min. 30 punts)	49.8 yd	Reggie Roby (Iowa)	1981

NEW RUSHING RECORD of 2,105 yds in one season was set by Eric Dickerson (LA Rams) in 1984, eclipsing O.J. Simpson's record of 2,003 which held for 11 years. (UPI—Bettmann Archive)

ALL-TIME NATIONAL FOOTBALL LEAGUE RECORDS
(Through 1984 Season)

SERVICE

Most Seasons, Active Player
26 George Blanda, Chi Bears, 1949–58; Balt, 1950; AFL: Hou, 1960–66; Oak, 1967–75

Most Games Played, Lifetime
340 George Blanda, Chi Bears, 1949–58; Balt, 1950; AFL: Hou, 1960–66; Oak, 1967–75

Most Consecutive Games Played, Lifetime
282 Jim Marshall, Cleve, 1960; Minn, 1961–79

Most Seasons, Head Coach
40 George Halas, Chi Bears, 1920–29, 33–42, 46–55, 58–67

SCORING

Most Seasons Leading League
5 Don Hutson, GB, 1940–44
Gino Cappelletti, Bos, 1961, 63–66 (AFL)

Most Points, Lifetime
2,002 George Blanda, Chi Bears, 1949–58; Balt, 1950; AFL: Hou, 1960–66; Oak, 1967–75 (9-td, 943-pat, 335-fg)

Most Points, Season
176 Paul Hornung, GB, 1960 (15-td, 41-pat, 15-fg)

Most Points, Rookie Season
132 Gale Sayers, Chi, 1965 (22-td)

Most Points, Game
40 Ernie Nevers, Chi Cards vs Chi Bears, Nov 28, 1929 (6-td, 4-pat)

Most Points, One Quarter
29 Don Hutson, GB vs Det, Oct 7, 1945 (4-td, 5-pat) 2nd Quarter

Touchdowns

Most Seasons Leading League
8 Don Hutson, GB, 1935–38, 41–44

Most Touchdowns, Lifetime
126 Jim Brown, Cleve, 1957–65 (106-r, 20-p)

Most Touchdowns, Season
24 John Riggins, Wash (24-r), 1983

Most Touchdowns, Rookie Season
22 Gale Sayers, Chi, 1965 (14-r, 6-p, 1-prb, 1-krb)

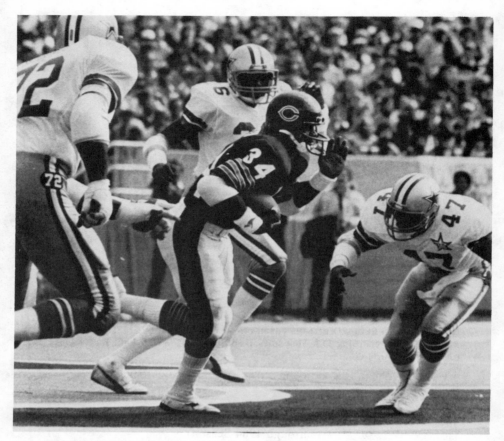

RUSHING RECORDHOLDER: Walter Payton (Chicago Bears) on his way through the Dallas Cowboy defense in 1984 to setting a record for 58 games with 100 yds or more gained. In 1977 he broke the record for yds gained in one game (275). (UPI—Bettmann Archive)

Touchdowns (continued)

Most Touchdowns, Game
  6 Ernie Nevers, Chi Cards vs Chi Bears, Nov 28, 1929 (6-r)
     William (Dub) Jones, Cleve vs Chi Bears, Nov 25, 1951 (4-r, 2-p)
     Gale Sayers, Chi vs SF, Dec 12, 1965 (4-r, 1-p, 1-prb)

Most Consecutive Games Scoring Touchdowns
  18 Lenny Moore, Balt, 1963–65

Points After Touchdown

Most Seasons Leading League
  8 George Blanda, Chi Bears, 1956; AFL: Hou, 1961–62; Oak, 1967–69, 72, 74

Most Points After Touchdown, Lifetime
  943 George Blanda, Chi Bears, 1949–58; Balt, 1950; AFL: Hou, 1960–66; Oak, 1967–75

Most Points After Touchdown, Season
  64 George Blanda, Hou, 1961 (AFL)

Most Points After Touchdown, Game
  9 Marlin (Pat) Harder, Chi Cards vs NY, Oct 17, 1948
     Bob Waterfield, LA vs Balt, Oct 22, 1950
     Charlie Gogolak, Wash vs NY, Nov 27, 1966

Most Consecutive Points After Touchdown
  234 Tommy Davis, SF, 1959–65

Most Points After Touchdown (no misses), Game
  9 Marlin (Pat) Harder, Chi Cards vs NY, Oct 17, 1948
     Bob Waterfield, LA vs Balt, Oct 22, 1950

Field Goals

Most Seasons Leading League
  5 Lou Groza, Cleve, 1950, 52–54, 57

COLLEGE STAR WHO JOINED NEW LEAGUE: Herschel Walker (left) rushed 1,616 yds as a freshman at Georgia in 1980 to set a record, and helped his team remain undefeated that year, including a Sugar Bowl victory. Going into the new pro World Football League, Walker became an instantaneous star for the New Jersey Generals. **STRONG ARM:** Fran Tarkenton set lifetime NFL records by attempting 6,467 passes and completing 3,686 of them during his 18-year career with the NY Giants and Minn Vikings. Tarkenton also holds career passing records for touchdowns and yards gained.

Most Field Goals, Lifetime
  338 Jan Stenerud KC 1967–69; Gr Bay 1980–83

Most Field Goals, Season
  35 Ali Haji-Sheikh, NY Giants, 1983

Most Field Goals, Game
  7 Jim Bakken, St L vs Pitt, Sept 24, 1967

Most Consecutive Games, Field Goals
  31 Fred Cox, Minn, 1968–70

Highest Field Goal Percentage, Season
95.24 Mark Mosely, Wash, 1982 (20–21)

Most Consecutive Field Goals
  23 Mark Mosely, Wash, 1981–82

Longest Field Goal
  63 yd Tom Dempsey, NO vs Det, Nov 8, 1970

RUSHING

Most Seasons Leading League
  8 Jim Brown, Cleve, 1957–61, 63–65

Most Yards Gained, Lifetime
13,309 Walter Payton, Chi, 1975–84

Most Yards Gained, Season
  2,105 Eric Dickerson, LA Rams, 1984

Most Yards Gained, Game
  275 Walter Payton, Chi vs Minn, Nov 20, 1977

Longest Run from Scrimmage
  99 yd Tony Dorsett, Dall vs Minn, Jan 3, 1983 (td)

Highest Average Gain, Lifetime
(799 att)
  5.2 Jim Brown, Cleve, 1957–65 (2,359–12,312)

Highest Average Gain, Game (10 att)
  17.1 Marion Motley, Cleve vs Pitt, Oct 29, 1950 (11–188)

Most Touchdowns Rushing, Lifetime
  106 Jim Brown, Cleve, 1957–65

Most Touchdowns Rushing, Season
  24 John Riggins, Wash, 1983

Most Touchdowns Rushing, Game
  6 Ernie Nevers, Chi Cards vs Chi Bears, Nov 28, 1929

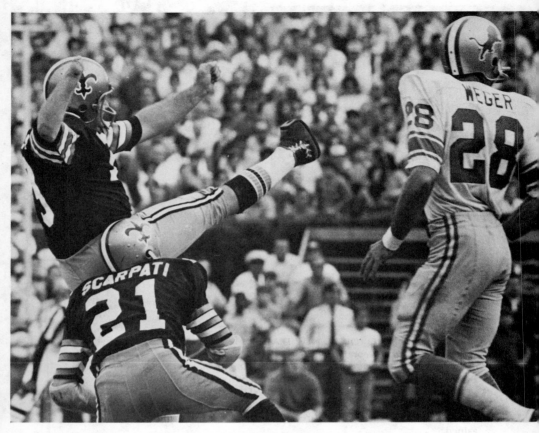

IN FRONT BY HALF A FOOT: Tom Dempsey (New Orleans Saints) kicked a record 63-yard field goal on the last play of an NFL game to beat the Detroit Lions 19–17 on Nov 8, 1970. Dempsey, who was born with only half a right foot and only part of his right arm, wore a special shoe for placekicking. He reportedly once kicked a 57-yarder without a shoe in a semipro game.

PASSING

Most Seasons Leading League
    6 Sammy Baugh, Wash, 1937, 40, 43, 45, 47, 49

Most Passes Attempted, Lifetime
6,467 Fran Tarkenton, Minn, 1961–66, 72–78; NY Giants, 1967–71 (3,686 completions)

Most Passes Attempted, Season
  609 Dan Fouts, SD, 1981 (360 completions)

Most Passes Attempted, Game
  68 George Blanda, Hou vs Buff, Nov 1, 1964 (AFL) (37 completions)

Most Passes Completed, Lifetime
3,686 Fran Tarkenton, Minn, 1961–66, 72–78; NY Giants, 1967–71 (6,467 attempts)

Most Passes Completed, Season
  362 Dan Marino, Miami, 1984 (564 attempts)

Most Passes Completed, Game
  42 Richard Todd, NY Jets vs SF, Sept 21, 1980 (59 attempts)

Most Consecutive Passes Completed
  20 Ken Anderson, Cin vs Hou, Jan 2, 1983

Longest Pass Completion (all tds)
  99 Frank Filchock (to Farkas), Wash vs Pitt, Oct 15, 1939
      George Izo (to Mitchell), Wash vs Cleve, Sept 15, 1963
      Karl Sweetan (to Studstill), Det vs Balt, Oct 16, 1966
      C. A. Jurgensen (to Allen), Wash vs Chi, Sept 15, 1968
      Jim Plunkett (to Branch) LA Raiders vs Wash Oct 2, 1983

Most Yards Gained Passing, Lifetime
47,003 Fran Tarkenton, Minn, 1961–66, 72–78; NY Giants, 1967–71

Most Yards Gained Passing, Game
554 Norm Van Brocklin, LA vs NY Yanks, Sept 28, 1951 (41–27)

Most Yards Gained Passing, Season
5,084 Dan Marino, Miami, 1984

Most Touchdown Passes, Lifetime
342 Fran Tarkenton, Minn, 1961–66, 72–78; NY Giants, 1967–71

Most Touchdown Passes, Season
48 Dan Marino, Miami, 1984

Most Touchdown Passes, Game
7 Sid Luckman, Chi Bears vs NY, Nov 14, 1943
Adrian Burk, Phil vs Wash, Oct 17, 1954
George Blanda, Hou vs NY, Nov 19, 1961 (AFL)
Y. A. Tittle, NY vs Wash, Oct 28, 1962
Joe Kapp, Minn vs Balt, Sept 28, 1969

Most Consecutive Games, Touchdown Passes
47 John Unitas, Balt, 1956–60

Passing Efficiency, Lifetime (1,500 att)
63.7 Joe Montana, SF 1979–84; (1,324–2,077)

Passing Efficiency, Season (100 att)
70.55 Ken Anderson, Cin, 1982 (309–218)

Passing Efficiency, Game (20 att)
90.9 Ken Anderson, Cin vs Pitt, Nov 10, 1974 (22–20)

Passes Had Intercepted

Most Passes Intercepted, Game
8 Jim Hardy, Chi Cards vs Phil, Sept 24, 1950 (39 attempts)

Most Consecutive Passes Attempted, None Intercepted
294 Bryan (Bart) Starr, GB, 1964–65

Fewest Passes Intercepted, Season (Qualifiers)
1 Joe Ferguson, Buff, 1976 (151 attempts)

Lowest Percentage Passes Intercepted, Lifetime (1,500 att)
3.3 Roman Gabriel, LA, 1962–72; Phil, 1973–77 (4,498–149)

Lowest Percentage Passes Intercepted, Season (Qualifiers)
0.66 Joe Ferguson, Buff, 1976 (151–1)

PASS RECEPTIONS

Most Seasons Leading League
8 Don Hutson, GB, 1936–37, 39, 41–45

Most Pass Receptions, Lifetime
657 Charley Joiner, SD, 1969–84

Most Pass Receptions, Season
106 Art Monk, Wash, 1984

Most Pass Receptions, Game
18 Tom Fears, LA vs GB, Dec 3, 1950 (189 yd)

Longest Pass Reception (all tds)
99 Andy Farkas (Filchock), Wash vs Pitt, Oct 15, 1939
Bobby Mitchell (Izo), Wash vs Cleve, Sept 15, 1963
Pat Studstill (Sweetan), Det vs Balt, Oct 16, 1966
Gerry Allen (Jurgensen), Wash vs Chi, Sept 15, 1968
Cliff Branch (Plunkett) LA Raiders vs Wash, Oct 2, 1983

Most Consecutive Games, Pass Receptions
127 Harold Carmichael, Phil, 1972–1980

Most Pass Receptions by a Running Back, Game
17 Clark Gaines, NY Jets vs SF, Sept 21, 1980

Most Yards Gained Pass Receptions, Game
303 Jim Benton, Cleve vs Det, Nov 22, 1945

Touchdowns Receiving

Most Touchdown Passes, Lifetime
99 Don Hutson, GB, 1935–45

Most Touchdown Passes, Season
18 Mark Clayton, Miami, 1984

Most Touchdown Passes, Game
5 Bob Shaw, Chi Cards vs Balt, Oct 2, 1950
Kellen Winslow, SD vs Oak, Nov 22, 1981

Most Consecutive Games, Touchdown Passes
11 Elroy (Crazy Legs) Hirsch, LA, 1950–51
Gilbert (Buddy) Dial, Pitt, 1959–60

PASS INTERCEPTIONS

Most Interceptions by, Lifetime
81 Paul Krause, Wash (28), 1964–67; Minn (53), 1968–79

Most Interceptions by, Season
14 Richard (Night Train) Lane, LA, 1952

PURPLE PEOPLE-EATER: Jim Marshall (dark uniform) played in 282 consecutive regular-season NFL games, to the consternation of quarterbacks around the league. Marshall scooped up a record 29 opponents' fumbles, the most famous of which he "returned" in the wrong direction. **(Minnesota Vikings)**

Highest Punting Average, Season (20 punts)
    51.4 yd Sammy Baugh, Wash, 1940 (35)

Highest Punting Average, Game (4 punts)
    61.8 yd Bob Cifers, Det vs Chi Bears, Nov 24, 1946

PUNT RETURNS

Yardage Returning Punts

Most Yards Gained, Lifetime
    3,008 Rick Upchurch, Den, 1975–83

Most Yards Gained, Season
    655 Neal Colzie, Oak, 1975

Most Yards Gained, Game
    205 George Atkinson, Oak vs Buff, Sept 15, 1968

Longest Punt Return (all tds)
    98 Gil LeFebvre, Cin vs Brk, Dec 3, 1933
    Charlie West, Minn vs Wash, Nov 3, 1968
    Dennis Morgan, Dall vs St L, Oct 13, 1974

Highest Average, Lifetime (75 or more returns)
    12.78 George McAfee, Chi Bears, 1940–41, 1945–50

Highest Average, Season (Qualifiers)
    23.0 Herb Rich, Balt, 1950

Highest Average, Game (3 returns)
    47.7 Chuck Latourette, St L vs NO, Sept 29, 1968

Touchdowns Returning Punts

Most Touchdowns, Lifetime
    8 Jack Christiansen, Det, 1951–58
    Rick Upchurch, Den, 1975–83

Most Touchdowns, Season
    4 Jack Christiansen, Det, 1951
    Rick Upchurch, Den, 1976

Most Touchdowns, Game
    2 Jack Christiansen, Det vs LA, Oct 14, 1951; vs GB, Nov 22, 1951
    Dick Christy, NY Titans vs Den, Sept 24, 1961
    Rick Upchurch, Den vs Cleve, Sept 26, 1976
    Leroy Irvin, LA vs Atl, Oct 11, 1981

Most Interceptions by, Game
    4 By many players, twice· by Jerry Norton St L vs Wash, Nov 20, 1960; St L vs Pitt, Nov 26, 1961

Most Touchdowns Interception Returns, Lifetime
    9 Ken Houston, Hou 1967–79; Wash 1973–80

PUNTING

Most Seasons Leading League
    4 Sammy Baugh, Wash, 1940–43
    Jerrel Wilson, AFL: KC, 1965, 68; NFL: KC, 1972–73

Most Punts, Season
    114 Bob Parsons, Chi, 1981

Most Punts, Game
    14 Dick Nesbitt, Chi Cards vs Chi Bears, Nov 30, 1933
    Keith Molesworth, Chi Bears vs GB, Dec 10, 1933
    Sammy Baugh, Wash vs Phil, Nov 5, 1939
    John Kinscherf, NY vs Det, Nov 7, 1943
    George Taliaferro, NY Yanks vs LA, Sept 28, 1951

Most Punts, Lifetime
    1,072 Jerrel Wilson, AFL: KC, 1963–69; NFL: KC, 1970–77; NE, 1978

Longest Punt
    98 yd Steve O'Neal, NY Jets vs Den, Sept 21, 1969 (AFL)

Average Yardage Punting

Highest Punting Average, Lifetime (300 punts)
    45.1 yd Sammy Baugh, Wash, 1937–52 (338)

PUTTING THE FOOT IN FOOTBALL: Steve O'Neal (#20) of the NY Jets follows through on his punt from the end zone in Denver's Mile High Stadium. The line of scrimmage (from which punts are measured) had been the 1-yd line. The ball, which sailed well over the receiver's head, bounced and rolled to the Denver 1-yd line—a 98-yd punt! (Pro Football Hall of Fame)

KICKOFF RETURNS

Yardage Returning Kickoffs

Most Yards Gained, Lifetime
6,922 Ron Smith, Chi, 1965, 70–72; Atl, 1966–67; LA, 1968–69; SD, 1973; Oak, 1974

Most Yards Gained, Season
1,317 Bobby Jancik, Hou, 1963 (AFL)

Most Yards Gained, Game
294 Wally Triplett, Det vs LA, Oct 29, 1950 (4)

Longest Kickoff Return for Touchdown
106 Al Carmichael, GB vs Chi Bears, Oct 7, 1956
Noland Smith, KC vs Den, Dec 17, 1967 (AFL)
Roy Green, St L vs Dall, Oct 21, 1979

Highest Average, Lifetime (75 returns)
30.6 Gale Sayers, Chi, 1965–71

Average Yardage Returning Kickoffs

Highest Average, Season (15 returns)
41.1 Travis Williams, GB, 1967 (18)

Highest Average, Game (3 returns)
73.5 Wally Triplett, Det vs LA, Oct 29, 1950 (4–294)

Touchdowns Returning Kickoffs

Most Touchdowns, Lifetime
6 Ollie Matson, Chi Cards, 1952 (2), 54, 56, 58 (2)
Gale Sayers, Chi, 1965, 66 (2), 67 (3)
Travis Williams, GB, 1967 (4), 69, 71

Kickoff Returns (*continued*)
Most Touchdowns, Season
    4   Travis Williams, GB, 1967
        Cecil Turner, Chi, 1970

Most Touchdowns, Game
    2   Thomas (Tim) Brown, Phil vs
        Dall, Nov 6, 1966
        Travis Williams, GB vs Cleve,
        Nov 12, 1967

FUMBLES

Most Fumbles, Lifetime
  105 Roman Gabriel, LA, 1962–72;
       Phil, 1973–77

Most Fumbles, Season
   17 Dan Pastorini, Hou, 1973

Most Fumbles, Game
    7   Len Dawson, KC vs SD, Nov 15,
        1964 (AFL)

Longest Fumble Run
  104 Jack Tatum, Oak vs GB, Sept 24,
       1972

Most Opponents' Fumbles Recovered, Lifetime
   29 Jim Marshall, Cleve, 1960; Minn,
       1961–79

Most Opponents' Fumbles Recovered, Season
    9   Don Hultz, Minn, 1963

Most Opponents' Fumbles Recovered, Game
    3   Corwin Clatt, Chi Cards vs Det,
       Nov 6, 1949
       Vic Sears, Phil vs GB, Nov 2, 1952
       Ed Beatty, SF vs LA, Oct 7, 1956
       Ron Carroll, Hou vs Cin, Oct 27,
       1974
       Maurice Spencer, NO vs Atl, Oct
       10, 1976
       Steve Nelson, NE vs Phil, Oct 8,
       1978
       Charles Jackson, KC vs Pitt, Sept
       6, 1981
       Willie Buchanon, SD vs Den, Sept
       27, 1981

NFL Champions

The Green Bay Packers have won a record 11 NFL titles from 1929 through 1967. The Packers also won the first two Super Bowls (instituted Jan 1967), when the games were a competition between NFL and AFL champions. The Pittsburgh Steelers have the most Super Bowl victories with 4 (1975–76, 79–80). The 1972 Miami Dolphins had the best record for one season, including playoffs and Super Bowl (played Jan 1973), with 17 wins and no losses or ties.

Super-Bowl Winners

1967 Green Bay Packers (NFL)
1968 Green Bay Packers (NFL)
1969 New York Jets (AFL)
1970 Kansas City Chiefs (AFL)
1971 Baltimore Colts (AFC)
1972 Dallas Cowboys (NFC)
1973 Miami Dolphins (AFC)
1974 Miami Dolphins (AFC)
1975 Pittsburgh Steelers (AFC)

1976 Pittsburgh Steelers (AFC)
1977 Oakland Raiders (AFC)
1978 Dallas Cowboys (NFC)
1979 Pittsburgh Steelers (AFC)
1980 Pittsburgh Steelers (AFC)
1981 Oakland Raiders (AFC)
1982 San Francisco 49ers (NFC)
1983 Washington Redskins (NFC)
1984 Los Angeles Raiders (AFC)
1985 San Francisco 49ers (NFC)

The highest aggregate score was in 1984 when the Raiders beat the Washington Redskins by 38–9.

GAMES AND PASTIMES

BACKGAMMON

Forerunners of the game have been traced back to a dice and a board game found in excavations at Ur, dated to 3000 BC. Later the Romans played a game remarkably similar to the modern one. The name "Backgammon" is variously ascribed to Welsh ("little battle"), or Saxon ("back game"). Modern variations include the American Acey Deucey.

At present there are no world championships held, but a points rating system may soon be introduced internationally, thereby enabling players to be ranked.

Marathon

Dick Newcomb and Greg Peterson of Rockford, Ill, played backgammon for 151 hours 11 min, June 30–July 6, 1978.

BRIDGE (CONTRACT)

Bridge (corruption of Biritch) is thought to be either of Levantine origin, similar games having been played there in the early 1870's, or to have come from the East—probably India.

Auction bridge (highest bidder names trump) was invented *c.* 1902. The contract principle, present in several games (notably the French game *Plafond, c.* 1917), was introduced to bridge by Harold S. Vanderbilt (US) on Nov 1, 1925, during a Caribbean voyage aboard the SS *Finland*. The new version became a world-wide craze after the US vs GB challenge match between Rumanian-born Ely Culbertson (1891–1955) and Lt-Col Walter Thomas More Buller (1887–1938) at Almack's Club, London, Sept 1930. The US won the 200-hand match by 4,845 points.

Most World Titles

The World Championship (Bermuda Bowl) has been won most often by Italy's Blue Team (*Squadra Azzura*), 1957–9, 61–3, 65–7, 69, 73–5,

BRIDGE MASTER: Giorgio Belladonna (center), world leader with 1,767 Master Points, played on all 13 of Italy's world championship Blue Teams.

whose team also won the Olympiad in 1964, 68 and 72. Giorgio Belladonna (b 1923) was on all these winning teams.

Most Durable Player

Oswald Jacoby (b 1903, Dallas, Tex, d 1984) was a world-rank competitor for 52 years after winning his first world title in 1931. He retired in July 1983 but came back in Nov 1983 to be part of a team that won the North America team championship. (He also won the World Backgammon title.)

Most Master Points

In the latest ranking list based on Master Points awarded by the World Bridge Federation, the leading male player in the world was Giorgio Belladonna, a member of Italy's Blue Team, with 1,766¼ points, followed by four more Italians. The world's leading woman player is Dorothy Hayden Truscott (US) with 331 points.

As for master points awarded by the American Contract Bridge League, the leader is Barry Crane of Los Angeles who won his 31,989th point in Apr 1984. Crane, who expects to hit 40,000 before the end of the 1980's, is far ahead of everyone else. Only two other players have even reached 20,000.

Youngest Life Masters

Dougie Hsieh (NYC) was 11 years 306 days when he reached the rank of Life Master in the ACBL, and youngest ever to win a regional championship.

Adair Gellman of Bethesda, Md, became the youngest-ever female life master at age 14 years 6 months 4 days on Oct 24, 1983, breaking a record that had stood for 6 years. Then on Nov 5, 1983, just 12 days later, she was toppled from her peak by a still younger lady, Patricia Thomas of Las Cruces, NM, who was 14 years and 28 days. According to bridge columnist Alan Truscott of *The NY Times,* Miss Thomas joined the ACBL when barely 10 and became a senior master at the age of 11.

Marathon

The longest recorded session is one of 180 hours by four students at Edinburgh University, Scotland, Apr 21–28, 1972.

CHECKERS

Checkers, also known as draughts, has origins earlier than chess. It was played in Egypt in the second millennium BC. The earliest book on the game was by Antonio Torquemada of Valencia, Spain in 1547. There have been four US vs GB international matches (crossboard) in 1905, 27, 73, and 83, three won by the US and one by GB.

Walter Hellman (1916–75) (US) won a record 6 world championships, 1948–67. Melvin Pomeroy (US) was internationally undefeated from 1914 until his death in 1933. Marion Tinsley (Tallahassee, Fla) has been the world champion since 1975.

CHESS MATES: Russians Anatoliy Karpov (left) and Victor Korchnoi (right) claim not to like each other. Karpov, world champion since 1975, has always emerged the winner. In the 1984-85 world championship matches Karpov and fellow Russian Gary Kasparov set a record for duration and number of draws.

Most Opponents

Con McCarrick (Ireland) was reported as having played a record 154 games simultaneously, winning 136, drawing 17, and losing one, in 4½ hours at Dundalk, County Louth, Ireland, Mar 14, 1982.

Newell W. Banks (b Detroit, Mich, Oct 10, 1887) played 140 games simultaneously, winning 133 and drawing 7, in Chicago in 1933. His playing time was 145 min, so averaging about one move per sec. In 1947 he played blindfolded for 4 hours per day for 45 consecutive days, winning 1,331 games, drawing 54 and losing only 2, while playing six games at a time.

Longest and Shortest Games

In competition the prescribed rate of play is not less than 30 moves per hour with the average game lasting about 90 min. In 1958 a match between Dr Marion Tinsley (US) and Derek Oldbury (GB) lasted 7 hours 30 min. The shortest possible game is one of 17 moves, composed by Gerhard Visscher of The Netherlands in 1983.

The longest session is 75 hours by Cees van der Jagt and Pim Keerssemeeckers at Vlissingen, The Netherlands Apr 5–8, 1983.

CHESS

The game originated in ancient India under the name Chaturanga (literally "four-corps")— an army game. The name chess is derived from the Persian word *shah*. The earliest reference is from the Middle Persian Karnamak (*c.* 590–628), though there are grounds for believing its origins are from the 2nd century, owing to the discovery, announced in Dec 1972, of two ivory chessmen in the Uzbek Soviet Republic, datable to that century. The *Fédération Internationale des Echecs* was established in 1924. There were an estimated 7 million registered players in the USSR in 1973.

Most Opponents

Vlastimil Hort (b Jan 12, 1944) (Czechoslovakia), in Seltjarnes, Iceland, Apr 23–24, 1977, played 550 opponents, including a record 201 simultaneously. He only lost ten games.

Dimitrije Bjelica (Yugoslavia) played 301 opponents simultaneously (258 wins, 36 draws, 7 losses) in 9 hours on Sept 18, 1982, at Sarajevo, Yugoslavia. Bjelica's weight dropped by 4½ lb as he walked a total of 12.4 miles.

The record for most consecutive games played is 605 (535 wins, 42 draws, 28 losses) by José Luis Larrañaga at Azkoitia, Guinpuzcoa, Spain, during 31 hours 42 min Nov 27–29, 1982.

George Koltanowski (Belgium, later of US) tackled 56 opponents "blindfold" and won 50, drew 6, lost 0 in 9¾ hours at the Fairmont Hotel, San Francisco, on Dec 13, 1960.

Longest Games

The master game with the most moves on record was when Yedael Stepak (b Aug 21, 1940) (Israel) beat Yaakov Mashian (b Dec 17, 1943) (Iran, later Israel) in 193 moves in Tel Aviv, Israel, March 23–Apr 16, 1980. The total playing time was 24½ hours.

The slowest reported move (before modern rules) in an official event is reputed to have been played by Louis Paulsen (1833–91) (Germany) against Paul Charles Morphy (1837–84) (US) on Oct 29, 1857. The game ended in a draw on move 56 after 15 hours of play, of which Paulsen used most of the allotted time. Grandmaster Friedrich Sämisch (1896–1975) (Germany) ran out of the allotted time (2½ hours for 45 moves) after only 12 moves, in Prague, Czechoslovakia, in 1938.

World Champions

World champions have been generally recognized since 1886. The longest undisputed tenure was 27 years by Dr Emanuel Lasker (1868–1941) of Germany, from 1894 to 1921. Robert J. (Bobby) Fischer (b Chicago, March 9, 1943) is reckoned on the officially adopted Elo system to be the greatest Grandmaster of all time, with a 2,785 rating. Currently, Anatoliy Karpov (USSR) (b May 23, 1951) has been world champion since 1975, with a 2,700 rating that is lower than that of 2,710 for Gary Kasparov (USSR) (b Apr 13, 1963).

The women's world championship was held by Vera Menchik-Stevenson (1906–44) (GB) from 1927 till her death, and was successfully defended a record 7 times. Nona Gaprindashvili (USSR) (b May 3, 1941) held the title from 1962 to 1978, and defended successfully 4 times.

The USSR has won the men's team title a record 13 times and the women's title 8 times.

The youngest world champion was Mikhail Nekhemevich Tal (USSR) (b Nov 9, 1936) when he took the title on May 7, 1960, aged 23 years 180 days. The oldest was Wilhelm Steinitz (1836–1900) who was 58 years old when he lost his title to Lasker in 1894.

José Raúl Capablanca (1888–1942) (Cuba) lost only 34 games in his adult career, 1909–39, for the fewest games lost by a world champion. He was unbeaten from Feb 10, 1916, to Mar 21, 1924, and was world champion from 1921 to 1927.

Marathon

The longest recorded session is one of 200 hours by Roger Long and Gordon Craft in Bristol, Eng, May 11–19, 1984.

CRIBBAGE

The invention of the game (once called Cribbidge) is credited to the English dramatist Sir John Suckling (1609–42). It is estimated that some ten million people play in the US alone.

Rare Hands

Edward Morawski of Greenfield, Mass, Eleanor Jonsson of Saskatoon, Canada and F. Art Skinner, of Alberta, Canada, were reported to have had three maximum 29-point hands. Paul Nault of Athol, Mass, had two such hands within eight games in a tournament on March 19, 1977. Derek Hearne dealt two hands of six clubs with the turn-up card the remaining club on Feb 8, 1976, in Blackpool, Lancashire, England. Bill Rogers of Burnaby, BC, Canada scored 29 in the crib in 1975.

Marathon

Geoff Lee, Ken Whyatt, Ray Charles and Paul Branson played for 120 hours at the RAOB Club, Mapperley, England, Mar 16–21, 1982.

DARTS*

The origins of darts date from the use by archers of heavily weighted 10-in throwing arrows for self-defense in close quarters fighting. The "dartes" were used in Ireland in the 16th century and darts was played on the *Mayflower* by the Plymouth pilgrims in 1620. The modern game dates from at least 1896 when Brian Gamlin of Bury, Lancashire, England, is credited with inventing the present numbering system on the board. The first recorded score of 180 (three triple 20's) was by John Reader at the Highbury Tavern in Sussex, England, in 1902.

Most Titles

Eric Bristow (b Apr 25, 1957) (GB) has the most wins in the World Masters Championships (instituted 1974) with 4, in 1977, 79, 81 and 83. He has also won the World Professional Championship (instituted 1978) three times, 1980, 81, 83. In 1983 he also won the World Cup Singles. John Lowe (b July 21, 1945) (GB) is the only man to have won each of the four major world titles: World Masters (1976 and 80), World Professional (1979), World Cup Singles (1981), and *News of the World* (1981).

---

* For more detailed information about darts, see *The Guinness Book of Darts,* available from Sterling.

DARTS QUEEN: Maureen Flowers, one of the few women in the game who can match all but the very best of the men. Here she is holding the British Ladies Pony Individual trophy after her second win in 1980.

Fastest Match

The fastest time taken for a match of three games of 301 is 1 min 58 sec by Ricky Fusco (GB) at the Perivale Residents Association Club, Middlesex, England, on Dec 30, 1976.

Fastest "Round the Board"

The record time for going round the board clockwise in "doubles" at arm's length is 9.2 sec by Dennis Gower at the Millers Arms, Hastings, England on Oct 12, 1975 and 14.5 sec in numerical order by Jim Pike (1903–60) at the Craven Club, Newmarket, England in March 1944. The record for this feat at the 9-ft throwing distance, retrieving own darts, is 2 min 13 sec by Bill Duddy (b Sept 29, 1932) at The Plough, Harringey, London, England on Oct 29, 1972.

Lowest Possible Scores

Scores of 201 in four darts, 301 in six darts, 401 in seven darts and 501 in nine darts, have been achieved on numerous occasions. The lowest number of darts thrown for a score of 1,001 is 19 by Cliff Inglis (b 1935) (160, 180, 140, 180, 121, 180, 40) at the Bromfield Men's Club, Devon, England on Nov 11, 1975. A score of 2,001 in 52 darts was achieved by Alan Evans (b 1949) at Ferndale, Glamorgan on Sept 3, 1976. A score of 3,001 in 79 darts was thrown by Charlie Ellix (b 1941) at The Victoria Hotel, Tottenham, London on Apr 29, 1977.

24-Hour Scores

Eight players from the Royal Hotel, Newsome, England, scored, on one board, 1,358,731 in 24 hours, May 26–27, 1981.

Million-and-One

Eight players from The Grapevine, S Oxhey, Hertfordshire, England, scored 1,000,001 with 38,925 darts in one session Aug 26–28, 1983.

Marathon

Trevor Blair and David Howe played for 127 hours 9 min at Bingham Leisure Centre, Notts, Eng, Aug 6–11, 1984.

FLYING DISC (formerly Frisbee®)

Competitive play began in 1957. Championships are now supervised by the World Flying Disc Federation.

Skills

Don Cain of New Brunswick, NJ set the record for maximum time aloft by keeping a Frisbee disc in the air for 16.72 sec in Phila, Pa, on May 26, 1984. For women, the time-aloft record is 11.47 sec, set in Sonoma, Calif, by Denise Garfield on Oct 5, 1980.

The greatest distance achieved for throwing a Frisbee disc, running, and catching it is 272.6 ft by Steve Bentley on Apr 8, 1982, at Sacramento, Calif.

Distance

The world record for outdoor distance is 550.8 ft by Frank Aquilera of LaPuente, Calif at Las Vegas, Nev, Feb 4, 1984. The indoor distance

DISC CATCHER: "Martha Faye" and master John Pickerill display the form which gave "Martha" and Dave Johnson the world record for canine distance Frisbee throw and catch, a remarkable 334.6 feet on June 11, 1978, in Wilmette, Illinois.

record is held by Van Miller of Tempe, Ariz, with a 399-ft toss at Flagstaff, Ariz, on Sept 18, 1982.

Liz Reeves holds the women's outdoor distance record (401.5 ft, set in Surrey, England, June 14, 1980), while the women's indoor distance record belongs to Suzanne Fields, of Boston, who threw 229.6 ft in Cedar Falls, Iowa, Apr 26, 1981.

The 24-hour group distance record is 428.02 miles set in Vernon, Conn, by the South Windsor Ultimate Frisbee disc Team, July 8–9, 1977. Dan Roddick and Alan Bonopane of Pasadena, Calif, hold the outdoor world record for 24-hour pair distance with 250.02 miles, Dec 30–31, 1979. Jamie Knerr and Keith Biery set the indoor 24-hour pair distance mark with 298.37 miles, Aug 14–15, 1982, at Allentown, Pa.

Marathons

The Prince George's Community College Flying High Club set the group marathon mark with 1,198 hours, June 1–July 22, 1981. The two-person marathon record is held by Jamie Knerr and Keith Biery, who played 110 hours 40 min in Allentown, Pa, Aug 23–27, 1981.

Fastest Guts Catch

Alan Bonopane threw a professional model Frisbee disc at a speed of 74 mph and his teammate Tim Selinske made a clean catch of the throw on Aug 25, 1980 in San Marino, Calif.

MONOPOLY®

The patentee of Monopoly, the world's most popular proprietary board game of which Parker Brothers has sold in excess of 80 million copies, was Charles Darrow (1889–1967). He invented the patented version of the game in 1933, while an unemployed heating engineer, using the street names of Atlantic City, NJ, where he spent his vacations.

Marathon

The longest game by four players ratified by Parker Brothers is 660 hours by Caara Fritz, Randy Smith, Phil Bennett, and Terry Sweatt in Atlanta, Ga July 12–Aug 8, 1981.

POKER

In the 1983 World Series of Poker held in Las Vegas, Nev, Tom McEvoy, a former Mich accountant, topped 107 other contestants, and with a $100 buy-in won the $540,000 top prize.

POOL AND BILLIARDS

Pool

Pool or championship pocket billiards with numbered balls began to become standardized c. 1890. The greatest exponents were Ralph Greenleaf (US) (1899–1950), who won the "world" professional title 19 times (1919–1937), and "Willie" Mosconi (US), who dominated the game from 1941 to 1957.

TV POOL: Willie Mosconi (right) came out of retirement to meet the challenge of Minnesota Fats (left) for the ABC cameras in 1978. William D. Cayton (center) is not only the promoter but the inventor of "7-Ball Pool," a new game they play on TV.

Michael Eufemia holds the record for the greatest continuous run in a straight pool match, pocketing 625 balls without a miss on Feb 2, 1960 before a large crowd at Logan's Billiard Academy, Brooklyn, New York.

The greatest number of balls to be pocketed in 24 hours is 13,437 by Patrick Young at the Lord Stanley, Plaistow, London, England, July 20–21, 1981.

The record time for pocketing all 15 balls in a speed competition is 40.06 sec by Ross McInnes (b Jan 19, 1955) at Clacton, Essex, Eng on Sept 11, 1983.

The longest game is 300 hours 16 min by Barry Wicks and Derek Shaw; also by Paul Haslam and Vincent Moore; all at the New Inn, Galgate, Lancaster, Eng, May 21–June 2, 1984.

3-Cushion Billiards

This pocketless variation dates back to 1878. The world governing body, *Union Mondiale de Billiard*, was formed in 1928. The most successful exponent, 1906–52, was William F. Hoppe (b Oct 11, 1887, Cornwall-on-Hudson, NY; d Feb 1, 1959) who won 51 billiards championships in all forms. The most UMB titles have been won by Raymond Ceulemans (Belgium) (b 1937) with 16 (1963–66, 1968–73, 1975–80), with a peak average of 1.679 in 1978.

SCRABBLE® CROSSWORD GAME

The crossword game was invented by Alfred M. Butts in 1931 and was developed, refined and trademarked as Scrabble Crossword Game by James Brunot in 1948. He sold the North American rights to Selchow & Righter Company, NY, the European rights to J. W. Spears & Sons, London, and the Australian rights to Murfett Pty Ltd, Melbourne.

BIGGEST MASS TWISTER GAME: 1,036 Colgate University students played for 3½ hours in Hamilton, NY, on May 5, 1984.

Marathon

The longest Scrabble Crossword Game is 129 hours 42 min by Marie Warrell and Carol Brockie at The Cock Inn, Sarratt, England, Aug 27–Sept 1, 1981.

TWISTER

Twister is played on a mat of 24 colored dots. Players place their hands and feet on the dots and move them to other dots according to the results of an arrow spun on a board. As hands and feet become twisted, players fall and are eliminated. The last one to remain on all fours is the winner.

Mass Twister games are played with contestants starting with three players per mat and consolidating as some are eliminated. The record for the greatest number of participants in one game was set on May 5, 1984 by 1,036 students at Colgate University, Hamilton, NY and lasted 3½ hours.

GLIDING

Man has sought to emulate the birds from early times, and the first successful "glider pilot" may well have been the mythical Daedalus, of Athens, who made wings for himself and his son Icarus to escape captivity. Icarus soared too near the sun and melted the wax with which the wings were fastened, but according to legend his father flew from Crete to Sicily. In Italy, about 1500 AD Leonardo da Vinci defined the difference between gliding and powered flight in some drawings, and at the same period Danti of Perugia, an Italian mathematician, is said to have actually flown.

Emanuel Swedenborg (1688–1772) of Sweden made sketches of gliders *c.* 1714. The earliest man-carrying glider was designed by Sir George Cayley (1773–1857) and carried his coachman (possibly John Appleby) about 500 yd across a valley in Brompton Dale, Yorkshire, England, in the summer of 1853. Gliders now attain speeds claimed at over 200 mph.

Most World Titles

The most world individual championships (instituted 1948) won is 3 by Helmut Reichmann (b 1942) (W Germany) in 1970, 74 and 78; and Douglas George Lee (b Nov 7, 1945) (GB) in 1976, 78 and 81.

HANG GLIDER shows how to take off down a sloping runway to achieve the nearest that man has come to emulating the birds.

HANG GLIDING

In the 11th century, the monk Eilmer is reported to have flown from the 60-ft-tall tower of Malmesbury Abbey, Wiltshire, England. The earliest modern pioneer was Otto Lilienthal (1848–96) of Germany who made about 2,500 flights in gliders of his own construction between 1891 and 1896. Professor Francis Rogallo of NASA developed a flexible "wing" in the 1950's from his research into space capsule re-entries.

The official FAI record for the farthest distance covered is 186.80 mi by John Pendry (GB) in an Airwave Magic 3, Horseshoe Meadows, Calif, to Summit Mt, Nev in July 1983.

The official FAI height gain record is 4,175.76 meters (13,699.8 ft) by Ian Kibblewhite (NZ) at Owens Valley, Calif, on July 22, 1981. The height gain record for a flex-wing micro-light glider is 16,168 ft by Bob Calvert (GB).

For distance to declared goal Klaus Kohmstedt (W Ger) glided 139.8 mi to a record over Owens Valley, Calif on July 13, 1983. He also holds the out-and-return distance to a goal record of 109.3 mi over Owens Valley set on June 15, 1983.

The women record holders are Judy Leden (GB) for 144.7 mi distance record and 50.97 mi for out-and-return, both over Owens Valley in June–July, 1983; Jean Little (US) for 27.99 mi for distance to declared goal over Cerro Gordo, Calif on June 15, 1983; and Page Pfieffer (US) for 10,800 ft gain of height over Owens on July 12, 1980.

SELECTED SOARING WORLD RECORDS (SINGLE-SEATERS)

DISTANCE
907.7 miles   Hans-Werner Grosse (W Germany) in an ASW-12 on Apr 25, 1972, from Lübeck to Biarritz.

DECLARED GOAL FLIGHT
779.4 miles   Bruce Drake, David Speight, S. H. "Dick" Georgeson (all NZ) all in Nimbus 2s, from Te Anau to Te Araroa, Jan 14, 1978.

ABSOLUTE ALTITUDE
46,266 ft   Paul F. Bikle, Jr (US) in a Schweizer SGS 1-23E over Mojave, Calif (released at 3,963 feet) on Feb 25, 1961 (also record altitude gain—42,303 ft).

(women) 41,460 ft   Sabrina Jackintell (US) in an Astir CS Feb 14, 1979.

GOAL AND RETURN
1,023.2 miles   Tom Knauff (US) in a Nimbus 3 from Williamsport, Pa, to Knoxville, Tenn on April 25, 1983.

SPEED OVER TRIANGULAR COURSE

100 km	121.28 mph	Ingo Renner (Australia) in a Nimbus 3 on Dec 14, 1982.
300 km	98.59 mph	Hans-Werner Grosse (W Germany) in an ASW-17 over Australia on Dec 24, 1980.
500 km	99.20 mph	Hans-Werner Grosse (W Germany) in an ASW-22 on Dec 20, 1983.
750 km	89.25 mph	Hans-Werner Grosse (W Germany) in an ASW-17 over Australia, on Jan 6, 1982.
1,000 km	90.29 mph	Hans-Werner Grosse (W Germany) in an ASW-17 over Australia, on Jan 3, 1979.
1,250 km	82.79 mph	Hans-Werner Grosse (W Germany) in an ASW-17 over Australia, on Dec 9, 1980.

GOLFING FIRSTS: The young Mary, Queen of Scots, playing golf at St Andrews in 1563, following in the footsteps of her grandfather, James IV, who was the first golfer in history that we know by name. She was accused of playing golf only a few days after her husband's death.

GOLF*

Origins

It has been suggested that golf originated with Scottish shepherds using their crooks to knock pebbles into rabbit holes. This may be apocryphal, but somewhat firmer evidence exists. A stained glass window in Gloucester Cathedral, dating from 1350, portrays a golfer-like figure, but the earliest mention of golf occurs in a prohibiting law passed by the Scottish Parliament in March 1457, under which "golff be utterly cryit doune and not usit."

The Romans had a cognate game called *paganica,* which may have been carried to Britain before 400 AD. The Chinese National Golf Association claims the game is of Chinese origin ("*Ch'ui Wan*—the ball-hitting game") from the 3rd or 2nd century BC. There were official ordinances prohibiting a ball game with clubs in Belgium and Holland from 1360. Gutta-percha balls succeeded feather balls in 1848, and were in turn succeeded in 1902 by rubber-cored balls, invented in 1899 by Coburn Haskell (US). Steel shafts were authorized in the US in 1925.

Golf was first played on the moon in Feb 1971 by Capt Alan Shepard (US), commander of the Apollo XIV spacecraft.

---

* For more detailed information about golf, see *Golf Facts and Feats* (Sterling).

TOP TITLISTS: Bobby Jones (left) won the US Open 4 times and the US Amateur 5 times. In 1930 he won golf's "Grand Slam," which then consisted of the British and US Amateur and Open championships. Glenna Collett Vare (right) won the US Women's Amateur title a record 6 times, 1922–35.

Oldest Clubs

The oldest club of which there is written evidence is the Gentleman Golfers (now the Honourable Company of Edinburgh Golfers) formed in March 1744—10 years prior to the institution of the Royal and Ancient Club of St Andrews, Fife, Scotland. However, the Royal Burgess Golfing Society of Edinburgh claim to have been founded in 1735. The oldest existing club in North America is the Royal Montreal Club (Nov 1873) and the oldest in the US is St Andrews, Westchester County, NY (1888). An older claim is by the Foxbury Country Club, Clarion County, Pa (1887).

Highest and Lowest Courses

The highest golf course in the world is the Tuctu Golf Club in Morococha, Peru, which is 14,335 ft above sea level at its lowest point. Golf has, however, been played in Tibet at an altitude of over 16,000 ft.

The lowest golf course in the world was that of the now defunct Sodom and Gomorrah Golfing Society at Kallia (Qulya), on the northern shores of the Dead Sea, 1,250 ft below sea level. Currently the lowest is the par-70 Furnace Creek Golf Course, Death Valley, Calif, at a disputed average of 178–272 ft below sea level.

Longest Course

The world's longest course is the par-77, 8,325-yd International GC, Bolton, Mass, from the "Tiger" tees, remodeled in 1969 by Robert Trent Jones.

MOST WINS IN MAJOR TOURNAMENTS

US Open	Willie Anderson (1880–1910)	4	1901–03–04–05
	Robert Tyre Jones, Jr (1902–71)	4	1923–26–29–30
	W. Ben Hogan (b Aug 13, 1912)	4	1948–50–51–53
	Jack William Nicklaus (b Jan 21, 1940)	4	1962–67–72–80
US Amateur	R. T. Jones, Jr	5	1924–25–27–28–30
British Open	Harry Vardon (1870–1937)	6	1896–98–99, 1903–11–14
British Amateur	John Ball (1861–1940)	8	1888–90–92–94–99, 1907–10–12
PGA Championship (US)	Walter C. Hagen (1892–1969)	5	1921–24–25–26–27
	Jack W. Nicklaus	5	1963–71–73–75–80
Masters Championship (US)	Jack W. Nicklaus	5	1963–65–66–72–75
US Women's Open	Elizabeth (Betsy) Earle-Rawls (b May 4, 1928)	4	1951–53–57–60
	"Mickey" Wright (b Feb 14, 1935)	4	1958–59–61–64
US Women's Amateur	Mrs Glenna Vare (*née* Collett) (b June 20, 1903)	6	1922–25–28–29–30–35

Biggest Bunker

The world's biggest trap is Hell's Half Acre on the 585-yd 7th hole of the Pine Valley course, Clementon, NJ, built in 1912 and generally regarded as the world's most trying course.

RECORDS IN THE 20's: Walter Hagen (US) blasting out of a bunker at the 17th green at Hoylake in the 1924 British Open. He did not win that year but he did win that event 3 times, the US Open twice and the PGA 5 times. (Radio Times—Hulton)

ON COURSE: "Slammin' " Sam Snead (left) carded a 59 for 18 holes and 122 for 36 in the 1959 Greenbrier Open. Snead has been credited with 134 tournament victories since 1934. Mickey Wright (above) celebrates her record-tying 4th US Women's Open title. Her 62 is the all-time women's best for a full-size 18-hole course, and her 82 pro tournament wins is also tops.

Longest Hole

The longest hole in the world is the 7th hole (par 7) of 909 yd at the Sano Course, Satsuki GC, Japan.

Largest Green

Probably the largest green in the world is that of the par-6, 695-yd 5th hole at International GC, Bolton, Mass, with an area greater than 28,000 sq ft.

Lowest Scores for 9 and 18 Holes

Three professional players are recorded to have played a long course (over 6,000 yd) for a score of 57: Bill Burke at the Normandie Golf Club, St Louis (6,389 yds, par 71) on May 20, 1970; Tom Ward at the Searcy (Ark) Country Club (6,098 yds, par 70) in 1981; Augie Navarro at the Sim Park Golf Course (Wichita, Kans) in 1982.

Alfred Edward Smith (b 1903), the English professional at Woolacombe, achieved an 18-hole score of 55 (15 under bogey 70) on his home course on Jan 1, 1936.

Nine holes in 25 (4, 3, 3, 2, 3, 3, 1, 4, 2) was recorded by A. J. "Bill"

Burke in his round of 57 (32 + 25) (see above), and by teenager Douglas Beecher at the Pitman (NJ) Country Club (3,150 yd, par 35) in 1976. The tournament record is 27 by Mike Souchak (US) (b May 1927) for the second nine (par 35) first round of the 1955 Texas Open; Andy North (US) (b Mar 9, 1950) second nine (par 34), first round, 1975 BC Open at En-Joie GC, Endicott, NY; and Jose Maria Canizares (Spain) (b Feb 18, 1947), first nine, third round, in the 1978 Swiss Open on the 6,811-yd Crans-Sur course.

The US PGA tournament record for 18 holes is 59 (30 + 29) by Al Geiberger (b Sept 1, 1937) in the second round of the Danny Thomas Classic, on the 72-par, 7,249-yd Colonial CC course, Memphis, Tenn, June 10, 1977.

In non-PGA tournaments, Sam Snead (b May 27, 1912) had 59 in the Greenbrier Open (now called the Sam Snead Festival), at White Sulphur Springs, W Va, on May 16, 1959; Gary Player (South Africa) (b Nov 1, 1935) carded 59 in the second round of the Brazilian Open in Rio de Janeiro on Nov 29, 1974; and David Jagger (GB) also had 59 in a Pro-Am tournament prior to the 1973 Nigerian Open at Ikoyi Golf Club, Lagos.

Women's Lowest Scores

The lowest recorded score on an 18-hole course (over 6,000 yd) for a woman is 62 (30 + 32) by Mary (Mickey) Kathryn Wright (b Feb 14, 1935), of Dallas, on the Hogan Park Course (6,286 yd) at Midland, Tex, in Nov 1964.

Wanda Morgan (b March 22, 1910) recorded a score of 60 (31 + 29) on the Westgate and Birchington Golf Club course, Kent, England, over 18 holes (5,002 yd) on July 11, 1929.

Lowest Scores for 36 Holes

The record for 36 holes is 122 (59 + 63) by Sam Snead in the 1959 Greenbrier Open (now called the Sam Snead Festival) (non-PGA) (see above), May 16–17, 1959. Horton Smith (see below) scored 121 (63 + 58) on a short course on Dec 21, 1928.

Lowest Scores for 72 Holes

The lowest recorded score on a first-class course is 255 (29 under par) by Leonard Peter Tupling (b Apr 6, 1950) (GB) in the Nigerian Open at Ikoyi Golf Club, Lagos, in Feb 1981, made up of 63, 66, 62 and 64 (average 63.75 per round). Horton Smith (1908–63), twice US Masters Champion, scored 245 (63, 58, 61 and 63) for 72 holes on the 4,700-yd course (par 64) at Catalina Country Club, Calif, to win the Catalina Open, Dec 21–23, 1928.

The lowest 72 holes in a US professional event is 257 (60, 68, 64 and 65) by Mike Souchak in the 1955 Texas Open at San Antonio.

The lowest 72 holes in an Open championship in Europe is 262 by Percy Alliss (1897–1975) of Britain, with 67, 66, 66 and 63 in the Italian Open Championship at San Remo in 1932, and by Lu Liang Huan (b Dec 10, 1935) (Taiwan) in the 1971 French Open at Biarritz. Kelvin D. G. Nagle (b Dec 21, 1920) of Australia shot 261 in the Hong Kong Open in 1961.

DIFFERENT STROKES: Ireland's Tommie Campbell (left) holds the world record for the longest drive with a distance of 392 yards in Dublin in 1964. Cary Middlecoff (right) holed an 86-foot putt on the 13th green at the Augusta National, Georgia, in 1955. The record putt helped him to win the Masters.

Longest Drive

In long-driving contests 330 yd is rarely surpassed at sea level.

In officially regulated long-driving contests over level ground the greatest distance recorded is 392 yd by Tommie Campbell (b July 24, 1927) (Foxrock Golf Club), a member of the Irish PGA, made at Dun Laoghaire, Co Dublin, in July 1964.

The USPGA record is 341 yd by Jack William Nicklaus (b Columbus, Ohio, Jan 21, 1940), then weighing 206 lb, in July 1963.

Valentin Barrios (Spain) drove a Slazenger B51 ball 568½ yd on an airport runway at Palma, Majorca, on March 7, 1977.

The longest on an ordinary course is 515 yd by Michael Hoke Austin (b Feb 17, 1910) of Los Angeles, in the US National Seniors Open Championship at Las Vegas, Nev, Sept 25, 1974. Aided by an estimated 35-mph tailwind, the 6-ft-2-in 210-lb golfer drove the ball on the fly to within a yard of the green on the par-4, 450-yd 5th hole of the Winterwood Course. The ball rolled 65 yd past the flagstick.

Arthur Lynskey claimed a drive of 200 yd out and 2 miles down off Pikes Peak, Colo, June 28, 1968.

A drive of 2,640 yd (1½ miles) across ice was achieved by an Australian meteorologist named Nils Lied at Mawson Base, Antarctica, in 1962. On the moon, the energy expended on a mundane 300-yd drive would achieve, craters permitting, a distance of a mile.

WELL SEASONED: Byron Nelson (left) had a good year in 1945. He won 18 tournaments that year (plus one unofficial), including 11 in a row. He might have won
more, but the Masters and the British and US Opens were not contested during the
war years. (Right) Jack Nicklaus' career golf earnings reached nearly $5 million by the
end of 1984. Nicklaus has stormed to 19 major tournament victories, including 4 US
Open titles and 5 victories in both the PGA and Masters. A consistent long hitter, the
"Golden Bear" holds the US record for longest drive (341 yd) and is also a master
putter. (E. D. Lacey)

Longest Hitter

The golfer regarded as the longest consistent hitter the game has ever
known is the 6-ft-5-in-tall, 230-lb George Bayer (US) (b Sept 17, 1925),
the 1957 Canadian Open Champion. His longest measured drive was one
of 420 yd at the fourth in the Las Vegas Invitational in 1953. It was measured as a precaution against litigation since the ball struck a spectator.
Bayer also drove a ball pin high on a 426-yd hole in Tucson, Ariz. Radar
measurements show that an 87-mph impact velocity for a golf ball falls to
46 mph in 3.0 sec.

Most Tournament Wins

The record for winning tournaments in a single season is 18 (plus one
unofficial), including a record 11 consecutively, by Byron Nelson (b Feb
4, 1912) (US), March 8–Aug 4, 1945.

Sam Snead has won 84 official USPGA tour events to Dec 1979, and
has been credited with a total 134 tournament victories since 1934.

Kathy Whitworth (b Sept 27, 1939) (US) topped this with her 87th LPGA victory through 1984, her 22nd year on the tour. Mickey Wright (US) won a record 13 tournaments in one year, 1963.

Jack Nicklaus (US) is the only golfer who has won all five major titles (British Open, US Open, Masters, PGA and US Amateur) twice, while setting a record total of 19 major tournament victories (1959–80). His remarkable record in the US Open is 4 firsts, 8 seconds and 2 thirds. Nicklaus has accumulated 70 PGA tournament wins in all.

In 1930 Bobby Jones achieved a unique "Grand Slam" of the US and British Open and Amateur titles.

Longest Putt

The longest recorded holed putt in a major tournament was one of 86 ft on the vast 13th green at the Augusta National, Ga, by Cary Middlecoff (b Jan 1921) in the 1955 Masters Tournament.

Bobby Jones was reputed to have holed a putt in excess of 100 ft on the 5th green in the first round of the 1927 British Open at St Andrews, Scotland.

Highest Earnings

The greatest amount ever won in official USPGA golf prizes is $4,520,824 by Jack Nicklaus through 1984.

The record for a year is $530,808 by Tom Watson (US) in 1980.

The highest LPGA career earnings by a woman is $1,789,264 by JoAnne Carner (b Apr 4, 1939) through 1984. She also holds the LPGA record for one season at $310,399 (1982).

Biggest Prize Putt

Jack Nicklaus' total earnings went up by $240,000 when he sank an 8-foot putt on the 18th green of the Desert Highlands course in Scottsdale, Ariz, on Nov 25, 1984 in a "Skins" match against Arnold Palmer, Gary Player and Tom Watson. All three of his opponents missed their birdie putts from further distances and Nicklaus won the accumulated prize money.

Most Rounds in a Day

The greatest number of rounds played on foot in 24 hours is 22 rounds plus 5 holes (401 holes) by Ian Colston, 35, at Bendigo GC, Victoria, Australia (6,061 yd), Nov 27–28, 1971. He covered more than 100 miles.

The most holes played on foot in a week (168 hours) is 1,128 by Steve Hylton at the Mason Rudolph Golf Club (6,060 yd), Clarksville, Tenn, Aug 25–31, 1980.

US Open

This championship was inaugurated in 1895. The lowest 72-hole aggregate is 272 (63, 71, 70, 68) by Jack Nicklaus on the Lower Course (7,015 yd) at Baltusrol Golf Club, Springfield, NJ, June 12–15, 1980. The lowest score for 18 holes is 63 by Johnny Miller (b Apr 29, 1947) of Calif on the 6,921-yd, par-71 Oakmont, Pa, course on June 17, 1973, and Jack Nicklaus and Tom Weiskopf (b Nov 9, 1942), both on June 12, 1980.

The longest delayed result in any national open championship occurred in the 1931 US Open at Toledo, Ohio. George von Elm (1901–61) and Bill Burke (1902–72) tied at 292, then tied the first replay at 149. Burke won the second replay by a single stroke after 72 extra holes.

Winners:

	Score		Score
1895 Horace Rawlins	173	1939 Byron Nelson	284
1896 James Foulis	152	1940 Lawson Little	287
1897 Joe Lloyd	162	1941 Craig Wood	284
1898 Fred Herd	328	1946 Lloyd Mangrum	284
1899 Willie Smith	315	1947 Lew Worsham	282
1900 Harry Vardon (GB)	313	1948 Ben Hogan	276
1901 Willie Anderson	331	1949 Cary Middlecoff	286
1902 Laurie Auchterlonie	307	1950 Ben Hogan	287
1903 Willie Anderson	307	1951 Ben Hogan	287
1904 Willie Anderson	303	1952 Julius Boros	281
1905 Willie Anderson	314	1953 Ben Hogan	283
1906 Alex Smith	295	1954 Ed Furgol	284
1907 Alex Ross	302	1955 Jack Fleck	287
1908 Fred McLeod	322	1956 Cary Middlecoff	281
1909 George Sargent	290	1957 Dick Mayer	282
1910 Alex Smith	298	1958 Tommy Bolt	283
1911 John McDermott	307	1959 Billy Casper	282
1912 John McDermott	294	1960 Arnold Palmer	280
1913 Francis Ouimet	304	1961 Gene Littler	281
1914 Walter Hagen	290	1962 Jack Nicklaus	283
1915 Jerome Travers	297	1963 Julius Boros	293
1916 Charles Evans, Jr	286	1964 Ken Venturi	278
1919 Walter Hagen	301	1965 Gary Player (S Afr)	282
1920 Edward Ray (GB)	295	1966 Billy Casper	278
1921 Jim Barnes	289	1967 Jack Nicklaus	275
1922 Gene Sarazen	288	1968 Lee Trevino	275
1923 Robert T. Jones, Jr	296	1969 Orville Moody	281
1924 Cyril Walker	297	1970 Tony Jacklin (GB)	281
1925 Willie Macfarlane	291	1971 Lee Trevino	280
1926 Robert T. Jones, Jr	293	1972 Jack Nicklaus	290
1927 Tommy Armour	301	1973 Johnny Miller	279
1928 Johnny Farrell	294	1974 Hale Irwin	287
1929 Robert T. Jones, Jr	294	1975 Lou Graham	287
1930 Robert T. Jones, Jr	287	1976 Jerry Pate	277
1931 Billy Burke	292	1977 Hubert Green	278
1932 Gene Sarazen	286	1978 Andy North	285
1933 John Goodman	287	1979 Hale Irwin	284
1934 Olin Dutra	293	1980 Jack Nicklaus	272
1935 Sam Parks, Jr	299	1981 David Graham (Aust)	273
1936 Tony Manero	282	1982 Tom Watson	282
1937 Ralph Guldahl	281	1983 Larry Nelson	280
1938 Ralph Guldahl	284	1984 Fuzzy Zoeller	276

US Masters

The lowest score in the US Masters (instituted at the 6,980-yd Augusta National Golf Course, Ga, in 1934) was 271 by Jack Nicklaus in 1965 and Raymond Floyd (b Sept 4, 1942) in 1976. Jack Nicklaus has won most often—5 times. The lowest rounds have been 64 by Lloyd Mangrum (1914–74) (1st round, 1940), Jack Nicklaus (3rd round, 1965), Maurice Bembridge (GB) (b Feb 21, 1945) (4th round, 1974), Hale Irwin (b June 3, 1945) (4th round, 1975), Gary Player (S Africa) (4th round, 1978), and Miller Barber (b March 31, 1931) (2nd round, 1979). The oldest champion was Gary Player (S Africa) at 42 years 5 months 9 days in 1978, and the youngest was Severiano Ballesteros (Spain) aged 23 years 4 days in 1980.

The Winners:

	Score		Score
1934 Horton Smith	284	1962 Arnold Palmer	280
1935 Gene Sarazen	282	1963 Jack Nicklaus	286
1936 Horton Smith	285	1964 Arnold Palmer	276
1937 Byron Nelson	283	1965 Jack Nicklaus	271
1938 Henry Picard	285	1966 Jack Nicklaus	288
1939 Ralph Gudahl	279	1967 Gay Brewer	280
1940 Jimmy Demaret	280	1968 Bob Goalby	277
1941 Craig Wood	280	1969 George Archer	281
1942 Byron Nelson	280	1970 Billy Casper	279
1946 Herman Keiser	282	1971 Charles Coody	279
1947 Jimmy Demaret	281	1972 Jack Nicklaus	286
1948 Claude Harmon	279	1973 Tommy Aaron	283
1949 Sam Snead	282	1974 Gary Player (S Afr)	278
1950 Jimmy Demaret	283	1975 Jack Nicklaus	276
1951 Ben Hogan	280	1976 Ray Floyd	271
1952 Sam Snead	286	1977 Tom Watson	276
1953 Ben Hogan	274	1978 Gary Player (S Afr)	277
1954 Sam Snead	289	1979 Fuzzy Zoeller	280
1955 Cary Middlecoff	279	1980 Severiano Ballesteros (Spain)	275
1956 Jack Burke	289	1981 Tom Watson	280
1957 Doug Ford	283	1982 Craig Stadler	284
1958 Arnold Palmer	284	1983 Severiano Ballesteros (Spain)	280
1959 Art Wall	284	1984 Ben Crenshaw	277
1960 Arnold Palmer	282		
1961 Gary Player (S Afr)	280		

IN THE CUP: Arnold Palmer prepares to putt as his many followers, known as Arnie's Army, look on. Palmer won the Masters 4 times and played on 6 winning teams in World Cup play. He was the first golfer to reach $1 million in career earnings.

US Amateur

Initially held in the same week and at the same venue as the first US Open in 1895. Bobby Jones won a record five times between 1924 and 1930, having first qualified for the tournament in 1916, aged 14 yr 5½ months, the youngest ever to do so. The oldest player to win the title was Jack Westland, aged 47 years 8 months 9 days in 1952, while the youngest was Robert Gardner at 19 years 5 months in 1909. (Three years later, in 1912, Gardner broke the world pole vault record becoming the first man to clear 13 ft.)

The Winners:

1895 Charles Macdonald	1939 Marvin Ward
1896 H. J. Whigham	1940 Richard Chapman
1897 H. J. Whigham	1941 Marvin Ward
1898 Findlay Douglas	1946 Stanley Bishop
1899 H. M. Harriman	1947 Robert Riegel
1900 Walter Travis	1948 William Turnesa
1901 Walter Travis	1949 Charles Coe
1902 Louis James	1950 Sam Urzetta
1903 Walter Travis	1951 Billy Maxwell
1904 Chandler Egan	1952 Jack Westland
1905 Chandler Egan	1953 Gene Littler
1906 Eben Byers	1954 Arnold Palmer
1907 Jerome Travers	1955 Harvie Ward
1908 Jerome Travers	1956 Harvie Ward
1909 Robert Gardner	1957 Hillman Robbins
1910 William Fownes, Jr	1958 Charles Coe
1911 Harold Hilton (GB)	1959 Jack Nicklaus
1912 Jerome Travers	1960 Deane Beman
1913 Jerome Travers	1961 Jack Nicklaus
1914 Francis Ouimet	1962 Labron Harris
1915 Robert Gardner	1963 Deane Beman
1916 Charles Evans, Jr	1964 Bill Campbell
1919 Davidson Herron	1965 Bob Murphy
1920 Charles Evans, Jr	1966 Gary Cowan (Can)
1921 Jesse Gullford	1967 Bob Dickson
1922 Jesse Sweetser	1968 Bruce Fleisher
1923 Max Marston	1969 Steve Melnyk
1924 Robert T. Jones, Jr	1970 Lanny Wadkins
1925 Robert T. Jones, Jr	1971 Gary Cowan (Can)
1926 George Von Elm	1972 Marvin Giles
1927 Robert T. Jones, Jr	1973 Craig Stadler
1928 Robert T. Jones, Jr	1974 Jerry Pate
1929 Harrison Johnston	1975 Fred Ridley
1930 Robert T. Jones, Jr	1976 Bill Sander
1931 Francis Ouimet	1977 John Fought
1932 Ross Somerville (Can)	1978 John Cook
1933 George Dunlap, Jr	1979 Mark O'Meara
1934 Lawson Little	1980 Hal Sutton
1935 Lawson Little	1981 Nathaniel Crosby
1936 John Fisher	1982 Jay Sigel
1937 John Goodman	1983 Jay Sigel
1938 William Turnesa	1984 Scott Vertplank

US PGA Championship

The Professional Golfers' Association championship was first held in 1916 as a match play tournament but since 1958 it has been contested over 72 holes of stroke play. It has been won a record five times by Walter Hagen between 1921 and 1927, and Jack Nicklaus between 1963 and 1980. The oldest champion was Julius Boros at 48 years 18 days in 1968 and the youngest was Gene Sarazen aged 20 years 5 months 20 days in 1922. Since 1958 the greatest margin of victory has been the seven-stroke lead by Nicklaus in 1980. The lowest aggregate was 271 by Bobby Nichols at Columbus, Ohio in 1964, and the lowest round was 63 by Bruce Crampton in 1975 and Ray Floyd in 1982. The lowest score for 36 holes has been 131 by Hal Sutton (65, 66) in 1983. The 54-hole mark is 202 (69, 66, 67) by Raymond Floyd in 1969.

				Score
1916 James Barnes		1951 Sam Snead		
1919 James Barnes		1952 Jim Turnesa		
1920 Jock Hutchison		1953 Walter Burkemo		
1921 Walter Hagen		1954 Chick Harbert		
1922 Gene Sarazen		1955 Doug Ford		
1923 Gene Sarazen		1956 Jack Burke		
1924 Walter Hagen		1957 Lionel Hebert		
1925 Walter Hagen		1958 Dow Finsterwald		276
1926 Walter Hagen		1959 Bob Rosburg		277
1927 Walter Hagen		1960 Jay Hebert		281
1928 Leo Diegel		1961 Jerry Barber		277
1929 Leo Diegel		1962 Gary Player (S Afr)		278
1930 Tommy Armour		1963 Jack Nicklaus		279
1931 Tom Creavy		1964 Bob Nichols		271
1932 Olin Dutra		1965 Dave Marr		280
1933 Gene Sarazen		1966 Al Geiberger		280
1934 Paul Runyan		1967 Don January		281
1935 Johnny Revolta		1968 Julius Boros		281
1936 Denny Shute		1969 Ray Floyd		276
1937 Denny Shute		1970 Dave Stockton		279
1938 Paul Runyan		1971 Jack Nicklaus		281
1939 Henry Picard		1972 Gary Player (S Afr)		281
1940 Byron Nelson		1973 Jack Nicklaus		277
1941 Vic Ghezzi		1974 Lee Trevino		276
1942 Sam Snead		1975 Jack Nicklaus		276
1943 Not held		1976 Dave Stockton		281
1944 Bob Hamilton		1977 Lanny Wadkins		282
1945 Byron Nelson		1978 John Mahaffey		276
1946 Ben Hogan		1979 David Graham (Aus)		272
1947 Jim Ferrier		1980 Jack Nicklaus		274
1948 Ben Hogan		1981 Larry Nelson		273
1949 Sam Snead		1982 Ray Floyd		272
1950 Chandler Harper		1983 Hal Sutton		274
		1984 Lee Trevino		273

Fastest Rounds

With such variations in lengths of courses, speed records, even for rounds under par, are of little comparative value. Rick Baker completed 18 holes (6,142 yd) in 25 min 48.47 sec at Surfer's Paradise, Queensland, Australia, Sept 4, 1982, but this test permitted striking the ball while it was still moving. The record for a still ball is 28.09 min by Gary Wright (b Nov 27, 1946) at Tewantin-Noosa Golf Club, Queensland, Australia (18 holes, 6,039 yd), on Dec 9, 1980.

Eighty-three players completed the 18-hole 6,412-yd Prince George Golf and Country Club course, BC, Canada, in 12 min 14.5 sec in 1973, using only one ball.

US Women's Open

This tournament was first held in 1946, and currently is played over 72 holes of stroke play. Betsy Rawls won a record four times between 1951 and 1960, and this was equalled by Mickey Wright between 1958 and 1964. The oldest champion was Fay Crocker (Uru) at 40 years 11 months in 1955, while the youngest was Catherine Lacoste (France) at 22 years 5 days in 1967, when she became the only amateur player to win the title. The greatest margin of victory was by Babe Didrikson Zaharias who beat Betty Hicks by 12 strokes in 1954. The lowest aggregate score has been 280 (70, 70, 68, 72) by Amy Alcott in 1980, and the lowest round was 65 by Sally Little in 1978. The record for 36 holes is 139 by Carol Mann and Donna Caponi in 1970, the latter going on to a 54-hole score of 210.

	Score		Score
1946 Patty Berg beat		1966 Sandra Spuzich	297
Betty Jameson 5 and 4		1967 Catherine Lacoste (France)	294
1947 Betty Jameson	295	1968 Sue Berning	289
1948 Mildred Zaharias	300	1969 Donna Caponi	294
1949 Louise Suggs	291	1970 Donna Caponi	287
1950 Mildred Zaharias	291	1971 JoAnne Carner	288
1951 Betsy Rawls	293	1972 Sue Maxwell Berning	290
1952 Louise Suggs	284	1973 Sue Maxwell Berning	290
1953 Betsy Rawls	302	1974 Sandra Haynie	295
1954 Mildred Zaharias	291	1975 Sandra Palmer	295
1955 Fay Crocker (Uru)	299	1976 JoAnne Carner	292
1956 Kathy Cornelius	302	1977 Hollis Stacy	298
1957 Betsy Rawls	299	1978 Hollis Stacy	289
1958 Mickey Wright	290	1979 Jerilyn Britz	284
1959 Mickey Wright	287	1980 Amy Alcott	280
1960 Betsy Rawls	292	1981 Pat Bradley	279
1961 Mickey Wright	293	1982 Janet Alex	283
1962 Murle Lindstrom	301	1983 Jan Stephenson	290
1963 Mary Mills	289	1984 Hollis Stacy	290
1964 Mickey Wright	290		
1965 Carol Mann	290		

Most Shots One Hole

The highest number of strokes taken at a single hole in a major tournament was achieved in the inaugural Open Championship at Prestwick, Scotland, in 1860, when an unnamed player took 21. In the 1938 US Open, Ray Ainsley achieved instant fame when he took 19 strokes at the par-4 16th hole. Most of them were in an attempt to hit the ball out of a fast-moving brook. At Biarritz, France in 1888 it was reported that Chevalier von Cittern took 316 for 18 holes, thus averaging 17.55 strokes per hole.

The story to top them all concerns a lady player in the qualifying round of a tournament in Shawnee-on-Delaware, Pa in the early part of the century. Her card showed she took 166 strokes for the short 130-yd 16th hole. Her tee shot landed and floated in a nearby river, and, with her meticulous husband, she set out in a boat and eventually beached the ball 1½ mi downstream. From there she had to play through a forest until finally she holed the ball. It is reported that A. J. Lewis, playing at Peacehaven, Sussex, Eng, in 1890 had 156 putts on one green without holing the ball.

US Women's Amateur Championship

Instituted in Nov 1895, and currently 36 final holes of match play after 36 qualifying holes of stroke play. Glenna Collett Vare won a record 6 titles between 1922 and 1935. The oldest champion was Dorothy Campbell-Hurd (GB) aged 41 years 4 months when winning her third title in 1924, and the youngest was Laura Baugh at 16 years 2 months 21 days in 1971. Margaret Curtis beat her sister, Harriot, in the 1907 final—they later presented the Curtis Cup for competition between the US and GB.

1895 C. S. Brown
1896 Beatrix Hoyt
1897 Beatrix Hoyt
1898 Beatrix Hoyt
1899 Ruth Underhill
1900 Frances Griscom
1901 Genevieve Hecker
1902 Genevieve Hecker
1903 Bessie Anthony
1904 Georgianna Bishop
1905 Pauline Mackay
1906 Harriot Curtis
1907 Margaret Curtis
1908 Catherine Harley
1909 Dorothy Campbell (GB)
1910 Dorothy Campbell (GB)
1911 Margaret Curtis
1912 Margaret Curtis
1913 Gladys Ravenscroft (GB)
1914 Catherine Harley-Jackson
1915 C. H. Vanderbeck
1916 Alexa Stirling
1919 Alexa Stirling
1920 Alexa Stirling
1921 Marion Hollins
1922 Glenna Collett
1923 Edith Cummings
1924 Dorothy Campbell-Hurd
1925 Glenna Collett
1926 Helen Stetson
1927 Miriam Burns Horn
1928 Glenna Collett
1929 Glenna Collett
1930 Glenna Collett
1931 Helen Hicks
1932 Virginia van Wie
1933 Virginia van Wie
1934 Virginia van Wie
1935 Glenna Collett Vare
1936 Pamela Barton (GB)
1937 Estelle Page
1938 Patty Berg

1939 Betty Jameson
1940 Betty Jameson
1941 Elizabeth Hicks Newell
1942-45 No Championship
1946 Mildred Zaharias
1947 Louise Suggs
1948 Grace Lencyzk
1949 Dorothy Germain Porter
1950 Beverly Hanson
1951 Dorothy Kirby
1952 Jacqueline Pung
1953 Mary Lena Faulk
1954 Barbara Romack
1955 Patricia Lesser
1956 Marlene Stewart (Can)
1957 JoAnne Gunderson
1958 Anne Quast
1959 Barbara McIntire
1960 JoAnne Gunderson
1961 Anne Quast Decker
1962 JoAnne Gunderson
1963 Anne Quast Welts
1964 Barbara McIntire
1965 Jean Ashley
1966 JoAnne Gunderson Carner
1967 Mary Lou Dill
1968 JoAnne Gunderson Carner
1969 Catherine Lacoste (France)
1970 Martha Wilkinson
1971 Laura Baugh
1972 Mary Ann Budke
1973 Carol Semple
1974 Cynthia Hill
1975 Beth Daniel
1976 Donna Horton
1977 Beth Daniel
1978 Cathy Sherk (Can)
1979 Carolyn Hill
1980 Juli Inkster
1981 Juli Inkster
1982 Juli Inkster
1983 Joanne Pacillo
1984 Deb Richard

Ryder Cup

The biennial Ryder Cup (instituted 1927) professional match between the US and GB (Europe since 1979) has been won by the US 21½–3½. William Earl "Billy" Casper (b San Diego, Calif, June 24, 1931) has the record of winning most matches, with 20 won out of 37 (1961–75). Neil Cales (GB) played in a record 40 matches (1961–77).

World Cup (formerly Canada Cup)

The World Cup (instituted 1953), contested over 72 holes of stroke play by teams of two with scores aggregated, has been won most often by the US with 16 victories between 1955 and 1983. The only men on six winning teams have been Arnold Palmer (b Sept 10, 1929) (1960, 62–64, 66–67) and Jack Nicklaus (1963–64, 66–67, 71, 73). The only man to take the individual title three times is Jack Nicklaus (US) in 1963–64, 1971. The lowest aggregate score for 144 holes is 545 by Australia, Bruce Devlin (b Oct 10, 1937) and David Graham (b May 23, 1946) at San Isidro, Buenos Aires, Argentina, Nov 12–15, 1970, and the lowest score by an individual winner was 269 by Roberto de Vicenzo (b Buenos Aires, Argentina, Apr 14, 1923) on the same occasion.

Walker Cup

The US versus Great Britain–Ireland series instituted in 1921 (for the Walker Cup since 1922), now biennial, has been won by the US 25½–2½ to date. Joe Carr (GB–I) played in 10 contests (1947–67).

Biggest Victory Margin

The greatest margin of victory in a major tournament is 21 strokes by Jerry Pate (b Sept 16, 1953) (US) in the Colombian Open with 262, Dec 10–13, 1981.

Youngest and Oldest Champions

The youngest winner of the British Open was Tom Morris, Jr (1851–75) at Prestwick, Ayrshire, Scotland, in 1868, aged 17 years 249 days. The oldest British Open champion was "Old Tom" Morris (1821–1908) who was aged 46 years 99 days when he won in 1867. In modern times, the oldest was 1967 champion Roberto de Vicenzo (Argentina), when aged 44 years 93 days. The oldest US Amateur Champion was Jack Westland (b Dec 14, 1904) at Seattle, Wash, on Aug 23, 1952, aged 47 years 253 days.

Longest Span

Jacqueline Ann Mercer (*née* Smith) (b Apr 5, 1929) won her first South African title at Humewood GC, Port Elizabeth, in 1948, and her fourth title at Port Elizabeth GC on May 4, 1979, 31 years later.

Richest Prize

The greatest first-place prize money was $500,000 (total purse $1.1 million) won by Johnny Miller (US) (b Apr 29, 1947) at Sun City, Bophuthatswana, S Africa, in 1982, and by Raymond Floyd (b Sept 4, 1942) in 1983. After 72-hole scores of 277, Miller beat Severiano Ballesteros (Spain) (who won $160,000 for second place) and Floyd beat Craig Stadler in playoffs.

DRIVING ACROSS THE RIVER THAMES: Tony Jacklin (GB), winner of the 1969 British Open and 1970 US Open, drives from the roof of the Savoy Hotel, London, 125 ft above street level. His longest drive was about 353 yds but it fell short of the opposite bank. (Daily Express)

British Open

The Open Championship was inaugurated in 1860 at Prestwick, Strathclyde, Scotland. The lowest score for 9 holes is 29 by Tom Haliburton (Wentworth) and Peter W. Thomson (Australia) (b Aug 23, 1929) at Royal Lytham and St Anne's, Lancashire, England, on July 10, 1963; by Tony Jacklin (GB, b July 7, 1944) on July 8, 1970 at St Andrews, Scotland; and by Bill Longmuir (b June 10, 1953) on the Royal Lytham and St Anne's course on July 18, 1979.

The lowest scoring round in the Open itself is 63 by Mark Hayes (US, b July 12, 1949) at Turnberry, Strathclyde, Scotland, in the second round on July 7, 1977, and by Isao Aoki (Japan) (b Aug 31, 1942) in the third round in Muirfield, July 19, 1980. Henry Cotton (GB) at Royal St George's, Sandwich, Kent, England, completed the first 36 holes in 132 (67 + 65) on June 27, 1934.

The lowest 72-hole aggregate is 268 (68, 70, 65, 65) by Tom Watson (US) (b Sept 4, 1949) at Turnberry, Scotland, ending on July 9, 1977.

The winners (GB unless specified):

	Score		Score
1860 Willie Park, Sr	174	1874 Mungo Park	159
1861 Tom Morris, Sr	163	1875 Willie Park, Sr	166
1862 Tom Morris, Sr	163	1876 Robert Martin	176
1863 Willie Park, Sr	168	1877 Jamie Anderson	160
1864 Tom Morris, Sr	167	1878 Jamie Anderson	157
1865 Andrew Strath	162	1879 Jamie Anderson	170
1866 Willie Park, Sr	167	1880 Robert Ferguson	162
1867 Tom Morris, Sr	170	1881 Robert Ferguson	170
1868 Tom Morris, Jr	170	1882 Robert Ferguson	171
1869 Tom Morris, Jr	154	1883 Willie Fernie	159
1870 Tom Morris, Jr	149	1884 Jack Simpson	160
1871 Not held		1885 Bob Martin	171
1872 Tom Morris, Jr	166	1886 David Brown	157
1873 Tom Kidd	179	1887 Willie Park, Jr	161

	Score		Score
1888 Jack Burns	171	1936 Alfred Padgham	287
1889 Willie Park, Jr	155	1937 Henry Cotton	283
1890 John Ball	164	1938 Reg Whitcombe	295
1891 Hugh Kirkaldy	169	1939 Richard Burton	290
1892 Harold Hilton	305	1946 Sam Snead (US)	290
1893 William Auchterlonie	322	1947 Fred Daly	293
1894 John Taylor	326	1948 Henry Cotton	284
1895 John Taylor	322	1949 Bobby Locke (S Afr)	283
1896 Harry Vardon	316	1950 Bobby Locke (S Afr)	279
1897 Harry Hilton	314	1951 Max Faulkner	285
1898 Harry Vardon	307	1952 Bobby Locke (S Afr)	287
1899 Harry Vardon	310	1953 Ben Hogan (US)	282
1900 John Taylor	309	1954 Peter Thomson (Aus)	283
1901 James Braid	309	1955 Peter Thomson (Aus)	281
1902 Alexander Herd	307	1956 Peter Thomson (Aus)	286
1903 Harry Vardon	300	1957 Bobby Locke (S Afr)	279
1904 Jack White	296	1958 Peter Thomson (Aus)	278
1905 James Braid	318	1959 Gary Player (S Afr)	284
1906 James Braid	300	1960 Kel Nagle (Aus)	278
1907 Arnaud Massy (France)	312	1961 Arnold Palmer (US)	284
1908 James Braid	291	1962 Arnold Palmer (US)	276
1909 John Taylor	295	1963 Bob Charles (NZ)	277
1910 James Braid	299	1964 Tony Lema (US)	279
1911 Harry Vardon	303	1965 Peter Thomson (Aus)	285
1912 Edward (Ted) Ray	295	1966 Jack Nicklaus (US)	282
1913 John Taylor	304	1967 Robert de Vicenzo (Arg)	278
1914 Harry Vardon	306	1968 Gary Player (S Afr)	299
1920 George Duncan	303	1969 Tony Jacklin	280
1921 Jock Hutchinson (US)	296	1970 Jack Nicklaus (US)	283
1922 Walter Hagen (US)	300	1971 Lee Trevino (US)	278
1923 Arthur Havers	295	1972 Lee Trevino (US)	278
1924 Walter Hagen (US)	301	1973 Tom Weiskopf (US)	276
1925 James Barnes (US)	300	1974 Gary Player (S Afr)	282
1926 Robert T. Jones, Jr (US)	291	1975 Tom Watson (US)	279
1927 Robert T. Jones, Jr (US)	285	1976 Johnny Miller (US)	279
1928 Walter Hagen (US)	292	1977 Tom Watson (US)	268
1929 Walter Hagen (US)	292	1978 Jack Nicklaus (US)	281
1930 Robert T. Jones, Jr (US)	291	1979 Severiano Ballesteros (Spain)	283
1931 Tommy Armour (US)	296	1980 Tom Watson (US)	271
1932 Gene Sarazen (US)	283	1981 Bill Rogers (US)	276
1933 Denny Shute (US)	292	1982 Tom Watson (US)	284
1934 Henry Cotton	283	1983 Tom Watson (US)	275
1935 Alfred Perry	283	1984 Severiano Ballesteros (Spain)	276

WINNING THE BIG ONES: Lee Trevino has won the British Open (twice), the US Open (twice), and the PGA Championship (once).

LARGEST DRIVING RANGE: This 3-tier structure in Toyko, Japan, accommodates 300 golfers at a time.

Largest Tournament

The Volkswagen Grand Prix Open Amateur Championship in the UK attracted a record 228,320 (172,640 men and 55,680 women) competitors in 1982.

HOLES-IN-ONE

In 1983, *Golf Digest* was notified of 40,473 holes-in-one, so averaging over 110 per day.

Longest

The longest straight hole shot in one is the 10th hole (447 yd) at Miracle Hills GC, Omaha, Neb. Robert Mitera achieved a hole-in-one there on Oct 7, 1965. Mitera, aged 21 and 5 ft·6 in tall, weighed 165 lb. A two-handicap player, he normally drove 245 yd. A 50-mph gust carried his shot over a 290-yd drop-off. The group in front testified to the remaining distance.

The longest dogleg achieved in one is the 480-yd 5th hole at Hope CC, Ark, by L. Bruce on Nov 15, 1962.

The women's record is 393 yd by Marie Robie of Wollaston, Mass, on the first hole of the Furnace Brook GC, Sept 4, 1949.

Most

The greatest number of holes-in-one in a career is 66 by Harry Lee Bonner from 1967 to 1983, most at his home 9-hole course of Las Gallinas, San Rafael, Calif.

Douglas Porteous, 28, aced 4 holes over 39 consecutive holes—the 3rd and 6th on Sept 26, and the 5th on Sept 28 at Ruchill GC, Glasgow,

Scotland, and the 6th at the Clydebank and District GC Course on Sept 30, 1974. Robert Taylor holed the 188-yd 16th hole at Hunstanton, Norfolk, England, on three successive days—May 31, June 1 and 2, 1974. On May 12, 1984, Joe Lucius of Tiffin, Ohio, aced for the 13th time the par-3, 141-yd 15th hole at the Mohawk Golf Club. Lucius has 10 aces for the 10th hole on the same course, and 31 aces in all.

Consecutive

There is no recorded instance of a golfer performing three consecutive holes-in-one, but there are at least 16 cases of "aces" being achieved in two consecutive holes, of which the greatest was Norman L. Manley's unique "double albatross" on two par-4 holes (330-yd 7th and 290-yd 8th) on the Del Valle CC course, Saugus, Calif, on Sept 2, 1964.

The only woman ever to card consecutive aces is Sue Prell, on the 13th and 14th holes at Chatswood GC, Sydney, Australia, on May 29, 1977.

The closest recorded instances of a golfer getting 3 consecutive holes-in-one were by the Rev Harold Snider (b July 4, 1900) who aced the 8th, 13th and 14th holes of the par-3 Ironwood course in Phoenix, Ariz, on June 9, 1976, and the late Dr Joseph Boydstone on the 3rd, 4th and 9th at Bakersfield GC, Calif on Oct 10, 1962.

Youngest and Oldest

The youngest golfer recorded to have shot a hole-in-one was Coby Orr (aged 5) of Littleton, Colo, on the 103-yd fifth hole at the Riverside GC, San Antonio, Tex, in 1975. *Golf Digest* credits Tommy Moore (6 yrs 1 month 7 days) of Hagerstown, Md with being the youngest for an ace he shot on a 145-yd hole in 1969.

The oldest golfer to have performed the feat is George Selbach, 97, on the 110-yd 9th hole at Indian River (Mich) Golf Club on July 6, 1983.

The oldest woman to score an ace is Ruth Needham, 87, who holed-in-one on the 91-yd 3rd hole of the Escanaba (Mich) Country Club on July 11, 1983.

BEST ALL-AROUND OLYMPIC GYMNAST: Mary Lou Retton (US) won the gold medal in this category, silver medal in the vault and bronze medal in the uneven parallel bars in the 1984 Games.

GYMNASTICS

Earliest References

Tumbling and similar exercises were performed *c* 2600 BC as religious rituals in China, but it was the Greeks who coined the word gymnastics. A primitive form was practiced in the ancient Olympic Games, but it was not until Johann Friedrich Simon began to teach at Basedow's Gymnasium in Dessau, Germany, in 1776 that the foundations of the modern sport were laid. The first national federation was formed in Germany in 1860 and the International Gymnastics Federation was founded in Liège, Belgium in 1881. The sport was included at the first modern Olympic Games at Athens in 1896.

Current events for men are: floor exercises, horse vault, rings, pommel horse, parallel bars and horizontal bar, while for women they are: floor exercises, horse vault, asymmetrical bars, and balance beam.

World Championships

In Olympic years, the Olympic title is the World Championship title.

The greatest number of individual titles won by a man in the World Championships including Olympics is 10 by Boris Shakhlin (USSR) between 1954 and 1964. He was also on three winning teams. The women's record is 12 individual wins and 5 team titles by Larissa Semyonovna Latynina (b Dec 27, 1934, retired 1966) of the USSR, between 1956 and 1964. She has the most medals, 31, of which 18 are Olympic medals.

Olympic Games

The 1984 gold medalists:

Men

Individual All-Round
Koji Gushiken (Jap) 118,700 pts

Floor Exercises
Li Ning (China) 19,925 pts

Pommel Horse
tie Li Ning (China) 19,950 pts
tie P. Vidmar (US) 19,950 pts

Rings
tie Koji Gushiken (Jap) 19,850 pts
tie Li Ning (China) 19,850 pts

Horse Vault
Lou Yun (China) 19,950 pts

Parallel Bars
Bart Conner (US) 19,950 pts

Horizontal Bar
Shinji Morisue (Jap) 20,000 pts

Women

Individual All-Round
Mary Lou Retton (US) 79,175 pts

Floor Exercises
Ecaterina Szabo (Romania) 19,975 pts

Horse Vault
Ecaterina Szabo (Romania) 19,875 pts

Balance Beam
tie Simona Pauca (Romania) 19,800 pts
tie Ecaterina Szabo (Romania) 19,800 pts

Asymmetrical Bars
tie Ma Yauhong (China) 19,950 pts
tie J. McNamara (US) 19,950 pts

Rhythmic Individual All-Around
Lori Fung (Can) 5,795 pts

The only men to win 6 individual gold medals are Boris Shakhlin (b Jan 21, 1932) (USSR), with one in 1956, 4 (2 shared) in 1960 and one in 1964; and Nikolai Andrianov (b Oct 14, 1952) (USSR) with one in 1972, 4 in 1976 and one in 1980.

The most successful woman has been Vera Caslavska-Odlozilova (b May 3, 1942) (Czechoslovakia), with 7 individual gold medals, 3 in 1964 and 4 (one shared) in 1968. Larissa Latynina of the USSR won 6 individual and 3 team gold medals for a total of 9. She also won 5 silver and 4 bronze for an all-time record total of 18 Olympic medals.

Ecaterina Szabo (Romania) won 4 gold medals and a silver—the most in the 1984 Games at any sport.

The most medals for a male gymnast is 15 by Nikolai Andrianov (USSR), 7 gold, 5 silver and 3 bronze, 1972–80. Alexander Ditiatin (USSR) (b Aug 7, 1957) is the only man to win a medal in all eight categories in the same Games, with 3 gold, 4 silver and 1 bronze at Moscow in 1980.

A PERFECT "10": Nadia Comaneci (Romania) was 14 years old when she made Olympic history as the first gymnast ever to be awarded a perfect score. Her unprecedented feat came during the 1976 Olympics in Montreal. She went on to earn 6 more 10's for a remarkable total of 7 flawless routines (4 on uneven parallel bars and 3 on the balance beam).

STYLE in Gymnastics: Nelli Kim (USSR) (left) shows why she won 1976 and 1980 Olympic golds. (Right) Erica Schiller (USSR) demonstrates Rhythmic Gymnastics, first included in Olympic Games of 1984.

Nadia Comaneci (b Nov 12, 1961) (Romania) was the first gymnast to be awarded a perfect score of 10.00 in the Olympic Games, in the 1976 Montreal Olympics. She ended the competition with a total of 7 such marks (4 on the uneven parallel bars, 3 on the balance beam). Since then Nelli Kim (USSR) in the same Games, and a number of others have received marks of 10.00.

In the 1984 Olympics a record 16 perfect marks of 10.00 were awarded.

Modern Rhythmic Gymnastics

This recent addition to the female side of the sport incorporates exercises with different hand-held apparatus, including ribbons, balls, ropes, hoops and Indian clubs. The most overall titles won in world championships is 3 by Maria Gigova (Bulgaria) while the most individual apparatus titles is 9 by Gigova and Galina Shugurova (USSR). The latter has also won a record total of 14 medals. This category of the sport was included in the Olympic Games for the first time in 1984.

Youngest International Competitors

Pasakevi "Voula" Kouna (b Dec 6, 1971) was aged 9 years 299 days at the start of the Balkan Games at Serres, Greece on Oct 1–4, 1981, when she represented Greece. Olga Bicherova (b Oct 26, 1966) won the women's world title at 15 years 1 month in Nov 1981. The youngest men's champion was Dmitri Relozerchev (USSR) at 16 years 315 days at Budapest, Hungary in 1983.

OLYMPIC WINNERS: (Left) Alexander Ditiatin (USSR) is the only man to win a medal in all 8 gymnastic categories in one Games (1980) in Moscow. (Right) Boris Shakhlin (USSR) earned 6 individual golds in Olympics and also 10 in World Championships, a feat that is unmatched.

ROPE-JUMP CHAMP: Katsumi Suzuki (Japan), amazes spectators when he performs this quintuple turn in which he jumps about 4 ft in the air and turns the rope 5 times under his feet and around his body before landing back on the floor. He performed this feat 5 times in a row for a world record in 1975. He has also beaten all competitors in making consecutive quadruple turns (51), treble turns (381) and double turns (10,133)—all without a stop or a miss. (Photo by Dean Moon)

Largest Gymnastic Display

The greatest number of gymnasts to give a display at the same time are the 30,000–40,000 from the Sokol movement who perform annually in the Strahov Stadium in Prague, Czechoslovakia before some 240,000 spectators.

Chinning the Bar

The greatest number of continuous chin-ups (from a dead hang position) is 170 by Lee Chin Yong (b Aug 15, 1925) at Backyon Gymnasium, Seoul, Korea on May 10, 1983. Robert Chisholm (b Dec 9, 1952) performed 22 one-arm (his right) chin-ups, from a ring, 18 two-finger chins and 12 one-finger chins, from a nylon strap on Dec 3, 1982 at Queen's Univ, Kingston, Ont, Canada.

Sit-Ups

The greatest recorded number of consecutive sit-ups without feet pinned down or knees bent is 30,052 by Capt Michael Fields (US Army) at Fort Polk, La, on Nov 17, 1984.

As for leg raises, Louis Screpa, Jr. did 21,598 in 6 hours in Fairfield, Calif on Dec 8, 1983.

Rope Climbing

The US Amateur Athletic Union (AAU) records are tantamount to world records: 20 ft (hands alone) 2.8 sec, by Don Perry, at Champaign, Ill, on Apr 3, 1954; 25 ft (hands alone), 4.7 sec, by Garvin S. Smith at Los Angeles, on Apr 19, 1947.

Parallel Bar Dips

Roger Perez (b July 11, 1962) of Sacramento, Calif, performed a record 718 parallel bar dips in 30 min 40 sec on Dec 14, 1983. Jack LaLanne (b 1914) is reported to have done 1,000 in Oakland, Calif, in 1945.

SOMERSAULTS FOR 10 MILES through NYC's Central Park is only one of the records held by Ashrita Furman. He also walked with a milk bottle balanced on his head for 24 miles.

Sargent Jump

Devised by, and named after, an eminent American professor of physical education in the 1920s, this exercise measures the differential between the height reached by a person's finger tips with feet flat on the ground, and that reached by jumping. The record is 48 in by Darrell Griffith (US) of the University of Louisville in 1976. Olympic Pentathlon champion Mary E. Peters (GB) reportedly jumped 30 in in Calif in 1972.

Push-Ups

Colin Hewick, 23, did 10,029 consecutive press-ups at the South Holderness Sports Centre, Humberside, England, July 18, 1982. At the Riverside Gymnasium, Putney, London, he did 1,100 finger-tip press-ups on Sept 30, 1983.

Paul Henry Allen Lynch (GB) performed 1,753 finger-tip push-ups at Streatham, London on July 19, 1984. He also set a record of 2,754 one-arm push-ups on July 15, 1984 at Bedford Hotel, London. Danny Castoldi (US) did 500 consecutive hand-stand push-ups at USC, Los Angeles, July 9, 1983. Mick Gooch (GB) did 45 one-finger push-ups at Crystal Palace, London on May 26, 1984.

Jumping Jacks

The greatest number of consecutive side-straddle hops is 40,014 in 4 hours 43 min by August John Hoffman Jr at Van Nuys, Calif, on Dec 4, 1982.

Somersaults

Ashrita Furman performed 6,773 forward rolls over 10 miles in Central Park, NYC, on Nov 19, 1980.

Corporal Wayne Wright (GB) of the Royal Engineers, made a successful dive-and-tucked somersault over 37 men at Old Park Barracks, Dover, Kent, England on July 30, 1980.

Shigeru Iwasaki (b 1960) backwards somersaulted over 50 m (54.68 yd) in 10.8 sec in Tokyo, March 30, 1980.

ROPE JUMPING

The longest recorded non-stop rope-jumping marathon was one of 12 hours 8 min by Frank P. Olivieri (estimated 120,744 turns) at Great Lakes Training Center, Chicago, Ill, on June 13, 1981.

Other rope-jumping records made without a break:

Most quintuple turns	5	Katsumi Suzuki (Japan)	Saitama, Japan	May 29, 1975
Most turns in 1 minute	418	Tyrone Krohn	Middletown (NY) HS	July 10, 1984
Most turns in 10 seconds	108	Albert Rayner	Wakefield, Eng	June 28, 1978
Most doubles (with cross)	830	Mark W. de C. Baker	Cattai, NSW, Aust	Feb 20, 1983
Double turns	10,133	Katsumi Suzuki (Japan)	Saitama	Sept 29, 1979
Treble turns	381	Katsumi Suzuki (Japan)	Saitama	May 29, 1975
Quadruple turns	51	Katsumi Suzuki (Japan)	Saitama	May 29, 1975
Quintuple turns	6	Hidasama Tateda (Japan)	Aomori	June 19, 1982
Duration	1,264 miles	Tom Morris (Aust)	Brisbane-Cairns	1963
Most on a single rope (minimum 12 turns obligatory)	160	(50 m rope) Shimizu Iida Junior High School	Shizuoka-ken, Japan	Dec 10, 1982
Most turns on single rope (team of 90)	97	Erimomisaki School	Hokkaido, Japan	May 28, 1983
On a tightrope (consecutive)	58	Bryan Andrew (né Dewhurst)	TROS TV, Holland	Aug 6, 1981

HANDBALL

Origin

Handball is a game of ancient Celtic origin. In the early 19th century only a front wall was used, but later side and back walls were added. The court is now standardized 60 feet by 30 feet in Ireland, Ghana and Australia, and 40 feet by 20 feet in Canada, Mexico and the US. The game is played with both a hard and soft ball in Ireland, and a soft ball only elsewhere.

The earliest international contest was in New York City in 1887, between the champions of the US and Ireland.

Championship

World championships were inaugurated in New York in October, 1964, with competitors from Australia, Canada, Ireland, Mexico and the US. The US is the only nation to have won twice, with victories in 1964 and 1967 (shared).

Most Titles

The most successful player in the U.S.H.A. National Four-Wall Championships has been James Jacobs (US), who won a record 6 singles titles (1955–56–57–60–64–65) and shared in 6 doubles titles (1960–62–63–65–67–68). Martin Decatur has won 8 doubles titles (1962–63–65–67–68–75–78–79), 5 of these with Jacobs as his partner. Fred Lewis has also won 6 singles titles (1972–74–75–76–78–81).

Olympics

Yugoslavia won both men's and women's events in 1984, which with their men's win in 1972 ties the record number of Olympic wins.

U.S. Handball Association National Champions

PROFESSIONAL SINGLES
1951   Walter Plekan
1952   Vic Hershkowitz
1953   Bob Brady
1954   Vic Hershkowitz
1955–57 Jim Jacobs
1958–59 John Sloan
1960   Jim Jacobs
1961   John Sloan
1962–63 Oscar Obert
1964–65 Jim Jacobs
1966–67 Paul Haber
1968   Simon (Stuffy) Singer
1969–71 Paul Haber
1972   Fred Lewis
1973   Terry Mack
1974–76 Fred Lewis
1977   Naty Alvarado
1978   Fred Lewis
1979–80 Naty Alvarado
1981   Fred Lewis
1982–84 Naty Alvarado

FOUR-WALL DOUBLES
1951–52 Frank Coyle and Bill Baier
1953   Sam Haber and Harry Dreyfus
1954–56 Sam Haber and Ken Schneider
1957–59 Phil Collins and John Sloan
1960   Jim Jacobs and Dick Weisman
1961   John Sloan and Vic Hershkowitz
1962–63 Jim Jacobs and Marty Decatur
1964   John Sloan and Phil Elbert
1965   Jim Jacobs and Marty Decatur
1966   Pete Tyson and Bob Lindsay
1967–68 Jim Jacobs and Marty Decatur
1969   Lou Kramberg and Lou Russo
1970   Carl Obert and Rudy Obert
1971   Ray Neveau and Simie Fein
1972   Kent Fusselman and Al Drews
1973–74 Ray Neveau and Simie Fein
1975   Steve Lott and Marty Decatur
1976   Dan O'Connor and Gary Rohrer
1977   Matt Kelley and Skip McDowell
1978–79 Marty Decatur and Simon (Stuffy) Singer
1980   Skip McDowell and Harry Robertson
1981   Jack Roberts and Tom Kopatich
1982–84 Vern Roberts and Naty Alvarado

OFF THE WALL: Jim Jacobs has been the most successful player in the USHA National Four-Wall Championships with 6 singles and 6 doubles titles.

HARNESS RACING

Origins

Trotting races were held in Valkenburg, Netherlands, in 1554. In England the trotting gait (the simultaneous use of the diagonally opposite legs) was known in the 16th century. The sulky first appeared in harness racing in 1829. Pacers thrust out their fore and hind legs simultaneously on one side.

Greatest Winnings

The greatest amount won by a trotting horse is $3,041,262 by "Ideal du Gazeau" (France) to July 23, 1983. The record for a pacing horse is $2,041,367 by "Cam Fella" (US).

The greatest award won by a harness horse in a single season is $1,414,313 by "Niatross" during 1980. He won $2,019,213 in just two years, 1979 and 1980.

The largest purse ever was $2,011,000 for the Woodrow Wilson 2-year-olds race at Meadowlands, NJ, on Aug 6, 1980, of which a record $1,005,000 went to the winner "Land Grant" driven by Del Insko.

HARNESS RACING RECORDS AGAINST TIME

TROTTING

Time Trial (mile track)	1:54.0	"Arndon" (driver, Delvin Miller) (US), at Lexington, Ky	Oct 6, 1982
Race Record (mile)	1:54.8	"Lindy's Crown" (driver, Howard Beissinger) (US) at Du Quoin, Ill	Aug 30, 1980

PACING

Time Trial (mile track)	1:49.2	"Niatross" (driver, Clint Galbraith) (US) at Lexington, Ky	Oct 1, 1980
Race Record (mile)	1:51.6	"Trenton" (driver, Tom Haughton) (US), at Springfield, Ill	Aug 21, 1982

Highest Price

The highest price paid for a trotter is $5.25 million for "Mystic Park" by Lana Lobell Farms from Allen, Gerald and Irving Wechter of NY and Robert Lester of Florida, announced on July 13, 1982. The highest price ever paid for a pacer is $8.25 million for "Merger" by Finder/Guida of NY from John Campbell, David Morrisey and Peter Oud of Canada in 1982.

Most Successful Driver

The most successful sulky driver in North America has been Herve Filion (Canada) (b Quebec, Feb 1, 1940) who reached a record of 8,731 wins and $42,123,469 in purse money by the end of 1983, after a record 637 victories in the 1974 season. Filion won the North American championship for the twelfth time in 1982. The greatest earnings in a year is $6,104,082 by John Campbell in 1983.

ROCKET MAN: Maurice "Rocket" Richard beats the Boston goaltender to score one of his record 82 Stanley Cup goals, this one in the 1953 finals. Of those 82 goals, 18 were game winners with 6 coming in overtime. Maurice Richard's brother, Henri "Pocket Rocket" Richard, played in 11 finals as part of his record 180 playoff-game appearances.

HOCKEY

Origins

There is pictorial evidence of a hockey-like game (Kalv) being played on ice in the Netherlands in the early 16th century. The game probably was first played in North America on Dec 25, 1855, at Kingston, Ontario, Canada, but Halifax also lays claim to priority.

The International Ice Hockey Federation was founded in 1908. The National Hockey League was inaugurated in 1917. The World Hockey Association was formed in 1971 and disbanded in 1979 when 4 of its teams joined the NHL.

Olympic Games

In 1984, the USSR won the Olympic title for the 6th time (1956, 64, 68, 72, 76, 84), tying the record set by Canada, who won in 1920, 24, 28, 32, 48, and 52, and who won the world title 19 times, the last being at Geneva in 1961. The longest Olympic career is that of Richard Torriani (Switzerland) from 1928 to 1948. The most gold medals won by any player is 3; this was achieved by 4 USSR players in the 1964, 68 and 72 Games—Vitaliy Davidov, Aleksandr Ragulin, Anatoliy Firssov and Viktor Kuzkin.

GOAL ORIENTED: Wayne Gretzky, who surprised NHL fans when he set assist and point records in the 1980–81 season, showed he was no flash in the pan when, in 1981–82, he broke those records and also set a goal-scoring record by netting 92 goals, including a record 10 hat tricks. Between Oct 1983 and Jan 1984, he scored one or more points in 51 consecutive games for a total of 153 points.
(Edmonton Oilers)

50 OR MORE GOALS in each of his first 7 NHL seasons 1977–84 is the record held by the Islanders' high-scoring right wing Mike Bossy.

Goalie Vladimir Tretiak (USSR) won 3 golds (1972, 1976 and 1984) as well as a silver in 1980.

Stanley Cup

This cup, presented by the Governor-General Lord Stanley (original cost $48.67), became emblematic of world professional team supremacy 33 years after the first contest at Montreal in 1893. It has been won most often by the Montreal Canadiens, with 22 wins in 1916, 24, 30–31, 44, 46, 53, 56–60 (a record 5 straight), 65–66, 68–69, 71, 73, 76–79. Henri Richard played in his eleventh finals in 1973.

Winners from 1970 are:

1970 Boston Bruins
1971 Montreal Canadiens
1972 Boston Bruins
1973 Montreal Canadiens
1974 Philadelphia Flyers
1975 Philadelphia Flyers
1976 Montreal Canadiens
1977 Montreal Canadiens

1978 Montreal Canadiens
1979 Montreal Canadiens
1980 New York Islanders
1981 New York Islanders
1982 New York Islanders
1983 New York Islanders
1984 Edmonton Oilers

Longest Game

The longest game was 2 hours 56 min 30 sec (playing time) when the Detroit Red Wings eventually beat the Montreal Maroons 1-0 in the 17th minute of the sixth period of overtime at the Forum, Montreal, at 2:25 a.m. on March 25, 1936, 5 hours 51 min after the opening faceoff. Norm Smith, goaltender for the Red Wings, turned aside 92 shots in registering the NHL's longest single shutout.

Fastest Player

The highest speed measured for any player is 29.7 mph (without the puck) for Bobby Hull (then of the Chicago Black Hawks) (b Jan 3, 1939). The highest puck speed is also attributed to Hull, whose left-handed slap shot has been measured at 118.3 mph. Also known as the "Golden Jet," Hull is the only player besides Gordie Howe to score over 1,000 goals in NHL and WHA play.

Longest Career

Gordie Howe (b March 31, 1928, Floral, Saskatchewan, Canada) skated 25 years for the Detroit Red Wings from 1946–47 through the 1970–71 season, playing in a total of 1,687 NHL regular-season games. During that time he also set records for most career goals, assists, and scoring points; was selected as an all-star a record 21 times; and collected 500 stitches in his face (see also *Individual Scoring*).

After leaving the Red Wings, he ended a 2-year retirement to skate with his two sons as teammates and played for 6 more seasons with the Houston Aeros and the New England Whalers of the World Hockey Association, participating in 497 games.

With the incorporation of the (now Hartford) Whalers into the NHL for the 1979–80 season, Gordie Howe skated in all 80 regular season

LONGEST CAREER: In a career that spanned 5 decades, Gordie Howe skated for 26 years in the NHL and 6 seasons in the now-defunct WHA. As a 52-year-old grandfather during the 1979–80 season, Howe was selected as an NHL all-star for the 22nd time. He holds NHL regular-season records for service, goals, assists and points. For all games in both leagues, Howe notched 1,071 goals and 1,518 assists for 2,589 points in 2,421 "major league" games.

games (for a record total of 1,767) in his record 26th year in that league, and the remarkable 52-year-old grandfather was again selected as an NHL all-star, a record 22nd time. Including Howe's 157 NHL playoff appearances, he skated in 2,421 "major league" games.

Most Consecutive Games

Garry Unger, playing for Toronto, Detroit, St Louis, and Atlanta, skated in 914 consecutive NHL games without a miss during 13 seasons from Feb 24, 1968, to Dec 21, 1979, when a torn shoulder muscle kept him on the bench.

The most consecutive complete games by a goaltender is 502, set by Glenn Hall (Detroit, Chicago), beginning in 1955 and ending when he suffered a back injury in a game against Boston on Nov 7, 1962.

Longest Season

The only man ever to play 82 games in a 78-game season is Ross Lonsberry. He began the 1971–72 season with the Los Angeles Kings where he played 50 games. Then, in January, he was traded to the Philadelphia Flyers (who had played only 46 games at the time) where he finished out the season (32 more games).

Brad Marsh (b Mar 31, 1958) played 83 games (17 with Calgary and 66 with Philadelphia) during an 80-game season in 1981–82.

Team Scoring

The greatest number of goals recorded in a World Championship match has been 47-0 when Canada beat Denmark on Feb 12, 1949.

The Edmonton Oilers set an NHL record of 446 goals in the 1983–84 season.

The NHL record for both teams is 21 goals, scored when the Montreal Canadiens beat the Toronto St Patricks at Montreal 14-7 on Jan 10, 1920. The most goals ever scored by one team in a single game was set by the Canadiens, when they defeated the Quebec Bulldogs on March 3, 1920 by a score of 16-3.

The most goals in a period is 9 by the Buffalo Sabres in the second period of their 14–4 victory over Toronto on March 19, 1981.

The Detroit Red Wings scored 15 consecutive goals without an answering tally when they defeated the NY Rangers 15-0 on Jan 23, 1944.

Longest Streaks

In the 1981–82 season, the NY Islanders won 15 consecutive games, Jan 21–Feb 20, 1982. The longest a team has ever gone without a defeat is 35 games, set by the Philadelphia Flyers with 25 wins and 10 ties from Oct 14, 1979, to Jan 6, 1980.

Fastest Scoring

Toronto scored 8 goals against the NY Americans in 4 min 52 sec on March 19, 1938.

The fastest goal ever scored from the opening whistle came at 5 sec of the first period. This occurred twice, most recently by Bryan Trottier of the NY Islanders vs Boston Bruins on Mar 22, 1984. The previous time was by Doug Smail of the Winnipeg Jets against St Louis on Dec 20,

FASTEST SKATER: Bobby Hull (left) was timed at 29.7 mph. His slap shot went screaming at goaltenders at 118.3 mph. Hull was the only player besides Gordie Howe to score 1,000 NHL and WHA goals. FASTEST GOAL: Bryan Trottier (right) of the NY Islanders scored a goal 5 sec after the opening whistle on Mar 22, 1984.

1981. Claude Provost of the Canadiens scored a goal against Boston after 4 sec of the opening of the second period on Nov 9, 1957.

The fastest scoring record is held by Bill Mosienko (Chicago) who scored 3 goals in 21 sec against the NY Rangers on March 23, 1952. In a playoff game Pat LaFontaine of the NY Islanders scored 2 goals in 22 sec vs Edmonton Oilers, May 19, 1984.

Gus Bodnar (Toronto Maple Leafs) scored a goal against the NY Rangers at 15 sec of the first period of *his first NHL game* on Oct 30, 1943. Later in his career, while with Chicago, Bodnar again entered the record book when he assisted on all 3 of Bill Mosienko's quick goals.

Several fast scoring feats have been reported from non-NHL competition: Kim D. Miles scored in 3 sec for Univ of Guelph vs Univ of W Ontario on Feb 11, 1975; Steve D'Innocenzo scored 3 goals in 12 sec for Holliston vs Westwood in a high school game in Mass on Jan 9, 1982; Clifford "Fido" Purpur, 38, scored 4 goals in 25 sec for the Grand Forks AMerks vs Winnipeg All Stars in Grand Forks, ND, on Jan 29, 1950. In team play, the Skara Ishockeyclubb, Sweden, scored 3 goals in 11 sec against Orebro IK at Skara on Oct 18, 1981; the Vernon Cougars scored 5 goals in 56 sec against Salmon Arm Aces at Vernon, BC, Canada, on Aug 6, 1982; the Kamloops Knights of Columbus scored 7 goals in 2 min 22 sec vs Prince George Vikings on Jan 25, 1980.

Goaltending

The longest any goalie has gone without a defeat is 32 games, a record set by Gerry Cheevers of Boston in 1971–72. The longest a goalie has ever kept successive opponents scoreless is 461 min 29 sec by Alex Connell of the Ottawa Senators in 1927–28. He registered 6 consecutive shutouts in this time.

The most shutouts ever recorded in one season is 22 by George Hainsworth of Montreal in 1928–29 (this is also a team record). This feat is even more remarkable considering that the season was only 44 games long at that time, compared to the 80-game season currently used.

Terry Sawchuk registered a record 103 career shutouts in his 20 seasons in the NHL. He played for Detroit, Boston, Toronto, Los Angeles, and the NY Rangers during that time. He also appeared in a record 971 games.

The only goaltender to score a goal in an NHL game is Bill Smith (NY Islanders), against the Colorado Rockies in Denver, Nov 28, 1979. After the Rockies had removed their goaltender in favor of an extra skater during a delayed penalty, a Colorado defenseman's errant centering pass sent the puck skidding nearly the full length of the ice and into his own untended goal. Goalie Smith was the last Islander to touch the puck and was credited with the goal even though he did not take the actual "shot."

Penalties

The most any team has been penalized in one season is the 2,621 min assessed against the Philadelphia Flyers in 1980–81. The most penalty-filled game was a contest between Boston and Minnesota in Boston on Feb 26, 1981, with a total of 84 penalties (42 by each team) for 406 min (211 min by Minnesota).

David "Tiger" Williams (Toronto, Vancouver) has amassed 2,994 penalty min over 10 seasons, 1974–75 to 1983–84. Dave Schultz (Philadelphia) earned 472 min of penalties in the 1974–75 season. Randy Holt (LA) was assessed 67 penalty min in a game against Philadelphia on Mar 11, 1979.

Individual Scoring

The career record in the NHL for regular season goals is 801 by Gordie Howe of the Detroit Red Wings and Hartford Whalers. Howe has scored 1,850 points in his NHL career, with 1,049 assists. With 68 goals, 92 assists, and 160 points in Stanley Cup competition; and 202 goals, 377 assists, and 579 points in WHA season and playoff games, Howe's unequaled professional career scoring totals are 1,071 goals and 1,518 assists, for 2,589 points.

Wayne Gretzky (b Jan 26, 1961) of the Edmonton Oilers set NHL season records by scoring 92 goals and 212 total points in 1981–82. He set the season record for assists with 125 in 1982–83.

Mike Bossy (b Jan 22, 1957) of the NY Islanders has scored 50 or more goals in each of his first 7 NHL seasons, 1977–78 through 1983–84. Marcel Dionne (b Aug 3, 1951) (Detroit, LA) notched 100 or more points in 7 seasons.

The most goals ever scored in one game is 7 by Joe Malone of the Quebec Bulldogs against the Toronto St Patricks on Jan 31, 1920. Ma-

THE PUCK STOPS HERE: Goaltender Gerry Cheevers (left) went 32 games without a loss. Whenever a puck struck his mask, Cheevers drew stitchmarks in honor of the injury not suffered. Bill Smith (right) became the only goaltender to be credited with scoring an NHL goal. He was the last Islander to touch the puck (in making a save) before the Colorado Rockies accidentally put the puck in their own net.

lone, playing for the Montreal Canadiens in 1917–18, had a season record 2.2 goals-per-game average (44 goals in 20 games).

The most points scored in one NHL game is 10, a record set by Darryl Sittler of the Toronto Maple Leafs, on Feb 7, 1976, against the Boston Bruins. He had 6 goals and 4 assists.

Charlie Simmer of the LA Kings had 56 goals on 171 shots in the 1980–81 season to record the best shooting percentage—32.7%.

In 1921–22, Harry (Punch) Broadbent of the Ottawa Senators scored 25 goals in 16 consecutive games to set an all-time "consecutive game goal-scoring streak" record.

Wayne Gretzky (Edmonton) earned one or more points in 51 consecutive games Oct 5, 1983—Jan 27, 1984, with 61 goals and 92 assists for 153 points during his record streak.

The most assists recorded in an NHL game is 7 by Billy Taylor of Detroit on March 16, 1947 against Chicago (Detroit won 10-6); and by Wayne Gretzky for Edmonton vs Washington, Feb 15, 1980.

Most 3-Goal Games

In his 18-year NHL career, Phil Esposito of Chicago, Boston and the NY Rangers, scored 3 or more goals in 32 games. Five of these were 4-goal efforts. Wayne Gretzky (Edmonton) scored 3 or more goals in 10 games during the 1981–82 season, and equaled the feat in 1983–84. The term "hat-trick" properly applies when 3 goals are scored consecutively by one player in a game without interruption by either an answering score by the other team or a goal by any other player on his own team. In general usage, a "hat-trick" is any 3-goal effort by a player in one game.

HORSE RACING

Origins

There is evidence that men were riding horses, as distinct from riding in chariots pulled by horses, in Assyria and Egypt c 1400 BC. However, early organized racing appears to have been confined to chariots, for which the Roman method used riders with a foot on each of two horses. The first racing on horseback was by the Greeks in the 33rd Olympic Games in 648 BC. The earliest recorded race in Britain was at Netherby, Cumbria in 210 AD between Arabian horses brought to Britain by the Roman Emperor, Lucius Septimius Severus. The first recognizable regular race meeting was that held at Smithfield, London at the weekly horse fairs on Fridays in 1174. The first known prize money was a purse of gold presented by Richard I (the Lion-heart) in 1195 for a race between knights over a distance of 3 mi.

Organized horse racing began in New York State at least as early as March 1668. The original Charleston (Va) Jockey Club, organized in 1734, was the world's first.

Racing colors (silks) became compulsory in 1889.

All thoroughbred horses in the world today are descended from at least one of three great stallions, which were imported into Britain in the 17th and 18th centuries. The "Darley Arabian" was brought from Aleppo, Syria by the British Consul Richard Darley of Yorkshire c 1704; the "Byerley Turk" was brought to England from Turkey c 1685 and used by Captain Byerley as a charger in Ireland; and the Godolphin Barb—the latter word derived from the Barbary Coast of North Africa—was originally brought from France by Edward Coke in about 1735 and then acquired by the Earl of Godolphin.

HORSES' SPEED RECORDS

Distance	Time	mph	Name	Course	Date
¼ mile	20.8s.	43.26	Big Racket (Mex)	Mexico City, Mex	Feb 5, 1945
½ mile	44.4s.	40.54	Sonido (Ven)	‡Caracas, Ven	June 28, 1970
	44.4s.	40.54	Western Romance (Can)	Calgary, Can	Apr 19, 1980
	44.4s.	40.54	Northern Spike (Can)	Winnipeg, Can	Apr 23, 1982
⅝ mile	53.6s.	41.98†	Indigenous (GB)	‡*Epsom, Eng	June 2, 1960
	53.89s.	41.75††	Raffingora (GB)	‡*Epsom, Eng	June 5, 1970
	55.2s.	40.76	Chinook Pass (US)	Seattle, Wash	Sept 17, 1982
¾ mile	1m. 06.2s.	40.78	Broken Tendril (GB)	*Brighton, Eng	Aug 6, 1929
	1m. 07.2s.	40.18	Grey Papa (US)	Longacres, Wash	Sept 4, 1972
	1m. 07.2s.	40.18	Petro D. Jay (US)	Phoenix, Ariz	May 9, 1982
Mile	1m. 31.8s.	39.21	Soueida (GB)	*Brighton, Eng	Sept 19, 1963
	1m. 31.8s.	39.21	Loose Cover (GB)	*Brighton, Eng	June 9, 1966
	1m. 32.2s.	39.04	Dr. Fager (US)	Arlington, Ill	Aug 24, 1968
1¼ miles	1m. 57.4s.	38.33	Double Discount (US)	Arcadia, Calif	Oct 9, 1977
1½ miles	2m. 23.0s.	37.76	Fiddle Isle (US)	Arcadia, Calif	Mar 21, 1970
			John Henry (US)	Arcadia, Calif	Mar 16, 1980
2 miles**	3m. 15.0s.	36.93	Polazel (GB)	Salisbury, Eng	July 8, 1924
2½ miles	4m. 14.6s.	35.35	Miss Grillo (US)	Pimlico, Md	Nov 12, 1948
3 miles	5m. 15.0s.	34.29	Farragut (Mex)	Aguascalientes, Mex	Mar 9, 1941

* Course downhill for ¼ of a mile.
** A more reliable modern record is 3 min 16.75 sec by *Il Tempo* (NZ) at Trentham, Wellington, New Zealand, on Jan 17, 1970.
† Hand-timed.　　†† Electrically timed.　　‡ Straight courses.

GREATEST MONEY-WINNING HORSE AND JOCKEY: "John Henry," who won almost $5 million in purses, with jockey Willie Shoemaker, who earned $96,508,751 in 35 years of riding 36,989 mounts. (Gerry Cranham)

Victories

The horse with the best win-loss record was "Kincsem," a Hungarian mare foaled in 1874, who was unbeaten in 54 races (1876–79), including the English Goodwood Cup of 1878.

"Camarero," foaled in 1951, won his first 56 races, 1953–56, and had 73 wins in 77 starts altogether.

Dead Heats

There is no recorded case in turf history of a quintuple dead heat. The nearest approach was in the Astley Stakes, at Lewes, England, on Aug 6, 1880, when "Mazurka," "Wandering Nun" and "Scobell" triple dead-heated for first place, just ahead of "Cumberland" and "Thora," who dead-heated for fourth place. Each of the five jockeys thought he had won. The only three known examples of a quadruple dead heat were between "Honest Harry," "Miss Decoy," "Young Daffodil" and "Peteria" at Bogside, England, on June 7, 1808; between "Defaulter," "The Squire of Malton," "Reindeer" and "Pulcherrima" in the Omnibus Stakes at The Hoo, England, on Apr 26, 1851; and between "Overreach," "Lady Go-Lightly," "Gamester" and "The Unexpected" at Newmarket, England, on Oct 22, 1855.

Since the introduction of the photo-finish, the highest number of horses in a dead heat has been three, on several occasions.

Greatest Winnings

The greatest amount ever won by a horse is $4,882,797 by the gelding "John Henry" (foaled 1975) from 1977 to July 25, 1984.

The most won in a year is $2,138,963 by the 4-year-old "All Along" in 1983 in France and the US.

"Trinycarol" is the leading money-winning mare with $2,644,516 from 18 wins in 26 races 1981–83 in Venezuela. A horse must make at least one start in North America before the Jockey Club will recognize career earnings as official, a condition "Trinycarol" satisfied at Belmont Park, NY, June 24, 1984.

Triple Crown

Eleven horses have won all three races in one season which constitute the American Triple Crown (Kentucky Derby, Preakness Stakes and the Belmont Stakes). This feat was first achieved by "Sir Barton" in 1919, and most recently by "Seattle Slew" in 1977 and "Affirmed" in 1978.

The only Triple Crown winner to sire another winner was "Gallant Fox," the 1930 winner, who sired "Omaha," who won in 1935. The only jockey to ride two Triple Crown winners is Eddie Arcaro (b Feb 19, 1916), on "Whirlaway" (1941) and "Citation" (1948).

Most Valuable Horse

The most expensive horse ever is the 1983 Irish Derby winner "Shareef Dancer." Reportedly 40 shares in the horse were sold at $1 million each in 1983.

The highest price for a yearling is $10.2 million for a colt by "Northern Dancer"—"My Bupers" (later named "Snaafi Dancer") bought at auction July 20, 1983, at Keeneland, Lexington, Ky, by Aston Upthorpe Stud of England, owned by Sheik Muhammed al-Maktoum, Defense Minister of Dubai, United Arab Emirates, who also owned and sold "Shareef Dancer" (see above).

The record auction price for a yearling filly was set on July 18, 1984, at Keeneland, when Aston Upthorpe Stud (see above) paid $3,750,000 for a filly by "Seattle Slew"–"Fine Prospect."

Largest Prizes

The richest race ever held was the Breeders' Cup Classic, run at Hollywood Park, Calif, on Nov 10, 1984 which paid $3 million in prize money. It was won by "Wild Again," a 31-to-1 shot. Altogether $10 million was paid out in prize money that day.

Most Horses in a Race

In the Grand National (England) on Mar 22, 1929, there were 66 horses.

BIG YEAR: "All Along" won more than $2 million in one year (1983) as a 4-year-old in France and the US.

Jockeys

The most successful jockey of all time is Willie Shoemaker (b weighing 2½ lb on Aug 19, 1931) now weighing 94 lb and standing 4 ft 11 in. (His wife is nearly 1 ft taller than he is.) From March 1949 to June 1984, he rode 8,366 winners from 36,989 mounts, earning $96,508,751.

Chris McCarron (US), 19, won a total of 546 races in 1974 out of 2,199 mounts, an average of 6 races a day.

The greatest amount ever won by any jockey in a year is $10,116,697 by Angel Cordero (b May 8, 1942) in 1983.

The most winners ridden on one card is 8 by Hubert S. Jones, 17, out of 13 mounts at Caliente, Calif, on June 11, 1944 (of which 5 were photo-finishes); by Oscar Barattuci at Rosario City, Argentina, on Dec 15, 1957; and by Dave Gall from 10 mounts at Cahokia Downs, East St Louis, Ill, on Oct 18, 1978, and Chris Loseth, 29, out of 10 mounts at Exhibition Park in Vancouver, BC, Canada on Apr 9, 1984.

The longest winning streak is 12 races by Sir Gordon Richards (GB) who won the last race at Nottingham, Eng, on Oct 3, 1933, 6 out of 6 at Chepstow on Oct 4, and the first 5 races the next day at Chepstow.

The oldest jockey was Harry Beasley, who rode his last race at Baldoyle, County Dublin, Ireland, on June 10, 1935, aged 83. The youngest

Kentucky Derby Winners

1¼ miles at Churchill Downs, Louisville, Kentucky; first held in 1875.

Year	Winner, Jockey	Year	Winner, Jockey
1875	*Aristides*, O. Lewis	1931	*Twenty Grand*, C. Kurtsinger
1876	*Vagrant*, R. Swim	1932	*Burgoo King*, E. James
1877	*Baden Baden*, W. Walker	1933	*Brokers Tip*, D. Meade
1878	*Day Star*, J. Carter	1934	*Cavalcade*, M. Garner
1879	*Lord Murphy*, C. Schauer	1935	*Omaha*, W. Saunders
1880	*Fonso*, G. Lewis	1936	*Bold Venture*, I. Hanford
1881	*Hindoo*, J. McLaughlin	1937	*War Admiral*, C. Kurtsinger
1882	*Apollo*, B. Hurd	1938	*Lawrin*, E. Arcaro
1883	*Leonatus*, W. Donohue	1939	*Johnstown*, J. Stout
1884	*Buchanan*, I. Murphy	1940	*Gallahadion*, C. Bierman
1885	*Joe Cotton*, E. Henderson	1941	*Whirlaway*, E. Arcaro
1886	*Ben Ali*, P. Duffy	1942	*Shut Out*, W. D. Wright
1887	*Montrose*, I. Lewis	1943	*Count Fleet*, J. Longden
1888	*Macbeth II*, G. Covington	1944	*Pensive*, C. McCreary
1889	*Spokane*, T. Kiley	1945	*Hoop, Jr.*, E. Arcaro
1890	*Riley*, I. Murphy	1946	*Assault*, W. Mehrtens
1891	*Kingman*, I. Murphy	1947	*Jet Pilot*, E. Guerin
1892	*Azra*, A. Clayton	1948	*Citation*, E. Arcaro
1893	*Lookout*, E. Kunze	1949	*Ponder*, S. Brooks
1894	*Chant*, F. Goodale	1950	*Middleground*, W. Boland
1895	*Halma*, J. Perkins	1951	*Count Turf*, C. McCreary
1896	*Ben Brush*, W. Simms	1952	*Hill Gail*, E. Arcaro
1899	*Manuel*, F. Taral	1953	*Dark Star*, H. Moreno
1900	*Lieutenant Gibson*, J. Boland	1954	*Determine*, R. York
1901	*His Eminence*, J. Winkfield	1955	*Swaps*, W. Shoemaker
1902	*Alan-a-Dale*, J. Winkfield	1956	*Needles*, D. Erb
1903	*Judge Himes*, H. Booker	1957	*Iron Liege*, W. Hartack
1904	*Elwood*, F. Prior	1958	*Tim Tam*, I. Valenzuela
1905	*Agile*, J. Martin	1959	*Tomy Lee*, W. Shoemaker
1906	*Sir Huon*, R. Troxler	1960	*Venetian Way*, W. Hartack
1907	*Pink Star*, A. Minder	1961	*Carry Back*, J. Sellers
1908	*Stone Street*, A. Pickens	1962	*Decidedly*, W. Hartack
1909	*Wintergreen*, V. Powers	1963	*Chateaugay*, B. Baeza
1910	*Donau*, F. Herbert	1964	*Northern Dancer*, W. Hartack
1911	*Meridian*, G. Archibald	1965	*Lucky Debonair*, W. Shoemaker
1912	*Worth*, C. H. Shilling	1966	*Kauai King*, D. Brumfield
1913	*Donerail*, R. Goose	1967	*Proud Clarion*, R. Ussery
1914	*Old Rosebud*, J. McCabe	1968	*Forward Pass* *, I. Valenzuela
1915	*Regret*, J. Nutter	1969	*Majestic Prince*, W. Hartack
1916	*George Smith*, J. Loftus	1970	*Dust Commander*, M. Manganello
1917	*Omar Khayyam*, C. Borel	1971	*Canonero II*, G. Avila
1918	*Exterminator*, W. Knapp	1972	*Riva Ridge*, R. Turcotte
1919	*Sir Barton*, J. Loftus	1973	*Secretariat*. R. Turcotte
1920	*Paul Jones*, T. Rice	1974	*Cannonade*, A. Cordero
1921	*Behave Yourself*, C. Thompson	1975	*Foolish Pleasure*, J. Vasquez
1922	*Morvich*, A. Johnson	1976	*Bold Forbes*, A. Cordero
1923	*Zev*, E. Sande	1977	*Seattle Slew*, J. Cruguet
1924	*Black Gold*, J. D. Mahoney	1978	*Affirmed*, S. Cauthen
1925	*Flying Ebony*, E. Sande	1979	*Spectacular Bid*, R. Franklin
1926	*Bubbling Over*, A. Johnson	1980	*Genuine Risk*, J. Vasquez
1927	*Whiskery*, L. McAtee	1981	*Pleasant Colony*, J. Velasquez
1928	*Reigh Count*, C. Lang	1982	*Gato del Sol*, E. Delahoussaye
1929	*Clyde Van Dusen*, L. McAtee	1983	*Sunny's Halo*, E. Delahoussaye
1930	*Gallant Fox*, E. Sande	1984	*Swale*, L. Pincay

* *Dancer's Image* finished first but was disqualified after drug tests.

THE DANCER FAMILY: This colt, sired by "Northern Dancer," brought $10.2 million—an auction record for a yearling—at the Keeneland sales in 1983. "Northern Dancer," who won the Kentucky Derby and Preakness Stakes in 1964, was also the sire of two fillies and a colt that each brought record prices. (AP)

jockey was Frank Wootton (1893–1940) (English Champion jockey 1909–12), who rode his first winner in South Africa aged 9 years 10 months. The lightest recorded jockey was Kitchener (d 1872), who won the Chester Cup in England on "Red Deer" in 1844 at 49 lb. He was said to have weighed only 40 lb in 1840. Of modern-day jockeys, Lester Piggott at 64 lb in 1984 is the lightest.

Trainers

The greatest number of wins by a trainer is 494 in one year by Jack Van Berg in 1976, and over 4,200 in his career to 1984. The greatest amount won in a year is $4,588,897 by Charley Wittingham (US) in 1982.

Owners

The most winners by an owner in one year is 494 by Dan R. Lasater (US) in 1974, when he also won a record $3,022,960 in prize money.

Largest Grandstand

The largest at a racecourse is at Belmont Park, Long Island, NY, which seats 30,000 and is 440 yd long.

Longest Race

The longest recorded horse race was one of 1,200 miles in Portugal, won by "Emir," a horse bred from Egyptian-bred Blunt Arab stock. The holder of the world record for long distance racing and speed is "Champion Crabbet," who covered 300 miles in 52 hours 33 min, carrying 245 lb, in 1920.

ICE SKATING

Origins

The earliest skates were made of animal bones, such as those found in France and thought to be 20,000 years old. The first reference to skating is in early Norse literature *c* 200 AD but the earliest report of skating as a sport or pastime is in a British chronicle by William Fitzstephen of 1175. The first club was founded in Edinburgh in 1742, and the earliest artificial ice rink was opened in London in December 1842.

Speed skating or racing must have taken place from the earliest times, although curved rinks, especially for racing, did not appear until the 1880s. Two Americans developed figure skating into an art. E. W. Bushnell invented steel blades in 1850 and thereby provided the precision skate needed for ever more intricate figures, and the first true innovator and teacher was Jackson Haines. He was a ballet master who transferred the artistry of the dance to the ice when he went to Vienna in 1864. One of his pupils, Louis Rubinstein, was a founder of the Amateur Skating Association of Canada in 1878, the first national governing body in the world. In 1892 the International Skating Union was set up at Scheveningen, Netherlands.

Longest Race

The longest race regularly held was the "Elfstedentocht" ("Tour of the Eleven Towns") in the Netherlands, covering 200 km (124 miles 483 yd). The fastest time was 7 hours 35 min by Jeen van den Berg (b Jan 8, 1928) on Feb 3, 1954. The race has now been transferred to Lake Vesivärji near Lahti, Finland.

Largest Rink

The world's largest indoor artificial ice rink is in the Moscow Olympic indoor arena which has an ice area of 86,800 sq ft. The largest outdoors is the Fujikyu Highland Promenade Rink complex in Japan with 285,244 sq ft.

Marathon

The longest recorded skating marathon is 109 hours 5 min by Austin McKinley of Christchurch, NZ, June 21–25, 1977.

FIGURE SKATING

Most Difficult Jumps

Many of the most difficult jumps in skating are named after their originators, such as the Axel (after Axel Paulsen of Norway) and the Salchow (after Ulrich Salchow of Sweden).

The first woman to attempt a jump in major competition is said to have been Theresa Weld (US) who was reprimanded for her "unfeminine behavior" in the 1920 Olympic events. Cecilia Colledge (GB) was the first woman to achieve two turns in the air a few years later. In the 1962 World championships Donald Jackson (Can) performed the first triple Lutz in a major competition and in the 1978 championships Vern Taylor, another Canadian, achieved the first triple Axel. Among women, the first

HIGHEST SCORES in Europe and Canada were awarded to the British pair Jayne Torvill and Christopher Dean in ice dancing tournaments, and they went on to win the gold medal in the 1984 Winter Olympics.

triple Salchow was done by Sonja Morgenstern (E Ger) in 1972, and the first triple Lutz by Denise Beilmann (Swi) in the 1978 European championships. Incidentally, the latter has a spin named after her.

The first quadruple twist was performed by Marina Tcherkasova and Sergei Shakrai (USSR) in a pairs competition in Helsinki in 1977. They were able to achieve this because of the unusual difference in size between the tiny 12-year-old girl and her tall male partner.

A backward somersault jump was successfully negotiated by Terry Kubicka (US) in the 1976 world championships but it was immediately banned as being too dangerous.

Highest Marks

The highest score from a single set of marks in any world figure skating competition was gained by Jayne Torvill (b Oct 7, 1957) and Christopher Dean (b July 27, 1958) of Great Britain when awarded maximum sixes by all 9 judges for artistic presentation of their free dance "Barnum-on-ice" routine in the World Ice-Dance championships at Helsinki, Finland, Mar 12, 1983.

The highest number of maximum sixes awarded for one performance

ICE SHOW STARS: Winning the women's Olympic figure skating gold medal is a good way to capture the attention of the American public, as Dorothy Hamill (left) and Peggy Fleming (right) both discovered. Fleming won the gold in Grenoble in 1968, plus 3 world titles. Hamill's gold medal came in 1976 at Innsbruck, and she also won the world title that year. Both skaters graduated to lucrative ice show careers.

in an international championship was 13 to Torvill and Dean in the World Ice Dancing Competition in Ottawa, Canada, on Mar 24, 1984.

Donald Jackson (Canada) was awarded 7 "sixes" (the most by a soloist) in the world men's championship at Prague, Czechoslovakia, in 1962.

Distance

Robin Cousins (GB) (b Mar 17, 1957) achieved 19 ft 1 in in an Axel jump and 18 ft with a back flip at Richmond Ice Rink, Surrey, Eng on Nov 16, 1983.

World Titles

The greatest number of individual world men's figure skating titles (instituted 1896) is 10 by Ulrich Salchow (1877–1949), of Sweden, in 1901–05, 07–11. The women's record (instituted 1906) is also 10 individ-

MOVIE STAR Sonja Henie (Norway) (left) earned an estimated $47 million in ice shows and films after winning 3 Olympic golds in 1928-32-36 and 10 world titles. GOLD MEDALIST Scott Hamilton (right) was the only American ice skater to win a gold medal in the 1984 Olympics.

ual titles, by Sonja Henie (Apr 8, 1912–Oct 12, 1969), of Norway, between 1927 and 1936. Irina Rodnina (b Sept 12, 1949), of the USSR, has won 10 pairs titles (instituted 1908)—four with Aleksiy Ulanov (1969–72) and six with her husband Aleksandr Zaitsev (1973–77). The most ice dance titles (instituted 1950) won is 6 by Aleksandr Gorshkov (b Dec 8, 1946) and Ludmilla Pakhomova (b Dec 31, 1946), both of the USSR, in 1970–74 and 76.

Olympic Titles in Figure Skating

The most Olympic gold medals won by a figure skater is 3 by Gillis Grafström (1893–1938), of Sweden, in 1920, 24 and 28 (also silver medal in 1932); by Sonja Henie (see above) in 1928, 32 and 36; and by Irina Rodnina (see above) in the pairs event in 1972, 76 and 80.

The 1984 gold medal winners were: Scott Hamilton (US) in the men's singles, Katarina Witt (E Ger) in the women's singles, Elena Valova and Oleg Vasselyev (USSR) in the pairs, and Torvill and Dean (GB) in the ice dance.

Barrel Jumping

Yvon Jolin (Can) jumped over 18 barrels, a record distance of 29 ft 5 in at Terrebonne, Quebec in Jan 1981. The best jump by a female skater is 11 barrels, measuring 20 ft 4½ in by Janet Hainstock (US) in March 1980.

AMERICAN SPEEDSTERS: His unprecedented 5-event sweep of the 1980 Olympic speed skating competition made Eric Heiden (left) the first Olympic athlete to earn 5 individual (that is, not relay or team) gold medals at one Games. Sheila Young (right) achieved the rare distinction of holding world titles simultaneously in 2 different sports. In 1976, she won the 500-meter Olympic speed skating gold medal (plus a silver and a bronze), and the world sprint titles in both speed skating and cycling.

SPEED SKATING

World Titles

The greatest number of world overall titles (instituted 1893) won by any skater is 5 by Oscar Mathisen (Norway) (1888–1954) in 1908–09, 12–14, and Clas Thunberg (b Apr 5, 1893) of Finland, in 1923, 25, 28–29 and 31. The most titles won by a woman is 4 by Mrs Inga Voronina, *née* Artomonova (1936–66) of Moscow, USSR, in 1957–58, 62 and 65, and Mrs Atje Keulen-Deelstra of the Netherlands (b Dec 31, 1938) in 1970, 72–74.

The record score achieved in the world overall title is 162.973 points by Eric Heiden (US) at Oslo, Norway, Feb 10–11, 1979.

Olympic Titles

The most Olympic gold medals won in speed skating is 6 by Lidia Skoblikova (b March 8, 1939), of Chelyabinsk, USSR, in 1960 (2) and 1964 (4). The male record is held by Clas Thunberg (see above) with 5 gold (including 1 tied gold) and also 1 silver and 1 tied bronze in 1924–28;

and by Eric Heiden (US) (b June 14, 1958) who won 5 gold medals, all at Lake Placid, NY, in 1980.

The 1984 gold medal winners in men's speed skating are: Sergei Fokichev (USSR) 38.18 sec at 500 meters; Gaetan Boucher (Canada) 1 min 15.80 sec at 1,000 meters and 1 min 58.36 sec at 1,500 meters; Tomas Gustafson (Sweden) 7 min 12.28 sec in the 5,000 meters; Igor Malkov (USSR) 14 min 39.90 sec in the 10,000 meters. In the women's speed skating, Christa Rothenburger (E Ger) 41.02 sec at 500 meters; Karin Enke (E Ger) 1 min 21.61 sec at 1,000 meters and 2 min 03.42 sec at 1,500 meters; Andrea Schöne (E Ger) 4 min 24.79 sec at 3,000 meters.

WORLD SPEED SKATING RECORDS
(Ratified by the I.S.U.)

Distance	min:sec	Name and Nationality	Place	Date
MEN				
500 m	36.57*	Pavel Pegov (USSR)	Medeo, USSR	Mar 26, 1983
1,000 m	1:12.58	Pavel Pegov (USSR)	Medeo, USSR	Mar 25, 1983
1,500 m	1:53.26	Oleg Bozhyev (USSR)	Medeo, USSR	Mar 24, 1984
3,000 m	4:04.06	Dmitri Ogloblin (USSR)	Medeo, USSR	Mar 28, 1979
5,000 m	6:49.15	Victor Shoshein (USSR)	Medeo, USSR	Mar 24, 1984
10,000 m	14:17.61 (unofficial)	Konstantin Kadhov (USSR)	Medeo, USSR	Dec 31, 1982
WOMEN				
500 m	39.69	Christa Rothenburger (E Ger)	Medeo, USSR	Mar 25, 1983
1,000 m	1:19.31	Natalia Petruseva (USSR)	Medeo, USSR	Mar 26, 1983
1,500 m	2:03.34	Andrea Schöne (E Ger)	Medeo, USSR	Mar 24, 1984
3,000 m	4:20.91	Andrea Schöne (E Ger)	Medeo, USSR	Mar 23, 1984
5,000 m	7:34.52	Andrea Schöne (E Ger)	Heerenveen, Neth	Mar 24, 1984

* represents an average speed of 30.58 mph

MOST DIFFICULT JUMP-LIFT: Marina Tcherkasova was only 12 years old when she and Sergei Shakrai first performed their unique quadruple twist lift in 1977. Shakrai was only 18 years old at the time. (Popperfoto)

JUDO

Origins

Judo is a modern combat sport which developed out of an amalgam of several old Japanese fighting arts, the most popular of which was *ju-jitsu* (*jiu-jitsu*), which is thought to be of Chinese origin. Judo has developed greatly since 1882, when it was first devised by Dr. Jigoro Kano (1860–1938). World Championships were inaugurated in Tokyo on May 5, 1956. The International Judo Federation was founded in 1951.

Grades

The efficiency grades in Judo are divided into pupil (*kyu*) and master (*dan*) grades. A white belt signifies a beginning student. The next 3 grades upwards are a brown belt, and the highest grade or black belt (*dan*) is divided into 10 degrees, with the 6th, 7th and 8th entitled to wear a red and white belt, and the 9th and 10th degrees a solid red belt. The solid red has been given to only 7 men. The highest degree for a woman is 6th *dan* and only 3 Japanese have attained it.

Marathon

The longest recorded Judo marathon with continuous play by two of six Judoka in 5-minute stints is 216 hours by the Wanganui Judo Club, New Zealand, Aug 29–Sept 7, 1980.

Olympics

Included since 1964, with the exception of 1968. Only Wim Ruska (Neth) has won more than one title, with the over 93 kg and the Open classes in 1972. One of the biggest upsets to national pride in any sport occurred in 1964 when the giant 6 ft 6 in Dutchman, Anton Geesink, won the Open category in Tokyo before some 15,000 partisan Japanese spectators. Yasuhiro Yamashita (Japan) (b June 1, 1957) added to his 7-year unbeaten record by winning the Open category.

Open
1964 Anton Geesink (Neth)
1972 Wim Ruska (Neth)
1976 Haruki Uemura (Jap)
1980 Dietmar Lorenz (E Ger)
1984 Yasuhiro Yamashita (Jap)

Over 95 kg (formerly over 93 kg)
Isao Inokuma (Jap)
Wim Ruska (Neth)
Sergei Novikov (USSR)
Angelo Parisi (France)
Hitoshi Saito (Jap)

95 kg (formerly 93 kg)
1964 Not held
1972 Shota Chochoshvili (USSR)
1976 Kazuhiro Ninomiya (Jap)
1980 Robert van de Walle (Belgium)
1984 Ha Hyoung-Zoo (S Korea)

86 kg (formerly 80 kg)
Isao Okano (Jap)
Shinobu Sekine (Jap)
Isamu Sonoda (Jap)
Jürg Röthlisberger (Swi)
Peter Seisenbacher (Austria)

78 kg
1980 Shota Khabareli (USSR)
1984 Frank Wiencke (W Ger)

65 kg
Nikolai Soludkhin (USSR)
Yoshiyuki Matsucka (Japan)

70 kg (formerly 71 kg)
1964 Not held
1972 Kazutoyo Nomura (Jap)
1976 Vladimir Nevzorov (USSR)
1980 Ezio Gamba (Italy)
1984 Byeong Kuen Ahu (S Korea)

60 kg (formerly 63 kg)
Takehide Nakatani (Jap)
Takao Kawaguchi (Jap)
Hector Rodriguez (Cuba)
Thierry Ray (France)
Shinji Hosokawa (Jap)

FLIPPERS: Japan's Shinobu Sekine (above, left) beat Brian Jacks in this semi-final match enroute to the middleweight gold medal in the 1972 Olympics. Wilhelm (Wim) Ruska (right) celebrates his second gold medal in the same (1972) Games, this one in the Open division. Ruska won an additional 2 world titles.

World Champions

Judo World Championships were first held in Tokyo in 1956 and are now held biennially, but were cancelled in 1977. New weight categories were applied to the 1979 competition and there are now 8 weight classes. Women's championships were first held in NYC in 1980.

Three men have won 4 world titles. Yasuhiro Yamashita won heavyweight in 1979, 1981, 1983 and Open 1981, Wilhelm Ruska (b Aug 29, 1940) of the Netherlands won the 1967 and the 1971 heavyweight and the 1972 Olympic heavyweight and Open titles, and Shozo Fujii (Japan) (b May 12, 1950) won the middleweight title in 1971, 1973, 1975, and 1979. Ingrid Berghmans (Belgium) with 4 has won most medals by a woman, gold and bronze in 1980, gold and silver in 1982.

MIDDLEWEIGHT TITLE WINNER 4 times: Shozo Fujii (Japan) stands on his head at times. (All-Sport)

KARATE

Origins

Originally *karate* (empty hand) is known to have been developed by the unarmed populace as a method of attack on, and defense against, armed Japanese aggressors in Okinawa, Ryukyu Islands, based on techniques devised from the 6th century Chinese art of Shaolin boxing (Kempo). Transmitted to Japan in the 1920's by Funakoshi Gichin, this method of combat was refined and organized into a sport with competitive rules.

The five major schools of *karate* in Japan are *Shotokan, Wado-ryu, Goju-ryu, Shito-ryu,* and *Kyokushinkai,* each of which places different emphasis on speed, power, etc. Other styles include *Sankukai, Shotokai* and *Shukokai.* The military form of *Tae-kwan-do* with 9 *dans* is a Korean equivalent of *karate. Kung fu* is believed to have originated in Nepal or Tibet but was adopted within Chinese temples *via* India, and has in recent years been widely popularized through various martial arts films.

Wu shu is a comprehensive term embracing all Chinese martial arts.

Grades

The white belt in karate signifies beginner grade 9. As the student progresses he rises to grades 8 and 7 (yellow belt), 6 and 5 (green), 4 (purple), 3, 2, and 1 (brown) and finally black belt.

Most Titles

The only winner of 3 All-Japanese titles has been Takeshi Oishi, who won in 1969–70–71.

The leading exponents among karatekas are a number of 10th *dans* in Japan.

TWO OF THE GREATEST KARATEKAS: Masotashi Nakoyama (left) and Hirokazu Kanazawa (right) demonstrate their art.

NATIVE SPORT: Lacrosse was derived from a game played by Iroquois Indians, whose contests would cover several miles and last several days. This illustration depicts a contest between Iroquois and early Canadian settlers.

LACROSSE

Origin

The game is of American Indian origin, derived from the inter-tribal game *baggataway,* and was played by Iroquois Indians at lower Ontario, Canada, and upper NY State, before 1492. The French named it after their game of *Chouler à la crosse,* known in 1381. The game was included in the Olympic Games of 1904 and 1908, and featured as an exhibition sport in 1928 and 1948 Games.

World Championship

The US won the first two Men's World Championships, in 1967 and 1974. Canada won the third in 1978, beating the US 17–16 in overtime—this was the first drawn international match. World Championships for women were instituted in 1969, and have been contested twice. Great Britain won the first title and the US the other in 1974.

Highest Score

The highest score in any international match was US over Canada, 28–4, at Stockport, Eng, on July 3, 1978. The highest total goal output in the World Games competition was seen in Australia's win over Canada, 24–18, in the 1982 World Games in Baltimore.

USILA National Champions

The Wingate Trophy, emblematic of the championship of the US Intercollegiate Lacrosse Association, was first awarded in 1936. It is given each year in perpetual competition.

Since 1971, the NCAA assumed responsibility for national championship competition.

1881 Harvard
1882 Harvard
1883 Yale
1884 Princeton
1885 Harvard
1886 Harvard
1887 Harvard
1888 Princeton
1889 Princeton
1890 Lehigh
1891 Johns Hopkins
1892 Stevens
1893 Lehigh
1894 Stevens
1895 Lehigh
1896 Lehigh
1897 Lehigh
1898 Johns Hopkins
1899 Johns Hopkins
1900 Johns Hopkins
1901 no records
1902 Johns Hopkins
1903 Johns Hopkins
1904 Swarthmore
1905 Columbia, Cornell, Harvard, Swarthmore
1906 Cornell, Johns Hopkins
1907 Cornell, Johns Hopkins
1908 Harvard, Johns Hopkins
1909 Harvard, Columbia, Johns Hopkins
1910 Harvard, Swarthmore
1911 Harvard, Johns Hopkins
1912 Harvard
1913 Harvard, Johns Hopkins
1914 Cornell, Lehigh
1915 Harvard, Johns Hopkins
1916 Cornell, Lehigh
1917 Stevens, Lehigh
1918 Stevens, Johns Hopkins
1919 Johns Hopkins
1920 Syracuse, Lehigh
1921 Lehigh
1922 Syracuse
1923 Johns Hopkins
1924 Syracuse, Johns Hopkins
1925 Syracuse, Maryland
1926 Johns Hopkins
1927 Johns Hopkins
1928 Johns Hopkins, Maryland, Rutgers, Navy
1929 Navy, Union*
1930 St. John's
1931 Johns Hopkins

1932 No champion†
1933 No champion#
1934 No champion‡
1935 No champion§
1936 Maryland
1937 Maryland, Princeton
1938 Navy
1939 Maryland
1940 Maryland
1941 Johns Hopkins
1942 Princeton
1943 Navy
1944 Army
1945 Army, Navy
1946 Navy
1947 Johns Hopkins
1948 Johns Hopkins
1949 Johns Hopkins, Navy
1950 Johns Hopkins
1951 Army, Princeton
1952 Virginia, RPI
1953 Princeton
1954 Navy
1955 Maryland
1956 Maryland
1957 Johns Hopkins
1958 Army
1959 Army, Maryland, Johns Hopkins
1960 Navy
1961 Army, Navy
1962 Navy
1963 Navy
1964 Navy
1965 Navy
1966 Navy
1967 Maryland, Navy, Johns Hopkins
1968 Johns Hopkins
1969 Johns Hopkins, Army
1970 Johns Hopkins, Navy, Virginia
1971 Cornell
1972 Virginia
1973 Maryland
1974 Johns Hopkins
1975 Maryland
1976 Cornell
1977 Cornell
1978 Johns Hopkins
1979 Johns Hopkins
1980 Johns Hopkins
1981 North Carolina
1982 North Carolina
1983 Syracuse
1984 Johns Hopkins

* St. John's, not a member of the USILA, generally was recognized as the national champion but was ineligible for official recognition.
† Johns Hopkins won Olympic playoff.
# Johns Hopkins, Princeton, Dartmouth were undefeated. Hopkins played strongest schedule.
‡ Johns Hopkins, Maryland, St. John's each won all games but one.
§ St. John's, Maryland, Navy each won all games but one, while Princeton was unbeaten. St. John's played strongest schedule.

CHAMPS: The Tar Heels of North Carolina rose to the top in 1981 and 1982 over defending champion Johns Hopkins in the NCAA championship game, but Johns Hopkins came back in 1984.

Collegiate

Johns Hopkins University has won or shared 39 national championships.

John Cheek (Washington College) netted 200 career goals, while Doug Fry (Maryland-Baltimore County) holds the collegiate record with 70 goals in one season.

Rick Gilbert (Hobart) holds the USILA record for single season assists (88) and points (122). He also holds career records with 287 assists and a remarkable 444 points.

Jeff Singer made a record 909 career saves as goaltender for MIT.

Women's Championship

The Association for Intercollegiate Athletics for Women (founded 1971) and the US Women's Lacrosse Association (founded 1931) jointly sponsored collegiate championships from 1978 to 1980. In 1981, the tournament was run solely by the A.I.A.W. Since then it has been sponsored by the National Collegiate Athletic Association.

1978 Penn State	1980 Penn State	1982 Massachusetts	1984 Temple
1979 Penn State	1981 Maryland	1983 Delaware	

DOUBLE VICTORIES: Candy Finn (in white) achieved an unusual double when Penn State won the AIAW titles in both field hockey and lacrosse. Finn scored the winning goals in both championship games.

Lacrosse ◆ 161

MODERN PENTATHLON

Origins

In the ancient Olympics the Pentathlon was the most prestigious event of the Games. Traditionally inspired by the city of Sparta, it consisted of the discus and javelin throws, running, jumping and wrestling, and the competitors were eulogized by Aristotle. The concept of the five-event all-round sporting contest was held dear by the founder of the modern Games, Baron de Coubertin, but it was not until 1912 that it was first held. The events of the Modern Pentathlon are riding (an 800 meter course with 15 fences), fencing, shooting, swimming (300 meter freestyle), and finally a 4000 meter cross-country run, each event held on a different day. There is a story that the competitor is supposed to represent a King's messenger. First he rides like the wind to outdistance his pursuers, then when his horse is brought down, he fences his way out of trouble, following up with some good shooting to drive back the enemy's reserves. Then he crosses the final obstacle, a river, and finally runs home to deliver his message. Certainly the qualities required of a Modern Pentathlete are not far removed from those of the messenger in the story. Points are awarded for each activity and the winner is the one with the highest total after the five events. Initially only military personnel competed, but since the founding of the Union Internationale de Pentathlon Moderne et Biathlon (UIPMB) in 1948 non-military competitors have been allowed.

RIDE, FENCE, SHOOT, SWIM AND RUN: András Balczó (left) of Hungary won a record 6 world titles and 3 Olympic gold medals (team) as well as the 1972 Olympic individual title, an extraordinary feat in this multifaceted event. Lars Hall (right) of Sweden has won 2 individual Olympic golds, 1952 and 1956.

Most World Championship Titles

World championships were first held in 1949 and annually since, except in Olympic years, when the Olympic and world titles are held simultaneously.

The record number of world titles won is 6 by András Balczó (Hungary) in 1963, 65–67 and 69, and the Olympic title in 1972.

Olympic Titles

The greatest number of Olympic gold medals won is three by Balczó, a member of Hungary's winning team in 1960 and 68, and the 1972 individual champion. Lars Hall (Sweden) uniquely has won two individual championships (1952 and 56). Pavel Lednev (USSR) (b Mar 25, 1943) has won a record 7 medals (2 gold, 2 silver, 3 bronze), 1968–80.

Probably the greatest margin of victory was by William Oscar Guernsey Grut (b Sept 17, 1914) (Sweden) in the 1948 Games in London, when he won three events and placed fifth and eighth in the other two events.

The gold medal winner in 1984 was Daniele Masala of Italy with 5,469 points. The Italian team won with 16,060 points, the highest number of points scored in any Games.

Highest Scores

Point scores in riding, fencing, cross-country and hence overall scores have no comparative value between one competition and another. In shooting and swimming (300 m), where measurements are absolute, the point scores are of record significance.

	Points	Name and Nationality	Date and Place
Shooting			
200/200	—[1]	Charles Leonard (US) (b Feb 23, 1913)	Aug 3, 1936 W Berlin, Germ
200/200	1,132	Daniele Masala (Italy) (b Feb 12, 1955)	Aug 21, 1978 Jönkoping, Swed
200/200	1,132	Geo Horvath (Swed) (b Mar 14, 1960)	July 22, 1980 Moscow, USSR
Swimming			
3 min 08.22 sec	1,368	John Scott (US)	Aug 27, 1982 London, Eng

[1] points not given in 1936 Olympic Games.

MOTORCYCLING *

Earliest Races and Circuits

The first motorcycle race was held on an oval track of 1 mi at Sheen House, Richmond, Surrey, England, on Nov 29, 1897, won by Charles Jarrott (1877–1944) on a Fournier.

In the early days many races were for both motorcycles and cars, and often took the form of long-distance inter-city or inter-country events. These were heavily criticized following the aborted Paris to Madrid race of 1903 which resulted in a number of deaths of competitors and spectators. In 1904 the International Cup Race was held in France for motorcycles only, and on a closed road circuit. However, in 1905 the race was held again, and this is recognized as the first international motorcycling event. The venue was Dourdon near Paris, and it was organized by the newly formed Fédération Internationale des Clubs Motocyclistes (FICM), the predecessor of the Fédération Internationale Motocycliste (FIM). The race was a success and was won by an Austrian named Wondrick.

The Auto-Cycle Union Tourist Trophy (TT) series was first held on the 15.81-mile "Peel" ("St John's") course on the Isle of Man on May 28, 1907, and is still run on the island, on the "Mountain" circuit.

The 37.73-mile "Mountain" circuit, over which the two main TT races have been run since 1911, has 264 curves and corners and is the longest used for any motorcycle race.

Fastest Circuits

The highest average lap speed attained on any closed circuit is 160.288 mph by Yvon du Hamel (Canada) (b 1941) on a modified 903-cc four-cylinder Kawasaki Z1 on the 31-degree banked 2.5-mile Daytona International Speedway, Fla, in March 1973. His lap time was 56.149 sec.

The fastest road circuit is the Francorchamps circuit near Spa, Bel-

DOUBLE WINNER: World champion Barry Sheene (GB) holds both the lap and race records for the Belgian Grand Prix, the road race held at Francorchamps, the world's fastest circuit.

---

* For more detailed information about motorcycling, see *The Guinness Book of Motorcycling Facts and Feats,* available from Sterling.

gium. It is 14.12 km (8 miles 1,340 yd) in length and was lapped in 3 min 50.3 sec (average speed of 137.150 mph) by Barry S. F. Sheene (b Holborn, London, England, Sept 11, 1950) on a 495-cc four-cylinder Suzuki during the Belgian Grand Prix on July 3, 1977.

The TT circuit speed record is 116.19 mph by Norman Brown on a Suzuki on June 10, 1983.

Fastest Race

The fastest track race in the world was held at Grenzlandring, W Germany, in 1939. It was won by Georg "Schorsh" Meier (b Germany Nov 9, 1910) at an average speed of 134 mph on a supercharged 495-cc flat-twin BMW.

The fastest road race is the 500-cc Belgian Grand Prix on the Francorchamps circuit (see above). The record time for this 10-lap 87.74-mile race is 38 min 58.5 sec (average speed of 135.068 mph) by Barry Sheene (UK) on a 495-cc four-cylinder Suzuki on July 3, 1977.

Longest Race

The longest race is the Liège 24 Hours. The greatest distance ever covered is 2,761.9 miles (average speed 115.08 mph) by Jean-Claude Chemarin and Christian Leon of France on a 941-cc four-cylinder Honda on the Francorchamps circuit on Aug 14–15, 1976 (see above).

Most Successful Machines

Italian MV-Agusta motorcycles won 37 world championships between 1952 and 1973 and 276 world championship races between 1952 and 1976. Japanese Honda machines won 29 world championship races and 5 world championships in 1966. In the 7 years Honda contested the championship (1961–67) its annual average was 20 race wins. In the sidecar class BMW machines won an unprecedented 19 consecutive championships between 1955 and 1973.

Speed Records

Official world speed records must be set with two runs over a measured distance within a time limit (one hour for FIM records, two hours for AMA records).

Donald Vesco (b Loma Linda, Calif, Apr 8, 1939) riding his 21-ft-long *Lightning Bolt* streamliner, powered by two 1,016-cc Kawasaki engines on Bonneville Salt Flats, Utah, on Aug 28, 1978, set AMA and FIM absolute records with an overall average of 318.598 mph and had a fastest run at an average of 318.66 mph.

The world record average speed for two runs over 1 km (1,093.6 yd) from a standing start is 16.68 sec by Henk Vink (b July 24, 1939) (Netherlands) on his supercharged 984-cc 4-cylinder Kawasaki, at Elvington Airfield, Yorkshire, England, on July 24, 1977. The faster run was made in 16.09 sec.

The world record for two runs over 440 yd from a standing start is 8.805 sec by Henk Vink on his supercharged 1,132-cc 4-cylinder Kawasaki, at Elvington Airfield, Yorkshire, England, on July 23, 1977. The faster run was made in 8.55 sec.

The fastest time for a single run over 440 yd from a standing start is 7.08 sec by Bo O'Brechta (US) riding a supercharged 1,200-cc Kawasaki-

QUICK AS A VINK: Henk Vink (Neth) set the world record for 1 kilometer by averaging 16.68 sec in his 2-way run. The faster run was made in 16.09 secs. He also set the record for 440 yd in 8.805 sec.

based machine at Ontario, Calif, in 1980. The highest terminal velocity recorded at the end of a 440-yd run from a standing start is 201.34 mph by Elmer Trett at Indianapolis, on Sept 5, 1983.

World Championships

Races are currently held for the following classes of motorcycles: 50 cc, 125 cc, 250 cc, 350 cc, 500 cc, and sidecars.

Most world championship titles (instituted by the *Fédération Internationale Motocycliste* in 1949) won are 15 by Giacomo Agostini (b Lovere, Italy, June 16, 1942) in the 350-cc class 1968–74 and in the 500-cc class 1966–72 and 75. Agostini is the only man to win two world championships in five consecutive years (350 and 500 cc titles 1968–72). Agostini won 122 races in the world championship series between Apr 24, 1965, and Aug 29, 1976, including a record 19 in 1970, also achieved by Stanley Michael Bailey "Mike" Hailwood, (b Oxford, England, Apr 2, 1940) in 1966.

Yrjo Vesterinen (Finland) won a record 3 world trials championships, 1976–8. Samuel Hamilton Miller (b Belfast, N Ireland, Nov 11, 1935) won 11 A-CU Solo Trials Drivers' Stars in 1959–69.

Klaus Enders (Germany) (b 1937) won 6 world sidecar titles, 1967, 69–70, 72–74.

Joël Robert (b Chatelet, Belgium, Nov 11, 1943) has won six 250-cc moto-cross (also known as "scrambles") world championships (1964, 68–72). Between Apr 25, 1964, and June 18, 1972, he won a record fifty 250-cc Grands Prix. He became the youngest moto-cross world champion on July 12, 1964, when he won the 250-cc championship aged 20 years 244 days.

Alberto "Johnny" Cecotto (b Caracas, Venezuela, Jan 25, 1956) was the youngest person to win a world championship. He was aged 19 years 211 days when he won the 350-cc title on Aug 24, 1975. The oldest was Hermann-Peter Müller (1909–76) of W Germany, who won the 250-cc title in 1955, aged 46.

Moto-Cross (Scrambling)

This is a very specialized sport in which the competitors race over rough country including steep climbs and drops, sharp turns, sand, mud and water. The sport originated in Eng, in 1924 when some riders competed in "a rare old scramble." Until the second World War it remained mainly a British interest but the Moto-Cross des Nations was inaugurated in 1947, and became an annual event, with the current rules formulated in 1963. In 1961 the Trophée des Nations, for 250 cc machines, was introduced by the FIM. World championships had been instituted in 1957. The most titles won are six by Joël Robert (Belgium) between 1964 and 1972, during which period he also won a record fifty 250 cc Grands Prix. The youngest to win a world championship was Joël Robert (Belgium) who was 20 yr 8 months when he won the 250 cc title in 1964. *Winners from 1970:*

Moto-Cross des Nations	*Trophée des Nations*
1970 Sweden	1970 Belgium
1971 Sweden	1971 Belgium
1972 Belgium	1972 Belgium
1973 Belgium	1973 Belgium
1974 Sweden	1974 Belgium
1975 Czechoslovakia	1975 Belgium
1976 Belgium	1976 Belgium
1977 Belgium	1977 Belgium
1978 USSR	1978 Belgium
1979 Belgium	1979 USSR
1980 Belgium	1980 Belgium
1981 US	1981 US
1982 US	1982 US
1983 US	1983 US

MOTO-CROSS RACE in process. André Malherbe (Belgium) almost takes flight on his way to victory in the 500-cc contest in 1980.

CONQUEROR OF MT. EVEREST NO. 24: No, it's not the abominable snowman, and it's not an alien. It's Teruo Matsuura atop the mountain on May 11, 1970. Bitter cold, high winds and thin air make heavy clothing and oxygen important aids.

MOUNTAINEERING

Origins

Although bronze-age artifacts have been found on the summit (9,605 ft) of the Riffelhorn, Switzerland, mountaineering, as a sport, has a continuous history dating back only to 1854. Isolated instances of climbing for its own sake exist back to the 13th century. The Atacamenans built sacrificial platforms near the summit of Llullaillaco in South America (22,058 ft) in late pre-Columbian times, c. 1490.

Greatest Wall

The highest final stage in any wall climb is that on the south face of Annapurna I (26,545 ft). It was climbed by the British expedition led by Christian John Storey Bonington (UK) (b Aug 6, 1934) when from Apr 2–May 27, 1970, Donald Whillans, 36, and Dougal Haston, 27, scaled to the summit. They used 18,000 ft of rope.

The longest wall climb is on the Rupal-Flank from the base camp at 11,680 ft to the South Point (26,384 ft) of Nanga Parbat—a vertical ascent of 14,704 ft. This was scaled by the Austro-Germano-Italian Expedition led by Dr Karl Maria Herrligkoffer in Apr 1970.

The most demanding free climbs are those rated at 5.13, the premier location for these being in the Yosemite Valley, Calif.

Mount Everest

Mount Everest (29,028 ft) was first climbed at 11:30 a.m. on May 29, 1953, when the summit was reached by Edmund Percival Hillary (b July 20, 1919), of New Zealand, and the Sherpa, Tenzing Norgay (b as Namgyal Wangdi, in Nepal in 1914, formerly called Tenzing Khumjung Bhutia). The successful expedition was led by Col (later Hon Brigadier) Henry Cecil John Hunt (b June 22, 1910).

The first climber to succeed three times was the Sherpa, Sundare (or Sungdare) on Oct 5, 1982. The first to succeed via three different routes was Yasuo Kato (Japan) (1949–82), who died shortly after his third ascent on Dec 27, 1982.

Franz Oppurg (1948–81) (Austria) was the first to make the final ascent solo, on May 14, 1978, while Reinhold Messner (Italy) was the first to make the entire climb solo on Aug 20, 1980. Messner and Peter Habeler (b July 22, 1942) (Austria) made the first entirely oxygen-less ascent on May 8, 1978.

Four women have reached the summit, the first being Junko Tabei (b Sept 22, 1939) (Japan) on May 16, 1975. The oldest person was Dr Gerhard Schmatz (W Germany) (b June 5, 1929) aged 50 years 88 days on Oct 1, 1979.

Reinhold Messner, with his ascent of Kangchenjunga in 1982, became the first person to climb the world's three highest mountains, having earlier reached the summits of Everest and K2. He has successfully scaled a record 7 of the world's 14 main summits of over 8,000 m (26,250 ft).

Highest Bivouac

Two Japanese, Hironobu Kamuro (1951–83) and Hiroshi Yoshino (1950–83), bivouacked at 28,870 ft on Mt. Everest on the night of Oct 8/9, 1983. Yoshino died on Oct 9 while Kamuro died either during the bivouac night or next day.

Progressive Mountaineering Altitude Records

ft	Mountain	Climbers	Date	
17,887	Popocatépetl, Mexico	Francisco Montano		1521
18,400	Mana Pass, Zaskar Range, Kashmir	A. de Andrade, M. Morques	July	1624
18,893	On Chimborazo, Ecuador	Dr. Alexander Von Humboldt, Aimé Bonpland, Carlos Montufar	June 23	1802
19,411	On Leo Pargyal Range, Himalaya	Garrard and Lloyd		1818
22,260	On E. Abi Gamin, Garhwal Himalaya	A. & R. Schlagintweit	Aug	1855
22,606	Pioneer Peak on Baltoro Kangri, Kashmir	William M. Conway, Matthias Zurbiggen	Aug 23	1892
22,834	Aconcagua, Andes	Matthias Zurbriggen	Jan 14	1897
23,394	On Pyramis Peak, Karakoram, Tibet	William H. Workman, J. Petigax Snr & Jnr, C. Savoie	Aug 12	1903
23,787	On Gurla Mandhata, Tibet	Thomas G. Longstaff, Alexis & Henri Brocherel	July 23	1905
c.23,900	On Kabru, Sikkim-Nepal	Carl W. Rubenson and Monrad Aas	Oct 20	1907
24,607	On Chogolisa, Karakoram, Tibet	Duke of the Abruzzi, J. Petigax, H. & E. Brocherel	July 18	1909
c.24,900	Camp V. Everest. Tibet-Nepal	G. L. Mallory, E. F Norton, T. H. Somervell, H. T. Morshead	May 20	1922
26,986	On Everest (North Face), Tibet	George L. Mallory, Edward F. Norton, T. Howard Somervell	May 21	1922
c.27,300	On Everest (North Face), Tibet	George I. Finch, J. Granville Bruce	May 27	1922
28,126	On Everest (North Face), Tibet	Edward Felix Norton	June 4	1924
28,215	South Shoulder on Everest, Nepal	Raymond Lambert, Tenzing Norgay	May 28	1952
28,721	South Shoulder on Everest, Nepal	Thomas D. Bourdillon, Robert C. Evans	May 26	1953
29,028	Everest, Nepal-Tibet	Edmund P. Hillary, Tenzing Norgay	May 29	1953

OLYMPIC GAMES

Note: These records include the un-numbered Games held at Athens in 1906. World Records set at the 1984 Olympiad in Los Angeles will be found under each sport.

Origins

The earliest celebration of the ancient Olympic Games of which there is a certain record is that of July 776 BC (when Coroibos, a cook from Elis, won a foot race), though their origin probably dates from perhaps as early as *c.* 1370 BC. The ancient Games were terminated by an order issued in Milan in 393 AD by Theodosius I, "the Great" (*c.* 346–95), Emperor of Rome. At the instigation of Pierre de Fredi, Baron de Coubertin (1863–1937), the Olympic Games of the modern era were inaugurated in Athens on Apr 6, 1896.

Olympic Sports

There are 21 different sports currently on the Summer Games program and eight on the Winter Games schedule, as follows (with year of first inclusion):

Summer

Archery (1900)
Basketball (1936)
Boxing (1904)
Canoeing (1936)
Cycling (1896)
Equestrianism (1900)
Fencing (1896)
Field Hockey (1908)
Gymnastics (1896)
Handball (1972)
Judo (1964)
Modern Pentathlon (1912)
Rowing (1900)
Shooting (1896)
Soccer (1900)

Swimming (including Diving & Water Polo) (1896)
Track and Field (1896)
Volleyball (1964)
Weightlifting (1896)
Wrestling (1896)
Yachting (1900)

Winter

Alpine Skiing (1936)
Bobsledding (1924)
Figure Skating (1908)
Ice Hockey (1920)
Nordic Skiing (including Ski-jumping & Biathlon) (1924)
Speed Skating (1924)
Luging (Tobogganing) (1964)

Most Medals

In the ancient Olympic Games, victors were given a chaplet (head garland) of olive leaves. Leonidas of Rhodos won 12 running titles from 164 to 152 BC.

The most individual gold medals won by a male competitor in the modern Games is 10 by Raymond Clarence Ewry (US) (b Oct 14, 1874, at Lafayette, Ind; d Sept 27, 1937), a jumper (see *Track and Field*). The female record is seven by Vera Caslavska-Odlozil (b May 3, 1942) of Czechoslovakia (also see *Gymnastics*).

The only Olympian to win 4 consecutive individual titles in the same event has been Alfred A. Oerter (b Sept 19, 1936, NYC) who won the discus title in 1956, 60, 64 and 68.

The only man to win a gold medal in both the Summer and Winter Games is Edward F. Eagan (US) (1898–1967) who won the 1920 light-heavyweight boxing title and was a member of the winning four-man bob in 1932.

Gymnast Larissa Latynina (b Dec 27, 1934) (USSR) won a record 18

HIS MEDALS RESTORED: Jim Thorpe, the American Indian who pole-vaulted to a gold medal in the decathlon of the 1912 Olympics (above) and a second gold that year, only to have them revoked because he had once received $25 for playing semi-pro baseball, received his medals back post-mortem in 1982, seventy years later.

medals (see *Gymnastics*). The record at one celebration is 8 medals by gymnast Aleksandr Ditiatin (b Aug 7, 1957) (USSR) in 1980.

Most Olympic Gold Medals at One Games

Mark Spitz (US), the swimmer, won a record 7 gold medals at one celebration (4 individual and 3 relay) at Munich in 1972.

The most gold medals won in individual events at one celebration is 5 by speed skater Eric Heiden (b June 14, 1958) (US) at Lake Placid, NY in 1980.

Olympic Medals Restored

The star of the 1912 Olympic Games was an American Indian named Jim Thorpe. Held in Stockholm, the Games provided him with an opportunity to win two gold medals, one in the decathlon and one in the pentathlon. He also placed well in the high jump and long jump. He was greeted in New York with a ticker-tape parade, but in 1913 the International Olympic Committee demanded his medals back after it had come to light that prior to the Olympics he had played baseball for $25 a week and therefore was not strictly an amateur athlete. On Oct 13, 1982, 29 years after Thorpe's death, the I.O.C. presented his gold medals to his children and reinstated his name in the record books.

Youngest and Oldest Medalists

The youngest woman to win a gold medal is Marjorie Gestring (US) (b Nov 18, 1922) aged 13 years 9 months, in the 1936 women's springboard event.

The oldest person was Oscar Swahn (Swe) who won a silver medal for shooting in 1920, aged 72 years 280 days. Swahn had won a gold medal in 1912 at the record age of 65 years 258 days.

The youngest male to win an Olympic gold medal was a French boy who coxed the winning Dutch rowing pairs crew in the 1900 Games. His name is not known as he was a last-minute substitute but he was no more than 10 years old and may even have been as young as seven.

Longest Span

The longest competitive span of any Olympic competitor is 40 years by Dr Ivan Osiier (Denmark) (1888–1965), in fencing, 1908–32 and 48, and by Magnus Konow (Norway) (1887–1972) in yachting, 1908–20 and 36–48. The longest span for a woman is 24 years (1932–56) by the Austrian fencer Ellen Müller-Preiss. Raimondo d'Inzeo (b Feb 8, 1925) competed for Italy in equestrian events in a record 8 celebrations (1948–76), gaining one gold medal, 2 silver and 3 bronze medals. Janice Lee York Romary (b Aug 6, 1928), the US fencer, competed in all 6 Games from 1948 to 1968, and Lia Manoliu (Romania) (b Apr 25, 1932) competed 1952–72, winning the discus title in 1968.

Largest Crowd

The largest crowd at any Olympic site was 150,000 at the 1952 ski-jumping at the Holmenkollen, outside Oslo, Norway. Estimates of the number of spectators of the marathon race through Tokyo on Oct 21, 1964, have ranged from 500,000 to 1,500,000.

Most and Fewest Competitors

The greatest number of competitors in any Summer Olympic Games has been 7,147 at Munich in 1972. A record 122 countries competed in the 1972 Munich Games. The fewest was 311 competitors from 13 countries in 1896. In 1904 only 12 countries participated. The largest team was 880 men and 4 women from France at the 1900 Games in Paris.

Most Participations

Four countries have never failed to be represented at the 20 celebrations of the Summer Games: Australia, Greece, Great Britain and Switzerland. Of these, only Great Britain has been present at all Winter celebrations as well.

National Medals

Although tables of medals by countries are frowned upon by the Olympic authorities—the Games are, in their eyes, for individuals—such compilations are nevertheless of considerable interest. The lists below give the top 10 countries, by total medals, in the Summer and in the Winter Games from 1896 to 1984. It should be noted that the GDR (or East Germany) was only counted separately from 1968.

KING MEETS DUKE: In the 1912 Olympics in Stockholm, King Gustavus V presented Duke Kahanamoku of Hawaii—his first name was Duke—with the gold medal he won in the 100-m freestyle swim. No Games in 1916 but in 1920 Duke won the gold again, and a silver in 1924 when Johnny Weissmuller outswam him.

Summer Games 1896–1984

	Gold	Silver	Bronze	Total
US*	627†	468	417	1512
USSR	340	292	253	885
Great Britain*	163	201	176	540
Germany	129	174	169	472
France	142	156	155	453
Sweden	129	125	156	410
Hungary	113	106	130	349
Italy	127	111	108	346
E Germany	116	94	97	307
Finland	92	72	102	266

Winter Games 1924–1984

	Gold	Silver	Bronze	Total
USSR	68	48	50	166
Norway	54	57	52	163
US	40	46	31	117
Finland	29	42	32	103
Austria	25	33	30	88
Sweden	32	25	29	86
E Germany	30	26	29	85
Germany	24	22	21	67
Switzerland	18	20	20	58
Canada	12	10	15	37
France	12	10	15	37

The Games of the XXIII Olympiad were held in Los Angeles from July 28 to Aug 12, 1984. A record 140 countries and about 7,400 athletes participated. Total spectator attendance was given as a record 5,767,923 including 1,421,627 for soccer and 1,129,465 for track and field events. The highest attendance for one event was 101,799 at the Rose Bowl, Pasadena for the soccer final in which France beat Brazil 2–0. The 1984 Games generated a surplus of $215 million for the LA Organizing Committee which will be paid out to amateur athletic organizations in the US, if all goes according to plan.

The medal results:

	Gold	Silver	Bronze	Total
US	83	61	30	174
West Germany	17	19	23	59
Romania	20	16	17	53
Canada	10	18	16	44
Great Britain	5	11	21	37

* Excludes medals won in official art competitions, 1912–48.
† The International Olympic Committee, on Oct 13, 1982, agreed to restore the 2 gold medals won by James F. Thorpe (1888–1953) in the 1912 decathlon and pentathlon.

Olympic Games ◆ 173

ORIENTEERING

Origins

Orienteering is basically a combination of cross-country running and map reading. Competitors in this unrenowned sport are given a map, marked with the locations of control points, and a compass. In some versions of the sport, the control points must be achieved in specified order, and the fastest time wins. In other versions, a time limit is declared and point values are assigned to the control points, so competitors must decide which control points they can get to to amass the highest score.

Orienteering as now known was invented by Major Ernst Killander in Sweden in 1918. It was based on military exercises of the 1890's. The term was first used for an event at Oslo, Norway, on October 7, 1900.

World Championships

World championships were inaugurated in 1966 and are held biennially under the auspices of the International Orienteering Federation (founded 1961), located in Sweden. The US Orienteering Federation was founded in 1971 to serve as the governing body for the sport in America and to choose teams for world championship competition. Winners:

	Men's Individual	*Women's Individual*
1966	Aage Hadler (Nor)	Ulla Lindqvist (Swe)
1968	Karl Johansson (Swe)	Ulla Lindqvist (Swe)
1970	Stig Berge (Nor)	Ingred Hadler (Nor)
1972	Aage Hadler (Nor)	Sarolta Monspart (Fin)
1974	Bernt Frilen (Swe)	Mona Norgaard (Den)
1976	Egil Johansen (Nor)	Liisa Veijalainen (Fin)
1978	Egil Johansen (Nor)	Anne Berit Eid (Nor)
1979	Oyvin Thon (Nor)	Outi Bergonstrom (Fin)
1981	Oyvin Thon (Nor)	Annichen Kringstad (Swe)
1983	Morton Berglia (Nor)	Annichen Kringstad-Svennson (Swe)

Sweden has won the men's relay six times between 1966 and 1979 and the women's relay six times, 1966, 1970, 1974–6, 1981 and 1983.

U.S. Champions

1973	Jerry Rice, Quantico	Heidi Green, Trojan OC, NC
1974–75	Bob Turbyfill, Quantico	Cindy Prince (Fuller), Grazoo
1975–76	Bob Turbyfill, Quantico	Joannie Pezdir (Gunther), Quantico
1976–77	Peter Gagarin, New Eng	Jenny Tuthill, New Eng
1977	Peter Gagarin, New Eng	Sharon Crawford, New Eng
1978	Peter Gagarin, New Eng	Sharon Crawford, New Eng
1979	Peter Gagarin, New Eng	Sharon Crawford, New Eng
1980	Eric Weyman, Hudson Valley	Sharon Crawford, New Eng
1981	Eric Weyman, Hudson Valley	Sharon Crawford, New Eng
1982	Eric Weyman, Hudson Valley	Sharon Crawford, New Eng
1983	Peter Gagarin, New Eng	Virginia Lehman, New Eng

OUT OF THE WOODS: Sweden's Ulla Lindqvist won back-to-back women's orienteering world titles.

LANDING ON A DIME: Staff Sergeant Dwight Reynolds of the Golden Knights at Fort Bragg, NC demonstrates accuracy landing. Reynolds holds the record of 105 day-time dead centers.

PARACHUTING

Origins

Parachuting became a regulated sport with the institution of world championships in 1951. A team title was introduced in 1954, and women's events were included in 1956.

Most Titles

The USSR won the men's team titles in 1954, 58, 60, 66, 72, 76, 80, and the women's team titles in 1956, 58, 66, 68, 72, 76. Nikolai Ushamyev (USSR) has won the individual title twice, 1974 and 1980.

Most Jumps

The greatest number of consecutive jumps completed in 24 hours is 236 by Alan Jones (Capt America) of Bellevue, Wash, over Issaquah Parachute Center near Seattle, July 13–14, 1984.

A record 10,000 jumps have been made by Yuri Baranov (USSR) and Anatoli Ossipov (USSR) to the end of 1980. The women's record is 8,000 by Valentina Zakoretskaya (USSR) 1964–80.

First from Tower	Louis-Sébastien Lenormand (1757–1839)	quasi-parachute	Montpellier, France	1783
First from Balloon	André-Jacques Garnerin (1769–1823)	2,230 ft	Monçeau Park, Paris	Oct 22, 1797
First from Aircraft (man)	"Capt" Albert Berry	aerial exhibitionist	St Louis	Mar 1, 1912
(woman)	Mrs Georgina "Tiny" Broadwick		Griffith Park, Los Angeles	June 21, 1913
First Free Fall	Mrs Georgina "Tiny" Broadwick	pilot, Glenn L. Martin	North Island, San Diego	Sept 13, 1914
Lowest Escape	Squad Leader T. Spencer, RAF	30–40 ft	Wismar Bay, Baltic Sea	Apr 19, 1945
Longest Duration Fall	Lt Col Wm. H. Rankin, USMC	40 min, due to thermals	North Carolina	July 26, 1956
Highest Escape	Flt Lt J. de Salis and Fg Off P. Lowe, RAF	56,000 ft	Monyash, Derby, Eng	Apr 9, 1958
Longest Delayed Drop (man)	Capt Joseph W. Kittinger[1]	84,700 ft (16.04 miles) from balloon at 102,800 ft	Tularosa, NM	Aug 16, 1960
(woman)	O. Kommissarova (USSR)	46,250 ft	over USSR	Sept 21, 1965
(civilian)	R. W. K. Beckett (GB) and Harry Ferguson (GB)	30,000 ft from 32,000 ft	D. F. Malan Airport, Capetown, So Africa	Nov 23, 1969
Most Southerly	T/Sgt Richard J. Patton (d 1973)	Operation Deep Freeze	South Pole	Nov 25, 1956
Most Northerly	Dr Jack Wheeler (US)	Pilot, Capt Rocky Parsons (−25 °F)	In Lat 90° 00′ N	Apr 15, 1981
Highest Landing	Ten USSR parachutists[2]	23,405 ft	Lenina Peak	May 1969
Heaviest Load	US Space Shuttle Columbia (external rocket retrieval)	80 ton capacity triple array each 120 ft dia	Atlantic, off Cape Canaveral, Fla	Apr 12, 1981
Highest from Bridge	Donald R. Boyles	1,053 ft	Royal Gorge, Colo	Sept 7, 1970
Highest Tower Jump	Herbert Leo Schmidtz (US)	KTUL-TV Mast 1,984 ft	Tulsa, Okla	Oct 4, 1970
Connected Free Fall (Biggest Star)	72-man team	Formation held 3.4 sec (FAI rules)	De Land, Fla	Apr 3, 1983
Highest Column	14-member team		Zephyrhills, Fla	Oct 1981
Most Traveled	Kevin Seaman from a Cessna Skylane (pilot, Charles Merritt)	12,186 miles	Jumps in all 50 US states	July 26–Oct 15, 1972
Oldest Man	Edwin C. Townsend	85 years 1 day	Riverview, Fla	Feb 6, 1982
Oldest Woman	Mrs Stella Davenport (GB)	75 years 8 mos	Humberside, Eng	June 27, 1981

[1] Maximum speed in rarefied air was 625.2 mph at 90,000 ft—marginally supersonic. [2] Four were killed.

Greatest Accuracy

Jacqueline Smith (GB) (b March 29, 1951) scored ten consecutive dead center strikes (4-inch disk) in the World Championships at Zagreb, Yugoslavia, September 1, 1978. At Yuma, Arizona, in March, 1978, Dwight Reynolds scored a record 105 daytime dead centers, and Bill Wenger and Phil Munden tied with 43 nighttime DCs, competing as members of the US Army team, the Golden Knights. With electronic measuring the official FAI record is 50 DCs by Alexander Aasmiae (USSR) at Ferghana, USSR, in October, 1979.

The Men's Night Accuracy Landing Record on an electronic score pad is 27 consecutive dead centers by Cliff Jones (US) in 1981.

ELEPHANT POLO: Polo was first played on elephant-back in Jaipur, India in 1976. The World Elephant Polo Association was formed on Apr 1, 1982 and their first championships were staged at Tiger Tops, Nepal on Apr 1, 1983, when the winners were the Tiger Tops Tuskers captained by Mark Payne. The Hurlingham Polo Association "takes no cognisance" of elephant polo.

POLO

Earliest Games

Polo is usually regarded as being of Persian origin, having been played as *Pulu c.* 525 BC. Other claims have come from Tibet and the Tang dynasty of China 250 AD.

The earliest club of modern times was the Kachar Club (founded in 1859) in Assam, India. The game was introduced into England from India in 1869 by the 10th Hussars at Aldershot, Hampshire, and the earliest match was one between the 9th Lancers and the 10th Hussars on Hounslow Heath, west of London, in July, 1871. The earliest international match between England and the US was in 1886.

Playing Field

The game is played (by two teams of four) on the largest field of any ball game in the world. The ground measures 300 yards long by 160 yards wide with side-boards or, as in India, 200 yards twice without boards.

Highest Handicap

The highest handicap based on eight 7½-minute "chukkas" is 10 goals, introduced in the US in 1891 and in the United Kingdom and in Argentina in 1910. The latest of the 41 players to have received 10-goal handicaps are Thomas Wayman (US) and Guillermo Gracida, Jr (Mex). A match of two 40-goal handicap teams was staged for the first time ever at Palermo, Buenos Aires, Argentina, in 1975.

Highest Score

The highest aggregate number of goals scored in an international match is 30, when Argentina beat the US 21–9 at Meadowbrook, Long Island, NY, in Sept, 1936.

Most Olympic Medals

Polo has been part of the Olympic program on five occasions: 1900, 1908, 1920, 1924 and 1936. Of the 21 gold medalists, a 1920 winner, John Wodehouse, the 3rd Earl of Kimberley (b. 1883–d. 1941) uniquely also won a silver medal (1908).

Most Internationals

Thomas Hitchcock, Jr. (1900–44) played five times for the US vs. England (1921–24–27–30–39) and twice vs. Argentina (1928–36).

Polo on Elephant Back

A crowd of 40,000 watched a game played at Jaipur, India, in 1976, when elephants were used instead of ponies and longer than normal polo sticks were used.

Largest Crowd

Crowds of more than 50,000 have watched flood-lit matches at the Sydney, Australia, Agricultural Shows.

1910 British old Contabs Polo Four ready to go into action.

START OF A POWERBOAT RACE: This 1978 Cowes–Torquay contest in England was won by a woman for the first time at a then record average speed of 77.42 mph.

POWERBOAT RACING

Origins

The first recorded race by powered boats was for steamboats at the Northern Yacht Club Regatta at Rothesay, Scotland in 1827. It was won by *Clarence,* a locally built vessel. Paddle steamers on the Mississippi were often pitted against each other in the 1840s for purely commercial reasons, such as getting to the markets first with their cargoes. In 1870 the *Robert E. Lee* had her famous race with the *Natchez* from New Orleans to St Louis, a distance of 1,027 miles, which the former won in 90 hours 30 min. This time was not beaten by any boat until 1929.

The earliest application of the gasoline engine to a boat was by Jean Joseph Etienne Lenoir (1822–1900) on the River Seine, Paris, in 1865, and the first race of motor launches took place in 1889. By 1908 the sport had progressed enough to be included in the Olympic Games.

The sport was given impetus by the presentation of a championship cup by Sir Alfred Harmsworth of England in 1903, which was also the year of the first offshore race from Calais to Dover across the Eng Channel.

Highest Speeds

The official water speed record is 319.627 mph by Ken Warby (Aust) in a jet-propelled hydroplane *Spirit of Australia* on Blowering Dam Lake, NSW in Oct 1978. However, he had unofficially attained a speed of approximately 345 mph in Nov 1977. The official record for a woman is 116.279 mph by Fiona Brothers (GB) in a Seebold marathon hull at Holme Pierrepont, Nottingham Eng, on Sept 1, 1981. However, the fastest attained on water by a woman driver is 190 mph by Mary Rife (US) in a drag boat.

Records are recognized by the Union Internationale Motonautique. The recognized speed record for an outboard-powered boat in Class OZ unlimited, a circuit boat, is 144.16 mph by Rick Frost in a Burgess catamaran powered by a 3.5-litre Johnson V8 engine, on Lake Windermere, Eng, on Oct 11, 1983.

The fastest speed recognized for an offshore boat was set by *Innovation,* a 35-ft Maelstrom boat powered by three Johnson Evinrude outboard engines each of 214 cu in driven by Mike Drury at a mean speed for two runs of 131.088 mph at New Orleans, La on March 31, 1984.

The diesel speed record is 132.40 mph by Carlo Bonomi at Venice on Dec 5, 1982 in a 24-ft BU221 hydroplane *Rothman's World Leader.*

Harmsworth Trophy

Of the 25 international contests from 1903 to 1961, the US won the most with 16. The greatest number of wins was achieved by Garfield A. Wood (US) with 8 (1920–21, 26, 28–30, 32–33). The only boat to win three times is *Miss Supertest III,* owned by James G. Thompson (Canada), driven by the late Bob Hayward (Canada), in 1959–61. This boat also achieved the record speed of 119.27 mph at Picton, Ontario, Canada, in 1961.

Competition for the Trophy was revived after a lapse from 1961 to 1977. The winners have been:

	Boat	Nation	Driver		Boat	Nation	Driver
1977	Limit-Up	Eng	Michael Doxford & Tim Powell	1980	Satisfaction	US	Bill Elswick
				1981	Satisfaction	US	Paul Clauser
1978	Limit-Up	Eng	Michael Doxford & Tim Powell	1982	Popeye	US	Al Copeland
1979	Uno-Mint-Jewellery	Eng	Derek Pobjoy	1983	Fayva Shoes Supercat	US	George Morales

Gold Cup

The Gold Cup (instituted 1903 by the American Power Boat Association) was won 8 times by Bill Muncey (1929–81) (US) (1956–57, 61–62, 72, 77–79). The highest lap speed reached in the competition is 128.338 mph by the hydroplane *Atlas Van Lines,* driven by Muncey in a qualifying round on the Columbia River, Wash in July 1977, and again in July 1978. Three boats have won on four occasions, *Slo-Mo-Shun IV* 1950–53, *Miss Budweiser* in 1969–70, 1973 and 1980, and *Atlas Van Lines* in 1972, 1977–79. The race speed record is 117.391 mph by *Miss Budweiser* driven by Dean Chenoweth in 1980.

RIDING THE AIRWAVES: From a takeoff speed of 55 mph, Peter Horak jumped his powerboat 120 feet through the air for a TV documentary.

Cowes International Offshore Powerboat Classic

Instituted in 1961, and originally held from Cowes to Torquay, Eng in 1968 it was extended to include the return journey, a total distance of 246.13 miles. In 1982 the race became the Cowes International Powerboat Classic. The record for the race is 3 hours 4 min 35 sec by *Satisfaction* driven by Bill Elswick (US) averaging 79.64 mph in Aug 1980. The only three-time winner has been Tommy Sopwith (b Nov 15, 1932) (GB) in 1961, 68 and 70.

Longest Race

The longest race has been the Port Richborough (London) to Monte Carlo Marathon Offshore International event. The race extended over 2,947 miles in 14 stages, June 10–25, 1972. It was won by *H.T.S.* (GB), driven by Mike Bellamy, Eddie Chater and Jim Brooks in 71 hours 35 min 56 sec (average speed 41.15 mph).

Dragsters

The highest speed recorded by a propeller-driven boat is 229.00 mph by Eddie Hill in his Kurtis Top Fuel Hydro Drag Boat *The Texan* at Chowchilla, Calif on Sept 5, 1982. He also set a 440-yd elapsed time record of 5.16 sec at Firebird Lake, Ariz, on Nov 13, 1983.

Longest Jump

The longest jump achieved by a jetboat has been 120 ft by Peter Horak (b May 7, 1943) (US) in a Glastron Carlson CVX 20 Jet Deluxe with a 460 Ford V8 engine (takeoff speed 55 mph) for a documentary TV film "The Man Who Fell from the Sky," at Salton Sea, Calif, on Apr 26, 1980.

The longest boat jump on to land is 172 ft by Norm Bagvie (NZ) from the Shotover River on July 1, 1982, in the 1½-ton jetboat *Valvdene*.

RODEO

Origins

While there is no known "first rodeo," as early as 1860 cowboys were competing at railheads and on trails for unofficial titles for bronc riding and other skills of their trade. After the great cattle drives were eliminated, due to the introduction of more and more railroads, large ranches began to "give a rodeo." As towns developed, they adopted the rodeo with Cheyenne, Wyo, claiming to have had the first in 1872.

A rodeo has been held each year in Prescott, Ariz, on the Fourth of July since 1888.

The sport was not organized until 1936 when a group of rodeo contestants founded the Cowboys Turtle Association (now the Professional Rodeo Cowboys Association) to standardize the sport. The official events now are saddle bronc riding, bareback riding, bull riding, calf roping, steer wrestling, and, in some states, team roping.

The largest rodeo in the world is the U.S. National Finals Rodeo, held in Oklahoma City annually in Dec. The total prize money in 1982 was $700,860.

Most World Titles

The record number of all-round titles in the Professional Rodeo Cowboys Association world championships is 6 by Larry Mahan (US) (b Nov 21, 1943) in 1966–70 and 1973 and, consecutively, 1974–9 by Tom Ferguson (b Dec 20, 1950). Jim Shoulders (b 1928) of Henryetta, Okla, won a record 16 world championships between 1949 and 1959.

Highest Earnings

The record figure for prize money in a single season is $153,391 by Roy Cooper in 1983. The greatest earnings in a rodeo career is $909,089 by Tom Ferguson to May 28, 1984. The record for the most money won at

STAYING POWER: Larry Mahan shares the record for most all-round world titles with 6.

POWER STEERING: This steer has cause for concern as 6-time world champion Tom Ferguson gets ahold of it. In 1980, Ferguson reached the top of the list in career rodeo earnings, and by May 1984 he had won more than $900,000 for his participation in this legacy of the Old West.

HORSING AROUND: Metha Brorsen of Perry, Oklahoma, was only 11 years old when she became the International Rodeo Association's champion cowgirl barrel racer in 1975. The young 4-ft-9-in, 66-lb rider earned over $15,000 that year.

one rodeo is $29,268 by Jimmie Cooper at the National Finals Rodeo in Oklahoma City in Dec 1982, where the total in prize money offered was $700,860.

Youngest Champion

The youngest winner of a world title is Metha Brorsen of Okla, who was only 11 years old when she won the International Rodeo Association Cowgirls barrel-racing event in 1975.

The youngest women's champion in the female division of the Professional Rodeo Cowboys Association competition is Jackie Jo Perrin of Antlers, Okla, who won the barrel-racing title in 1977 at age 13.

Champion Bull

The top bucking bull was probably "Honky Tonk," an 11-year-old Brahma, who unseated 187 riders in an undefeated eight-year career to his retirement in Sept 1978.

Champion Bronc

Traditionally a bronc called "Midnight" owned by Jim McNab of Alberta, Canada, was never ridden in 12 appearances at the Calgary Stampede.

Time Records

Records for timed events, such as calf roping and steer wrestling, are not always comparable, because of the widely varying conditions due to the size of arenas and amount of start given the stock. The fastest time recently recorded for roping a calf is 5.7 sec by Lee Phillips in Assiniboia, Saskatchewan, Canada, in 1978, and the fastest time for overcoming a steer is 2.4 sec by James Bynum at Marietta, Okla, in 1955; by Carl Deaton at Tulsa, Okla, in 1976; and by Gene Melton at Pecatonica, Ill, in 1976.

The standard required time to stay on in bareback, saddle bronc and bull riding events is 8 sec. In the now discontinued ride-to-a-finish events, rodeo riders have been recorded to have survived 15 min or more, until the mount had not a buck left in it.

The highest score in bull riding was 98 points out of a possible 100 by Denny Flynn on "Red Lightning" at Palestine, Ill, in 1979.

ROLLER SKATING

Origin

The first roller skate was undoubtedly a pair of wooden spools, attached to a pair of ice skates, sometime around 1700. The first recorded use of roller skates was in a play by Tom Hood, performed in 1743 at the Old Drury Lane Theatre, London, England. The first documented roller skate was invented by Jean Joseph Merlin of Huy, Belgium, in 1760, and demonstrated by him in London but with disastrous results. The forerunner of the modern four-wheel skate was invented by James L. Plimpton of Medfield, Mass, patented in 1863. The first indoor rink was opened in the Haymarket, London, in about 1824.

Largest Rink

The largest indoor rink ever to operate was located in the Grand Hall, Olympia, London, England. It had an actual skating area of 68,000 sq ft. It first opened in 1890 for one season, then again from 1909 to 1912.

The largest rink now in operation is the Fireside Roll-Arena in Hoffman Estates, Ill, which has a total skating surface of 29,859 sq ft.

Most Titles

Most world speed titles have been won by Alberta Vianello (Italy) with 16 between 1953 and 1965. The records for figure titles are 5 by Karl Heinz Losch in 1958–59, 61–62, 66, and 4 by Astrid Bader, both of W Germany, in 1965–68. Most world pair titles have been taken by Dieter Fingerle (W Germany) with 4 in 1959, 65–67.

Speed Records

The fastest speed (official world's record) is 25.78 mph by Giuseppe Cantarella (Italy) who recorded 34.9 sec for 440 yd on a road at Catania, Italy, on Sept 28, 1963. The mile record on a rink is 2 min 25.1 sec by Gianni Ferretti (Italy). The greatest distance skated in one hour on a rink by a woman is 21.995 miles by Marisa Danesi at Inzell, W Germany, on Sept 28, 1968. The men's record on a track is 23.133 miles by Alberto Civolani (Italy) at Inzell, W Germany, on Sept 28, 1968. He went on to skate 50 miles in 2 hours 20 min 33.1 sec.

Marathon

The longest recorded continuous roller skating marathon was one of 344 hours 18 min by Isamu Furugen at Naka Roller Skate Land, Okinawa, Japan, Dec 11–27, 1983.

Endurance

Theodore J. Coombs (b 1954) of Hermosa Beach, Calif, skated 5,193 miles from Los Angeles to NYC and back to Yates Center, Kan, from May 30 to Sept 14, 1979. His longest 24-hour distance was 120 mi, June 27–28.

ROWING

Oldest Race

The Sphinx stela of Amenhotep II (1450–1425 BC) records that he *stroked* a boat for some three miles. Warships were driven by human power in ancient times. The earliest literary reference to rowing is by the Roman poet, Virgil in the *Aeneid,* published after his death in 19 BC. Rowing regattas were held in Venice *c* 300 AD. The world's oldest annual race was inaugurated on Aug 1, 1716 by Thomas Doggett, an Irish-born actor. He presented "an Orange Colour Livery with a Badge" for the winner of a competition for London watermen over a 4½-mi course from London Bridge to Chelsea. The world governing body, FISA, was founded in 1892, and the first major international meeting, the European championships, was held a year later.

Olympic and World Championships

Five oarsmen have won 3 gold medals: John B. Kelly (US) (1889–1960), father of Princess Grace of Monaco, in the sculls (1920) and double sculls (1920 and 24); his cousin Paul V. Costello (US) (b Dec 27, 1899) in the double sculls (1920, 24 and 28); Jack Beresford, Jr (GB) (1899–1977) in the sculls (1924), coxless fours (1932) and double sculls (1936); Vyacheslav Ivanov (USSR) (b July 30, 1938) in the sculls (1956, 60 and 64); Siegfried Brietzke in the coxless pairs (1972) and the coxless fours (1976 and 80); and Pertti Karppinen (Finland) in the single sculls (1976, 1980, 1984).

1984 gold medal winners were:

Men	Women
Single Sculls	*Single Sculls*
Pertti Karppinen (Fin) 7 min 0.24 sec	Valeria Racila (Romania) 3 min 40.68 sec
Double Sculls	*Double Sculls*
US 6 min 36.87 sec	Romania 3 min 26.75 sec
Coxless Quadruple Sculls	*Coxless Pairs*
W Germany 5 min 57.55 sec	Romania 3 min 32.60 sec
Coxless Pairs	*Coxed Quadruple Sculls*
Romania 6 min 45.39 sec	Romania 3 min 14.11 sec
Coxed Pairs	*Coxed Fours*
Italy 7 min 5.99 sec	Romania 3 min 19.30 sec
Coxless Fours	*Eights*
New Zealand 6 min 3.48 sec	US 2 min 59.80 sec
Coxed Fours	
Great Britain 6 min 18.64 sec	
Eights	
Canada 5 min 41.32 sec	

Olympic Championships were first held in 1900. Separate world championships were first held for men in 1962 and for women in 1974. The East German coxless pairs team of Bernd and Jorg Landvoigt have won

BY A NOSE: The US won a close finish in the Eights race for a gold medal in the 1932 Olympics at Los Angeles.

their event 4 times in world championships and twice in Olympic competition, setting a record for any event. The female sculler Christine Scheiblich-Hann (E Ger) nearly matched this with one Olympic and four world titles.

> John Kelly was thought to be a victim of class distinction when he was refused entry into the Diamond Sculls at Henley, Eng, in 1920, being unofficially informed that the muscles he had developed as a bricklayer gave him an unfair advantage over "gentlemen" competitors. Later, as a rich businessman, he saw his son John Kelly Jr win the Diamond Sculls twice, in 1947 and 1949, and his film-star daughter become Princess Grace of Monaco. Benjamin Spock, later author of a best-selling baby and child care book, was a member of the Yale crew which represented the US and won the 1924 Olympic Eights.

Highest Speed

Speeds in tidal or flowing water are of no comparative value. The greatest speed attained on non-tidal water, over the standard men's rowing distance of 2000 m (2,187 yd), is 13.68 mph by the US eight on the Rootsee, Lucerne, Switzerland, in June 1984 when they clocked 5 min 27.14 sec. A team from the Penn AC (US) was timed in 5 min 18.8 sec (14.03 mph) in the FISA Championships on the Meuse River, Liège, Belgium, on Aug 17, 1930, but with the help of the river current.

The fastest by a female eight is also by a US crew, who clocked 2 min 54.05 sec for the standard women's distance of 1000 m (1,093.6 yd), achieving an average of 12.85 mph on the Rootsee, Lucerne in 1984. The fastest time over 2000 m by a single sculler, 6 min 49.68 sec by Nikolai Dovgan (USSR) in 1978, represents an average speed of 10.92 mph. The

GOLD OAR: This East German crew won the Eights gold medal in 1976, the first year of women's rowing competition in the Olympics. Sports officials, traditionally male and conservative, long maintained that women could not compete in the most strenuous events, but women have been proving them wrong.

best by a female sculler over 1000 m, 3 min 30.74 sec by Cornelia Linse (E Ger) in 1984, represents an average of 10.61 mph.

Heaviest Oarsman

The heaviest man ever to row in a British Boat Race has been Stephen G. H. Plunkett (Queen's) the No 5 in the 1976 Oxford boat at 229 lb. The 1983 Oxford crew averaged a record 204.3 lb.

Longest Race

The longest rowing race is the annual Tour du Lac Léman, Geneva, Switzerland for coxed fours (the five-man team taking turns as cox) over 99 miles. The record winning time is 12 hours 52 min by LAGA, Delft, Netherlands, Oct 3, 1983.

The longest distance rowed in 24 hours by a crew of 8 is 130 mi by members of the Renmark Rowing Club of S Australia Apr 1, 1984.

Sculling

The record number of wins in the Wingfield Sculls on the Thames in London (Putney to Mortlake) (instituted 1830) is 7 by Jack Beresford, Jr 1920–26. The fastest time has been 21 min 11 sec by Leslie Frank Southwood (b Jan 18, 1906) on Aug 12, 1933. The most world professional sculling titles (instituted 1831) won is 7 by William Beach (Australia) (1850–1935), 1884–87.

SHOOTING

Earliest Club

The Lucerne Shooting Guild (Switzerland) was formed *c.* 1466, and the first recorded shooting match was held at Zurich in 1472. Early contests had to be over very short range as it was not until rifling, to spin the bullet, was introduced to gun barrels in *c.* 1480 that accuracy over greater distances could be achieved.

Trap-shooting was introduced in the US in 1830, and skeet shooting in 1915, "skeet" being the old Norse word for "shoot."

Olympic Games

The record number of medals won is 11 by Carl Townsend Osburn (US) (1884–1966) in 1912, 1920 and 1924, consisting of 5 gold, 4 silver and 2 bronze. Six other marksmen have won 5 gold medals. The only marksman to win 3 individual gold medals has been Gudbrand Gudbrandsönn, Skatteboe (Norway) (1875–1965) in 1906.

> The first woman to win a medal at shooting was Margaret Murdock (US) in the small-bore rifle (3 positions) event in 1976. It was originally announced that she had won by a single point, but an error was discovered and she was tied with her teammate Lonny Bassham. Then an examination of the targets indicated that one of the latter's shots was 1/25th of an inch closer to the center than previously determined, and so the gold medal was given to Bassham, who gallantly invited Murdock to share first place position on the award rostrum.

INDIVIDUAL WORLD SHOOTING RECORDS
(as ratified by the International Shooting Union—UIT)

			Max-Score		
Free Rifle	300m	3 × 40 shots	1200–1160	Lones W. Wigger (US)	Seoul, 1978
			1160	Lones W. Wigger (US)	Rio de Janeiro, 1981
		60 shots prone	600–595	K. Leskinen (Finland)	Oslo, Norway, 1983
			595	T. Muller (Switz)	Oslo, Norway, 1983
Standard Rifle	300m	3 × 20 shots	600–580	Lones W. Wigger (US)	Rio de Janeiro, 1981
Small-Bore Rifle	50m	3 × 40 shots	1200–1180	Kiril Ivanov (USSR)	Lvov, USSR, Dec 1982
	50m	60 shots prone	600–600	Alistair Allan (GB)	Titograd, Yugo, 1981
			600	Ernest Van de Zande (US)	Rio de Janeiro, 1981
Free Pistol	50m	60 shots	600–581	Aleksandr Melentev (USSR)	Moscow, 1980
Rapid-Fire Pistol	25m	60 shots	600–599	Igor Puzyrev (USSR)	Titograd, Yugo, 1981
Center-Fire Pistol	25m	60 shots	600–597	Thomas D. Smith (US)	São Paulo, Brazil, 1963
Standard Pistol	25m	60 shots	600–584	Eric Buijong (US)	Caracas, Venez, 1983
Running Target	50m	60 shots "normal runs"	600–595	Igor Sokolov (USSR)	Miskulc, Hungary, 1981
Trap	—	200 birds	200–200	Danny Carlisle (US)	Caracas, Venez, 1983
Skeet	—	200 birds	200–200	Matthew Dryke (US)	São Paulo, Brazil, 1981
Air Rifle	10m	60 shots	600–590	Harald Stenvaag (Norway)	The Hague, Neth, 1982
Air Pistol	10m	60 shots	600–591	Vladas Tourla (USSR)	Caracas, Venez, 1983

Trick Shooting

The greatest rapid-fire feat was by Ed McGivern (US), who twice fired from 15 ft in 0.45 sec 5 shots which could be covered by a silver half-dollar piece at the Lead Club Range, SD, on Aug 20, 1932. On another occasion he fired 10 shots, using 2 pistols, in 1.2 sec into 2 playing cards at the same range.

Sgt. Joe Walsh, of Morris County Sheriff's Dept, Morristown, NJ, fired 10 shots in 0.9 sec from two guns at the same time (five shots from each), no draw, with all 10 shots hitting within the area of two 2½ × 3½ in play-

TWO WORLD RECORDS with a rifle are held by Lones W. Wigger (far left). TRICK SHOOTING made Annie Oakley (right) famous in the late 19th and early 20th century. She was a central attraction of the Buffalo Bill Wild West show that performed in front of European royalty and became the inspiration for a Broadway musical and a TV series.

ing cards, which were 15 ft away from Walsh. The feat was performed at the Shongum Sportsman shooting range in Ledgewood, NJ, on Oct 30, 1983.

The most renowned trick shot of all time was Annie Oakley (*née* Mozee) (1860–1926). She demonstrated the ability to shoot 100 of 100 in trap shooting for 35 years, aged between 27 and 62. At 30 paces she could split a playing card end-on, hit a dime in mid-air or shoot a cigarette from the lips of her husband—one Frank Butler.

Bench Rest Shooting

The smallest group on record at 1,000 yd is 5.093 in by Rick Taylor with a 300 Weatherby at Williamsport, Pa, on Aug 24, 1980.

Small-Bore Rifle Shooting

Richard Hansen shot 5,000 bull's-eyes in 24 hours at Fresno, Calif, on June 13, 1929.

Highest Score in 24 Hours

The Easingwold (England) Rifle & Pistol Club team of John Smith, Edward Kendall, Paul Duffield and Philip Kendall scored 120,242 points (averaging 95.66 per card) on Aug 6–7, 1983.

Clay Pigeon Shooting

The record number of clay birds shot in an hour is 2,215 by Joseph Kreckman at the Paradise Shooting Center, Cresco, Pa, Aug 28, 1983. Graham Douglas Geater (b July 21, 1947) shot 2,264 targets in an hour on a trap-shooting range at the NILO Gun Club, Papamoa, NZ on Jan 17, 1981.

Most world titles have been won by Susan Nattrass (Canada) with 6, 1974–5, 77–9, 81.

A unique maximum 200/200 was achieved by Ricardo Ruiz Rumoroso at the Spanish clay pigeon championships at Zaragoza on June 12, 1983.

Olympic Gold Medalists 1984

Men

Free Pistol

Xu Haifeng (China) 566 pts

Small-bore Rifle (Prone)

Ed Etzel (US) 599 pts

Small-bore Rifle (Three positions)

Malcolm Cooper (GB) 1173 pts

Rapid-fire Pistol

Takeo Kamachi (Jap) 595 pts

Running Game Target

Li Yuwei (China) 587 pts

Air Rifle

Philippe Heberle (France) 589 pts

Women

Small-bore Standard Rifle

Wu Xiaoxuan (China) 581 pts

Air Rifle

Pat Spurgin (US) 393 pts

Pistol Match

Linda Thom (Can) 585 pts

Mixed

Skeet

Matthew Dryke (US) 198 pts

Trap

Luciano Giovannetti (Ita) 192 pts

GAME SHOOTING

Record Heads

The world's finest head is the 23-pointer stag head in the Maritzburg collection, E Germany. The outside span is 75½ in, the length 47½ in and the weight 41½ lb. The greatest number of points is probably 33 (plus 29) on the stag shot in 1696 by Frederick III (1657–1713), the Elector of Brandenburg, later King Frederick I of Prussia.

Largest Shoulder Guns

The largest bore shoulder guns made were 2-bore. Less than a dozen of these were made by two English wildfowl gunmakers *c.* 1885. Normally the largest guns made are double-barrelled 4-bore weighing up to 26 lb which can be handled only by men of exceptional physique. Larger smooth-bore guns have been made, but these are for use as punt-guns.

Biggest Bag

The largest animal ever shot by any big game hunter was a bull African elephant (*Loxodonta africana africana*) shot by E. M. Nielsen of Columbus, Neb, 25 miles north-northeast of Mucusso, Angola, on Nov 7, 1974. The animal, brought down by a Westley Richards 0.425, stood 13 ft 8 in tall at the shoulder.

In Nov 1965, Simon Fletcher, 28, a Kenyan farmer, claims to have killed two elephants with one 0.458 bullet.

The greatest recorded lifetime bag is 556,000 birds, including 241,000 pheasants, by the 2nd Marquess of Ripon (1852–1923) of England. He himself dropped dead on a grouse moor after shooting his 52nd bird on the morning of Sept 22, 1923.

TRIPLE WINNER IN 1984 OLYMPICS: Marja-Liisa Hamalainen (Finland) dominated the women's cross-country skiing events, taking all three individual gold medals.

SKIING

Origins

The most ancient ski in existence was found well preserved in a peat bog at Höting, Sweden, dating from *c.* 2500 BC. However, in 1934 a Russian archaeologist discovered a rock carving of a skier at Bessovysledki, USSR, which dates from *c.* 6000 BC. These early skiers used the bones of animals whereas wooden skis appear to have been introduced to Europe from Asia. The first reference in literature is in a work by Procopius *c.* AD 550 who referred to "Gliding Finns." Additionally in the Scandinavian sagas there occur gods of skiing. By 1199, the Danish historian Saxo was reporting the military use of troops on skis by Sigurdsson Sverrir, the Norwegian King.

The modern sport did not develop until 1843 when the first known competition for civilians took place at Tromsó, Norway. The first ski club, named the Trysil Shooting and Skiing Club, was founded in Norway in 1861. Twenty years later ski bindings were invented by Sondre Nordheim, from Morgedal in the Telemark area, and the people of this region were the pioneers of the sport. The legendary "Snowshoe" Thompson, whose parents were Norwegian, was the earliest well-known skier in the US (1856) although skiing took place here in the 1840s. It was not until Olaf Kjeldsberg went to Switzerland in 1881 that the sport began to take hold in that country, and in 1889 one of the earliest of British exponents, Arthur Conan Doyle, began skiing at Davos, Switz. The

TWINS WIN gold and silver in Giant Slalom in 1984 Olympics: Phil Mahre (left) beat his twin brother Steve by 21/100ths of a second.

first downhill race—as opposed to the Scandinavian races across country—was held at Kitzbuhel, Austria in 1908. The first modern slalom event was run at Mürren, Switzerland, on Jan 21, 1922. The International Ski Federation (FIS) was founded on Feb 2, 1924. The Winter Olympics were inaugurated on Jan 25, 1924, and Alpine events have been included since 1936. The FIS recognizes both the Winter Olympics and the separate World Ski Championships as world championships.

Most Alpine World Titles

The World Alpine Championships were inaugurated at Mürren, Switzerland, in 1931. The greatest number of titles won has been 13 by Christel Cranz (b July 1, 1914), of Germany, with 7 individual—4 Slalom (1934, 37–39) and 3 Downhill (1935, 37, 39); and 5 Combined (1934–35, 37–39). She also won the gold medal for the Combined in the 1936 Olympics. The most titles won by a man is 7 by Anton "Toni" Sailer (b Nov 17, 1935), of Austria, who won all 4 in 1956 (Giant Slalom, Slalom, Downhill and the non-Olympic Alpine Combination) and the Downhill, Giant Slalom and Combined in 1958.

Olympic Alpine Gold Medalists 1984

Men

Giant Slalom

Max Julen (Switz) 2 min 41.18 sec

Slalom

Phil Mahre (US) 1 min 39.41 sec

(Silver medal winner was his twin brother Steve)

Downhill

Bill Johnson (US) 1 min 45.59 sec

Women

Giant Slalom

Debbie Armstrong (US) 2 min 20.98 sec

Slalom

Paoletta Magoni (Italy) 1 min 36.47 sec

Downhill

Michela Figini (Switz) 1 min 13.36 sec

SKI STARS: (Left) Ingemar Stenmark (Sweden) has won 79 World Cup events and 2 Olympic gold medals. Christel Cranz (lower left) of Germany won 12 Alpine World titles, and an Olympic gold medal. Toni Sailer (right, below) of Austria won 7 Alpine World titles and 3 Olympic golds.

Most Olympic Victories

Marja-Liisa Haemaelainen (Fin), after having twice won the women's World Cup title in Nordic, 1983–84, won all 3 individual gold medals in the 1984 Olympics.

The most Olympic gold medals won by an individual for skiing is 4 by Sixten Jernberg (b Feb 6, 1929), of Sweden, in 1956–64 (including one for a relay). In addition, Jernberg has won 3 silver and 2 bronze medals for a record 9 Olympic medals. Four were also won by Nikolai Zimjatov (b June 28, 1955) (USSR) in 1980 (30 km, 50 km and on the team for 4 × 10-km relay) and in 1984 (30 km).

CONSISTENT WINNER: Jean-Claude Killy (France) thrilled his countrymen when he swept all 3 Olympic gold medals in the 1968 Winter Olympics in Grenoble, France. Killy also won the Alpine Combination world title that year and 2 other world titles in 1966.

The only woman to win 4 gold medals is Galina Koulakova (b Apr 29, 1942) of USSR who won the 5 km and 10 km (1972) and was a member of the winning 3 × 5-km relay team in 1972 and the 4 × 5-km team in 1976. Koulakova also has won 2 silver and 2 bronze medals, 1968–80.

The most Olympic gold medals won in men's Alpine skiing is 3, by Anton "Toni" Sailer in 1956 and Jean-Claude Killy in 1968.

Olympic Nordic Gold Medalists 1984

Men

15,000 Meters

Gunde Svan (Swe) 41 min 25.6 sec

30,000 Meters

Nikolai Zimyatov (USSR) 1 hour 28 min 56.3 sec

50,000 Meters

Thomas Wassberg (Swe) 2 hours 15 min 55.8 sec

4 × 10,000 Meters Relay

Sweden 1 hour 55 min 06.3 sec

Nordic Combination

Tom Sandberg (Nor) 422.595 pts

70-Meter Ski Jump

Jens Weissflog (E Ger) 215.2 pts

90-Meter Ski Jump

Matti Nykanen (Fin) 231.2 pts

Women

5,000 Meters

Marja-Liisa Hämäläinen (Fin) 17 min 04.0 sec

10,000 Meters

Marja-Liisa Hämäläinen (Fin) 31 min 44.2 sec

20,000 Meters

Marja-Liisa Hämäläinen (Fin) 1 hour 01 min 45.0 sec

4 × 5,000 Meters Relay

Norway 1 hour 06 min 49.7 sec

Most Nordic World Titles

The first world Nordic championships were those of the 1924 Winter Olympics at Chamonix, France. The greatest number of titles won is 9 by Galina Koulakova (b Apr 29, 1942) (USSR), 1968–78. She also won 4 silver and 4 bronze medals for a record total of 17. The most won by a man is 8, including relays, by Sixten Jernberg (b Feb 6, 1929) (Sweden), 1956–64. Johan Grottumsbraaten (1899–1942), of Norway, won 6 individual titles (2 at 18 km cross-country and 4 Nordic Combined) in 1926–32. The record for a jumper is 5 by Birger Ruud (b Aug 23, 1911), of Norway, in 1931–32 and 1935–37. Ruud is the only person to win Olympic titles in each of the dissimilar Alpine and Nordic disciplines. In 1936 he won the ski-jumping and the Alpine downhill (which was not then a separate event, but only a segment of the Combined event).

World Cup

The Alpine World Cup, instituted in 1967, has been won 4 times by Gustavo Thoeni (Italy) (b Feb 28, 1951) in 1971–73, and 75. The women's cup has been won 6 times by the 5-ft-6-in 150-lb Annemarie Moser (née Pröll) (Austria) in 1971–75 and 79. From Dec 1972 to Jan 1974 she completed a record sequence of 11 consecutive downhill victories. She holds the women's record of 62 individual event wins (1970–79). The most by a man is 79 by Ingemar Stenmark (b Mar 18, 1956) (Sweden), 1974–84, including a record 14 in one season in 1979.

Alexander Zavialov (USSR) (b June 2, 1955) has a record two wins, 1981 and 1983, in the cross-country or Nordic World Cup (inst 1979). The jumping World Cup (inst 1980) has been twice won by Armin Kogler (Austria) (b Sept 4, 1959) 1981–2.

WINTER WONDERS: Gustavo Thoeni (left) used his slalom expertise to win 4 Alpine World Cups. The Italian skier also captured 4 world titles and an Olympic gold. Russia's Galina Koulakova (right) pushes on to one of her record 4 Olympic gold medals. The most titled Nordic skier, she won 9 world championships as well.

Closest Verdict

The narrowest winning margin in a championship ski race was one hundredth of a second by Thomas Wassberg (Sweden) (b March 23, 1956) over Juha Mieto (Finland) in the Olympic 15 km cross-country race at Lake Placid, NY on Feb 17, 1980. His winning time was 41 min 57.63 sec.

The narrowest margin of victory in an Olympic Alpine event was 2/100ths of a sec by Barbara Cochran (US) over Daniele De Bernard (France) in the 1972 slalom at Sapporo, Japan.

Highest Speed

The highest speed ever achieved by any skier is 129.827 mph by Franz Weber (b Austria 1957) on Apr 21, 1984 at Les Arcs, France. The fastest by a woman is 124.759 mph by Melissa Dimino (US) Apr 19, 1984 at Les Arcs, France.

The highest average race speed in the Olympic downhill was 64.95 mph by Bill Johnson (US) (b Mar 30, 1960) at Sarajevo, Yugo, on Feb 16, 1984. The fastest in a World Cup downhill is 67.00 mph by Harti Weirather (Austria) (b Jan 25, 1958) at Kitzbuhl, Austria on Jan 15, 1982.

Highest Speed—Cross Country

Bill Koch (US) (b Apr 13, 1943) on Mar 26, 1981 skied ten times around a 5-km (3.11-mi) loop on Marlborough Pond, near Putney, Vt. He completed the 50 km in 1 hour 59 min 47 sec, an average speed of 15.57 mph. A race includes uphill and downhill sections; the record time for a 50 km race is 2 hours 15 min 55.8 sec by Thomas Wassberg (Swe) (b Mar 27, 1956) in the 1984 Olympics, an average speed of 13.71 mph. The record for a 15-km Olympic or World Championship race is 38 min 52.5 sec by Oddvar Braa (Nor) (b Mar 16, 1951) at the 1982 World Championships, an average speed of 14.38 mph.

Longest Jump

The longest ski jump ever recorded is 185 m (606 ft 11 in) by Matti Nykanen (Finland) Mar 17, 1984 at Oberstdorf, W Germany.

The women's record is 110 m (361 ft) by Tiina Lehtola (Fin) (b Aug 3, 1962) at Ruka, Finland, on Mar 29, 1981.

The longest dry ski jump is 92 m (301 ft 10 in) by Hubert Schwarz (W Germany) at Berchtesgaden, W Germany, on June 30, 1981.

Longest Races

The world's longest ski races are the Grenader, run just north of Oslo, Norway, and the König Ludwig Lauf in Oberammergau, W Germany. Both are 90 km (55.9 miles). The Canadian Ski Marathon at 160 km (99 miles) is longer, but is run in two parts on consecutive days.

The world's greatest Nordic ski race is the Vasaloppet, which commemorates an event in 1521 when Gustavus Vasa (1496–1560), later King of Sweden, fled 85.8 km (53.3 miles) from Mora to Sälen, Sweden. He was overtaken by loyal, speedy scouts on skis, who persuaded him to return eastwards to Mora to lead a rebellion and become the king of Sweden. The re-enactment of this journey is an annual event, with a

BIATHLON: Aleksandr Tikhonov (left) shoots for his 4th Olympic gold medal. The biathlon event was introduced to the Olympics in 1960, and Tikhonov was on all 4 winning Soviet teams (1968–80). NORDIC SKIING: Sweden's Sixten Jernberg (right) also earned 4 Olympic golds, and he dominated the sport (1956–64) with a total of 9 Olympic medals.

record 12,000 entrants (including 188 women) in 1981. The record time is 3 hours 58 min 8 sec by Konrad Hallenbarter (Switz) on Mar 6, 1983.

The Vasaloppet is now the longest of 10 long distance races, constituting the world loppet, staged in 10 countries.

The longest downhill race is the *Inferno* in Switzerland, 8.7 miles from the top of the Schilthorn to Lauterbrunnen. In 1981 there was a record entry of 1,401, with Heinz Fringen (Switz) winning in a record 15 min 44.57 sec.

Steepest Descent

Sylvain Saudan (b Lausanne, Switzerland, Sept 23, 1936) achieved a descent of Mt Blanc on the northeast side down the Couloir Gervasutti from 13,937 ft on Oct 17, 1967, skiing gradients of about 60 degrees.

Longest Run

The longest all-downhill ski run in the world is the Weissfluhjoch-Küblis Parsenn course (7.6 miles long), near Davos, Switzerland. The run from the Aiguille du Midi top of the Chamonix lift (vertical lift 8,176 ft) across the Vallée Blanche is 13 miles.

Duration

The record distance covered in 48 hours of Nordic skiing is 319 mi 205 yd by Bjorn Lokken (Norway) (b Nov 27, 1937) Mar 11–13, 1982.

In 24 hours Alf Waaler covered 188 miles 122 yds at Sanderstolen (Norway) Mar 24–25, 1984.

The longest time spent in downhill skiing under regulated conditions is 82 hours 9 min by two members of the Canadian Ski Patrol, Andrew Hempel and John Nicholas Rutter at Silverwood Winter Park, Fredericton, New Brunswick, Jan 25–28, 1984. The ski lift was exclusively confined to the record attempt and no time was wasted waiting for the lift, nor did the skiers sit down on the lift (no seats), but they did take the allowed rest breaks of 5 min after each hour of skiing.

A record of 123 hours under less rigid conditions was set by Christopher Ganong and Alfred Williams at Jiminy Peak, Hancock, Mass on Mar 19, 1982.

A record of 138 hours by Luc Labrie at Daie Comeau, Quebec, Feb 20–25, 1984 with unknown lift conditions has been received.

Longest Lift

The longest gondola ski lift is 3.88 mi long at Grindelwald-Männlichen, Switzerland (in two sections, but one gondola). The longest chair lift is the Alpine Way to Kosciusko Châlet lift above Thredbo, near the Snowy Mountains, NSW, Australia. It takes from 45 to 75 min to ascend the 3.5 mi, according to the weather. The highest is at Chacaltaya, Bolivia, rising to 16,500 ft.

Backflip on Skis

The greatest number of skiers to perform a back layout flip while holding hands is 28 at Bromont, Quebec, Canada, on Feb 10, 1982.

BACKFLIP: The record for this popular stunt has increased from 19 (as shown here) to 28 in just a few years. (Gary McMillin)

Highest Altitude

Jean Atanassieff and Nicolas Jaeger (both France) skied down from 26,900 ft to 20,340 ft on Mt Everest in 1978.

Ski Parachuting

The greatest recorded vertical descent in parachute ski-jumping is 3,300 ft by Rick Sylvester (b Apr 3, 1942) (US), who on July 28, 1976, skied off the 6,600-ft summit of Mt Asgard in Auyuittuq National Park, Baffin Island, Canada, landing on the Turner Glacier. The jump was made for a sequence in the James Bond film *The Spy Who Loved Me*.

BIATHLON

The biathlon, which combines skiing and shooting, was first included in the Olympic Games in 1960, and world championships were first held in 1958.

The most biathlon titles, now competed over 10 km, 20 km and a 4 × 7.5 km relay, have been won by Aleksandr Tikhonov (USSR). He won individual championships in 1969, 1970, 1973 and 1977, and was on the winning relay teams 10 times between 1968 and 1980 to make a grand total of 14 titles.

Most Olympic Titles

Magnar Solberg (Norway) (b Feb 4, 1937), in 1968 and 1972, is the only man to have won two Olympic individual titles. The USSR has won all four 4 × 7.5 km relay titles, 1968–80. Aleksandr Tikhonov (b Jan 2, 1947) who was a member of each team also won a silver in the 1968 20 km.

Olympic Gold Medalists 1984

10,000 Meters
Erik Kvalfoss (Norway) 30 min 53.8 sec

20,000 Meters
Peter Angever (W Ger) 1 hour 11 min 52.7 sec

4 × 7,500 Meter Relay
USSR 1 hour 38 min 51.7 sec

Most World Championships

Frank Ullrich (E Ger) (b Jan 24, 1958) has won a record six individual world titles, at 10 km, 1978–81, including the 1980 Olympics, and at 20 km 1982–83. Aleksandr Tikhonov was in ten winning USSR relay teams, 1968–80 and won four individual titles.

BIATHLON CHAMP: Frank Ullrich (E Ger), who has won 6 titles including Olympics, shows how he handles the gun while on a ski run.

SNOWMOBILING

The record speed for a snowmobile is 148.6 mph, set by Tom Earhart (US) in a Budweiser-Polaris snowmobile designed and owned by Bob Gaudreau, at Lake Mille Lacs, Minn, on Feb 25, 1982.

Richard and Raymond Moore and Loren Matthews drove their snowmobile 5,876 miles from Fairbanks, Alaska, to Fenton, Mich, in 39 days, from Feb 3 to Mar 13, 1980.

SNOWSHOE RACING

Records set in competition, recognized by the US Snowshoe Association are:

Men	100 m	Gary Nadeau	17 sec	1979
	200 m	David Lee	40.34 sec	1984
	400 m	Steve Mackey	1 min 28.81 sec	1984
	1,600 m	Mark Lessard	7 min 56 sec	1979
Women	100 m	Edna Kayes	23.49 sec	1984
	200 m	Gwenne Church	49.87 sec	1984
	400 m	Gwenne Church	2 min 5.23 sec	1984

RACING THROUGH THE SNOW: Snowshoe racing is a grueling sport that is attracting increasing numbers of enthusiasts throughout the snowy sections of the world. Most participants use specially designed snowshoes in the five officially sanctioned events: sprint, relay, hurdle, slalom, and biathlon (David Verner/AMPS)

BALL JUGGLERS: The Brazilian youngster (left) in the street in Rio dreams of being a star soccer player like his fellow countryman Pelé. Mikael Palmqvist (Sweden) has kept a soccer ball in midair for 12 hours 15 min non-stop.

SOCCER

Origins

Ball-kicking games were played very early in human history.

A game with some similarities termed *Tsu-chu* was played in China in the 3rd and 4th centuries BC. One of the earliest references to the game in England is a Royal Proclamation by Edward II in 1314 banning the game in the City of London. A soccer-type game called Calcio was played in Italy in 1410. The earliest clear representation of the game is in a print from Edinburgh, Scotland, dated 1672–73. The game became standardized with the formation of the Football Association in England on Oct 26, 1863. Eleven players on a side was standardized in 1870.

The sport is nationally governed by the US Soccer Federation with headquarters in NYC, which is affiliated with the *Fédération Internationale de Football Association*. The North American Soccer League is affiliated with the USSF.

Highest Team Scores

The highest score recorded in any first-class match is 36. This occurred in the Scottish Cup match between Arbroath and Bon Accord on Sept 5, 1885, when Arbroath won 36–0 on their home ground. But for the lack of nets and the consequent waste of retrieval time, the score might have been even higher.

The highest goal margin recorded in any international match is 20, when England beat France in an amateur match by 20–0 in 1910 at Ipswich, England. In a "promotion" match in Yugoslavia in 1979, two teams connived with the help of the referee to set a record score of 134–1.

Individual Scoring

The most goals scored by one player in a first-class match is 16 by Stephan Stanis (*né* Stanikowski, b Poland, July 15, 1913) for Racing Club de Lens vs Aubry-Asturies, in Lens, France, on Dec 13, 1942.

The record number of goals scored by one player in an international match is 10 by Sofus Nielsen (1888–1963) for Denmark vs France (17–1) in the 1908 Olympics and by Gottfried Fuchs for Germany, which beat Russia 16–0 in the 1912 Olympic tournament (consolation event) in Sweden.

The most goals scored in a specified period is 1,216 by Edson Arantes do Nascimento (b Baurú, Brazil, Oct 23, 1940), known as Pelé, the Brazilian inside left, in the period Sept 7, 1956, to Oct 2, 1974 (1,254 games). His best year was 1959 with 127 goals. His *milesimo* (1,000th) came in a penalty for his club, Santos, in the Maracaña Stadium, Rio de Janeiro, on Nov 19, 1969, when he was playing in his 909th first-class match. He came out of retirement in 1975 to add to his total with the New York Cosmos of the North American Soccer League. By his retirement on Oct 1, 1977 his total had reached 1,281 in 1,363 games. He added 4 more goals later in special appearances.

Franz ("Bimbo") Binder (b Dec 1, 1911) scored 1,006 goals in 756 games in Austria and Germany between 1930 and 1950.

Ball Control

Mikael Palmqvist (Sweden) juggled a regulation soccer ball for 12 hours 15 min non-stop with feet, legs and head without the ball ever touching the ground at Zürich, Switzerland on Oct 7–8, 1983. He also headed a regulation soccer ball non-stop for 4½ hours at Göteborg, Sweden, in 1984.

Most Olympic Wins

The only country to have won the Olympic soccer title three times is Hungary in 1952, 1964 and 1968. The UK won in 1908 and 1912 and also the unofficial tournament of 1900. The highest Olympic score is Denmark 17 vs France "A" 1 in 1908.

Winners:

1908 Great Britain	1932 not held	1964 Hungary
1912 Great Britain	1936 Italy	1968 Hungary
1920 Belgium	1948 Sweden	1972 Poland
1924 Uruguay	1952 Hungary	1976 E Germany
1928 Uruguay	1956 USSR	1980 Czechoslovakia
	1960 Yugoslavia	1984 France

Fastest Goals

The record for an international match is 3 goals in 3½ min by Willie Hall (Tottenham Hotspur) for England against Ireland on Nov 16, 1938, at Old Trafford, Manchester, England.

The fastest authenticated time for a goal from kickoff is 6 sec by Albert Mundy (1958), Barnie Jones (1962), Keith Smith (1964) and Tommy

ATHLETE'S FEAT: Pelé celebrates one of his 1,285 goals, this one with the NY Cosmos of the NASL. In a seemingly premature poll of 20 international newspapers, the tremendously popular Brazilian soccer star was named "Athlete of the Century" by the French sports magazine "L'Equipe." Jesse Owens was runner-up.

Langley (1980). Wind-aided goals in 3 sec after kickoff have been scored by a number of players.

In amateur soccer, Tony Bacon, of Schalmont HS, scored three goals vs Ichabod Crane HS in 63 sec at Schenectady, NY on Oct 8, 1975.

Goalkeeping

The longest that any goalkeeper has succeeded in preventing any goals being scored past him in international matches is 1,142 min for Dino Zoff (Italy) from Sept 1972 to June 1974.

The biggest goalie on record was Willie J. ("Fatty") Foulke of England (1874–1916) who stood 6 ft 3 in and weighed 311 lb. By the time he died, he tipped the scales at 364 lb. He once stopped a game by snapping the cross bar.

Longest Matches

The world duration record for a first-class match was set in the Copa Libertadores championship in Santos, Brazil, Aug 2–3, 1962, when Santos drew 3–3 with Penarol FC of Montevideo, Uruguay. The game lasted 3½ hours (with interruptions), from 9:30 p.m. to 1 a.m.

A match between St Ignatius College Preparatory of San Francisco and Bellarmine College Preparatory of San Jose lasted 4 hours 56 min (230 min playing time) at San Francisco on Feb 6, 1982.

Most Postponements

In the winter of 1978–79, the tie-breaking match for the Scottish Cup between Inverness Thistle and Falkirk had to be postponed 29 times due to weather conditions.

Penalties

All 11 players and 2 substitutes were "booked" before the start of a game played by Glencraig United (UK) because the referee took exception to the chart which greeted his arrival.

Largest Tournament

In the Metropolitan Police 5-a-side Youth Competition in 1981 a record 7,008 teams entered.

Crowds

The greatest recorded crowd at any soccer match was 205,000 (199,854 paid) for the Brazil vs Uruguay World Cup final in Rio de Janeiro, Brazil, on July 16, 1950.

The greatest crowd to see a soccer game in the US and Canada was the 77,691 spectators at Giants Stadium, NJ, who watched an NASL playoff game between the NY Cosmos and Ft Lauderdale Strikers on Aug 14, 1977.

The highest attendance at any amateur match is 120,000 at Senayan Stadium, Djakarta, Indonesia, on Feb 26, 1976, for the Pre-Olympic Group II Final between North Korea and Indonesia.

World Cup

The *Fédération Internationale de Football Association* (FIFA) was founded in Paris on May 21, 1904, and instituted the World Cup Competition in 1930, in Montevideo, Uruguay. Cup competition is held every 4 years.

COSMOS' TOPPER: Giorgio Chinaglia holds NASL goal-scoring records for a career (195 through 1983), season (34) and game (7). After announcing his retirement as a player, he bought the Cosmos in mid-1984.

The only countries to win three times have been Brazil (1958, 62, 70) and Italy (1934, 38, 82). Brazil was also second in 1950, and third in 1938 and 1978, and is the only one of the 47 participating countries to have played in all 12 competitions, losing only 10 of a total of 57 matches played.

Antonio Carbajal (b 1923) played for Mexico in goal in a record 5 competitions, in 1950, 54, 58, 62 and 66.

The record goal scorer has been Just Fontaine (France) with 13 goals in 6 games in the final stages of the 1958 competition. The most goals scored in the final game is 3 by Geoffrey Hurst (West Ham United) for England vs W Germany in 1966. Gerd Müller (W Germany) scored a total of 14 goals in two World Cup finals (1970 and 74).

The highest score in a World Cup match is New Zealand's 13–0 defeat of Fiji in a qualifying match at Auckland on Aug 16, 1981. The highest score in the Finals Tournament is Hungary's 10–1 win over El Salvador at Elche, Spain, on June 15, 1982.

The fastest goal scored in World Cup competition was one in 27 sec by Bryan Robson for England vs France in Bilbao, Spain, on June 16, 1982.

NASL Records

The North American Soccer League was created in 1968 through the merger of the two competing professional soccer leagues: the United Soccer Association and the National Professional Soccer League.

The NY Cosmos have won a record 5 NASL championships, 1972, 77–78, 80 and 82.

Giorgio Chinaglia (b Jan 24, 1947) of the NY Cosmos scored a record 34 goals during the 1978 season. He also set the record for points that season with 79. (The NASL awards 2 points for a goal and 1 point for an assist.) Through 1983, Chinaglia had scored a league-record 195 goals in 213 regular-season games. Alan Hinton (Vancouver) had the most assists in a season with 30 in 1978.

Giorgio Chinaglia (NY) scored 7 goals in one playoff game against the Tulsa Roughnecks on Aug 31, 1980. He also added an assist, and his total points for a single game (15) is also a league record.

Steve Davis (LA) scored goals in 10 consecutive games in 1977, and Mike Stojanovic (San Diego) matched this feat in 1981.

NET WEIGHT: At 6 ft 3 in and 311 lb, Fatty Foulke was the most massive goalkeeper ever. One of his greatest exploits came off the field, however, when, appearing at the dinner table early one evening, Foulke ate the team's entire meal before any of his teammates arrived.

INDOOR SOCCER: The Kansas City Comets of the MISL are at home in Kemper Arena which holds 15,925 spectators. The surface is covered with artificial grass. (Kansas City Comets)

Peter Beardsley (Vancouver) scored the fastest goal, at 10 seconds against Toronto on June 5, 1983.

Goalkeeper Lincoln Phillips (Washington) went 528 consecutive minutes without allowing a goal in 1970. The fewest goals allowed in a season is 8 by Bob Rigby (Philadelphia) in 1973. The record for most saves in a game is 22, by Mike Winter (St Louis) vs Rochester, May 27, 1973.

Major Indoor Soccer League (MISL)

Founded in 1974, this league has a season with 48 games played by each team between Nov and Apr (playoffs continue until the end of May). There are 14 teams in the league, whose headquarters are in Bala Cynwyd, Pa. All-time career record holders to end of 1983–84 season are:

Most goals scored: Steve Zungul (NY) with 419 as compared to 259 for second place Fred Grgurev (Phil, NY, Mem). Zungul also shares the lead with 7 goals in a game (3/8/81), has most assists in a career with 222, points with 641, power play goals with 49, game-winning goals with 52, and hat tricks with 78. Grgurev is second in points, power play goals and hat tricks, and leads in number of games played with 230. Stan Stamenkovic (Balt), with most assists and scores, was chosen Most Valuable Player, 1983–84.

On defense, goalkeeper Shep Messing (NY) holds the all-time records in most games with 163, most wins with 104, most minutes played with

MISL STAR: Slobo Ilijevski of the St L Steamers, shown making a save in the 1984 All-Star game in St L, set an MISL record with 3.67 goals against average during the 1983–84 season. (Photo by Bill Brinson)

9,018, most shots with 5,796, most goals against, however, with 766, and second place in most saves with 2,684 and winning percentage with .680. Slobo Ilijevski (St L) was chosen top goalkeeper of 1983–84, with the record for lowest goals against, and most saves with 2,958.

Kenny Cooper of the Baltimore Blasts whose team won 20 games at home was selected coach of the year 1983–84.

Marathons

The longest outdoor game played was 74½ hours by two teams trying to establish a record at Liswerry Leisure Centre, Gwent, Wales, June 23–26, 1983. The indoor soccer record is 104 hours 10 min set by two teams of students at Summerhill College, Sligo, Ireland, Mar 27–31, 1983.

World Cup Winners

Winner	Locale
1930 Uruguay	Uruguay
1934 Italy	Italy
1938 Italy	France
1950 Uruguay	Brazil
1954 W Germany	Switzerland
1958 Brazil	Sweden
1962 Brazil	Chile
1966 England	England
1970 Brazil	Mexico
1974 W Germany	W Germany
1978 Argentina	Argentina
1982 Italy	Spain

SOFTBALL

Origins

Softball, as an indoor derivative of baseball, was invented by George Hancock at the Farragut Boat Club of Chicago, in 1887. Rules were first codified in Minneapolis in 1895 as Kitten Ball. The name Softball was introduced by Walter Hakanson at a meeting of the National Recreation Congress in 1926. The name was adopted throughout the US in 1930. Rules were formalized in 1933 by the International Joint Rules Committee for Softball and adopted by the Amateur Softball Association of America. The International Softball Federation was formed in 1950 as governing body for both fast pitch and slow pitch.

Marathons

The longest fast pitch marathon is 61 hours 36 min 33 sec by two teams of 9 (no substitutes) belonging to the Marines of the 2nd Radio Battalion at Camp Lejeune, NC, May 3–5, 1984. The game went 266 innings and the score was 343-296.

The longest for slow pitch is 95 hours by two teams of ten players (no substitutes) from the crew of the USS *Willamette* (A0180) at the US Naval Station, Pearl Harbor, Hawaii, Apr 26–30, 1984.

SOFTBALL STRIKEOUT ARTISTS: Joan Joyce (left) struck out 76 and pitched 2 perfect games in one season, and Ty Stofflet struck out 98 batters with his underhand fast pitch. Joyce once struck out Ted Williams and Hank Aaron. (Joyce photo—ASA)

WORLD CHAMPIONSHIP FAST PITCH SOFTBALL RECORDS

MEN
Batting

Highest batting average:	.556	Seiichi Tanka, Japan	1980
Most hits in a game:	17	Basil McLean, New Zealand	1976
Most runs scored in a game:	12	Generoso Lopez, Venezuela	1966
Most runs batted in in a game:	14	Chuck Teuscher US	1966
	14	Bob Burrows, Canada	1976
Most doubles in a game:	5	Hector Serranto, Puerto Rico	1966
	5	Luis Delgado, Mexico	1966
	5	Frank Hurtt, US	1968
	5	Filomeno Codinera, Philippines	1968
Most triples in a game:	3	Akira Nakagawa, Japan	1976
	3	Jesus Augon, Guam	1976
Most home runs in a game:	4	Bob Burrows, Canada	1976

Pitching (in a year)

Most wins:	6	Owen Walford, New Zealand	1976
	6	Owen Walford, US	1980
Most strikeouts, total:	99	Kevin Herlihy, New Zealand	1972
	98	Ty Stofflet, US	1976
Most strikeouts in one game:	33	Ty Stofflet, US	1976
		in 20 innings 1–0 win over New Zealand	
Most innings pitched in a year:	59	Ty Stofflet, US	1976
	58⅔	Kevin Herlihy, New Zealand	1972
Lowest earned run average:			
(59 innings pitched)	0.00	Ty Stofflet, US	1976
(32⅓ innings pitched)	0.00	Chuck Richard, US	1966
(34⅔ innings pitched)	0.00	Owen Walford, US	1980
Most consecutive wins:	12 in a row	Owen Walford, US	1976
	12 in a row	Owen Walford, New Zealand	1976
Perfect games:	1	Joe Lynch, US	1968
	1	Chuck Richard, US	1968
	1	Dave Ruthowsky, Canada	1976

WOMEN
Batting

Highest batting average:	.550	Tamara Bryce, Panama	1978
Most hits in a game:	17	Miyoko Naruse, Japan	1974
Most runs scored in a game:	13	Kathy Elliott, US	1974
Most runs batted in in a game:	11	Miyoko Naruse, Japan	1974
	11	Keiko Uoul, Japan	1974
	11	Kathy Elliott, US	1974
Most doubles in a game:	4	Vicki Murray, NZ	1983
	4	Suh-Chiung Ju, Taiwan	1983
Most triples in a game:	6	Miyoko Naruse, Japan	1974
	6	Yug Feng Yang, Taiwan	1982

Pitching

Most wins:	6	Lorraine Wooley, Australia	1965
	6	Nancy Welborn, US	1970
Most innings pitched:	50	Nancy Welborn, US	1970
Most strikeouts in a year:	76	Joan Joyce, US	1974
Most perfect games:	2	Joan Joyce, US	1974

World Championships

The US has won the men's world championship (instituted in 1966) four times, 1966, 68, 76 (shared) and 80. The US has also won the women's title (instituted in 1965) twice, in 1974 and 78.

SQUASH

Earliest Champion

Although racquets with a soft ball (called "squashy") was played in 1817 at Harrow School (England), there was no recognized champion of any country until J. A. Miskey of Philadelphia won the American Amateur Singles Championship in 1907.

World Titles

Geoffrey B. Hunt (b Mar 11, 1947) (Australia) won a record four World Open (inst 1976) titles, 1976–7 and 1979–80, and three World Amateur (inst 1967) titles. Australia has won a record four amateur team titles, 1967, 1969, 1971 and 1973.

Jahangir Khan (Pakistan) has won 3 times (1981–82–83), and was the youngest champion in 1981 at age 17 years 354 days.

Heather McKay (see below) won twice (1976 and 1979). No women's tournament was held in 1977 and 1978.

British Open Championship

The most wins in the Open Championship (amateur or professional), held annually in Britain, is 8 by Geoffrey Hunt in 1969, 74, and 76–81. Hashim Khan (b 1915) (Pakistan) won 7 times and has also won the Vintage title 5 times, 1978–82.

The most wins in the Women's Squash Rackets Championship is 16 by Heather McKay (*née* Blundell) (b July 31, 1941) of Australia, 1961 to 1977. She also won the World Open title in 1976 and 79. In her career from 1959 to 1980 she lost only two games.

Longest and Shortest Championship Matches

The longest recorded championship match was one of 2 hours 45 min when Jahangir Khan (b Dec 10, 1963) (Pakistan) beat Gamal Awad (Egypt) (b Sept 8, 1955) 9–10, 9–5, 9–7, 9–2, the first game lasting a record 1 hour 11 min, in the final of the Patrick International Festival at Chichester, W Sussex, England, Mar 30, 1983.

Deanna Murray beat Christine Rees in only 9½ min in a Ladies Welsh title match at Rhos-on-Sea, Clwyd, Wales, on Oct 21, 1979.

Marathon Record

The longest squash marathon has been 121 hours 16 min by Paul Holmes and Andy Head at Hove Squash Court, Hove, Sussex, Eng, Apr 18–23, 1984. (*This category is now confined to two players only.*)

HOLDING COURT: The winner of 16 British and 2 World Open championships, Heather McKay has not lost a match since 1961. She won all but 2 of the games she played.

SURFING

Origins

The traditional Polynesian sport of surfing in a canoe was first recorded by Captain James Cook (GB) (1728–79) on his first voyage at Tahiti in Dec 1771. Surfing on a board was first described "most perilous and extraordinary ... altogether astonishing and is scarcely to be credited" by Lt (later Capt) James King (GB) in Mar 1779 at Kealakekua Bay, Hawaii Island. A surfer was first depicted by this voyage's official artist John Webber. The sport was revived at Waikiki by 1900. Hollow boards were introduced in 1929 and the light plastic foam type in 1956.

Most Titles

World Amateur Championships were inaugurated in May 1964 at Sydney, Australia; the only surfer to win two titles has been Joyce Hoffman (US) in 1965 and 1966. A World Professional circuit was started in 1975 and Mark Richards (Australia) has won the men's title four times, 1979–82.

Highest Waves Ridden

Makaha Beach, Hawaii provides the reputedly highest consistently tall waves, often reaching the rideable limit of 30–35 ft. The highest wave ever ridden was the *tsunami* of "perhaps 50 ft," which struck Minole, Hawaii on Apr 3, 1868, and was ridden to save his life by a Hawaiian named Holua.

Longest Ride

About four to six times each year rideable surfing waves break in Matanchen Bay near San Blas, Nayarit, Mexico which makes a ride of *c.* 5,700 ft possible.

THRILL RIDE: This surfer is riding the waves much as the Hawaiians did over 200 years ago. A wave of reportedly 50 feet was the highest ever ridden.

SWIMMING

Earliest References

Egyptian hieroglyphics, c 3000 BC, indicate swimming figures, and a bronze of a diver dating from c 510 BC was found near Perugia, Italy. Both Julius Caesar and Charlemagne were known to be good swimmers. Competitions took place in Japan in 36 BC, and that country was the first to take to the sport in a major way with an Imperial edict by the Emperor G-Yozei decreeing its introduction in schools. In Britain, sea bathing was practiced as early as 1660 at Scarborough, but competitive swimming was not introduced until 1837, when competitions were held in London's artificial pools organized by the National Swimming Society, founded in that year. Australia was in the forefront of modern developments and an unofficial world 100-yd championship was held in Melbourne in 1858. With the foundation in Britain of the Amateur Swimming Association (though not known by this name till later) in 1869 came the distinction between amateurs and professionals.

The first recognizable stroke style seems to have been the breaststroke, although the "dog-paddle" technique may well have preceded it. From this developed the sidestroke, which is the breaststroke performed sideways, a style which was last used by an Olympic champion in 1904, when Emil Rausch (Ger) won the 1-mi event. About the middle of the 19th century, some American Indians had swum in London exhibiting a style resembling the crawl. An Englishman, John Trudgen, noted a variation of this style while on a trip to South America in the 1870s. His forerunner to the modern crawl used the legs in basically a breaststroke way. However, from ancient carvings and wall paintings it would seem that the trudgen stroke was in use in early times.

Another "throwback" was the front or Australian crawl which is credited to a British emigrant to Australia, Frederick Cavill, and his sons, who noticed the unusual style of South Sea Island natives, and modified it to their own use. American swimmers developed this even further by variations of the kicking action of the legs. At the beginning of the 20th century some had shown their prowess by attempting the breaststroke on their backs, and later the crawl action was tried in the same position. Thus the backstroke was born. In the 1930s the idea of recovering the arms over the water in the breaststroke was developed, and led to a drastic revision of the record book, until the new style was recognized as a separate stroke, the butterfly, in 1952. Also in the 1930s came the introduction, mainly in the US, of medley events in which swimmers use all four major strokes during one event, a real test of all-around ability.

Largest Pools

The largest swimming pool in the world is the salt-water Orthlieb Pool in Casablanca, Morocco. It is 480 m (1,574 ft) long, 75 m (246 ft) wide, and has an area of 8.9 acres.

The largest land-locked swimming pool with heated water was the Fleishhacker Pool on Sloat Boulevard, near Great Highway, San Francisco. It measures 1,000 ft by 150 ft (3.44 acres), is up to 14 ft deep, and

MOST RECORDS: A young Mark Spitz (17 years old in this photo) is congratulated after setting a world record early in his career. Spitz might be considered the most successful swimmer ever. Of his 9 Olympic gold medals (including the unequaled haul of 7 in 1972), 8 were won in world record time. In his 6-year career, Spitz set a total of 26 world records.

can contain 7,500,000 gallons of water. It was opened on May 2, 1925, but has now been abandoned.

The world's largest competition pool is at Osaka, Japan. It accommodates 13,614 spectators.

Fastest Swimmers

The fastest 50 m in a 50-m pool is 22.54 sec by Robin Leamy (b Apr 1, 1961) (US), averaging 4.96 mph, at Milwaukee, Wis, on Aug 15, 1981.

The fastest by a woman is 25.62 sec by Dara Torres (US), 15, of Beverly Hills, Calif, averaging 4.37 mph, at Clovis, Calif, on Aug 6, 1983.

Most World Records

Men: 32, Arne Borg (Sweden) (b 1901), 1921–29. Women: 42, Ragnhild Hveger (Denmark) (b Dec 10, 1920), 1936–42. Under modern condi-

FASTEST SPRINT: Robin Leamy, a student at UCLA, swam the length of a 50-meter pool in 22.54 seconds in Milwaukee, Wisconsin, in 1981.

tions (only metric distances in 50-meter pools) the most is 26 by Mark Spitz (US, b Feb 10, 1950), 1967–72, and 23 by Kornelia Ender (now Matthes) (E Germany, b Oct 25, 1958), 1973–76.

Hveger's record of 42 gained for her the name "Golden Torpedo." Her records came in 18 different events. She was a virtual certainty to win at the 1940 Olympic Games, but, of course, war intervened. Retiring in 1945, she made a comeback for the 1952 Games and placed fifth in the 400 m freestyle.

World Titles

In the world swimming championships (instituted in 1973), the greatest number of medals won is 10 by Kornelia Ender of E Germany (8 gold, 2 silver). The most by a man is 8 (5 gold, 3 silver) by Ambrose "Rowdy" Gaines (US, b Feb 17, 1959) in 1978 and 1982. The most gold medals is 6 by James Montgomery (b Jan 24, 1955) in 1973 and 1975.

The most medals in a single championship is 6 by Tracy Caulkins (US) (b Jan 11, 1963) in 1978 with 5 gold and a silver. She has won a record 47 US titles to 1983.

The most successful country in the championships has been the US with a total of 50 swimming, 9 diving and 8 synchronized swimming titles. However, in women's swimming events alone E Germany has a record total of 31 victories.

Other than relays, the only gold medalist in the same event at three championships is Phil Boggs (US) in springboard diving.

Most Individual Gold Medals

The record number of individual gold medals won is 4 shared by four swimmers: Charles M. Daniels (US) (1884–1973) (100 m freestyle 1906 and 1908, 220 yd freestyle 1904, 440 yd freestyle 1904); Roland Matthes (E Germany) (b Nov 17, 1950) with 100 m and 200 m backstroke 1968 and 1972; and Mark Spitz and Mrs Patricia McCormick (see below).

Most Olympic Gold Medals

The greatest number of Olympic gold medals won is 9 by Mark Andrew Spitz (US) (b Feb 10, 1950), as follows:

100 m freestyle	1972	4 × 100 m freestyle relay	1968 and 1972
200 m freestyle	1972	4 × 200 m freestyle relay	1968 and 1972
100 m butterfly	1972	4 × 100 m medley relay	1972
200 m butterfly	1972		

All but one of these performances (the 4 × 200 m relay of 1968) were also world records at the time.

The record number of gold medals won by a woman is 4 shared by Mrs Patricia McCormick (*née* Keller) (US) (b May 12, 1930) with the High and Springboard Diving double in 1952 and 1956 (also the women's record for individual golds); by Dawn Fraser (Australia) (b Sept 4, 1937) with the 100 m freestyle (1956, 60, 64) and the 4 × 100 m freestyle relay (1956); and by Kornelia Ender (E Germany) with the 100 and 200 m freestyle (1976), the 100 m butterfly (1976) and the 4 × 100 m medley relay (1976). Dawn Fraser is the only swimmer to win the same event on three successive occasions.

OLYMPIC GOLD MEDALISTS: Mrs. Pat McCormick (left) (US) and Dawn Fraser (right) (Aust) share the record, along with Kornelia Ender (E Ger) for the most gold medals won by a woman. McCormick uniquely won all 4 in individual events while Fraser is the only swimmer to win the same event at 3 consecutive Games.

Closest Race

In the women's 100 m freestyle final in the 1984 Olympics, Carrie Steinseifer (US) and Nancy Hogshead (US) won in a tie at 55.92 sec, and were both awarded gold medals. It was not in record time, but it was the first dead heat in Olympic swimming history.

BUTTERFLY CHAMPION: Since 1980, Mary Meagher (US) has been setting world records. In the 1984 Olympics, she set Olympic records in the 100 m and 200 m butterflies.

Gold Medal Winners in 1984 Olympics

Men

		min	sec	
100 m freestyle	Ambrose "Rowdy" Gaines (US)		49.80	OR
200 m freestyle	Michael Gross (W Ger)	1	47.44	WR
400 m freestyle	George DiCarlo (US)	3	51.23	OR
1500 m freestyle	Michael O'Brien (US)	15	05.20	
100 m backstroke	Richard "Rick" Carey (US)		55.79	
200 m backstroke	Richard "Rick" Carey (US)	2	00.23	
100 m breaststroke	Steve Lundquist (US)	1	01.65	WR
200 m breaststroke	Victor Davis (Can)	2	13.34	WR
100 m butterfly	Michael Gross (W Ger)		53.08	WR
200 m butterfly	John Sieben (Aust)	1	57.04	WR
200 m ind. medley	Alex Baumann (Can)	2	01.42	WR
400 m ind. medley	Alex Baumann (Can)	4	17.41	WR
4 × 100 m freestyle	US	3	19.03	WR
4 × 200 m freestyle	US	7	15.69	WR
4 × 100 m medley	US	3	39.30	WR

Women

		min	sec	
100 m freestyle	Carrie Steinseifer & Nancy Hogshead (US)		55.92	
200 m freestyle	Mary Wayte (US)	1	59.23	
400 m freestyle	Tiffany Cohen (US)	4	07.10	OR
800 m freestyle	Tiffany Cohen (US)	8	24.95	OR
100 m backstroke	Theresa Andrews (US)	1	02.55	
200 m backstroke	Jolanda De Rove (Neth)	2	12.38	
100 m breaststroke	Petra Van Staveren (Neth)	1	09.88	OR
200 m breaststroke	Anne Ottenbrite (Can)	2	30.38	
100 m butterfly	Mary Meagher (US)		59.26	OR
200 m butterfly	Mary Meagher (US)	2	06.90	OR
200 m ind. medley	Tracy Caulkins (US)	2	12.64	OR
400 m ind. medley	Tracy Caulkins (US)	4	39.24	
4 × 100 m freestyle	US	3	43.43	
4 × 100 m medley	US	4	08.34	
Synchronized duet	Candy Costie & Tracie Ruiz (US)		195.584 points	
Synchronized solo	Tracie Ruiz (US)		198.467 points	

WR = World Record   OR = Olympic Record

Most Olympic Medals

The most medals won is 11 by Spitz, who in addition to his 9 golds (see above), won a silver (100 m butterfly) and a bronze (100 m freestyle), both in 1968.

The most medals won by a woman is 8 by Dawn Fraser, who in addition to her 4 golds (see above) won 4 silvers (400 m freestyle 1956, 4 × 100 m freestyle relay 1960 and 1964, 4 × 100 m medley relay 1960); by Shirley Babashoff (US) who won 2 golds (4 × 100 m freestyle relay 1972 and 1976) and 6 silvers (100 m freestyle 1972, 200 m freestyle 1972 and 1976, 400 m and 800 m freestyle 1976, and 400 m medley 1976); and by Kornelia Ender (E Germany) who, in addition to her 4 golds (see above), won 4 silvers (200 m individual medley 1972, 4 × 100 m medley 1972, 4 × 100 m freestyle 1972 and 1976).

Swimming into the Movies

The ability to move well in water has been the key to a movie career for a number of champion swimmers. The first star was Australian Annette Kellerman who made a number of silent films, and was the first woman to wear a one-piece bathing suit. However, it was the 1924 and 1928 Olympic gold medalist, Johnny Weissmuller (US), who became the first major box-office attraction from the swimming world, playing the role of Tarzan in a dozen films. His 1928 Olympic teammate, Clarence "Buster" Crabbe, who later won the 1932 400 m freestyle title, also went to Hollywood, where he was the hero in the long-running Buck Rogers and Flash Gordon serials.

Another 1932 Olympic champion, the glamorous Eleanor Holm (US) made several movies, although she did not go to Hollywood until she was dropped from the 1936 team for disciplinary reasons. Perhaps the best known swimming star was Esther Williams, American 100 m champion in 1939 and favorite for the cancelled Olympics of 1940. Turning professional she created a new vogue in the cinema, the swimming musical, in which she was supreme throughout the 1940s. One of her co-stars was Fernando Lamas, who had been a national swimming champion in his native Argentina, and whom she later married.

SWIMMING WORLD RECORDS

At distances recognized by the Fédération Internationale de Natation Amateur as of July 16, 1983. FINA no longer recognizes any records made for non-metric distances. Only performances in 50-m pools are recognized as World Records.

MEN

Distance	min:sec	Name and Nationality	Place	Date
		FREESTYLE		
100 m	49.36	Ambrose (Rowdy) Gaines (US)	Austin, Tex	Apr 3, 1981
200 m	1:47.44	Michael Gross (W Ger)	Los Angeles	July 29, 1984
400 m	3:48.32	Vladimir Salnikov (USSR)	Moscow	Feb 19, 1983
800 m	7:52.33	Vladimir Salnikov (USSR)	Los Angeles	July 14, 1983
1,500 m	14:54.76	Vladimir Salnikov (USSR)	Moscow	Feb 22, 1983
4 × 100 m Relay	3:19.03	US National Team (Chris Cavanaugh, Michael Heath, Mathew Biondi, Ambrose "Rowdy" Gaines)	Los Angeles	Aug 2, 1984
4 × 200 m Relay	7:15.69	US National Team (Michael Heath, David Larson, Jeff Float, Bruce Hayes)	Los Angeles	July 30, 1984
		BREASTSTROKE		
100 m	1:01.65	Steve Lundquist (US)	Los Angeles	July 29, 1984
200 m	2:13.34	Victor Davis (Canada)	Los Angeles	Aug 2, 1984
		BUTTERFLY STROKE		
100 m	53.08	Michael Gross (W Ger)	Los Angeles	July 30, 1984
200 m	1:57.04	Jon Sieben (Australia)	Los Angeles	Aug 3, 1984
		BACKSTROKE		
100 m	55.19	Richard (Rick) Carey (US)	Caracas, Venezuela	Aug 21, 1983
200 m	1:58.41	Sergei Zabolotnov (USSR)	Moscow	Aug 21, 1984
		INDIVIDUAL MEDLEY		
200 m	2:01.42	Alex Baumann (Canada)	Los Angeles	Aug 4, 1984
400 m	4:17.41	Alex Baumann (Canada)	Los Angeles	July 30, 1984
		MEDLEY RELAY (Backstroke, Breaststroke, Butterfly Stroke, Freestyle)		
4 × 100 m	3:39.70	US National Team (Richard "Rick" Carey, Steven Lundquist, Pablo Morales, Ambrose "Rowdy" Gaines)	Los Angeles	Aug 4, 1984

Olympic Medals for Diving

Klaus Dibiasi (Italy, b Austria, Oct 6, 1947) won a total of 5 diving medals (3 gold, 2 silver) in 4 Games from 1964 to 1976. He is also the only

DIVING CHAMPION: Greg Louganis (US), considered the best diver in the world today, is one of two divers to earn perfect 10's from all 7 judges for one dive. He achieved the feat while winning his 2nd and 3rd world championships. In the 1984 Olympics he won 2 gold medals and set new world records for springboard and highboard.

diver to win the same event (highboard) at 3 successive Games (1968, 72 and 76). Pat McCormick (see above) won 4 gold medals.

In the 1984 Olympics, Greg Louganis (see below) won two gold medals and set record totals of 754.41 for springboard and 710.91 for highboard.

Diving Gold Medal Olympic Winners 1984

Men	Women
Springboard Diving	*Springboard Diving*
Greg Louganis (US) 754.41 pts	Sylvie Bernier (Can) 530.70 pts
High Diving	*High Diving*
Greg Louganis (US) 710.91 pts	Zhov Jihong (China) 435.51 pts

World Diving Titles

Phil Boggs (US) (b Dec 29, 1949) won 3 springboard gold medals, in 1973, 1975 and 1978, but Klaus Dibiasi (Italy) won 4 medals (2 gold, 2 silver) in 1973 and 1975. Irina Kalinina (USSR) (b Feb 8, 1959) has won 5 medals (three gold, one silver, one bronze) in 1973, 1975 and 1978. Greg Louganis (US) (b Jan 29, 1960), won one gold in 1978 and 2 in the 1982 world championships at Guayaquil, Ecuador, where he became the first to score over 700 points for the 11-dive springboard event with 752.67 on

Aug 1, 1982. He went on to be awarded a score of 10.0 by all 7 judges for his highboard inward 1½ somersault in the pike position.

Perfect Dive

In the 1972 US Olympic Trials, held in Chicago, Michael Finneran (b Sept 21, 1948) was awarded a score of 10 by all seven judges for a backward 1½ somersault 2½ twist (free) from the 10-m platform, an achievement then without precedent. Greg Louganis matched this feat in 1982.

SWIMMING WORLD RECORDS

WOMEN

Distance	min:sec	Name and Nationality	Place	Date
		FREESTYLE		
100 m	54.79	Barbara Krause (E Ger)	Moscow	July 21, 1980
200 m	1:57.75	Kristin Otto (E Ger)	Magdeburg, E Ger	May 23, 1984
400 m	4:06.28	Tracey Wickham (Aust)	W Berlin	Aug 24, 1978
800 m	8:24.62	Tracey Wickham (Aust)	Edmonton, Canada	Aug 5, 1978
1,500 m	16:04.49	Kim Linehan (US)	Ft Lauderdale	Aug 19, 1979
4 × 100 m Relay	3:42.41	East German National Team (Kristin Otto, Karen Konig, Heike Friedrich, Birgit Meineke)	Moscow	Aug 21, 1984
4 × 200 m Relay	8:02.27	E Germany (Kristin Otto, Karen Konig, Heike Friedrich, Birgit Meineke)	Moscow	Aug 21, 1984
		BREASTSTROKE		
100 m	1:08.29	Sylvia Gerasch (E Ger)	Moscow	Aug 22, 1984
200 m	2:28.36	Lina Kachushite (USSR)	Potsdam, E Germany	Apr 6, 1979
		BUTTERFLY STROKE		
100 m	57.93	Mary Meagher (US)	Milwaukee	Aug 16, 1981
200 m	2:05.96	Mary Meagher (US)	Milwaukee	Aug 13, 1981
		BACKSTROKE		
100 m	1:00.59	Ina Kleber (E Ger)	Moscow	Aug 24, 1984
200 m	2:09.91	Kornelia Sirch (E Ger)	Guayaquil, Ecuador	Aug 7, 1982
		INDIVIDUAL MEDLEY		
200 m	2:11.73	Ute Geweniger (E Ger)	E Berlin	July 4, 1981
400 m	4:36.10	Petra Schneider (E Ger)	Guayaquil, Ecuador	Aug 1, 1982
		MEDLEY RELAY (Backstroke, Breaststroke, Butterfly Stroke, Freestyle)		
4 × 100 m Relay	4:03.69	E German National Team (Ina Gelber, Sylvia Gerasch, Ines Geissler, Birgit Meineke)	Moscow	Aug 24, 1984

Long Distance Swimming

A unique achievement in long distance swimming was established in 1966 by Mihir Sen of Calcutta, India. He swam the Palk Strait from Sri Lanka to India (in 25 hours 36 min, Apr 5–6); the Straits of Gibraltar (Europe to Africa in 8 hours 1 min on Aug 24); the Dardanelles (Gallipoli, Europe, to Sedulbahir, Asia Minor, in 13 hours 55 min on Sept 12); the Bosphorus (in 4 hours on Sept 21) and the entire length of the Panama Canal (in 34 hours 15 min, Oct 29–31). He had earlier swum the English Channel in 14 hours 45 min on Sept 27, 1958.

The longest ocean swim claimed is one of 128.8 miles by Walter Poenisch (US) (b 1914), who started from Havana, Cuba, and arrived at Little

LONG-TIME CHAMPIONS: No one has been able to beat the record of Petra Schneider of E Germany (left) in the 400 m individual medley since 1982. Cindy Nicholas of Canada (right) was the first woman to make a double crossing of the English Channel in 1977, knocking 10 hours off the men's mark. She beat this by an hour in 1982.

Duck Key, Fla (in a shark cage and wearing flippers) 34 hours 15 min later, July 11–13, 1978.

The greatest recorded distance ever swum is 1,826 miles down the Mississippi from Ford Dam, near Minneapolis, to Carrollton Avenue, New Orleans, July 6 to Dec 29, 1930, by Fred P. Newton, then 27, of Clinton, Okla. He was in the water a total of 742 hours, and the water temperature fell as low as 47° F. He protected himself with petroleum jelly.

The longest swim using the highly exhausting butterfly stroke exclusively was 28.5 miles around Manhattan Island, NYC, in 9 hours 42 min by twins James and Jonathan di Donato (b Oct 24, 1953) (US) Aug 21, 1984.

The fastest swim around Manhattan was made by Drury J. Gallagher in 6 hours 41 min 35 sec on Sept 7, 1983. The women's record was set by Diddo Clark in 6 hours 52 min 15 sec on Oct 6, 1983.

The longest duration swim ever achieved was one of 168 continuous hours, ending on Feb 24, 1941, by the legless Charles Zibbelman, *alias* Zimmy (b 1894), of the US, in a pool in Honolulu, Hawaii.

The longest duration swim by a woman was 87 hours 27 min in a salt water pool at Raven Hall, Coney Island, NY by Mrs Myrtle Huddleston of NYC, in 1931.

The greatest distance covered in a continuous swim is 299 miles by Ricardo Hoffmann (b Oct 5, 1941) from Corrientes to Santa Elena, Argentina, in the River Parana in 84 hours 37 min, Mar 3–6, 1981.

J. Hestoy (Faroe Islands) was reported to have swum 55.41 miles in 24 hours in a pool in 1982.

TWIN BUTTERFLY STROKERS: James and Jonathan di Donato swam the 28+ miles around Manhattan in 9 hours 42 min using only the exhausting butterfly stroke.

The greatest lifetime distance by a swimmer is 37,073 miles recorded by Gustave Brickner (b Feb 10, 1912) of Charleroi, Pa, in 55 years to Oct 1982.

Earliest Channel Swimmers

The first to swim the English Channel (without a life jacket) was the merchant navy captain Matthew Webb (1848–83) (GB), who swam breaststroke from Dover, England, to Calais Sands, France, in 21 hours 45 min, Aug 24–25, 1875. Webb swam an estimated 38 miles to make the 21-mile crossing. Paul Boyton (US) had swum from Cap Gris Nez to the South Foreland in his patented lifesaving suit in 23 hours 30 min, May 28–29, 1875. There is good evidence that Jean-Marie Saletti, a French soldier, escaped from a British prison hulk off Dover by swimming to Boulogne in July or Aug 1815. The first crossing from France to England was made by Enrico Tiraboschi, a wealthy Italian living in Argentina, who crossed in 16 hours 33 min on Aug 12, 1923, to win a $5,000 prize. By the end of 1981 the English Channel had been swum by 228 persons on 366 occasions.

The first woman to succeed was Gertrude Ederle (b Oct 23, 1906) (US) who swam from Cap Gris Nez, France, to Deal, England, on Aug 6, 1926, in the then record time of 14 hours 39 min. The first woman to swim from England to France was Florence Chadwick of California, in 16 hours 19 min on Sept 11, 1951.

Youngest and Oldest Channel Swimmers

The youngest conqueror is Marcus Hooper (b June 14, 1967) of Eltham, England, who swam from Dover to Sangatte, France, in 14 hours 37 min, when he was aged 12 years 53 days. The youngest woman was Samantha Claire Druce (b Apr 21, 1971) aged 12 years 119 days when she swam from England to France in 15 hours 26 min on Aug 18, 1983.

The oldest is Ashby Harper (b Oct 1, 1916) of Albuquerque, N Mex, at 65 years 332 days. He swam from Dover to Cap Blanc Nez in 13 hours 52 min on Aug 28, 1983.

The oldest woman to conquer the Channel is Stella Ada Rosina Taylor (b Bristol, Avon, England, Dec 20, 1929), aged 45 years 350 days when she swam it in 18 hours 15 min on Aug 26, 1975.

Most Conquests of the English Channel

The greatest number of Channel conquests is 30 by Michael Read (GB), to July 8, 1984, including a record 6 in one year. Cindy Nicholas made her first crossing of the Channel on July 29, 1975, and her 19th (and fifth 2-way) on Sept 14, 1982.

Double Crossings of the Channel

Antonio Abertondo (Argentina), aged 42, swam from England to France in 18 hours 50 min (8:35 a.m. on Sept 20 to 3:25 a.m. on Sept 21, 1961) and after about 4 minutes' rest returned to England in 24 hours 16 min, landing at St Margaret's Bay at 3:45 a.m. on Sept 22, 1961, to complete the first "double crossing" in 43 hours 10 min.

Cynthia Nicholas (b Aug 20, 1957, Scarborough, Ont, Canada) became the first woman to complete a double crossing of the English Channel, Sept 7–8, 1977. Her astonishing time of 19 hours 55 min was more than 10 hours faster than the previous mark. She later set a speed record of 18 hours 55 min on Aug 28, 1982.

The relay record is 16 hours 5½ min (including a 2 min rest) by 6 Saudi Arabian men on Aug 11, 1977.

Triple Crossing of the Channel

The first triple crossing of the English Channel was by Jon Erikson (b Sept 6, 1954) (US) in 38 hours 27 min, Aug 11–12, 1981.

Fastest Channel Crossings

The official Channel Swimming Association record is 7 hours 40 min by Penny Dean (b March 21, 1955) of California, who swam from Shakespeare Beach, Dover, England to Cap Gris Nez, France on July 29, 1978.

CHANNEL ENERGY: Jon Erikson (right), the first swimmer to make a triple crossing of the English Channel, relaxes here with his father, Ted. Both had held records for the fastest double crossing.

The fastest crossing by a relay team is 7 hours 17 min by 6 Dover (Eng) lifeguards from England to France on Aug 9, 1981.

Underwater Swimming

Paul Cryne swam 44.79 mi underwater in a 24-hour period at Doha, Qatar on June 26–July 7, 1984 using sub-aqua equipment. He was swimming underwater for 89.1% of the time.

The first underwater cross-Channel swim was achieved by Fred Baldasare (US), aged 38, who completed a 42-mile swim from France to England with scuba in 18 hours 1 min, July 10–11, 1962.

Relay Records

The New Zealand national relay team of 20 swimmers swam a record 113.59 mi in Lower Hutt, NZ in 24 hours, passing 100 mi in 20 hours 47 min 13 sec on Dec 9–10, 1983.

The most participants in a swim relay is 1900 (38 teams of 50) in Sao Paulo, Brazil, on Apr 1, 1984. A team of 4 from Capalaba State Primary School, Kim Wilson, Tanya Obstoj, Paul Giles, Daren Sheldrick, set an endurance record of 168 hours with one of the team in the water at any time, covering 336 mi on Dec 12–19, 1983 at Sheldon, Queensland, Australia.

The fastest time recorded for 100 miles in a pool by a team of 20 swimmers is 21 hours 41 min 4 sec by the Dropped Sports Swim Club of Indiana State University at Terre Haute, Ind, Mar 12–13, 1982. Four swimmers from the Darien YMCA, Conn, covered 300 miles in relay in 122 hours 59 min 40 sec, Nov 25–30, 1980.

Peter Saville, John Mason, Robert Mortimer and Duncan Moulder, of Stratford-upon-Avon Sub Aqua Club, swam an underwater relay of 279.099 miles in 168 hours at the Holiday Inn, Birmingham, England, June 30–July 7, 1979.

Treading Water

The duration record for treading water (vertical posture in an 8-ft square without touching the pool sides or ropes or lane markers) is 81 hours 25 min set by Thiru Shanmugam at Anna Swimming Pool, Madras, India, June 26–29, 1983.

Albert Rizzu trod water in the sea at Gzira, Malta, for 108 hours 9 min Sept 7–12, 1983.

TABLE TENNIS

Earliest Reference

In 1879 some Cambridge University students indulged in a diversion in which they hit champagne corks to each other over a table, using cigar boxes as crude bats. From this humble beginning came a new sport. Rubber balls soon followed, but it was not until James Gibb, a former English world record-breaking runner, introduced a celluloid ball to the game that *gossima,* as the game had previously been called, took the name of *ping pong,* after the noise the ball made when hit back and forth. The game thrived for a period, and in 1902 the Ping Pong Association was formed in Britain. But the monotony of play due to plain wooden bats soon led to a decline in interest until the 1920s when E. C. Goode fixed a studded rubber mat, from a pharmacy, to his paddle and proceeded to sweep all before him with the spin thus imparted to the ball. In Apr 1927 the English Table Tennis Association was founded and rules were standardized. In view of their current dominance it is noteworthy that organized table tennis in China dates from 1923.

World Championships

Instituted in 1927, the world championships were held annually until 1957, when the competitions became biennial (rendering most of the following personal records virtually unbreakable). G. Viktor Barna (1911–72) (Hungary) won 5 men's singles titles (1930, 32–35) and 8 men's doubles titles (1929–35, 39). Including his 2 mixed doubles titles, Barna

CHINESE DOMINATION of table tennis began in the 1960's. Here Chuang Tse-tung (China) smashes his way to the world title in Prague in 1963. He won the 1961 and 1965 titles also, for 3 straight. His smash was reputed to have been the fastest in table tennis in his time.

won a total of 15 personal world championships. The most wins in the women's singles is 6 by Angelica Rozeanu (b Oct 15, 1921) (Romania), 1950–55. Maria Mednyanszky (1901–79) (Hungary) won 7 women's doubles titles (1928, 1930–35) and 6 mixed doubles titles (1927–28, 1930–31, 1933–34). Including her 5 wins in women's singles, Mednyanszky won 18 personal titles in the world championships.

The most victories in the men's team championships (Swaythling Cup) is 12 by Hungary from 1927 through 1979. The women's team title (Marcel Corbillon Cup, instituted in 1934) has been won most often by Japan, with 8 victories from 1952-1971.

Longest Match

In the Swaythling Cup final match between Austria and Romania in Prague, Czechoslovakia, in 1936, the play lasted for 11 hours, beginning Sunday, March 15, and completed the following Wednesday.

Longest Rally

In a Swaythling Cup match in Prague on March 14, 1936, between Alex Ehrlich (Poland) and Paneth Farcas (Romania), the opening rally lasted for 1 hour 58 min.

Rick Bowling and Richard De Witt staged a rally lasting 10 hours 9 min at the YWCA in New Haven, Conn, on July 26, 1983.

Youngest International Contestant

The youngest international (in any sport) was Joy Foster, aged 8, when she represented Jamaica in the West Indies Championships at Port of Spain, Trinidad, in Aug 1958.

Fastest Rallying

The record number of hits in 60 sec is 162 by Nicky Jarvis and Desmond Douglas in London, England, on Dec 1, 1976. This was equaled by Douglas and Paul Day at Blackpool, England, on March 21, 1977. The most by women is 148 by Linda Howard and Melodi Ludi at Blackpool, Lancashire, England, on Oct 11, 1977.

With a paddle in each hand, Gary D. Fisher of Olympia, Wash, completed 5,000 consecutive volleys over the net in 44 min 28 sec on June 25, 1979.

Highest Speed

No conclusive measurements have been published, but in a lecture M. Sklorz (W Germany) stated that a smashed ball had been measured at speeds up to 105.6 mph.

Marathon

The longest recorded time for a marathon singles match by two players is 147 hours 47 min by S. Unterslak and J. Boccia at Dewaal Hotel, Cape Town, S Africa, Nov 12–18, 1983.

The longest doubles marathon by 4 players is 101 hours 1 min 11 sec by Lance, Phil and Mark Warren and Bill Weir at Sacramento, Calif, Apr 9–13, 1979.

TENNIS IN ITS IN-FANCY: Leslie's magazine pictured women's entry into the sport in the late 19th century.

TENNIS

Origins

The modern game of lawn tennis is generally agreed to have evolved as an outdoor form of the French Royal Tennis or *Jeu de Paume* from the 11th century. "Field Tennis" was mentioned in an English magazine (*Sporting Magazine*) on Sept 29, 1793. In 1858 Major Harry Gem laid out a "court" on the lawn of a friend in Birmingham, Eng, and in 1872 he founded the Leamington Club. In Feb 1874, Major Walter Clopton Wingfield of England (1833–1912) patented a form called "sphairistike," which was nicknamed "sticky," but the game soon became known as lawn tennis. The US Lawn Tennis Association (USLTA) was founded in 1881.

Amateurs were permitted to play with and against professionals in Open tournaments starting in 1968.

"Grand Slams"

The "grand slam" is to hold at the same time all four of the world's major championship titles: Wimbledon, the US Open, Australian and French championships. The first time this occurred was in 1935 when Frederick John Perry (GB) (b 1909) won the French title, having won Wimbledon (1934), the US title (1933–34) and the Australian title (1934).

The first player to hold all four titles simultaneously was J. Donald Budge (US) (b June 13, 1915), who won the championships of Wimble-

FIRST "GRAND SLAMMERS": Fred Perry (GB) (left) won all 4 major titles in 1934–35. Don Budge (US) (right) in 1937–38 held all 4 simultaneously. (Perry photo, AP)

don (1937), the US (1937), Australia (1938), and France (1938). He subsequently retained Wimbledon (1938) and the US (1938). Rodney George Laver (Australia) (b Aug 9, 1938) achieved this grand slam in 1962 as an amateur and repeated as a professional in 1969 to become the first two-time grand slammer.

Three women players also have won all these four titles in the same tennis year. The first was Maureen Catherine Connolly (US). She won the US title in 1951, Wimbledon in 1952, retained the US title in 1952, won the Australian in 1953, the French in 1953, and Wimbledon again in 1953. She won her third US title in 1953, her second French title in 1954, and her third Wimbledon title in 1954. Miss Connolly (later Mrs Norman Brinker) was seriously injured in a riding accident shortly before the 1954 US championships; she died in June 1969, aged only 34.

The second woman to win the "grand slam" was Margaret Smith Court (Australia) (b July 16, 1942) in 1970. Martina Navratilova (US) (b Prague, Oct 18, 1956) became the most recent "grand slam" winner on June 9, 1984 when she won the French title, beating Christine Evert Lloyd (US), after winning the other three titles in 1983. She then went on to win at Wimbledon and in the US Open again in July 1984.

The most singles championships in "grand slam" tournaments is 24 by Margaret Court (11 Australian, 5 French, 5 US, 3 Wimbledon), 1960–73. The men's record is 12 by Roy Emerson (Australia) (b Nov 3, 1936) (6 Australian, 2 each French, US, Wimbledon), 1961–67.

In doubles, the only men to win a "grand slam" are Frank Sedgman (US) and Ken McGregor (Aust) in 1951. Margaret Smith Court (Aust) and Ken Fletcher (Aust) won it in mixed doubles in 1961. Martina

MORE "GRAND SLAMMERS": The only women before Martina Navratilova to win the "grand slam" were Maureen Connolly (left) and Margaret Smith Court (right). Connolly (US) performed the feat in 1953, and she might well have repeated had she not suffered a serious, career-ending injury in 1954. Court (Australia), who won the "grand slam" in 1970, is the all-time leading title winner. She won 22 titles in the Australian Open (including a record 10 in singles), 18 titles in the US Championships, and 13 titles in the French tournament (including 5 in singles).

Navratilova (US) and Pam Shriver (US) managed a "grand slam" in doubles in 1983–84, the same year Martina got her "grand slam" in singles.

HIGHEST EARNINGS: With official tennis earnings of $8,512,645 to Nov 1984, Martina Navratilova is easily the top money-winning woman athlete in the world. She is one of 3 women who have won the "grand slam" (1983–84). (USTA)

Davis Cup

The most wins in the Davis Cup (instituted 1900), the men's international team championship, have been (inclusive of 1982) by the US with 28.

Roy Emerson (b Nov 3, 1936) (Australia) played on 8 Cup-winning teams, 1959–62, 1964–67.

Nicola Pietrangeli (Italy) (b Sept 11, 1933) played a record 164 rubbers, 1954 to 1972, winning 120. He played 110 singles (winning 78) and 54 doubles (winning 42). He took part in 66 ties.

Wightman Cup

The most wins in the Wightman Cup, contested annually by women's teams from the US and GB (instituted 1923) have been 45 by the US through 1983. Virginia Wade (b July 10, 1945) (GB) played in a record 19 ties and 54 rubbers between 1965 and 1983. Christine Evert Lloyd won all 22 of her singles matches, 1971–82.

Federation Cup

The most wins in the Federation Cup (instituted 1963), the women's international team championship, is 11 by the US. Virginia Wade (GB) played each year from 1967 to 1983, in a record 55 ties, playing 100 rubbers, including 56 singles (winning 36) and 44 doubles (winning 30). Christine Evert Lloyd (b Dec 21, 1954) (US) won all of her 28 singles matches and 14 of 15 doubles, 1977–82.

Tennis Olympics

Tennis was part of the Olympic program up until 1924 and it was also a demonstration sport at Mexico City in 1968 and LA in 1984. It is likely to be reinstated to the Games proper in 1988.

The most gold and total medals won was by 1911 Wimbledon doubles champion Max Decugis (Fra) with 4 gold, one silver and one bronze in 1900, 1906 and 1920. Kitty McKane-Godfree (GB) set a women's record with one gold, 2 silver and 2 bronze in 1920 and 1924. In the latter year she won the first of her two Wimbledon singles championships. The 1908 Olympic tennis was played at the All-England Club, Wimbledon.

Greatest Crowd

The greatest crowd at a tennis match was the 30,472 who came to the Houston Astrodome in Houston, Tex, on Sept 20, 1973, to watch Billie Jean King (US, b Nov 22, 1943) beat Robert Larimore (Bobby) Riggs (US, b Feb 25, 1918), over 25 years her senior, in straight sets in the so-called "Tennis Match of the Century."

The record for an orthodox match is 25,578 at Sydney, Australia, on Dec 27, 1954, in the Davis Cup Challenge Round vs the US (1st day).

Highest Earnings

The greatest reward for playing a single match is the $500,000 won by James Scott (Jimmy) Connors (US) (b Sept 2, 1952) when he beat John Newcombe (Australia) (b May 23, 1944) in a challenge match at Caesars Palace Hotel, Las Vegas, Nev, Apr 26, 1975.

COLORFUL CHAMPIONS: John McEnroe (US) (left) has had a stormy career in winning Wimbledon, US Open and other titles in recent years. Francis Jean Borotra (right) was a spectacular performer in the era 1924–64. He made his 35th Wimbledon appearance in 1964. In the photo he is winning a semi-final in 1928.

The record for career earnings is held by Martina Navratilova, who won $8,512,645 by Nov 1984.

The single season record for men is $2,028,850 by Ivan Lendl (Czechoslovakia) in 1982 (and including the Volvo Masters tournament held in January 1983).

Fastest Service

The fastest service ever *measured* was one of 163.6 mph by William Tatem Tilden (1893–1953) (US) in 1931. The American professional Scott Carnahan, 22, was electronically clocked at 137 mph at Pauley Pavilion in Los Angeles during the third annual "Cannonball Classic" sponsored by *Tennis* magazine, and reported in the fall of 1976.

A serve by Steve Denton (Australia) (b Sept 5, 1956) was timed at 138 mph at Beaver Creek, Colo on July 29, 1984.

Longest Career

The championship career of C. Alphonso Smith (b March 18, 1909) of Charlottesville, Va, extended from winning the US National Boy's title at Chicago on Aug 14, 1924, to winning the National 70-and-over title at Santa Barbara, Calif, in Aug 1979. Smith has won 31 US National titles in all.

Dorothy May Bundy-Cheney (US) (b Sept 2, 1916) won 116 US titles at various age groups from 1941 to 1982.

Longest Game

The longest known singles game was one of 37 deuces (80 points) between Anthony Fawcett (Rhodesia) and Keith Glass (GB) in the first round of the Surrey championships at Surbiton, Surrey, England, on May 26, 1975. It lasted 31 min.

A junior game lasted 52 min (9 deuces) between Noelle Van Lottum and Sandra Begijn in the semi-finals of the under-13 Dutch National Indoor Championships in Ede, Gederland, Holland on Feb 12, 1984.

The longest tiebreaker was the 20–18 win to complete the third set by Bjorn Rune Borg (Sweden) (b June 6, 1956) over Prenjit Lall (India) in his 6–3, 6–4, 9–8 win in the first round of the 1973 Wimbledon Championships.

Tennis Marathons

The longest recorded tennis singles match is one of 116 hours 24 min by Mark Humes and Chris Long at Reno, Nevada, May 22–27, 1983.

The duration record for doubles is 91 hours 42 min by Jan Jefferis, George Milton, Ted Hollembeak, and Les Stafford of Kansas in October 1982.

WIMBLEDON RECORDS

The first Championship was in 1877. Professionals first played in 1968. From 1971 the tie-break system was introduced, which effectually prevents sets proceeding beyond a 17th game, i.e., 9–8.

Most Wins

Six-time singles champion Billie Jean King (*née* Moffitt) has also won 10 women's doubles and 4 mixed doubles during the period 1961 to 1979, to total a record 20 titles.

The greatest number of singles wins was 8 by Helen N. Moody (*née* Wills) (b Oct 6, 1905) (US), who won in 1927–30, 32–33, 35 and 38.

The greatest number of singles wins by a man since the Challenge Round (wherein the defending champion was given a bye until the final round) was abolished in 1922 is 5 consecutively by Bjorn Borg (Sweden) in 1976–80. The all-time men's record was seven by William C. Renshaw, 1881–86 and 1889.

The greatest number of doubles wins by men was 8 by the brothers Doherty (GB)—Reginald Frank (1872–1910) and Hugh Lawrence (1875–1919). They won each year from 1897 to 1905 except for 1902. Hugh Doherty also won 5 singles titles (1902–06) and holds the record for most men's titles with 13.

The most wins in women's doubles was 12 by Elizabeth "Bunny" Ryan (US) (1894–1979). The greatest number of mixed doubles wins was 7 by Elizabeth Ryan, giving her a record total of 19 doubles wins 1914–34.

The men's mixed doubles record is 4 wins: by Elias Victor Seixas (b Aug 30, 1923) (US) in 1953–56; by Kenneth N. Fletcher (b June 15, 1940) (Australia) in 1963, 65–66 and 68; and by Owen Keir Davidson (Australia) (b Oct 4, 1943) in 1967, 71 and 73–74.

SUPERSTAR 1916–26: Suzanne Lenglen (France) was unbeaten in singles in those years.

Youngest Champions

The youngest champion ever at Wimbledon was Charlotte (Lottie) Dod (1871–1960), who was 15 years 285 days old when she won in 1887.

The youngest male singles champion was Wilfred Baddeley (b Jan 11, 1872), who won the Wimbledon title in 1891 at the age of 19 years 175 days.

Richard Dennis Ralston (b July 27, 1942) (US) was 17 years 341 days old when he won the men's doubles with Rafael H. Osuna (1938–69), of Mexico, in 1960.

The youngest-ever player at Wimbledon is reputedly Miss Mita Klima (Austria), who was 13 years old in the 1907 singles competition. The youngest player to win a match at Wimbledon is Kathy Rinaldi (b March 24, 1967) (US), who was 14 years 91 days old on June 23, 1981.

DOUBLES VISION: "Bunny" Ryan is the all-time Wimbledon doubles champion with 19 titles (12 women's and 7 mixed). Her 19 victories were the overall record until Billie Jean King won the 1979 doubles title. Ryan, who had said she didn't want to live to see her record broken, died the night before King's 20th victory.

Tournament Winners at Wimbledon

Men's Singles

1877 Spencer W. Gore (GB)
1878 Frank Hadow (GB)
1879 Rev. John Hartley (GB)
1880 Rev. John Hartley (GB)
1881 William Renshaw (GB)
1882 William Renshaw (GB)
1883 William Renshaw (GB)
1884 William Renshaw (GB)
1885 William Renshaw (GB)
1886 William Renshaw (GB)
1887 Herbert Lawford (GB)
1888 Ernest Renshaw (GB)
1889 William Renshaw (GB)
1890 Wiloughby Hamilton (GB)
1891 Wilfred Baddeley (GB)
1892 Wilfred Baddeley (GB)
1893 Joshua Pim (GB)
1894 Joshua Pim (GB)
1895 Wilfred Baddeley (GB)
1896 Harold Mahony (GB)
1897 Reginald Doherty (GB)
1898 Reginald Doherty (GB)
1899 Reginald Doherty (GB)
1900 Reginald Doherty (GB)
1901 Arthur Gore (GB)
1902 Laurence Doherty (GB)
1903 Laurence Doherty (GB)
1904 Laurence Doherty (GB)
1905 Laurence Doherty (GB)
1906 Laurence Doherty (GB)
1907 Norman Brookes (Aus)
1908 Arthur W. Gore (GB)
1909 Arthur W. Gore (GB)
1910 Tony Wilding (NZ)
1911 Tony Wilding (NZ)
1912 Tony Wilding (NZ)
1913 Tony Wilding (NZ)
1914 Norman Brookes (Aus)
1919 Gerald Patterson (Aus)
1920 Bill Tilden (US)
1921 Bill Tilden (US)
1922 Gerald Patterson (Aus)
1923 William Johnston (US)
1924 Jean Borotra (Fra)
1925 René Lacoste (Fra)
1926 Jean Borotra (Fra)
1927 Henri Cochet (Fra)
1928 René Lacoste (Fra)
1929 Henri Cochet (Fra)
1930 Bill Tilden (US)
1931 Sidney Wood (US)
1932 Ellsworth Vines (US)
1933 Jack Crawford (Aus)
1934 Fred Perry (GB)
1935 Fred Perry (GB)
1936 Fred Perry (GB)
1937 Donald Budge (US)
1938 Donald Budge (US)
1939 Bobby Riggs (US)
1940–45 not held
1946 Yvon Petra (Fra)
1947 Jack Kramer (US)
1948 Bob Falkenburg (US)
1949 Ted Schroeder (US)
1950 Budge Patty (US)
1951 Dick Savitt (US)
1952 Frank Sedgman (Aus)
1953 Vic Seixas (US)
1954 Jaroslav Drobny (Cze)
1955 Tony Trabert (US)
1956 Lew Hoad (Aus)
1957 Lew Hoad (Aus)
1958 Ashley Cooper (Aus)
1959 Alex Olmedo (US)
1960 Neale Fraser (Aus)
1961 Rod Laver (Aus)
1962 Rod Laver (Aus)
1963 Chuck McKinley (US)
1964 Roy Emerson (Aus)
1965 Roy Emerson (Aus)
1966 Manuel Santana (Spa)
1967 John Newcombe (Aus)
1968 Rod Laver (Aus)
1969 Rod Laver (Aus)
1970 John Newcombe (Aus)
1971 John Newcombe (Aus)
1972 Stan Smith (US)
1973 Jan Kodes (Cze)
1974 Jimmy Connors (US)
1975 Arthur Ashe (US)
1976 Bjorn Borg (Swe)
1977 Bjorn Borg (Swe)
1978 Bjorn Borg (Swe)
1979 Bjorn Borg (Swe)
1980 Bjorn Borg (Swe)
1981 John McEnroe (US)
1982 Jimmy Connors (US)
1983 Jimmy Connors (US)
1984 John McEnroe (US)

Women's Singles

First played in 1884.
1884 Maud Watson (GB)
1885 Maud Watson (GB)
1886 Blanche Bingley (GB)
1887 Lottie Dod (GB)
1888 Lottie Dod (GB)
1889 Blanche Hillyard (née Bingley (GB)
1890 Helene Rice (GB-Ire)
1891 Lottie Dod (GB)
1892 Lottie Dod (GB)
1893 Lottie Dod (GB)
1894 Blanche Hillyard (GB)
1895 Charlotte Cooper (GB)
1896 Charlotte Cooper (GB)
1897 Blanche Hillyard (GB)
1898 Charlotte Cooper (GB)
1899 Blanche Hillyard (GB)
1900 Blanche Hillyard (GB)
1901 Charlotte Sterry (née Cooper) (GB)
1902 Muriel Robb (GB)
1903 Dorothea Douglass (GB)
1904 Dorothea Douglass (GB)
1905 May Sutton (US)
1906 Dorothea Douglass (GB)
1907 May Sutton (US)
1908 Charlotte Sterry (GB)
1909 Dora Boothby (GB)
1910 Dorothea Lambert Chambers (née Douglass) (GB)
1911 Dorothea Lambert Chambers (GB)
1912 Ethel Larcombe (GB)
1913 Dorothea Lambert Chambers (GB)
1914 Dorothea Lambert Chambers (GB)
1919 Suzanne Lenglen (Fra)
1920 Suzanne Lenglen (Fra)
1921 Suzanne Lenglen (Fra)

THE WINNING MOMENT: Billie Jean King jubilantly tosses her racket through the air because she knows, even if the scoreboard is a little slow, that she just won the championship point from Chris Evert in the 1975 women's singles finals at Wimbledon. The victory was her 19th at Wimbledon (6th in singles), tying her with "Bunny" Ryan for the most wins in that tournament. King then won the 1979 doubles title, for her 20th victory, and became the winningest player in Wimbledon's history.

1922 Suzanne Lenglen (Fra)
1923 Suzanne Lenglen (Fra)
1924 Kathleen McKane (GB)
1925 Suzanne Lenglen (Fra)
1926 Kathleen Godfree (née McKane) (GB)
1927 Helen Wills (US)
1928 Helen Wills (US)
1929 Helen Wills (US)
1930 Helen Wills Moody (US)
1931 Cilly Aussem (Ger)
1932 Helen Wills Moody (US)
1933 Helen Wills Moody (US)
1934 Dorothy Round (GB)
1935 Helen Wills Moody (US)
1936 Helen Jacobs (US)
1937 Dorothy Round (GB)
1938 Helen Wills Moody (US)
1939 Alice Marble (US)
1940–45 not held
1946 Pauline Betz (US)
1947 Margaret Osborne (US)
1948 Louise Brough (US)
1949 Louise Brough (US)
1950 Louise Brough (US)
1951 Doris Hart (US)
1952 Maureen Connolly (US)
1953 Maureen Connolly (US)
1954 Maureen Connolly (US)
1955 Louise Brough (US)

1956 Shirley Fry (US)
1957 Althea Gibson (US)
1958 Althea Gibson (US)
1959 Maria Bueno (Bra)
1960 Maria Bueno (Bra)
1961 Angela Mortimer (GB)
1962 Karen Susman (US)
1963 Margaret Smith (Aus)
1964 Maria Bueno (Bra)
1965 Margaret Smith (Aus)
1966 Billie Jean King (US)
1967 Billie Jean King (US)
1968 Billie Jean King (US)
1969 Ann Jones (GB)
1970 Margaret Court (née Smith) (Aus)
1971 Evonne Goolagong (Aus)
1972 Billie Jean King (US)
1973 Billie Jean King (US)
1974 Christine Evert (US)
1975 Billie Jean King (US)
1976 Christine Evert (US)
1977 Virginia Wade (GB)
1978 Martina Navratilova (Cze)
1979 Martina Navratilova (Cze)
1980 Evonne Cawley (née Goolagong) (Aus)
1981 Christine Evert-Lloyd (US)
1982 Christine Evert-Lloyd (US)
1983 Martina Navratilova (US)
1984 Martina Navratilova (US)

Wimbledon Winners (continued)

Men's Doubles

First held 1884.

Most wins: 8 Laurence Doherty and Reginald Doherty (GB): 1897–1901, 1903–05

Winners since 1965:
1965 John Newcombe and Tony Roche (Aus)
1966 Ken Fletcher and John Newcombe (Aus)
1967 Bob Hewitt and Frew McMillan (S Af)
1968 John Newcombe and Tony Roche (Aus)
1969 John Newcombe and Tony Roche (Aus)
1970 John Newcombe and Tony Roche (Aus)
1971 Roy Emerson and Rod Laver (Aus)
1972 Bob Hewitt and Frew McMillan (S Af)
1973 Jimmy Connors (US) and Ilie Nastase (Rom)
1974 John Newcombe and Tony Roche (Aus)
1975 Vitas Gerulaitis and Sandy Mayer (US)
1976 Brian Gottfried (US) and Raul Ramirez (Mex)
1977 Ross Case and Geoff Masters (Aus)
1978 Bob Hewitt and Frew McMillan (S Af)
1979 Peter Fleming and John McEnroe (US)
1980 Peter McNamara and Paul McNamee (Aus)
1981 Peter Fleming and John McEnroe (US)
1982 Peter McNamara and Paul McNamee (Aus)
1983 Peter Fleming and John McEnroe (US)
1984 Peter Fleming and John McEnroe (US)

Women's Doubles

First held 1899, but not a championship event until 1913.

Most wins: 12 Elizabeth (Bunny) Ryan (US): 1 with Agatha Morton 1914, 6 with Suzanne Lenglen 1919–23, 1925; 1 with Mary Browne 1926, 2 with Helen Wills Moody 1927, 1930; 2 with Simone Mathieu 1933–34

Winners since 1965:
1965 Maria Bueno (Bra) and Billie Jean Moffitt (US)
1966 Maria Bueno (Bra) and Nancy Richey (US)
1967 Rosemary Casals and Billie Jean King (née Moffitt) (US)
1968 Rosemary Casals and Billie Jean King (US)
1969 Margaret Court and Judy Tegart (Aus)
1970 Rosemary Casals and Billie Jean King (US)
1971 Rosemary Casals and Billie Jean King (US)
1972 Billie Jean King (US) and Betty Stove (Hol)
1973 Rosemary Casals and Billie Jean King (US)
1974 Evonne Goolagong (Aus) and Peggy Michel (US)
1975 Ann Kiyomura (US) and Kazuko Sawamatsu (Jap)
1976 Christine Evert (US) and Martina Navratilova (Cze)
1977 Helen Cawley (Aus) and Joanne Russell (US)
1978 Kerr Reid and Wendy Turnbull (Aus)
1979 Billie Jean King (US) and Martina Navratilova (Cze)
1980 Kathy Jordan and Anne Smith (US)
1981 Martina Navratilova (Cze) and Pam Shriver (US)
1982 Martina Navratilova (US) and Pam Shriver (US)
1983 Martina Navratilova (US) and Pam Shriver (US)
1984 Martina Navratilova (US) and Pam Shriver (US)

Mixed Doubles

First held 1900, but not a championship event until 1913.

Most wins: 7 Elizabeth Ryan (US): 1919, 1921, 1923, 1927–28, 1930, 1932 with 5 different partners

Winners since 1965:
1965 Ken Fletcher and Margaret Smith (Aus)
1966 Ken Fletcher and Margaret Smith (Aus)
1967 Owen Davidson (Aus) and Billie Jean King (US)
1968 Ken Fletcher and Margaret Court (née Smith) (Aus)
1969 Fred Stolle (Aus) and Ann Jones (GB)
1970 Ilie Nastase (Rom) and Rosemary Casals (US)
1971 Owen Davidson (Aus) and Billie Jean King (US)
1972 Ilie Nastase (Rom) and Rosemary Casals (US)
1973 Owen Davidson (Aus) and Billie Jean King (US)
1974 Owen Davidson (Aus) and Billie Jean King (US)
1975 Marty Riessen (US) and Margaret Court (Aus)
1976 Tony Roche (Aus) and Françoise Durr (Fra)
1977 Bob Hewitt and Greer Stevens (S Af)
1978 Frew McMillan (S Af) and Betty Stove (Hol)
1979 Bob Hewitt (S Af) and Greer Stevens (US)
1980 John Austin and Tracy Austin (US)
1981 Frew McMillan (S Af) and Betty Stove (Hol)
1982 Anne Smith (US) and Kevin Curren (S Af)
1983 Wendy Turnbull (Aus) and John Lloyd (GB)
1984 Wendy Turnbull (Aus) and John Lloyd (GB)

FIVE-TIME DOUBLES WINNERS at Wimbledon: Rosemary Casals (jumping) and Billie Jean King (US) won in 5 of the 7 years 1967–73. (Leon Serchuk)

Oldest Champions

The oldest champion was Margaret Evelyn du Pont (*née* Osborne) (b Mar 4, 1918) (US) who was 44 years 125 days old when she won the mixed doubles in 1962 with Neale Fraser (Aust). The oldest singles champion was Arthur Gore (GB) at 41 years 182 days in 1909.

Most Appearances

Arthur W. Gore (1868–1928) (GB) made 36 appearances between 1888 and 1927, and was in 1909 at 41 years the oldest singles winner ever. In 1964 Jean Borotra (b Aug 13, 1898) of France made his 35th appearance since 1922. In 1977 he appeared in the Veterans' Doubles, aged 78.

Most Wins in One Day

When rain delayed play in the Italian Open on May 27, 1984, Manuela Maleeva, a 17-year-old Bulgarian, had to finish the last set of her quarter-final match the next day against Romania's Virginia Ruzici (winning), then faced Canada's Carling Basset in a semifinal match (winning). In the final on the same day, after a half-hour nap, Manuela met the top-seeded Chris Evert Lloyd, and vanquished her in straight sets, 6–3, 6–3, to win the $150,000 tournament. It was the first time anyone had won 3 escalating singles matches in the same day.

Greatest Attendance

The record crowd for one day at Wimbledon is 38,291 on June 27, 1979. The total attendance record was set at the 1984 Championships with 391,673.

U S CHAMPIONSHIPS

Most Wins

Margaret Evelyn du Pont (*née* Osborne) won a record 25 titles between 1936 and 1962. She won a record 13 women's doubles (12 with Althea Louise Brough), 8 mixed doubles and 3 singles. The men's record is 16 by William Tatem Tilden, including 7 men's singles, 1920–25, 1929—a record for singles shared with Richard Dudley Sears (1861–1943), 1881–87; William A Larned (1872–1926), 1901–02, 1907–11; and at women's singles by Molla Mallory (*née* Bjurstedt) (1892–1959), 1915–16, 1918, 1920–22, 1926 and Helen Moody (*née* Wills), 1923–25, 1927–29, 1931.

Youngest and Oldest

The youngest champion was Vincent Richards (1903–59) who was 15 years 139 days when he won the doubles with Bill Tilden in 1918. The youngest singles champion was Tracy Ann Austin (b Dec 12, 1962) who was 16 years 271 days when she won the women's singles in 1979.

The oldest champion was Margaret du Pont who won the mixed doubles at 42 years 166 days in 1960. The oldest singles champion was William Larned at 38 years 242 days in 1911.

US Open Champions

The USTA Championships were first held in 1881 and continued until 1969. The Tournament was superseded in 1970 by the US Open Championships which had first been held in 1968. Now held at Flushing Meadow, New York.

Most wins in the USTA Championships:
Men's Singles: 7 Richard D. Sears 1881–87; 7 William A. Larned 1901–02, 1907–11; 7 William T. Tilden 1920–25, 1929
Women's Singles: 7 Helen Wills Moody 1923–25, 1927–29, 1931

Men's Singles
1920 Bill Tilden
1921 Bill Tilden
1922 Bill Tilden
1923 Bill Tilden
1924 Bill Tilden
1925 Bill Tilden
1926 René Lacoste
1927 René Lacoste
1928 Henri Cochet
1929 Bill Tilden
1930 John Doeg
1931 H. Ellsworth Vines
1932 H. Ellsworth Vines
1933 Fred Perry
1934 Fred Perry
1935 Wilmer Allison
1936 Fred Perry
1937 Don Budge
1938 Don Budge
1939 Robert Riggs
1940 Don McNeil
1941 Robert Riggs
1942 F. R. Schroeder Jr.
1943 Joseph Hunt
1944 Frank Parker
1945 Frank Parker
1946 Jack Kramer
1947 Jack Kramer
1948 Pancho Gonzales
1949 Pancho Gonzales
1950 Arthur Larsen
1951 Frank Sedgman
1952 Frank Sedgman
1953 Tony Trabert
1954 E. Victor Seixas Jr
1955 Tony Trabert
1956 Ken Rosewall
1957 Malcolm Anderson
1958 Ashley Cooper
1959 Neale A. Fraser
1960 Neale A. Fraser

SEVEN-TIME WINNER: Bill Tilden won the US Open singles 7 times in the 1920's. His serve was measured at 163.6 mph in 1931.

1961 Roy Emerson
1962 Rod Laver
1963 Rafael Osuna
1964 Roy Emerson
1965 Manuel Santana
1966 Fred Stolle
1967 John Newcombe
1968 Arthur Ashe
1969 Rod Laver
1970 Ken Rosewall
1971 Stan Smith
1972 Ilie Nastase
1973 John Newcombe
1974 Jimmy Connors
1975 Manuel Orantes
1976 Jimmy Connors
1977 Guillermo Vilas
1978 Jimmy Connors
1979 John McEnroe
1980 John McEnroe
1981 John McEnroe
1982 Jimmy Connors
1983 Jimmy Connors
1984 John McEnroe

Women's Singles
1935 Helen Jacobs
1936 Alice Marble
1937 Anita Lizana
1938 Alice Marble
1939 Alice Marble

1940 Alice Marble
1941 Mrs. Sarah P. Cooke
1942 Pauline Betz
1943 Pauline Betz
1944 Pauline Betz
1945 Sarah P. Cooke
1946 Pauline Betz
1947 A. Louise Brough
1948 Mrs. Margaret O. duPont
1949 Mrs. Margaret O. duPont
1950 Mrs. Margaret O. duPont
1951 Maureen Connolly
1952 Maureen Connolly
1953 Maureen Connolly
1954 Doris Hart
1955 Doris Hart
1956 Shirley J. Fry
1957 Althea Gibson
1958 Althea Gibson
1959 Maria Bueno
1960 Darlene Hard
1961 Darlene Hard
1962 Margaret Smith
1963 Maria Bueno
1964 Maria Bueno
1965 Margaret Smith
1966 Maria Bueno
1967 Billie Jean King
1968 Virginia Wade

NEVER A WINNER IN US OPEN: Bjorn Borg (Sweden) won 5 Wimbledon titles and many others though.

FAMILY COURT: Both Chris Evert-Lloyd (left) and Evonne Goolagong Cawley (right) came back with big victories after interrupting their successful careers to better enjoy their marriages. Evonne beat Chris in the 1980 Wimbledon finals, but shortly thereafter Chris won the US Open, her 5th singles title there.

US Open Champions (continued)

1969 Margaret Smith Court
1970 Margaret Smith Court
1971 Billie Jean King
1972 Billie Jean King
1973 Margaret Smith Court
1974 Billie Jean King
1975 Chris Evert
1976 Chris Evert
1977 Chris Evert
1978 Chris Evert
1979 Tracy Austin
1980 Chris Evert-Lloyd
1981 Tracy Austin
1982 Chris Evert-Lloyd
1983 Martina Navratilova
1984 Martina Navratilova

Men's Doubles

1922 Bill Tilden—Vincent Richards
1923 Bill Tilden—Brian Norton
1924 Howard Kinsey—Robert Kinsey
1925 R. Norris Williams—Vincent Richards
1926 R. Norris Williams—Vincent Richards
1927 Bill Tilden—Francis Hunter
1928 George Lott—John Hennessey
1929 George Lott—John Doeg
1930 George Lott—John Doeg
1931 Wilmer Allison—John Van Ryn
1932 H. Ellsworth Vines—Keith Gledhill
1933 George Lott—Lester Stoefen

1934 George Lott—Lester Stoefen
1935 Wilmer Allison—John Van Ryn
1936 Don Budge—C. Gene Mako
1937 Baron G. von Cramm—Henner Henkel
1938 Don Budge—C. Gene Mako
1939 Adrian Quist—John Bromwich
1940 Jack Kramer—Frederick Schroeder Jr.
1941 Jack Kramer—Frederick Schroeder Jr.
1942 Gardner Mulloy—William Talbert
1943 Jack Kramer—Frank Parker
1944 Don McNeill—Robert Falkenburg
1945 Gardner Mulloy—William Talbert
1946 Gardner Mulloy—William Talbert
1947 Jack Kramer—Frederick Schroeder Jr.
1948 Gardner Mulloy—William Talbert
1949 John Bromwich—William Sidwell
1950 John Bromwich—Frank Sedgman
1951 Frank Sedgman—Kenneth McGregor
1952 Mervyn Rose—E. Victor Seixas Jr.
1953 Rex Hartwig—Mervyn Rose
1954 E. Victor Seixas Jr.—Tony Trabert
1955 Kosel Kamo—Atsushi Miyagi
1956 Lewis Hoad—Ken Rosewall
1957 Ashley Cooper—Neale Fraser
1958 Hamilton Richardson—Alejandro Olmedo
1959 Neale A. Fraser—Roy Emerson
1960 Neale A. Fraser—Roy Emerson
1961 Dennis Ralston—Chuck McKinley
1962 Rafael Osuna—Antonio Palafox
1963 Dennis Ralston—Chuck McKinley

1964 Dennis Ralston—Chuck McKinley
1965 Roy Emerson—Fred Stolle
1966 Roy Emerson—Fred Stolle
1967 John Newcombe—Tony Roche
1968 Robert Lutz—Stan Smith
1969 Fred Stolle—Ken Rosewall
1970 Pierre Barthes—Nicki Pilic
1971 John Newcombe—Roger Taylor
1972 Cliff Drysdale—Roger Taylor
1973 John Newcombe—Owen Davidson
1974 Bob Lutz—Stan Smith
1975 Jimmy Connors—Ilie Nastase
1976 Marty Riessen—Tom Okker
1977 Bob Hewitt—Frew McMillan
1978 Stan Smith—Bob Lutz
1979 John McEnroe—Peter Fleming
1980 Stan Smith—Bob Lutz
1981 John McEnroe—Peter Fleming
1982 Kevin Curren—Steve Denton
1983 John McEnroe—Peter Fleming
1984 John Fitzgerald—Tomas Smid

Women's Doubles
1936 Mrs. M. G. Van Ryn—Carolin Babcock
1937 Mrs. Sarah P. Fabyan—Alice Marble
1938 Alice Marble—Mrs. Sarah P. Fabyan
1939 Alice Marble—Mrs. Sarah P. Fabyan
1940 Alice Marble—Mrs. Sarah P. Fabyan
1941 Mrs. S. P. Cooke—Margaret Osborne
1942 A. Louise Brough—Margaret Osborne
1943 A. Louise Brough—Margaret Osborne
1944 A. Louise Brough—Margaret Osborne
1945 A. Louise Brough—Margaret Osborne
1946 A. Louise Brough—Margaret Osborne
1947 A. Louise Brough—Margaret Osborne
1948 A. Louise Brough—Mrs. M. O. duPont
1949 A. Louise Brough—Mrs. M. O. duPont
1950 A. Louise Brough—Mrs. M. O. duPont
1951 Doris Hart—Shirley Fry
1952 Doris Hart—Shirley Fry
1953 Doris Hart—Shirley Fry
1954 Doris Hart—Shirley Fry
1955 A. Louise Brough—Mrs. M. O. duPont
1956 A. Louise Brough—Mrs. M. O. duPont
1957 A. Louise Brough—Mrs. M. O. duPont
1958 Darlene Hard—Jeanne Arth
1959 Darlene Hard—Jeanne Arth
1960 Darlene Hard—Maria Bueno
1961 Darlene Hard—Lesley Turner
1962 Maria Bueno—Darlene Hard
1963 Margaret Smith—Robyn Ebbern
1964 Billie Jean Moffitt—Karen Susman
1965 Carole C. Graebner—Nancy Richey
1966 Maria Bueno—Nancy Richey
1967 Rosemary Casals—Billie Jean King

1968 Maria Bueno—Margaret S. Court
1969 Françoise Durr—Darlene Hard
1970 M. S. Court—Judy Tegart Dalton
1971 Rosemary Casals—Judy Tegart Dalton
1972 Françoise Durr—Betty Stove
1973 Margaret S. Court—Virginia Wade
1974 Billie Jean King—Rosemary Casals
1975 Margaret Court—Virginia Wade
1976 Linky Boshoff—Ilana Kloss
1977 Betty Stove—Martina Navratilova
1978 Martina Navratilova—Billie Jean King
1979 Betty Stove—Wendy Turnbull
1980 Martina Navratilova—Billie Jean King
1981 Kathy Jordan—Anne Smith
1982 Rosemary Casals—Wendy Turnbull
1983 Martina Navratilova—Pam Shriver
1984 Martina Navratilova—Pam Shriver

Mixed Doubles
1946 Margaret Osborne—William Talbert
1947 A. Louise Brough—John Bromwich
1948 A. Louise Brough—Thomas Brown Jr.
1949 A. Louise Brough—Eric Sturgess
1950 Mrs. M. O. duPont—Kenneth MacGregor
1951 Doris Hart—Frank Sedgman
1952 Doris Hart—Frank Sedgman
1953 Doris Hart—E. Victor Seixas Jr.
1954 Doris Hart—E. Victor Seixas Jr.
1955 Doris Hart—E. Victor Seixas Jr.
1956 Mrs. M. O. duPont—Ken Rosewall
1957 Althea Gibson—Kurt Nielsen
1958 Mrs. M. O. duPont—Neale Fraser
1959 Mrs. M. O. duPont—Neale Fraser
1960 Mrs. M. O. duPont—Neale Fraser
1961 Margaret Smith—Robert Mark
1962 Margaret Smith—Fred Stolle
1963 Margaret Smith—Kenneth Fletcher
1964 Margaret Smith—John Newcombe
1965 Margaret Smith—Fred Stolle
1966 Donna Floyd Fales—Owen Davidson
1967 Billie Jean King—Owen Davidson
1968 Mary Ann Eisel—Peter Curtis
1969 Margaret S. Court—Marty Riessen
1970 Margaret S. Court—Marty Riessen
1971 Billie Jean King—Owen Davidson
1972 Margaret S. Court—Marty Riessen
1973 Billie Jean King—Owen Davidson
1974 Pam Teeguarden—Geoff Masters
1975 Rosemary Casals—Dick Stockton
1976 Billie Jean King—Phil Dent
1977 Betty Stove—Frew McMillan
1978 Betty Stove—Frew McMillan
1979 Greer Stevens—Bob Hewitt
1980 Wendy Turnbull—Marty Riessen
1981 Anne Smith—Kevin Curren
1982 Anne Smith—Kevin Curren
1983 Elizabeth Sayers—John Fitzgerald
1984 Manuela Maleeva—Tom Gullikson

TRACK AND FIELD

Earliest References

There is evidence that running was involved in early Egyptian rituals at Memphis c 3800 BC, but usually track and field athletics date from the ancient Olympic Games. The earliest accurately known Olympiad dates from July 776 BC, at which celebration Coroibos won the foot race of 164–169 yd. The oldest surviving measurements are a long jump of 23 ft 1½ in by Chionis of Sparta c. 656 BC, and a discus throw of 100 cubits (c. 152 ft) by Protesilaus.

Earliest Landmarks

The first time 10 sec ("even time") was bettered for 100 yd under championship conditions was when John Owen, then 30 years old, recorded 9 4/5 sec in the AAU Championships at Analostan Island, Wash, DC, on Oct 11, 1890. The first recorded instance of 6 ft being cleared in the high jump was when Marshall Jones Brooks (1855–1944) jumped 6 ft 0⅛ in at Marston, near Oxford, England, on March 17, 1876. (He is reputed to have done much of his jumping while wearing a high hat.) The first man over 7 ft was Charlie Dumas (US) who jumped 7 ft 0½ in in June 1956. The breaking of the "4-minute barrier" in the one mile was first achieved by Dr Roger Gilbert Bannister (b Harrow, England, March 23, 1929), when he recorded 3 min 59.4 sec on the Iffley Road track, Oxford, at 6:10 p.m. on May 6, 1954. Since then, 4 min has been broken by 423 athletes by the end of 1983.

Most Records

The greatest number of official world records (in events on the current schedule) broken by one athlete is 14, by Paavo Nurmi (Fin) at various events between 1921 and 1931, and by Iolanda Balas (Rom) in the high jump from 1956 to 1961. Nurmi also set eight marks in events no longer recognized, giving him a grand total of 22.

The only athlete to have his name entered in the record book 6 times in one day (in fact, within one hour) was J. C. "Jesse" Owens (US) (1913–80) who at Ann Arbor, Mich, on May 25, 1935, equaled the 100-yd running record with 9.4 sec at 3:15 p.m.; long-jumped 26 ft 8¼ in at 3:25 p.m.; ran 220 yd (straight away) in 20.3 sec at 3:45 p.m.; and 220 yd over low hurdles in 22.6 sec at 4 p.m. The two 220-yd runs were also ratified as 200-m world records.

Fastest Runners

Robert Lee Hayes (b Dec 20, 1942), of Jacksonville, Fla, may have reached a speed of about 27 mph at St Louis, on June 21, 1963, in his then world record 9.1 sec for 100 yd. Evelyn Ashford (b Apr 15, 1957) of Shreveport, La ran at an average speed of 20.73 mph in her world record 100 m in 10.79 sec at Colorado Springs on July 3, 1983.

Frederick Carl Lewis (b July 1, 1961) of Houston, Tex, when he ran the last leg of the 4 × 100 m relay as the US team set a world record, was clocked at 25.13 mph on the video tapes.

RUNNING AND JUMPING:
In the 1936 Olympics in Berlin, Jesse Owens (US) (left) won 4 gold medals, and in the 1984 Olympics in LA, Carl Lewis (US) (below) emulated that feat. Lewis jumped 28 ft 0¼ in, won the 100 m and 200 m sprints, and was the anchor man on the 4 x 100 m relay. Owens also set 6 world records in one hour at Ann Arbor, Mich in 1935. (Photos, courtesy Atlantic Richfield Co—ARCO Jesse Owens Games. Lewis, UPI)

22' **7** 24' |25' **8** 27' 28' **9**

DISTANCE RUNNER Paavo Nurmi is so famous in Finland that the entrance to the Helsinki stadium is adorned with a figure of Nurmi in action. He broke 14 world records between 1921 and 1931. (Finnish Tourist Assoc.)

NOTE: Records on opposite page, marked A, were set at high altitude—Mexico City 7,349 ft, Colorado Springs 7,201 ft. Best marks at low altitude have been: Carl Lewis (US) (b July 1, 1961) 100 m—9.97 Modesto, Cal, May 14, 1983; 200 m—19.75 and long jump—28 ft 10¼ in both at Indianapolis, June 19, 1983. Calvin Smith (US)—100 m—9.97, Zurich, Switzerland, Aug 24, 1983. Alberto Juantorena (Cuba) (b Nov 21, 1950) 400 m—44.26, Montreal, July 29, 1976. Willie Banks (US) (b Mar 11, 1956) triple jump—57 ft 7½ in, Sacramento, Cal, and the US 4 × 400 m relay team—2:58.65, Montreal, July 31, 1976.

OLDEST RACE RECORD: The three-legged race record of 100 yards in 11 seconds was set 76 years ago by Harry Hillman (left) and Lawson Robertson (right), both Olympic medalists in 1904.

WORLD TRACK AND FIELD RECORDS

World Records for the 32 men's events (excluding the walking records) scheduled by the International Amateur Athletic Federation. Note: On July 27, 1976, IAAF eliminated all records for races measured in yards, except for the mile (for sentimental reasons). All distances up to (and including) 400 m must be electrically timed to be records. When a time is given to one-hundredth of a second, it represents the official electrically-timed record. In one case, a professional performance has bettered or equaled the IAAF mark, but the same highly rigorous rules as to timing, measuring and weighing were not necessarily applied.

MEN

RUNNING

Event	min:sec	Name and Nationality	Place	Date
100 m	9.93A	Calvin Smith (US)	Colorado Springs	July 3, 1983
200 m (turn)	19.72A	Pietro Mennea (Italy)	Mexico City	Sept 12, 1979
400 m	43.86A	Lee Edward Evans (US)	Mexico City	Oct 18, 1968
800 m	1:41.73	Sebastian Coe (GB)	Florence, Italy	June 10, 1981
1,000 m	2:12.18	Sebastian Coe (GB)	Oslo	July 11, 1981
1,500 m	3:30.77	Steven Ovett (GB)	Rieti, Italy	Sept 4, 1983
1 mile	3:47.33	Sebastian Coe (GB)	Brussels	Aug 28, 1981
2,000 m	4:51.4	John Walker (NZ)	Oslo	June 30, 1976
3,000 m	7:32.1	Henry Rono (Kenya)	Oslo	June 27, 1978
5,000 m	13:00.41	David Moorcroft (GB & NI)	Oslo	July 7, 1982
10,000 m	27:13.81	Fernando Mamede (Portugal)	Stockholm	July 2, 1974
20,000 m	57:24.2	Jos Hermens (Neth)	Papendal, Neth	May 1, 1976
25,000 m	1 hr. 13:55.8	Toshihiko Seko (Japan)	Christchurch, NZ	Mar 22, 1981
30,000 m	1 hr. 29:18.8	Toshihiko Seko (Japan)	Christchurch, NZ	Mar 22, 1981
1 hour	13 miles 24 yd 2 ft	Jos Hermens (Neth)	Papendal, Neth	May 1, 1976

FIELD EVENTS

Event	ft	in	Name and Nationality	Place	Date
High Jump	7	10	Zhu Jian Hua (China)	Eberstadt, W Ger	June 10, 1984
Pole Vault	19	5¾	Sergei Bubka (USSR)	Rome	Aug 31, 1984
Long Jump	29	2½A	Robert Beamon (US)	Mexico City	Oct 18, 1968
Triple Jump	58	8½A	Joao de Oliveira (Brazil)	Mexico City	Oct 15, 1975
Shot Put	72	10¾	Udo Beyer (E Ger)	Los Angeles	June 25, 1983
Discus Throw	235	9‡	Yuri Dumchev (USSR)	Moscow	May 29, 1983
Hammer Throw	283	3	Yuri Sedykh (USSR)	Cork, Ireland	July 3, 1984
Javelin Throw	343	10	Uwe Hohn (E. Ger)	East Berlin	July 20, 1984

‡ Ben Plucknett (US) threw 237 ft 4 in at Stockholm on July 7, 1981 but was subsequently disqualified from competition.

Note: One professional performance which was equal or superior to the IAAF marks, but where the same highly rigorous rules as to timing, measuring and weighing were not necessarily applied, was the Shot Put of 75 ft by Brian Ray Oldfield (US), at El Paso, Tex, on May 10, 1975.

HURDLING

Event	min:sec	Name and Nationality	Place	Date
110 m (3'6")	12.93	Renaldo Nehemiah (US)	Zurich	Aug 19, 1981
400 m (3'0")	47.02	Edwin Corley Moses (US)	Coblenz, W Ger	Aug 31, 1983
3,000 m Steeplechase	8:05.4	Henry Rono (Kenya)	Seattle, Wash	May 13, 1978

RELAYS

			Place	Date
4 × 100 m	37.83	US Team (Sam Graddy, Ron Brown, Calvin Smith, Carl Lewis)	Los Angeles	Aug 11, 1984
4 × 200 m	1:20.26†	University of Southern California (US) (Joel Andrews, James Sanford, William Mullins, Clancy Edwards)	Tempe, Ariz	May 27, 1978
4 × 400 m	2:56.16A	US Olympic Team (Vincent Matthews, Ronald Freeman, G. Lawrence James, Lee Edward Evans)	Mexico City	Oct 20, 1968
4 × 800 m	7:03.89	Great Britain Team (Peter Elliott, Garry Cook, Steve Cram, Sebastian Coe)	London	Aug 30, 1982
4 × 1,500 m	14:38.8	W German Team (Thomas Wessinghage, Harald Hudak, Michael Lederer, Karl Fleschen)	Cologne, W Ger	Aug 17, 1977

† The time of 1:20.2 achieved by the Tobias Striders at Tempe, Ariz on May 27, 1978 was not ratified as the team was composed of varied nationalities.

DECATHLON

			Place	Date
8,798 points		Juergen Hingsen (W Ger)	Bernhausen, W Ger	June 9, 1984

WORLD TRACK AND FIELD RECORDS

RUNNING

Event	min:sec	Name and Nationality	Place	Date
100 m	10.76	Evelyn Ashford (US)	Zurich	Aug 22, 1984
200 m (turn)	21.71	Marita Koch (E Ger)	Potsdam, E Ger	July 21, 1984
400 m	47.99	Jarmila Kratochvilova (Czech)	Helsinki, Finland	Aug 10, 1983
800 m	1:53.28	Jarmila Kratochvilova (Czech)	Munich	July 26, 1983
1,500 m	3:52.47	Tatyana Kazankina (USSR)	Zurich, Switz	Aug 13, 1980
2,000 m	5:28.72	Tatyana Kazankina (USSR)	Moscow	Aug 4, 1984
1 mile	4:17.44	Maricica Puica (Romania)	Rieti, Italy	Sept 16, 1982
3,000 m	8:22.62	Tatyana Kazankina (USSR)	Leningrad	Aug 26, 1984
5,000 m	14:58.89	Ingrid Kristiansen (Norway)	Oslo, Norway	June 28, 1984
10,000 m	31:13.78	Olga Bondarenko (USSR)	Kiev, USSR	June 24, 1984

FIELD EVENTS

Event	ft	in	Name and Nationality	Place	Date
High Jump	6	9½	Ludmila Andanova (Bulgaria)	E Berlin	July 20, 1984
Long Jump	24	4½	Anisoara Cusmir (Romania)	Bucharest	June 4, 1983
Shot Put	73	11	Natalya Lisovskaya	Sochi, USSR	May 27, 1984
Discus Throw	241	11	Zdena Silhava (Czech)	Nitra, Czech	Aug 26, 1984
Javelin Throw	245	3	Ilse Kristiina (Tiina) Lillak (Finland)	Tampere, Finland	June 13, 1983

HEPTATHLON

	Name and Nationality	Place	Date
6,867 points	Sabine Paetz (E Ger)	Potsdam, E Ger	May 5–6, 1984

(100 m hurdles 13.42 sec, shot put 50 ft 0½ in, high jump 5 ft 11½ in, 200 m 23.49 sec, long jump 22 ft 3½ in, javelin 163 ft 10 in, 800 m 2 min 07.51 sec.)

HURDLES

Event	min:sec	Name and Nationality	Place	Date
100 m (2'9")	12.36	Grazyna Rabsztyn (Poland)	Warsaw	June 13, 1980
400 m (2'6")	53.58	Margarita Ponomaryeva (USSR)	Kiev	June 22, 1984

RELAYS

	min:sec		Place	Date
4 × 100 m	41.53	E Germany (Silke Gladisch, Marita Koch, Ingrid Auerswold, Marlies Göhr)	E Berlin	July 31, 1983
4 × 200 m	1:28.15	E Germany (Marlies Göhr, Romy Müller, Barbel Wöckel, Marita Koch)	Jena, E Ger	Aug 10, 1980
4 × 400 m	3:15.92	E Germany (Gesine Walther, Sabine Busch, Dagmar Ruebsam, Marita Koch)	Erfurt, E Ger	June 3, 1984
4 × 800 m	7:52.3	USSR (Nadezha Olizarenko, Lyubov Gunina, Lyudmila Borisova, Irina Padyalovskaya)	Moscow, USSR	Aug 5, 1984

World Championships

The first-ever track and field world championships were staged at Helsinki, Finland, Aug 7–14, 1983. The most gold medals won was 3 by Carl Lewis (US) in the 100 m dash, long jump, and 4 × 100 m relay; and by Marita Koch (E Ger) in the 200 m dash, 4 × 100 m relay, and 4 × 400 m relay. With a silver medal in the 100 m dash, Koch was the top medal winner with 4.

Standing High Jump

The best jump is 6 ft 2¾ in by Rune Almen (b Oct 20, 1952) (Sweden) at Karlstad, Sweden, on May 30, 1980. The best jump by a woman is 4 ft 11 in by Grete Bjørdalsbakke (b June 23, 1960) (Norway) at Orsta, Norway on Dec 12, 1979.

HISTORIC JUMP: Bob Beamon (US) is in mid-flight of his 29-foot-2½-inch long jump at the 1968 Olympics in Mexico City. The high altitude and a tail wind possibly helped Beamon shatter the record by over 2 feet. The next best jump has been 28 ft 10¼ in.

Standing Long Jump

Joe Darby (1861–1937), the famous Victorian professional jumper from Dudley, Worcestershire, England, jumped a measured 12 ft 1½ in *without* weights at Dudley Castle, on May 28, 1890. Arne Tverrvaag (Norway) jumped 12 ft 2¼ in in 1968. The best long jump by a woman is 9 ft 7 in by Annelin Mannes (Norway) at Flisa, Norway on March 7, 1981.

One-Legged High Jump

Arnie Boldt (b 1958), of Saskatchewan, Canada, cleared a height of 6 ft 8¼ in in Rome, Italy, on Apr 3, 1981, in spite of the fact that he has only one leg.

Oldest and Youngest Record Breakers

The greatest age at which anyone has broken a standard world record is 41 years 196 days in the case of John J. Flanagan (1868–1938), who set a world record in the hammer throw on July 24, 1909. The female record is 35 years 255 days for Dana Zátopkova (*née* Ingrova) (b Sept 19, 1922) of Czechoslovakia, who broke the women's javelin record with 182 ft 10 in at Prague, Czechoslovakia, on June 1, 1958.

The youngest individual record breaker is Carolina Gisolf (b July 13, 1913) (Netherlands) who set a women's high jump mark with 5 ft 3⅜ in at Maastricht, Netherlands, on July 18, 1925, aged 15 years 5 days. The male record is 17 years 198 days by Thomas Ray (1862–1904) when he pole vaulted 11 ft 2¼ in on Sept 19, 1879.

UNBEATABLE: Valerie Brisco-Hooks (left) became the first woman to win three gold medals, in the 200 m, 400 m and relay races in the 1984 Olympics. Edwin Moses (right, #943) has never been beaten in the 400 m low hurdles, beginning in 1977. He won gold medals in 1976, 1980 and 1984 Olympics. This photo is from 1976.

Oldest and Youngest Olympic Champions

The oldest Olympic medalist was Tebbs Lloyd Johnson (b Apr 7, 1900), aged 48 years 115 days when he was third in the 1948 50,000 m walk. The oldest woman medalist was Dana Zatopkova aged 37 years 248 days when she was second in the javelin in 1960.

The youngest gold medalist was Barbara Jones (US) (b March 26, 1937) who was a member of the winning 4 × 100 m relay team, aged 15 years 123 days, at Helsinki, Finland, on July 27, 1952. The youngest male champion was Robert Bruce Mathias (US) (b Nov 17, 1930) aged 17 years 263 days when he won the decathlon at London, Aug 5–6, 1948.

Most Olympic Gold Medals in Field and Track

The most Olympic gold medals won in field events is 10 individual medals by Ray C. Ewry (US) (b Oct 14, 1873, d Sept 29, 1937) with:

Standing High Jump	1900, 1904, 1906, 1908
Standing Long Jump	1900, 1904, 1906, 1908
Standing Triple Jump	1900, 1904

The most gold medals won by a woman is 4, a record shared by Francina E. Blankers-Koen (Netherlands) (b Apr 26, 1918) with 100 m, 200 m, 80 m hurdles and 4 × 100 m relay (1948); Betty Cuthbert (Australia) (b Apr 20, 1938) with 100 m, 200 m, 4 × 100 m relay (1956) and 400 m (1964); and Barbel Wöckel (née Eckert) (b March 21, 1955) (E Germany) with 200 m and 4 × 100 m relay in 1976 and 1980.

The most gold medals at one Olympic celebration is 5 by Nurmi in 1924 (see below) and the most individual is 4 by Alvin C. Kraenzlein (US) (1876–1928) in 1900 with 60 m, 110 m hurdles, 200 m hurdles and long jump.

Gold Medal Winners in 1984 Olympics

Men

		min	sec	
100 m	Carl Lewis (US)		9.99	
200 m	Carl Lewis (US)		19.80	OR
400 m	Alonzo Babers (US)		44.27	
800 m	Joachim Cruz (Brazil)	1	43.00	OR
1500 m	Sebastian Coe (GB)	3	32.53	OR
5000 m	Said Aouita (Morocco)	13	05.59	OR
10000 m	Alberto Cova (Ita)	27	47.54	
Marathon	Carlos Lopes (Portugal)	2 hr	9.21	OR
110 m hurdles	Roger Kingdom (US)		13.20	OR
400 m hurdles	Edwin Moses (US)		47.75	
3000 m steeplechase	Julius Korir (Ken)	8	11.80	
4 × 100 m relay	US		37.83	WR
4 × 400 m relay	US	2	57.91	
20 km road walk	Ernesto Canto (Mex)	1 hr	23.13	OR
50 km road walk	Raul Gonzalez (Mex)	3 hr	47.26	OR

		meters	
High Jump	Dietmar Mögenburg (W Ger)	2.35	
Pole Vault	Pierre Quinon (Fra)	5.75	
Long Jump	Carl Lewis (US)	8.54	
Triple Jump	Al Joyner (US)	17.26	
Shot Put	Alessandro Andrei (Ita)	21.26	
Discus	Rolf Danneberg (W Ger)	66.60	
Hammer	Juha Tiainen (Fin)	78.08	
Javelin	Arto Härkönen (Fin)	86.76	
Decathlon	Daley Thompson (GB)	8797 points	OR

Women

		min	sec	
100 m	Evelyn Ashford (US)		10.97	OR
200 m	Valerie Brisco-Hooks (US)		21.81	OR
400 m	Valerie Brisco-Hooks (US)		48.83	OR
800 m	Doina Melinte (Romania)	1	57.60	OR
1500 m	Gabriella Dorio (Ita)	4	03.25	
3000 m	Maricica Puica (Romania)	8	35.96	*
Marathon	Joan Benoit (US)	2 hr	24.52	*
100 m hurdles	Benita Fitzgerald-Brown (US)		12.84	
400 m hurdles	Nawal El Moutawakel (Morocco)		54.61	*
4 × 100 m relay	US		41.65	
4 × 400 m relay	US	3	18.29	OR

		meters	
High Jump	Ulrike Meyfarth (W Ger)	2.02	OR
Long Jump	Anisoara Stanciu (Romania)	6.96	
Shot Put	Claudia Losch (W Ger)	20.48	
Discus	Ria Stalman (Neth)	65.36	
Javelin	Tessa Sanderson (GB)	69.56	OR
Heptathlon	Glynis Nunn (Aust)	6390 points	*

* not previously held
WR = World Record   OR = Olympic Record

Most Olympic Medals in Track and Field

The most medals won in track is 12 (9 gold and 3 silver) by Paavo Johannes Nurmi (Finland) (1897–1973) with:

1920 Gold: 10,000 m; Cross-Country, Individual and Team; silver: 5,000 m
1924 Gold: 1,500 m; 5,000 m; 3,000 m Team; Cross-Country, Individual and Team.
1928 Gold: 10,000 m; silver: 5,000 m; 3,000 m steeplechase.

The most medals won by a woman athlete is 7 by Shirley de la Hunty (*née* Strickland) (b July 18, 1925) (Australia) with 3 gold, 1 silver and 3 bronze in the 1948, 1952 and 1956 Games. A recently discovered photo-finish indicates that she finished third, not fourth, in the 1948 200 m event, thus unofficially increasing her total to 8. Irena Szewinska (*née*

OLYMPIC INCIDENT at Los Angeles in 1984 caused Mary Decker (US) (left) to fall down in the 800-m race. She ran the world best mile (4 min 17.6 sec) but it is not a record because the indoor track was oversize. Marita Koch (E Ger) (above, #552) holds 200 m outdoor and 3 indoor world sprint records. Here, she is running with the great Polish sprinter Irena Szewinska, winner of 7 Olympic medals.

Kirszenstein) of Poland has also won 7 medals (3 gold, 2 silver, 2 bronze) in 1964, 1968, 1972 and 1976. She is the only woman ever to win Olympic medals in track and field in 4 successive Games.

Most Gold Medals in Track and Field in One Olympiad

Carl Lewis won 4 gold medals—in the 100 and 200 m sprints, the long jump, and as the anchor runner of the world-record-setting 4 × 100 m relay team in 1984—matching the record Jesse Owens (US) set in the 1936 Olympics.

Fastest Preparation for Olympics

Otis Davis was a 26-year-old Oregon basketball player when the track coach asked him to try out for the team in 1958. He ran mostly shorter sprints, used up his eligibility before his senior year, and got to compete in only about ten 440-yd events (or its 400-m Olympic equivalent) before the 1960 Olympics. At the Games that year in Rome, he ran the 400 m in a world-record 44.9 sec and won the gold medal.

GOLD MEDALISTS: Fanny Blankers-Koen (Neth) (left) and Betty Cuthbert (Aust) (far right) share, with Barbel Wöckel (E Ger), the women's record for most Olympic gold medals with 4 apiece. Blankers-Koen was 30 years old with 2 children when she captured her 4 golds, all in the 1948 Games. Cuthbert won 3 golds in 1956 and picked up her fourth 8 years later.

MILERS: Between them, Britishers Steve Ovett (left) and Sebastian Coe (right, #9) set 5 records for the mile run, including an amazing flurry of 3 records in 10 days during August, 1981. In their 1980 Olympic gold-medal runs, Ovett beat record-holder Coe at 800 meters before Coe beat record-holder Ovett at 1,500 meters. In 1984, Coe won the gold at 1,500 m and the silver at 800 m. Ovett did not race.

DISTANCE WORLD RECORD HOLDER: Jos Hermens (in the lead) ran the fastest time for 20,000 m and the farthest distance for one hour in 1976, and the records still stand.

Longest Race

The longest races ever staged were the 1928 (3,422 miles) and 1929 (3,665 miles) transcontinental races from NYC to Los Angeles. The Finnish-born Johnny Salo (1893–1931) was the winner in 1929 in 79 days, from March 31 to June 18. His elapsed time of 525 hours 57 min 20 sec gave a running average of 6.97 mph. His margin of victory was only 2 min 47 sec.

24-Hour Record

The greatest distance run on a standard track in 24 hours is 170 miles 974 yd by Dave Dowdle (b Nov 7, 1954) (Gloucester AC) at Blackbridge,

HIGH JUMP CHAMP: Zhu Jian Hua, first Chinese to set a world record in track and field, is here topping the bar at 7 ft 10 in in June 1984. The Olympic gold medalist couldn't beat 7 ft 7 in. (Agence Sam)

RUSSIAN FOR THE GOLD: Star Soviet distance runner Tatyana Kazankina (#340) is first across the finish line in the Olympic 800 m in 1976. Kazankina, who also won the 1,500 m in both 1976 and 1980, holds world records for 1,500 and 2,000 m set in 1984.

Gloucester, England, May 22–23, 1982. The best by a woman is 133 miles 939 yd by Lynn Fitzgerald (b Sept 9, 1947) (Highgate Harriers) in the same race.

Greatest Mileage

Jay F. Helgerson (b Feb 3, 1955) of Foster City, Calif, ran a certified marathon (26 miles 385 yd) or longer, each week for 52 weeks from Jan 28, 1979 to Jan 19, 1980, totalling 1,418 racing miles.

Douglas Alistair Gordon Pirie (b Feb 10, 1931) (GB), who set 5 world records in the 1950s, estimated that he had run a total distance of 216,000 miles in 40 years to 1981.

The greatest distance run in one year is 15,472 miles by Tina Maria Stone (b Naples, Italy, Apr 5, 1934) of Irvine, Calif, in 1983.

The longest-ever solo run is 10,608 miles by Robert J. Sweetgall (US) (b Dec 8, 1947) around the perimeter of the US, starting and finishing in Wash, DC, Oct 9, 1982–July 15, 1983.

Ron Grand (Aust) (b Feb 15, 1943) ran around Australia, 8,316 miles in 217 days 3 hours 45 min, running every day Mar 28–Oct 31, 1983.

Ernst Mensen (1799–1846) (Norway), a former seaman in the British Navy, is reputed to have run from Istanbul, Turkey, to Calcutta, in West Bengal, India, and back in 59 days in 1836, so averaging an improbable 92.4 miles per day.

Max Telford (b Hawick, Scotland, Feb 2, 1935) of New Zealand ran 5,110 miles from Anchorage, Alaska, to Halifax, Nova Scotia, in 106 days 18 hours 45 min from July 25 to Nov 9, 1977.

The greatest non-stop run recorded is 352.9 miles in 121 hours 54 min by Bertil Järlåker (Sweden) at Norrköping, Sweden, May 26–31, 1980. He was moving 95.04% of the time.

Fastest 100 Miles

The fastest recorded time for 100 miles is 11 hours 30 min 51 sec by Donald Ritchie (b July 6, 1944) at Crystal Palace, London, on Oct 15, 1977. The best by a woman is 15 hours 31 min 56 sec by Donna Hudson (US) at Shea Stadium, NYC, June 17–18, 1983.

GREATEST DISTANCE run in one year is 15,472 mi by Tina Maria Stone (left) who was born in Italy, but is now running in Irvine, Calif. RUNNING ACROSS CANADA took Beryl Stott (right) 6½ months. She ran through all 10 provinces from Victoria to Nova Scotia, a total of 3,824 mi.

Trans-America Run

The fastest time for the cross-US run is 46 days, 8 hours 36 min by Frank Giannino Jr (b 1952) (US) for the 3,100 miles from San Francisco to NYC, Sept 1–Oct 17, 1980.

When Johnny Salo won the 1929 Trans-America race from NYC to LA, his total elapsed time of 525 hours 57 min 20 sec gave him a margin of only 2 min 47 sec over second-place Peter Gavuzzi—after 3,665 miles.

Nicki Lewis, 50, of Santa Monica, Calif, is the first American woman to run across the continent, setting a speed record of 3,224 miles in 75 days, Aug 16, 1983–Oct 30, 1983, running an average of 42.8 miles per day from Santa Monica to NYC. She was escorted by David Hermitage (Eng). She wore out one pair of shoes and had two other pairs sent by Nike to her, enroute.

In an attempt to beat the record, three women sponsored by The Greyhound Corporation set out from Boston, Mass in the summer of 1984 for San Francisco. Two of the women finished, Caroline Merrill, 42, and Annabel Marsh, 61, after 130 days and 3,261 miles. They wore out 12 pairs of shoes each.

Running unaccompanied, Sandy Goldstein, 38, ran from Sacramento, Calif to Hyannis, Mass, her hometown, also in 1984 in 130 days, but covering 3,328 miles.

Trans-Canada Run

The only woman to have run across Canada from Victoria, BC, to Halifax, Nova Scotia, a distance of 3,824 mi in 6½ months, touching all 10 provinces, is Kanchan Beryl Stott of Ottawa, Ont. It was probably the longest run ever made by a woman.

Six-Day Race

The greatest distance covered by a man in six days (*i.e.* the 144 permissible hours between Sundays in Victorian times) was 623¾ miles by George Littlewood (England), who required only 141 hours 57½ min for this feat on Dec 3–8, 1888, at the old Madison Square Garden, NYC.

Downhill Mile

Mike Boit (Kenya) ran what is believed to be the fastest mile ever when he won the Molenberg Mile in 3 min 28.36 sec over a carefully measured downhill course along Queen Street, Auckland, NZ, on Apr 16, 1983. The course had an overall vertical drop of nearly 208 yd.

Mass Relay Record

The record for 100 miles by 100 runners belonging to one club is 7 hours 53 min 52.1 sec by Baltimore Road Runners Club of Towson, Md, on May 17, 1981. The women's mark is 10 hours 47 min 9.3 sec by a team from the San Francisco Dolphins Southend Running Club, on Apr 3, 1977.

The best club time for a 100 × 400 m relay is 1 hour 29 min 11.8 sec (average 53.5 sec) by the Physical Training Institute, Leuven, Belgium, on Apr 19, 1978. The best women's club time for 100 × 100 meters relay is 23 min 28 sec by Amsterdanse dames athletiekvereniging, on Sept 26, 1981, in Amsterdam, Netherlands.

The longest relay ever run was 9,357 mi by 20 members of the Melbourne Fire Brigade around Australia on Highway No. 1 in 43 days 23 hours 58 min, July 10–Aug 23, 1983. The most participants is 4,800 (192 teams of 25), in the Batavierenrace, 103.89 mi from Nijmegen to Enschede, The Netherlands, won in 9 hours 30 min 44 sec on Apr 23, 1983.

Running Backwards

The fastest time recorded for running 100 yd backwards is 12.8 sec by Ferdie Adoboe (Kenya) in Amherst, Mass, on July 28, 1983.

Donald Davis (b Feb 10, 1960) (US) ran the Honolulu marathon backwards in 4 hours 20 min 36 sec on Dec 12, 1982 and 1 mi backwards in 6 min 7.1 sec at the University of Hawaii on Feb 21, 1983.

Blind 100 Meters

The fastest time recorded for 100 m by a blind man is 11.4 sec by Graham Henry Salmon (b Sept 5, 1952) of Loughton, Essex, England, at Grangemouth, Scotland, on Sept 2, 1978.

Fastest 100 Kilometers

Donald Ritchie ran 100 km in a record 6 hours 10 min 20 sec at Crystal Palace, London, on Oct 28, 1978. The women's best, run on the road, is 7 hours 27 min 22 sec by Chantal Langlace (b Jan 6, 1955) (France) at Amiens, France on Sept 6, 1980.

Three-Legged Race

The fastest recorded time for a 100-yd three-legged race is 11.0 sec by Olympic medalists Harry L. Hillman (1881–1945) and Lawson Robertson (1883–1951) in Brooklyn, NYC, on Apr 24, 1909.

Ambidextrous Shot Put

Allan Feuerbach (US, b Jan 14, 1948) has put a 16-lb shot a total of 121 ft 6¾ in (51 ft 5 in with his left hand and 70 ft 1¾ in with his right) at Malmö, Sweden, on Aug 24, 1974.

Pancake Race Record

The annual "Housewives" Pancake Race at Olney, Buckinghamshire, England, was first mentioned in 1445. The record for the winding 415-yd course (three tosses mandatory) is 61.0 sec, set by Sally Ann Faulkner, 16, on Feb 26, 1974. The record for the counterpart race at Liberal, Kansas, is 58.5 sec by Sheila Turner (b July 9, 1953) in 1975.

Dale R. Lyons (b Feb 26, 1937) (GB) has run several marathons during which he tosses a 2-oz pancake repeatedly en route in a 1½ lb pan. His fastest time is 2 hours 57 min 16 sec on Mar 25, 1984 at Wolverhampton, England.

MARATHON PROGRESSIVE BEST PERFORMANCES

Men

2:55:18.4	Johnny Hayes (US)	1908	2:18:40.2	Jim Peters (GB)	1953
2:52:45.4	Robert Fowler (US)	1909	2:18:34.8	Jim Peters (GB)	1953
2:46:52.6	James Clark (US)	1909	2:17:39.4	Jim Peters (GB)	1954
2:46:04.6	Albert Raines (US)	1909	2:15:17.0	Sergey Popov (USSR)	1958
2:42:31.0	Fred Barrett (GB)	1909	2:15:16.2	Abebe Bikila (Eth)	1960
2:40:34.2	Thore Johansson (Swe)	1909	2:15:15.8	Toru Terasawa (Jap)	1963
2:38:16.2	Harry Green (GB)	1913	2:14:28.0*	Buddy Edelen (US)	1963
2:36:06.6	Alexis Ahlgren (Swe)	1913	2:13:55.0	Basil Heatley (GB)	1964
2:32:35.8	Hannes Kolehmainen (Fin)	1920	2:12:11.2	Abebe Bikila (Eth)	1964
2:29:01.8	Albert Michelsen (US)	1925	2:12:00.0	Morio Shigematsu (Jap)	1965
2:27:49.0	Fusashige Suzuki (Jap)	1925	2:09:36.4	Derek Clayton (Aus)	1967
2:26:44.0	Yasao Ikenaka (Jap)	1935	2:08:33.6	Derek Clayton (Aus)	1969
2:26:42.0	Kitei Son (Jap)	1935	2:08:13.0	Alberto Salazar (US)	1981
2:25:39.0	Yun Bok Suh (S Kor)	1947	2:08:05.0	Stephen Jones (GB)	1984
2:20:42.2	Jim Peters (GB)	1952			

* 36 yd (about 6 sec) under standard distance.

Women

3:40:22.0	Violet Piercy (GB)	1926	2:40:15.8	Christa Vahlensieck (W Ger)	1975
3:27:45.0	Dale Greig (GB)	1966	2:38:19.0	Jackie Hansen (US)	1975
3:19:33.0	Mildred Sampson (NZ)	1964	2:35:15.4	Chantal Langlace (Fra)	1977
3:15:22.0	Maureen Wilton (Can)	1967	2:34:47.5	Christa Vahlensieck (W Ger)	1977
3:07:26.0	Anni Pede-Erdkamp (Ger)	1967	2:32:30.0	Grete Waitz (Nor)	1978
3:02:53.0	Caroline Walker (US)	1970	2:27:33.0	Grete Waitz (Nor)	1979
3:01:42.0	Elizabeth Bonner (US)	1971	2:25:42.0	Grete Waitz (Nor)	1980
2:46:30.0	Adrienne Beames (Aus)	1971	2:25:29.0	Allison Roe (NZ)	1981
2:46:24.0	Chantal Langlace (Fra)	1974	2:25:29.0	Grete Waitz (Nor)	1983
2:43:54.5	Jackie Hansen (US)	1974	2:22:43.0	Joan Benoit (US)	1984
2:42:24.0	Liane Winter (W Ger)	1975			

MARATHON MAN: Clarence DeMar is first across the finish line in the 1930 Boston Marathon for his record 7th victory in the event that is believed to be America's oldest regularly contested foot race.

BALANCING A BOTTLE on a tray is the way Roger Bourban (above) runs in every marathon.

NEW YORK CITY'S MARATHON (right) annually draws between 16,000 and 20,000 runners, shown here starting at the Staten Island end of the Verrazano Bridge. The largest number of spectators ever to witness a sporting event (2,500,000) crowd the streets each October.

The Marathon

The inaugural marathon races were staged in Greece in 1896. They were two trial races before the first Olympic marathon at Athens. The race commemorated the legendary run of an unknown Greek courier, possibly Pheidippides, who in 490 BC ran some 24 miles from the Plain of Marathon to Athens with the news of a Greek victory over the numerically superior Persian army. Delivering his message—"Rejoice! We have won."—he collapsed and died. The Olympic races were run over varying distances until 1924 when the distance was standardized at 26 miles 385 yd, the distance first instituted in the 1908 Games in London.

There are no official records for the distance due to the variety of courses used and their varying severity, but the figures on p. 256 are generally accepted to be the progressive best-known times on record.

The NYC Marathon regularly draws the largest number of spectators to any sporting event—an estimated 2,500,000 people who line the route through city streets each year.

The most participants in any race (6.5 mi) is 80,000 in Auckland, NZ.

ROADRUNNERS: The international reputation of the NYC Marathon was bolstered when both the men's and women's marathon records fell in the 1981 race. Alberto Salazar (left), after boldly predicting a new record, made good on his promise by trimming 20 secs off Derek Clayton's 12-year-old mark. This mark was not broken until 1984 when the Welshman Stephen Jones knocked 8 sec off in the first Chicago Marathon.

Allison Roe (right, #F2), of New Zealand, lowered the women's mark by 13.3 secs after shin splints forced defending champion Grete Waitz to drop out of the race. Her record was tied by Waitz in 1983 and then beaten by Joan Benoit (the Olympic winner) in 1984.

Grete Waitz

TRAMPOLINING

Origins

The *sport* of trampolining (from the Spanish word *trampolin,* a springboard) dates from 1936, when the prototype "T" model trampoline was developed by George Nissen (US) in a garage in Cedar Rapids, Iowa. Trampolines were used in show business at least as early as "The Walloons" of the period, 1910–12.

World Championships

Instituted in 1964 and since 1968 held biennially:

Men	Women
1964 Danny Millman (US)	Judy Wills (US)
1965 George Irwin (US)	Judy Wills (US)
1966 Wayne Miller (US)	Judy Wills (US)
1967 Dave Jacobs (US)	Judy Wills (US)
1968 Dave Jacobs (US)	Judy Wills (US)
1970 Wayne Miller (US)	Renee Ransom (US)
1972 Paul Luxon (GB)	Alexandra Nicholson (US)
1974 Richard Tisson (Fra)	Alexandra Nicholson (US)
1976 Richard Tisson (Fra) / Evgeni Janes (USSR)	Svetlana Levina (USSR)
1978 Evgeni Janes (USSR)	Tatyana Anisimova (USSR)
1980 Stewart Matthews (GB)	Ruth Keller (Switz)
1982 Carl Furrer (GB)	Ruth Keller (Switz)

TWIST AND TURN: On the shores of the Konigsee, West Germany, Richard Tisson, a 2-time world champion, set a record by landing on his feet after performing a triple back somersault with 3 full twists. The Guinness TV cameras caught the action.

TRAMPOLINING LEAP: Marco Canestrelli imitates Superman flying through the air over the backs of 4 elephants in the Ringling Bros and Barnum & Bailey Circus.

Stunts

Septuple twisting back somersault to bed and quintuple twisting back somersault to shoulders was made by Marco Canestrelli to Belmonte Canestrelli at Madison Square Garden, NYC, on Jan 5 and Mar 28, 1979.

Richard Tisson performed a triple twisting triple back somersault for a Guinness TV program near Berchtesgaden, W Germany on June 30, 1981.

Richard Cobbing of Gateshead, Eng performed 1,610 consecutive somersaults at Gateshead July 22, 1984.

Marathon Record

The longest recorded trampoline bouncing marathon is one of 1,248 hours (52 days) set by a team of 6 in Phoenix, Ariz, from June 24 to Aug 15, 1974. The solo record is 266 hours 9 min by Jeff Schwartz, 19, at Glenview, Ill, Aug 14–25, 1981.

TRIATHLON

A new type of competition, the Triathlon, began in Feb 1978 in Hawaii when two Navy men challenged each other to a particularly strenuous test of all the major muscles of the body in strength and endurance: a swim of 2.4 miles in the ocean, followed immediately by a 112-mile bike race, and then a full marathon run of 26 miles 385 yd, with no time-outs.

They were joined by 13 others in the first two Triathlons in Feb 1978 and Feb 1979. Then, in 1980 ABC on its "Wide World of Sports" began televising what began to be called the Ironman Triathlon and 108 competed. Now there are hundreds of triathlons—but not all are Ironman Triathlons. The "tinman" races cut the distances in half or less.

In Oct 1984, in the Ironman Triathlon, Dave Scott (Davis, Calif) won in the men's division with a record time 8 hours 54 min 2 sec, shaving 11 min 37 sec off his previous record.

In the women's division a new record was also set in 1984. Sylviane Puntus (Montreal, Canada) finished in 10 hours 25 min 13 sec. Patricia, her identical twin sister, finished right behind her in 10:27:28.

Most in One Year

John C. Riley (Alamo, Calif) competed in 52 triathlons, one a week, in 1983 (a total of 210 hours) to celebrate his 52nd birthday.

1984 IRONMAN WINNERS: Dave Scott (left) in his 4th victory in this Triathlon set a record time of 8 hours 54 min 2 sec. (Photo by Reggie David) Sylviane Puntus of Montreal (right) was the winner in the women's division for the second time with a record of 10:25:13. Her twin sister took second place. (Photo by Noel Black) (Both photos, courtesy Foster-Gaffney Associates)

VIDEO GAMES

Highest score records are meaningless because of the tremendous variance between the games and cassettes available for play at home and in arcades. Each machine, each joy stick setting, each environment is different so that skill and endurance cannot be measured and compared with precision. Therefore the only records worth publishing are those of contest winners.

To ascertain what scores in video games are actually world records, competitions have been held under the auspices of Twin Galaxies with Walter Day as coordinator. On Jan 12 and 13, 1985 in LA, 22 of the top players of the US were selected to compete in an Invitational Player of the Year Contest. The results are:

Highest Percentages: Phil Britt (Riverside, Calif) 80.0%; Mike Sullivan (Riverside, Calif) 73.6%.

Highest scores in each game: "Mad Crasher": Jeff Peters (Etiwanda, Calif) 135,450; "Return of the Jedi": Phil Britt (see above) 1,638,780; "Karate Champ": Jack Gale (N Miami Beach, Fla) 227,300; "Cheyenne": Donn Nauert (Austin, Tex) 83,610,600.

A column about video games by Rawson Stovall of San Jose, Calif, who began his writing at age 10 in 1982, is being distributed by Universal Press Syndicate.

ONE-MAN VOLLEYBALL TEAM: Bob Schaffer of Newark, NJ (see inset) has won over 1,000 games with only 2 losses against 6-man teams.

VOLLEYBALL

Origins

The game was invented as Minnonette in 1895 by William G. Morgan at the YMCA gymnasium at Holyoke, Mass. The International Volleyball Association was formed in Paris in Apr 1947. The ball travels at a speed of up to 70 mph when smashed over the net, which stands 7 ft 11½ in high. In the women's game it is 7 ft 4¼ in high.

World Titles

World Championships were instituted in 1949. The USSR has won 5 men's titles (1949, 52, 60, 62 and 78). The USSR won the women's championship in 1952, 56, 60 and 70. The record crowd is 60,000 for the 1952 world title matches in Moscow, USSR.

Most Olympic Medals

In the 1984 Olympics the US won the gold medal in the men's game, and China won in the women's.

The sport was introduced to the Olympic Games for both men and women in 1964. The only volleyball player to win four medals is Inna Ryskal (USSR) (b June 15, 1944), who won a silver medal in 1964 and 76 and golds in 1968 and 72.

The record for medals for men is held by Yuriy Poyarkov (USSR), who won gold medals in 1964 and 68, and a bronze in 1972.

IN 1976 OLYMPICS, the USSR (left) won the silver medal. Here they are beating Cuba, 3-0 in a semi-final. Poland (right) after beating Japan in the other semi-final, went on to win the gold medal. In 1984, the US won the men's gold medal.

Marathon

The longest recorded volleyball marathon by two teams of six is 75 hours 30 min by 12 players from Kinston, NC, Jan 31–Feb 3, 1980.

WALKING

Longest Race

The Paris-Colmar event (until 1980 it was the Strasbourg-Paris event, instituted in 1926 in the reverse direction), now 322 miles, is the world's longest annual walk event. Gilbert Roger (France) has won 6 times (1949, 53–54, 56–58). The fastest performance is by Robert Pietquin (b 1938) (Belgium) who walked 315 miles in the 1980 race in 60 hours 1 min 10 sec (deducting 4 hours of compulsory stops), averaging 5.25 mph. The first woman to complete the race was Annie van den Meer (Neth) (b Feb 24, 1947) who was 10th in 1983 in 82 hours 10 min.

Dumitru Dan (1890–1978) of Romania was the only man of 200 entrants to succeed in walking 100,000 km (62,137 miles), in a contest organized by the Touring Club de France on Apr 1, 1910. By March 24, 1916, he had covered 96,000 km (59,651 miles), averaging 27.24 miles per day.

Longest in 24 Hours

The best official performance on a track is 133 miles 21 yd by Huw Neilson (GB) at Walton-on-Thames, Surrey, England, Oct 14–15, 1960. The best by a woman is 122.5 miles by Annie van den Meer (Netherlands) at Rouen, France, May 2–3, 1981, over a 1.185-km-lap road course.

WALKING FOR 24 HOURS: Huw Neilson (GB) covered more than 133 miles in 1960, a record that still stands.

WALKING THE DOG: When Sean Maguire (left) says he's taking his dog "Sweden" for a walk, he means it. They set out from the Yukon River, Alaska, and arrived at their destination (Key West, Florida) 10 months and 7,327 miles later.

John Lees (right) walked the 2,876 miles from LA to NYC in 53½ days. Lees' time was faster than the then-standing trans-America running record.

Most Olympic Medals

Walking races have been included in the Olympic schedule since 1906, but walking matches have been known since 1589. The only walker to win 3 gold medals has been Ugo Frigerio (Italy) (1901–68) with the 3,000 m and 10,000 m in 1920 and the 10,000 m in 1924. He also holds the record of most medals with 4 (having additionally won the bronze medal in the 50,000 m in 1932), which total is shared with Vladimir Golubnitschiy (USSR) (b June 2, 1936), who won gold medals for the 10,000 m in 1960 and 1968, the silver in 1972 and the bronze in 1964.

In the 1984 Olympics Ernesto Canto (Mex) won the 20,000 m in 1 hour 23 min 13 sec. Raul Gonzalez (Mex) won the 50,000 m walk in 3 hours 47 min 26 sec. Canto's world record at 20,000 m set May 5, 1984 in Fana, Norway, is 1 hour 18 min 39.9 sec. Gonzalez' world record at 50,000 m set May 25, 1979 at Fana, Norway, is 3 hours 41 min 38.4 sec.

"Non-Stop" Walking

Norman Fox, 35, of the 7th Regiment, Royal Horse Artillery (GB) walked 401.43 mi in 5 days 23 hours 29 min at Osnabrück, W Germany, Sept 1–7, 1982. This was 586 laps of a 1,102,412 m closed circuit. He was not permitted any stops for rest and was moving 98.07 percent of the time.

Most Titles

Four-time Olympian Ronald Owen Laird (b May 31, 1938) of the NYAC, won a total of 65 US National titles from 1958 to 1976, plus 4 Canadian championships.

Walking Backwards

The greatest exponent of reverse pedestrianism has been Plennie L. Wingo (b Jan 24, 1895) then of Abilene, Tex, who started on his 8,000-mile transcontinental walk on Apr 15, 1931, from Santa Monica, Calif, to Istanbul, Turkey, and arrived on Oct 24, 1932. He celebrated the walk's 45th anniversary by covering the 452 miles from Santa Monica to San Francisco, Calif, backwards, in 85 days, aged 81 years.

The longest distance recorded for walking backwards in 24 hours is 82.95 mi by Donald A. Davis in Honolulu, Hawaii, Apr 22–23, 1983.

Walking Around the World

The first person reported to have "walked around the world" is George M. Schilling (US), Aug 3, 1897–1904, but the first verified achievement was by David Kunst (b 1939), who started with his brother John from Waseca, Minn, on June 10, 1970. John was killed by Afghan bandits in 1972. David arrived home, after walking 14,500 miles, on Oct 5, 1974.

WALKED FOR SIX YEARS at a rate of 29.24 mph: Dumitru Dan (Romania) (left) covered 100,000 kilometers in a contest 1910–16.
WALKED BACKWARDS: Plennie Wingo (US) (right) walked 8,000 mi in reverse from Calif to Turkey in 1931–32. He carried a mirror in his cane.

Tomas Carlos Pereira (b Argentina, Nov 16, 1942) spent 10 years, Apr 6, 1968, through Apr 8, 1978, walking 29,825 miles around all 5 continents.

John Lees, 27, of Brighton, England, Apr 11–June 3, 1972, walked 2,876 miles across the US from City Hall, Los Angeles, to City Hall, NYC, in 53 days 12 hours 15 min (53.746 miles per day).

Sean Eugene Maguire (b Sept 15, 1956) (US) walked 7,327 miles from the Yukon River, north of Livengood, Alaska, to Key West, Fla, in 307 days, from June 6, 1978 to Apr 9, 1979.

The record for the trans-Canada (Halifax to Vancouver) walk of 3,764 miles is 96 days by Clyde McRae, 23, from May 1 to Aug 4, 1973.

1976 OLYMPIC GOLD MEDALIST in the 20,000 m walk in Montreal was Daniel Bautista of Mexico. He also holds the world record of 1:20:06.8, three min better than the 1984 Olympic winner walked.

WATER POLO

Origins

Water polo was developed in England as "Water Soccer" in 1869 and was first included in the Olympic Games in Paris in 1900.

Olympic Victories

Hungary has won the Olympic tournament most often with 6 wins, in 1932, 36, 52, 56, 64 and 76. Five players share the record of 3 gold medals: George Wilkinson (1879–1946) in 1900, 08 and 12; Paulo (Paul) Radmilovic (1886–1968) and Charles Sidney Smith (1879–1951) in 1908, 12 and 20—all GB; and the Hungarians Deszö Gyarmati (b Oct 23, 1927) and György Kárpáti (b June 23, 1935) in 1952, 56 and 64. Gyarmati's wife (Eva Szekely) and daughter (Andrea) won gold and silver medals respectively in swimming. Radmilovic also won a gold medal for the 4 × 200 m freestyle relay in 1908. Yugoslavia won the gold medal in 1984.

Marathon

Two teams of seven from the Manly-Warringah Amateur Water Polo Club played for 24 hours 10 min at the Aquatic Centre, French's Forest, NSW, Australia, Oct 3–4, 1980.

SLAM DUNK: Hungary's Gyorgy Karpati (#7) is one of the 5 players who have won 3 Olympic gold medals in water polo.

WATER SKIING

Origins

The sport originated with people walking on water with planks attached to their feet, possibly as early as the 14th century. A 19th century treatise on sorcerers refers to Eliseo of Tarentum who, in the 14th century, "walks and dances" on the water. The first report of aquaplaning on large boards behind a motorboat was from the Pacific coast of the US in the early 1900's. A photograph exists of a "plank-riding" contest in a regatta won by a Mr H. Storry at Scarborough, Yorkshire, England, on July 15, 1914. Competitors were towed on a *single* plank by a motor launch.

The present-day sport of water skiing was pioneered by Ralph W. Samuelson on Lake Pepin, Minn, on two curved pine boards in the summer of 1922, though unsubstantiated claims have been made for the birth of the sport on Lake Annecy (Haute-Savoie), France, in 1920.

One of the earliest British aquaplaners was the Duke of York, later King George VI, who was introduced to the fad at Cowes, Isle of Wight, Eng, in 1921 by Lord Louis Mountbatten, himself one of the early band of true water skiers. Other early *aficionados* of the new sport in the 1930s were film stars David Niven and Errol Flynn. The first national governing body was the American Water Ski Association founded in 1939, and they organized the first national championships in that year. The first World Water Ski Organization was formed in Geneva, Switzerland, on July 27, 1946.

Slalom

The world record for slalom is 4½ buoys at 10.75-m line by Kris La-Point (US) at the International Cup event at McCormick Lake, Seffner, Fla on Apr 29, 1984.

The women's record is 4 buoys, at 11.25-m line, on Oct 2, 1983, by Deena Brush (US) at Okeechellee Record Classic, W Palm Beach, Fla.

Highest Speed

The fastest water skiing speed recorded is 143.08 mph by Christopher Michael Massey (Australia) on the Hawkesbury River, NSW, Australia, Mar 6, 1983. His drag-boat driver was Stanley Charles Sainty. Donna Patterson Brice (US) (b 1953) set a feminine record of 111.11 mph at Long Beach, Calif, on Aug 21, 1977.

Longest Run

The greatest distance traveled is 1,304.6 miles by Will Coughey on Feb 18–19, 1984 on Lake Tikitapu, New Zealand.

Most Titles

World overall championships (instituted 1949) have been twice won by Alfredo Mendoza (US) in 1953 and 55, Mike Suyderhoud (US) in 1967 and 69, and George Athans (Canada) in 1971 and 73, and Sammy Duvall (US) in 1981 and 83. The women's title has been won three times by Mrs Willa McGuire Cook (*née* Worthington) of the US, in 1949–50 and 55, and Elizabeth Allan-Shetter (US) in 1965, 69, and 75. Allan-Shetter has

ROUNDING A BUOY in the record slalom run is Kris LaPoint (US) at the International Cup event in Florida in Apr 1984. (American Water Ski Association)

BAREFOOT AUSTRALIAN Brett Wing (above) set a record 61-ft 4-in jump in 1984.

SLALOM TWISTER: (left) Deena Brush (US) rounding 4 buoys at 11.25-m line set a women's world record in Oct 1983 in Florida.

also won a record 8 individual championship events. The US has won the team championship on 14 successive occasions, 1957–83.

Jumps

The first recorded jump on water skis was 50 ft by Ralph W. Samuelson, off a greased ramp at Lake Pepin in 1925, and this was not exceeded officially until 1947.

The longest jump recorded is one of 202 ft by Glenn Thurlow (Australia) at the Moomba Masters, Australia, on March 7, 1983. The women's record is 45.8 m (150.22 ft) by Sue Lipplegoes (Australia) at the Peter Stuyvesant International Jump Classic at Kirtons Farm, Reading, England, on July 31, 1983.

Barefoot

The first person to water ski barefoot is reported to be Dick Pope, Jr, at Lake Eloise, Fla, on March 6, 1947. The barefoot duration record is 2 hours 42 min 39 sec by Billy Nichols (US) (b 1964) on Lake Weir, Fla, on Nov 19, 1978. The backwards barefoot record is 39 min by Paul McManus (Australia). The best officially recorded barefoot jump is 61 ft 4 in by Brett Wing (Australia), 1984. The official barefoot speed record (two runs) is 110.02 mph by Lee Kirk (US) at Firebird Lake, Phoenix, Ariz, on June 11, 1977. His fastest run was 113.67 mph. The fastest by a woman is 73.67 mph by Karen Toms (Australia) on Mar 31, 1984 in New South Wales, Australia.

Tricks

The tricks or freestyle event involves various maneuvers for which points are awarded according to the degree of difficulty and the speed at which they are performed.

The tricks record is 10,000 points (pending) by Cory Pickos (b 1964) (US) at Lakeland, Fla on May 6, 1984.

The women's record is 7,850 points by Natalia Rumyantseva (USSR) in 1984.

BAREFOOT SPEED-STER: Lee Kirk (US) in a 2-run average speed 110.02 mph in Ariz in 1977 for a record that still stands.

STRONGEST WOMAN WEIGHTLIFTER: Lifting her 182-lb. brother was child's play to Katie Sandwina (1884–1952), who once unofficially lifted 312½ lbs. over her head. She herself weighed 210 lb. Her official record of 286 lb was surpassed on Dec 15, 1984 by Karyn Tarter with an overhead clean and jerk of 289 lb.

WEIGHT LIFTING and POWER LIFTING

Origins

Competitions for lifting weights of stone were held in the ancient Olympic Games. The first "world" championship was staged at the Café Monico, Piccadilly, London, on March 28, 1891, and the first official championships were held in Vienna, Austria, July 19–20, 1898. Prior to that time, weight lifting consisted of professional exhibitions in which some of the advertised poundages were open to doubt.

The first to raise 400 lb was Karl Swoboda (1882–1933) (Austria) in Vienna, with 401¼ lb in 1910, using the continental and jerk style.

Over the years competition in the lifting of weights has evolved into two different sports: weight lifting and power lifting. Weight lifting, an Olympic sport, depends more on technique. Two types of lifts are used, the "snatch and clean" which is accomplished in one movement and the "clean and jerk" which has two parts. The "press" has been discontinued in Olympic competition. Power lifting, not an Olympic event, depends more on sheer strength. It has three lifts, the "squat," "bench press," and "dead lift." No set style or technique is required in any of them.

WORLD WEIGHT LIFTING RECORDS (as of mid-1984)

Bodyweight Class	Lift	Lifted		Name and Country	Place	Date
52 kg 114½ lb	Snatch	115.5	254½	Neno Terzinski (Bulgaria)	San Marino	May 9, 1983
Flyweight	Jerk	152.5	336	Neno Terzinski (Bulgaria)	Vittoria, Spain	Apr 27, 1984
	Total	262.5	578½	Neno Terzinski (Bulgaria)	Vittoria, Spain	Apr 27, 1984
56 kg 123¼ lb	Snatch	131.5	289¾	Naim Suleimanov (Bulgaria)	Varna, Bulgaria	May 11, 1984
Bantamweight	Jerk	170	374¾	Naim Suleimanov (Bulgaria)	Varna, Bulgaria	May 11, 1984
	Total	300	661¼	Naim Suleimanov (Bulgaria)	Varna, Bulgaria	May 11, 1984
60 kg 132¼ lb	Snatch	138.5	305¼	Amir Arizov (USSR)	Minsk, USSR	Mar 15, 1984
Featherweight	Jerk	180	396¾	Stefan Topurov (Bulgaria)	Moscow	Oct 24, 1983
	Total	315	694¼	Stefan Topurov (Bulgaria)	Vittoria, Spain	Apr 28, 1984
67.5 kg 148¾ lb	Snatch	155.5	342¾	Vladimir Grachev (USSR)	Minsk, USSR	Mar 15, 1984
Welterweight	Jerk	196	432	Joachim Kunz (E Germany)	Karl Marx Stadt, E Germany	June 26, 1981
	Total	345	760½	Joachim Kunz (E Germany)	Karl Marx Stadt, E Germany	June 26, 1981
75 kg 165¼ lb	Snatch	167.5	369¼	Vladimir Kuznyetsov (USSR)	Moscow, USSR	Oct 26, 1983
Middleweight	Jerk	210	462¾	Aleksandr Varbanov (Bulgaria)	Moscow	Oct 26, 1983
	Total	370	815½	Aleksandr Varbanov (Bulgaria)	Moscow	Oct 26, 1983
82.5 kg 181¾ lb	Snatch	180.5	397¾	Yurik Vardanyan (USSR)	Moscow	Oct 27, 1983
Light-heavyweight	Jerk	223.5	492½	Aleksandr Pervi (USSR)	Frunze, USSR	Mar 5, 1982
	Total	400	881¾	Yurik Vardanyan (USSR)	Moscow, USSR	July 25, 1980
		400	881¾	Asen Zlatev (Bulgaria)	Ljubljana, Yugoslavia	Sept 23, 1982
90 kg 198¼ lb	Snatch	195.5	431	Blagoi Blagoyev (Bulgaria)	Varna, Bulgaria	May 1, 1983
Middle-heavyweight	Jerk	232.5	512½	Victor Solodov (USSR)	Vittoria, Spain	Apr 30, 1984
	Total	420	925¼	Blagoi Blagoyev (Bulgaria)	Varna, Bulgaria	May 1, 1983
100 kg 220½ lb	Snatch	200	440¼	Yuri Zakharevich (USSR)	Odessa, USSR	Mar 4, 1983
	Jerk	241	531¼	Pavel Kuznyetsov (USSR)	Minsk, USSR	Mar 17, 1984
	Total	440	970	Yuri Zakharevich (USSR)	Odessa, USSR	Mar 4, 1983
110 kg 242½ lb	Snatch	196.5	433	Leonid Taranenko (USSR)	Odessa, USSR	Mar 5, 1983
Heavyweight	Jerk	247.5	545½	Vyacheslav Klokov (USSR)	Moscow	Oct 30, 1983
	Total	440	970	Vyacheslav Klokov (USSR)	Moscow, USSR	Oct 30, 1983
Over 110 kg 242½ lb	Snatch	211	465	Alexander Gunyashev (USSR)	Rheims, France	June 1, 1984
Super-heavyweight	Jerk	261	575¼	Sergei Didyk (USSR)	Moscow, USSR	July 30, 1983
	Total	465	1,025	Alexander Gunyashev (USSR)	Rheims, France	June 1, 1984

Greatest Lift

The greatest weight ever raised by a human being is 6,270 lb in a back lift (weight raised off trestles) by the 364-lb Paul Anderson (US) (b Oct 17, 1932), the 1956 Olympic heavyweight champion, at Toccoa, Ga, on June 12, 1957. The greatest by a woman is 3,564 lb with a hip and harness lift by Mrs Josephine Blatt (*née* Schauer) (US) (1869–1923) at the Bijou Theatre, Hoboken, NJ, on Apr 15, 1895.

The greatest overhead lift ever made by a woman is 286 lb in a continental and jerk (a three-part lift no longer practiced) by Katie Sandwina, *née* Brummbach (Germany) (b Jan 21, 1884, d as Mrs Max Heymann in

PICKUPS: Norbert Schemansky (left) won 4 Olympic medals, the most by any lifter. He became the oldest weightlifter to break a world record when, aged 37 years 10 months, he set a heavyweight snatch mark in 1962. Powerlifter Jan Todd (right) possibly the strongest woman in the world, raised 545½ pounds in a squat lift in 1981. Todd was the first woman to exceed 1,200 pounds in the three-lift total. Jan has since lost 82 lb, but is still setting records.

GREATEST LIFT: (Below) Paul Anderson once raised 6,270 lb in a back lift from trestles. A gold medalist in the 1956 Olympics, he later turned professional, switching from weight lifting to power lifting, where he succeeded with a squat lift of 1,200 lb.

WORLD POWER LIFTING RECORDS (as at June 1, 1984) Figures in kilograms

Class	Squat	Bench Press	Dead Lift	Total
MEN				
52 kg	242.5 Joe Cunha (US) 1981	146.5 Joe Cunha 1982	232.5 Haruji Watanabe (Jap) 1980	567.5 Hideaki Inaba (Jap) 1980
56 kg	237.5 Hideaki Inaba (Jap) 1982	147.5 Hiroyaki Isagawa (Jap) 1981	289.5 Lamar Gant (US) 1982	625 Lamar Grant 1982
60 kg	295 Joe Bradley (US) 1980	180 Joe Bradley 1980	285 Lamar Gant 1980	707.5 Joe Bradley 1982
67.5 kg	297 Robert Wahl (US) 1982	194 Kristoffer Hulecki (Swe) 1982	312.5 Raimo Välineva (Fin) 1981	732.5 Joe Bradley 1981
75 kg	327.5 Mike Bridges (US) 1980	217.5 James Rouse 1980	325 Raimo Välineva 1982	850 Rick Gaugler (US) 1982
82.5 kg	379.5 Mike Bridges 1982	240 Mike Bridges 1981	357.5 Veli Kumpuniemi (Fin) 1980	952.5 Mike Bridges 1982
90 kg	375 Fred Hatfield (US) 1980	255 Mike MacDonald (US)	372.5 Walter Thomas (US) 1982	937.5 Mike Bridges 1980
100 kg	400 Fred Hatfield 1982	261.5 Mike MacDonald 1977	377.5 James Cash (US) 1982	952.5 James Cash 1982
110 kg	393.5 Dan Wohleber (US) 1981	270 Jeffrey Magruder (US) 1982	395 John Kuc (US) 1980	1,000 John Kuc 1980
125 kg	412.5 David Waddington (US) 1982	278.5 Tom Hardman (US) 1982	385 Terry McCormick (US) 1982	1,005 Ernie Hackett (US)
125+ kg	445 Dwayne Fely (US) 1982	300 Bill Kazmaier (US) 1981	402 Bill Kazmaier 1981	1,100 Bill Kazmaier 1981
WOMEN				
44 kg	133 Anna Liisa Prinkkala (Fin) 1983	75 Teri Hoyt (US) 1982	138? D. Wickler (US) 1983	317.5 Cheryl Jones 1983
48 kg	143 Diana Rowell (US) 1983	82.5 Michelle Evris (US) 1981	174.5 Majik Jones (US) 1983	382.5 Majik Jones 1983
52 kg	155 Sisi Dolman-Gricar (Hol) 1983	84 Lynda Chicado-Shendow (US) 1983	165 Vicki Steenrod (US) 1982	390 Kali Bogias (Can) 1983
56 kg	161.5 Debbie Candelaria (US) 1983	104.5 Juli Thomas (US) 1982	183 Tina van Duyn-Woodley (Hol) 1983	440 Juli Thomas 1983
60 kg	200.5 Ruthi Shafer (US) 1983	97.5 Eileen Todaro (US) 1981	213 Ruthi Shafer 1983	500 Ruthi Shafer 1983
67.5 kg	189.5 Angie Ross (US) 1983	105 Jennifer Weyland (US) 1981	215 Jan Todd (US) 1983	467.5 Jennifer Weyland 1981
75 kg	212.5 Beverley Francis (Aus) 1981	140 Beverley Francis 1981	212.5 L. Miller (Aus) 1983	550 Beverley Francis 1983
82.5 kg	218 Beverley Francis 1983	150 Beverley Francis 1981	227.5 Vicky Gagne (US) 1981	577.5 Beverley Francis 1983
90 kg	213 Gael Martin (Aus) 1983	120.5 Gael Martin 1983	210 Rebecca Waibler (W. Ger) 1982	525 Gael Martin 1982
90+ kg	247.5 Jan Todd (US) 1981	130 Gael Martin 1982	230 Wanda Sander (US) 1981	567.5 Gael Martin 1982

NYC, in 1952) *c.* 1911. She stood 5 ft 11 in tall, weighed 210 lb, and is reputed to have unofficially lifted 312½ lb and to have once shouldered a 1,200-lb cannon taken from the tailboard of a Barnum & Bailey circus wagon.

Most Olympic Medals

Winner of most Olympic medals is Norbert Schemansky (US) with 4: gold, middle-heavyweight 1952; silver, heavyweight 1948; bronze, heavyweight 1960 and 1964.

Olympic Gold Medal Winners 1984

Up to 52 kg	Up to 82.5 kg
Zeng Guoqiang (China) 235.0 kg	Petre Becheru (Romania) 355.0 kg
Up to 56 kg	Up to 90 kg
Wu Shude (China) 267.5 kg	Niku Vlad (Romania) 392.5 kg
Up to 60 kg	Up to 100 kg
Chen Weiqiang (China) 282.5 kg	Rolf Milser (W Ger) 385.0 kg
Up to 67.5 kg	Up to 110 kg
Yao Jingyuan (China) 320.0 kg	Norberto Oberburger (Ita) 390.0 kg
Up to 75 kg	Over 110 kg
Karl-Heinz Radschinsky (W Ger) 340.0 kg	Dinko Lukin (Australia) 412.5 kg

Most World Titles

The most world title wins, including Olympic Games, is 8 by John Davis (US) (b Jan 12, 1921) in 1938, 46–52; by Tommy Kono (US) (b June 27, 1930) in 1952–9; and by Vasili Alexeev (USSR) (b Jan 7, 1942) 1970–7.

Youngest World Record Holder

Naim Suleimanov (Bulgaria) (b Nov 23, 1967) set 56 kg world records for clean and jerk (160 kg) and total (285 kg) at 15 years 123 days at Allentown, NJ, Mar 26, 1983.

MOST WORLD TITLES: Tommy Kono of Hawaii (left) and Vasili Alexeev of the USSR (right), as well as John Davis (US) each has 8 world titles, earned in competition, including Olympics. Alexeev has set 80 official world records in the heavyweight class in his career, more than any other athlete.

Paul Anderson as a professional has bench-pressed 627 lb, achieved 1,200 lb in a squat, and deadlifted 820 lb, making a career aggregate of 2,647 lb.

Hermann Görner (Germany) performed a one-handed dead lift of 734½ lb in Dresden on July 20, 1920. He once raised 24 men weighing 4,123 lb on a plank with the soles of his feet, in London on Oct 12, 1927, and also carried on his back a 1,444-lb piano for a distance of 52½ ft on June 3, 1921.

Precious McKenzie (b June 6, 1936) was the first man to total 11 times his body weight (121 lb) with 1,339 lb at Honolulu, Hawaii on May 5, 1979. Lamar Grant (US) deadlifted five times his body weight (123¼ lb) with 617 lb at Dayton, Ohio on Nov 2, 1979. Mike Bridges (US) is the first to hold the total records in three classes simultaneously, on Nov 8, 1980.

The newly instituted two-man dead lift record was raised to 1,448 lb by Clay and Doug Patterson in Arlington, Tex, on Dec 15, 1979.

Peter B. Cortese (US) achieved a one-arm dead lift of 370 lb—22 lb over triple his body weight—at York, Pa, on Sept 4, 1954.

The greatest power lift by a woman is a squat of 545½ lb by Jan Suffolk Todd (b May 22, 1952) (US) (weighing 195 lb) at Columbus, Ga, in Jan 1981. The official power lifting record for the three-lift total is 1,273¼ lb by Bev Francis (b Feb 15, 1955) (Australia). Cammie Lynn Lusko (b Apr 5, 1958) (US) became the first woman to lift more than her body weight (131 lb vs 128.5 lb) at Milwaukee, Wis, May 21, 1983.

A dead lift record of 4,702,646.25 lb in 24 hours was set by a team of ten at the Darwin Weightlifting Club, Darwin, England, Aug 14–15, 1981.

FRENCH WINDSURFER Jenna de Rosnay has boardsailed at a record speed of 26.28 knots.

WINDSURFING (Boardsailing)

"Windsurfing" is the common name for this sport, although strictly speaking a "windsurfer" is a particular brand of sail board, first designed by Hoyle Schweitzer in 1968 and first made in California in 1964 by Newman Darby. The idea enabled surfriders to continue practicing their sport even when there were no waves. The sport was included in the Olympic Games for 1984.

World Championships

The world Windslider championships have been won five times, consecutively, by Stephen van den Berg (Neth) to 1983.

Highest Speed

The record speed for boardsailing is 30.82 knots by Fred Haywood (US) at Weymouth, England, on Oct 16, 1983 in a Force 7–8 wind. The women's record of 26.28 knots by Jenna de Rosnay (France) was set on Oct 14, 1982 at Weymouth, England.

Longest Sail

The longest verified distance covered in 24 hours (actually 23 hours 25 min) was a sail of 205 miles in the West Indies by Thomas Staltmaier (W Ger) on Feb 2–3, 1981.

1984 Olympics winners were: Stephan van den Berg (Neth) with 27.70 points, R. Scott Steele (US) second with 46.00 points, and Bruce Kendall (NZ) third with 46.60 points.

WRESTLING

Earliest References

The earliest depictions of wrestling holds and falls on wall plaques and a statue indicate that organized wrestling dates from c. 2750–2600 BC. It was the most popular sport in the ancient Olympic Games and victors were recorded from 708 BC. The Greco-Roman style is of French origin and arose about 1860. The International Amateur Wrestling Federation (FILA) was founded in 1912.

Best Records

In international competition, Osamu Watanabe (b Oct 21, 1940) (Japan), the 1964 Olympic freestyle featherweight champion, was unbeaten and unscored-upon in 187 consecutive matches.

Wade Schalles (US) has won 821 bouts from 1964 to 1984, with 530 of these victories by pin.

Most World Championships

The greatest number of world championships won by a wrestler is 10 by the freestyler Aleksandr Medved (USSR) (b Sept 16, 1937), with the light-heavyweight titles in 1964 (Olympic) and 66, the heavyweight 1967 and 68 (Olympic), and the super-heavyweight title 1969, 70, 71 and 72 (Olympic). The only wrestler to win the same title in 7 successive years has been Valeriy Rezantsev (b Feb 2, 1947) (USSR) in the Greco-Roman light-heavyweight class, 1970–76, including the Olympic Games of 1972 and 1976.

Most Olympic Titles

The 1984 Olympic gold medal winners are:

(Freestyle)	(Greco-Roman)
Up to 48 kg	*Up to 48 kg*
Robert Weaver (US)	Vicenzo Maenza (Ita)
Up to 52 kg	*Up to 52 kg*
Saban Trestena (Yugo)	Atsuji Miyahara (Jap)
Up to 57 kg	*Up to 57 kg*
Hideaki Tomiyama (Jap)	Pasquale Passarelli (W Ger)
Up to 62 kg	*Up to 62 kg*
Randy Lewis (US)	Weon-Kee Kim (S Korea)
Up to 68 kg	*Up to 68 kg*
Yo In-Tak (S Korea)	Vlado Lisjak (Yugo)
Up to 74 kg	*Up to 74 kg*
Dave Schultz (US)	Jouko Salomaki (Fin)
Up to 82 kg	*Up to 82 kg*
Mark Schultz (US)	Ion Draica (Romania)
Up to 90 kg	*Up to 90 kg*
Ed Banach (US)	Steven Fraser (US)
Up to 100 kg	*Up to 100 kg*
Lon Banach (US)	Vasile Andrei (Romania)
Over 100 kg	*Over 100 kg*
Bruce Baumgartner (US)	Jeff Blatnick (US)

MOST TITLES: Ten-time world champion Aleksandr Medved drives India's Maruti Mane to the mat. Three of Medved's record 10 titles came in Olympic competition, as he moved up in class from light-heavyweight to super-heavyweight.

Three wrestlers have won three Olympic gold medals. They are: Carl Westergren (1895–1958) (Sweden) in 1920, 24 and 32; Ivar Johansson (1903–79) (Sweden) in 1932 (two) and 36; and Aleksandr Medved (b Sept 16, 1937) (USSR) in 1964, 68 and 72.

Two wrestlers who won more medals are Imre Polyak (b Apr 16, 1932) (Hungary) who won the silver medal for the Greco-Roman featherweight in 1952, 56 and 60, and the gold in 1964, and Eino Leino (Finland) who won the gold in 1920, silver in 1924, and bronze in 1928 and 1932 as a freestyle middleweight.

Longest Bout

The longest recorded bout was one of 11 hours 40 min between Martin Klein (Estonia, representing Russia) and Alpo Asikáinen (Finland) in the Greco-Roman middleweight "A" event for the silver medal in the 1912 Olympic Games in Stockholm, Sweden. Klein won.

Fastest Pin

Don Brown, a 177-pound senior from the University of Oregon, broke a 52-year-old National Collegiate tournament record on March 13, 1980, when he pinned Jay Greiner of Ohio State in only 16 seconds. The previous record, set in 1928, was 19 seconds.

Sumo Wrestling

The sport's origins in Japan certainly date from *c.* 23 BC. The heaviest ever *sumotori* is Samoan-American Salevaa Fuali of Hawaii, also known as Konishki, who attained a height of 6 ft 1½ in and weight of 464 lb in 1984. Weight is amassed by overeating a high protein stew called *chankonabe*.

The most successful wrestlers have been Koki Naya (b 1940), *alias* Taiho ("Great Bird"), who won 32 Emperor's Cups until his retirement in 1971; Sadaji Akiyoshi (b 1912), *alias* Futabayama, who won 69 consecutive bouts in the 1930's; and the *ozeki* Torokichi, *alias* Raiden, who in 21 years (1789–1810) won 240 bouts and lost only 10 for the highest ever winning percentage of .962.

The youngest of the 59 men to attain the rank of *Yokozuna* (Grand Champion) was Toshimitsu Obata, *alias* Kitanoumi, in July 1974, aged 21 years 2 months. He set a record in 1978 winning 82 of the 90 bouts that top *rikishi* fight annually. Hawaiian-born Jesse Kuhaulua (b June 16, 1944), now a Japanese citizen named Daigoro Watanabe, *alias* Takamiyama, was the first non-Japanese to win an official tournament in July 1972 and in 1981 set a record of 1,231 consecutive top division bouts. He weighs at least 450 lb.

Heaviest Heavyweight

The heaviest wrestler in Olympic history is Chris Taylor (1950–79), bronze medalist in the super-heavyweight class in 1972, who stood 6 ft 5 in tall and weighed over 420 lb. FILA is introducing a top weight limit of 286 lb for international competition in 1985.

HEAVIES: Hawaiian-born Jesse Kuhaulua (left), known as Takamiyama, takes on 2 US Marines in a charity exhibition. Kuhualua, the first non-Japanese ever to win an official tournament, weighed as much as 450 lbs. Chris Taylor (US) (right) was the heaviest wrestler in Olympic history. At 6 ft 5 in tall, Taylor weighed over 420 lbs when he won the 1972 super-heavyweight bronze medal.

YACHTING

Origins

Yachting in England dates from the £100 stake race between King Charles II of England and his brother, James, Duke of York, on the Thames River, on Oct 1, 1661, over 23 miles, from Greenwich to Gravesend. The King won. The earliest club is the Royal Cork Yacht Club (formerly the Cork Harbour Water Club), established in Ireland in 1720, when the first recorded regatta was held.

The word "yacht" is from the Dutch, meaning to hunt or chase. The word "regatta"—meaning a gathering of boats—is Italian and was applied to the proceedings at Ranelagh on the Thames in June 1775. The sport did not really prosper until the seas became safer with the end of the Napoleonic Wars in 1815. That year The Yacht Club (later to become The Royal Yacht Squadron) was formed and organized races at Cowes, Isle of Wight, Eng, which was the beginning of modern yacht racing. In 1844 the New York YC was founded and held its first regatta the following year. The International Yacht Racing Union (IYRU) was established in 1907.

Highest Speed

The official world sailing speed record is 36.04 knots (41.50 mph) achieved by the 73½-ft *Crossbow II* over a 500-m (547-yd) course off Portland Harbor, Dorset, England, on Nov 17, 1980. The vessel, which had a sail area of 1,400 sq ft, was designed by Rod McAlpine-Downie and owned and steered by Timothy Colman. In an unsuccessful attempt on the record in Oct 1978, *Crossbow II* is reported to have momentarily attained a speed of 45 knots (51 mph).

The fastest 24-hour single-handed run by a sailing yacht was recorded by Nick Keig (b June 13, 1936), of the Isle of Man, who covered 340 nautical miles in a 37½-ft trimaran, *Three Legs of Mann I,* during the Falmouth to Punta, Azores, race, June 9–10, 1975, averaging 14.16 knots (16.30 mph). The fastest bursts of speed reached were about 25 knots (28.78 mph).

Longest Race

The longest regular sailing race is the quadrennial Whitbread Round the World race (instituted Aug 1973) organized by the Royal Naval Sailing Association. The distance is 26,180 nautical miles from Portsmouth, England, and return with stops and restarts at Cape Town, Auckland and Mar del Plata. The record (sailing) time is 120 days 6 hours 35 min by *Flyer* crewed by Cornelius van Rietschoten (Netherlands), finishing on Mar 29, 1982.

Most Competitors

The most competitors ever to start in a single race was 1,947 (of which 1,767 finished) sailing boats in the Round Zeeland (Denmark) race, June 17–20, 1983, over a course of 233 miles.

IN KNOTS: Crossbow II (above) broke its own sailing speed record in 1980 by clocking 36.04 knots (41.50 mph) over a 500-m course. Paul Elvstrom (right) was the first Olympian to win individual gold medals in 4 successive Games, with a gold in the Firefly class in 1948 and golds in the Finn class in 1952, 1956 and 1960.

Most Successful

The most successful racing yacht in history was the British Royal Yacht *Britannia* (1893–1935), owned by King Edward VII while Prince of Wales, and subsequently by King George V, which won 231 races in 625 starts.

America's Cup

The America's Cup was originally won as an outright prize by the schooner *America* on Aug 22, 1851, at Cowes, England, but was later offered by the NY Yacht Club as a challenge trophy. On Aug 8, 1870, J. Ashbury's *Cambria* (GB) failed to capture the trophy from the *Magic,* owned by F. Osgood (US). Since then the Cup has been challenged by GB in 16 contests, by Canada in 2 contests, and by Australia 7 times, but the US holders had never been defeated, winning 77 races in 132 years and only losing 8 until the 4–3 defeat in Sept 1983 of *Liberty* by *Australia II,* skippered by John Bertrand and owned by a syndicate headed by Alan Bond at Newport, RI. The closest race ever was the fourth race of the 1962 series, when the 12-m sloop *Weatherly* beat her Australian challenger *Gretel* by about 3½ lengths (75 yd), a margin of only 26 sec, on Sept 22, 1962. The fastest time ever recorded by a 12-m boat for the triangular course of 24.3 miles is 2 hours 27 min 42 sec by *Freedom* on Sept 25, 1980.

Olympic Victories

The first sportsman ever to win individual gold medals in four successive Olympic Games was Paul B. Elvström (b Feb 24, 1928) (Denmark) in the Firefly class in 1948 and the Finn class in 1952, 56 and 60. He has also won 8 other world titles in a total of 6 classes.

The lowest number of penalty points by the winner of any class in an Olympic regatta is 3 points (5 wins [1 disqualified] and 1 second in 7 starts) by *Superdocious* of the Flying Dutchman class sailed by Lt Rodney Stuart Pattison (b Aug 5, 1943), British Royal Navy, and Ian Somerled Macdonald-Smith (b July 3, 1945), in Acapulco Bay, Mexico, in Oct 1968.

In the 1984 Olympics the gold medal winners were:

International Soling	*International 470*
R. Haines (US) 33.20 pts	L. Doreste (Spain) 33.70 pts
International Star	*International Finn*
E. Buchan (US) 29.70 pts	Russell Coutts (NZ) 34.70 pts
International Flying Dutchman	*International Tornado*
J. McKee (US) 19.70 pts	R. Sellers (NZ) 14.70 pts

Admiral's Cup

The ocean racing series to have attracted the largest number of participating nations (three boats allowed to each nation) is the Admiral's Cup held by the Royal Ocean Racing Club in the English Channel in alternate years. Up to 1981, Britain had a record 8 wins. A record 19 nations competed in the 1975, 77 and 79 competitions.

Largest Marina

The largest marina in the world is that of Marina Del Rey, Los Angeles, Calif, which has 7,500 berths.

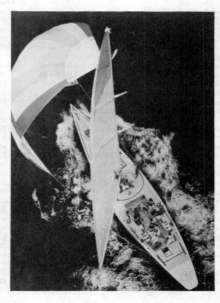

AUSTRALIA II in full sail. Winner of the America's Cup in 1983 churning through the waves on its way to defeat the US and take the cup away from the US for the first time in 132 years of racing.

INDEX

Aerobatics, earliest, world championships, inverted flight, loops 12

Archery, earliest sport 7, 13, flight records, highest scores and 24-hour scores 13, most titles, world records, Olympic medals, flight shooting, greatest pull 14

Auto Racing, largest crowd 8, earliest races, fastest circuits 15, Le Mans 16, 17, fastest races 16, toughest circuits, Indianapolis "500" 17, fastest pit stop, most successful drivers, oldest and youngest world champions, youngest and oldest Grand Prix winners and drivers 18, stock car racing, closest finishes, manufacturers, duration record 19; winners: Indianapolis "500," Le Mans 24-Hour Race, Daytona "500" 21; dragging: rocket or jet-engined 21, piston-engined 22; land speed records, Pikes Peak Race 22, earliest, longest rallies 23, fastest experimental car, Monte Carlo, worst disaster 24

Backgammon, origins, marathon 97

Badminton, origins, international championships, most titles, marathons, longest hit 25

Ball Field, largest 7, 177

Baseball, earliest games 26, home runs 26, 27, Japanese star, fastest base runner 28, shortest and tallest players 28, 31, most games played 28, 29, most at-bats, youngest and oldest players, most hit by pitcher, World Series attendance 29, do-nothing, do-everything records, tale of two cities record, base stealer supreme, consecutive game hitting record 30, managers, longest throws 31, strikeout and knuckleball pitchers 32, 33, fastest pitcher 33; major league all-time records: individual batting 33–35, base running 35, pitching 35–36; World Series records 37–38, longest and shortest games 38

Basketball, origins, 24-second rule change, most accurate shooting 39, longest field goal, individual scoring 40, 42, team scoring, youngest, oldest, tallest players, Olympic champions, world champions 41; NBA regular season records: service 42, scoring 42–44, rebounds 44, assists, personal fouls, disqualifications 45; marathon, greatest attendances 45

Biathlon, 200

Boardsailing, 279

Bobsledding, Luging and Tobogganing, origins, Olympic and world titles 46, 1984 gold medalists 47

Bowling, origins, organizations, lanes, world championships, marathons 48; ABC league records: highest scores, consecutive strikes, most perfect scores 49; ABC tournament records: highest individual, highest doubles scores, perfect scores, best finishes in one tournament, strikes and spares in a row 50, most tournament appearances, greatest attendance, youngest and oldest winners 51; WIBC records: highest scores, perfect games, consecutive strikes, spares and splits 52, championship tournament 53; PBA records: perfect games, most titles, consecutive titles, highest earnings, television bowling 53

Boxing, greatest earnings 9, 58, 61, early, organizations, longest fight 54, shortest fight, tallest boxer 55; world heavyweight champions: first title fight, roster of champions 55, heaviest and lightest, tallest and shortest 56, longest and shortest reigns, oldest and youngest, undefeated 57, recaptures 58, 59, knockout percentage 59; world champions (any weight): traveling champion, longest and shortest reigns, greatest "tonnage" 59, youngest and oldest 59, 62, smallest champions, longest fight, most recaptures, most titles simultaneously, most knockdowns in title fights, amateur world champions 60; all fights: largest purse, highest and lowest attendances 61,

most knockouts, most fights without loss 62, Olympic gold medals, 1984 Olympic gold medalists, time-keeping 63

Bridge (Contract), origins, most world titles 97, most durable player, most Master Points, youngest Life Masters, marathon 98

Canoeing and Kayaking, origins, Olympic and World titles, highest speed 64, longest open sea voyage 64, 65, longest race 65, longest journeys 65–66, Eskimo rolls 66

Checkers, origins, champions 98, most opponents, longest and shortest games 99

Chess, origins 99, world champions 99, 100, most opponents, longest games, marathon 101

Contract, biggest 8

Cribbage, invention of, rare hands, marathon 101

Croquet, origins 66, USCA national ratings 67, US Croquet Hall of Fame, USCA national champions, International Challenge Cup 68

Cross-Country Running, international championships, most appearances, most wins, largest entry field 69

Cycling, longest race 7, crowd size 8, earliest race, highest speed, Tour de France, greatest distances covered 70, most six-day race wins, most Olympic titles 71, 1984 Olympic winners 71, 72, longest one-day race, touring, cyclo-cross 72, endurance records, roller cycling, stationary cycling 73

Darts, origins, most titles 101, fastest match, fastest "round the board," lowest possible scores 102, 24-hour scores, million-and-one, marathon 103

Disasters, worst 9

Earnings, greatest 9, 58, 61

Equestrian Sports, origin, steeplechase jump 74, most Olympic medals 75, world titles, jumping records 76, 77, longest ride, first solo transcontinental journey, marathon 77

Fastest Speed, sky-diving, delayed drops, jai-alai ball, golf ball 7

Fencing, origins 78, most Olympic titles 78, 79, world championships 79

Fishing, origins 80, largest catches 80–81, 83, most fish caught in a season 80, 81, smallest catch, world records, freshwater casting, longest fight 81, world records, spear-fishing, bass-fishing 82, most valuable fish 83

Flying Disc (Frisbee), skills 103, distance 103–04, marathons, fastest guts catch 104

Football, heaviest player 10, origins, college series records, college record passer 84, famous West Pointers 85, coaching records 85, 86–87, Presidential football players 85, 86, All-America brothers, most prolific recordbreaker, shortest touchdown pass, worst attendance 86, highest score, first televised game, longest streaks, rules changes 87, All-America selections, Jim Thorpe vs Dwight Eisenhower, modern major-college individual records 88; all-time National Football League records: service 89, scoring 89–91, rushing 89, 90, 91, passing 91, 92–93, pass interceptions 93–94, punting 94, 95, punt returns 94, kickoff returns 95–96, fumbles 94, 96; NFL champions, Super-Bowl winners 96

Games and Pastimes, BACKGAMMON: origins, marathon 97; BRIDGE (Contract): origins, most world titles 97, most durable player, most Master Points, youngest Life Masters, marathon 98; CHECKERS: origins, champions 98, most opponents, longest and shortest games 99; CHESS: origins 99, world champions 99, 100, most opponents, longest games, marathon 101; CRIBBAGE: invention of, rare hands, marathon 101; DARTS: origins, most titles 101, fastest match,